The Congress Papers

Limerick 2015

The Congress Papers

Empowering Humanity, Inspiring Science

From the 10th International Congress
of the F. M. Alexander Technique
9–15 August 2015, Limerick, Ireland

edited by
Rachel Gering-Hasthorpe

STAT&Books

Published 2016 by

STAT Books

The Books Division of
The Society of Teachers of the Alexander Technique
Grove Business Centre, Unit W48, 560-568 High Road
London, N17 9TA
Great Britain

www.alexandertechnique.co.uk

This compilation
© STAT Books 2016

Copyright of each paper is held by the author or authors.

The views expressed in this volume are those of the authors and not necessarily those of STAT Books or of the Society of Teachers of the Alexander Technique.

The publication of this book was made possible by a donation from
The Alexander Technique Congress Association.

Photographs pp. 8, 322 courtesy of © Ralf Hiemisch 2015

British Library Cataloguing-in-Publication Data
A catalogue record for this book is available from the British Library.

ISBN 978-0-9562110-4-0 (paperback)
The Congress Papers. Empowering Humanity, Inspiring Science.

Text in New Baskerville
Front cover photo © iStockphoto LP
Design, lay-out, and typesetting by Jean M. O. Fischer.
Printed on 80gsm Munken Bookwove
and bound by ImprintDigital, Devon.

Contents

PART ONE
HOW WE WORK 11

International Panel: To Assess or not to Assess? That is the Question...... *Kathleen Ballard, Carol Boggs, Ed Bouchard, Terry Fitzgerald, Ann Rodiger and David Moore* 13

A Way of Practising the Alexander Technique through Linking Words (Guiding Orders or Direction) with Hands-on Experience...... *Anne Battye* 22

Teachable Moments...... *Pamela Blanc* 26

I Could Not Feel So I Learnt To Touch...... *Richard Brennan* 29

The Supreme Art of Education...... *Ted Dimon* 34

Miss Goldie's Understanding...... *Penelope Easten* 41

Slaying the Invisible Man...... *Henry Fagg* 47

Lighten Up!...... *Diane Gaary* 53

A 12 Step Programme for 21st Century Job Creation for Alexander Technique Teachers and Graduating Trainees *Monika Gross* 60

Getting out of Splendid Isolation...... *Nicola Hanefeld* 69

Introduction to the Alexander Technique: Returning to Your Essential Nature...... *Anne Johnson* 73

Beyond Posture ...... *Anthony Kingsley* 78

The Means–Whereby of Excellence...... *Brooke Lieb* 89

Chair Work: What is It? Why Do It?...... *Tom Vasiliades* 95

Practising Our Practice is Our Theory...... *Sharyn West* 98

PART TWO
TOUCH, DIRECTION, WORKING ON OURSELVES AND OTHERS 105

The Brain, Body, and Touch...... *Sarah Barker* 107

Timing and Touch...... *Erik Bendix* 116

Tapping into the Well of Chi...... *Alexander Farkas*   121

Thinking Hands and Thinking Hands Listening and Talking
    Brita Forsstrom   123

Working on Oneself – Widening the Field..... *Dorothea Magonet*   129

Be Here Now...... *Penny O'Connor*   136

PART THREE
CREATIVITY AND PERFORMANCE   141

Making a Mark...... *Jane Brucker with Jeremy Wasser*   143

Embodied Stage Presence...... *Corinne Cassini*   150

The Use of Breathing and the Body Vowels..... *Agnès de Brunhoff*   156

Seeds of Imagination: Developing Creativity in Teaching the
    Alexander Technique...... *Cathy Madden*   162

The Physicality of String Playing...... *Alun Thomas*   169

PART FOUR
ANATOMY AND MOVEMENT   175

Reasons for Thinking about Head and Support
    Paul Norikazu Aoki   177

Creativity in Motion...... *Korina Biggs*   181

Up Off Your Ankles!...... *Joan Frost*   185

Two Practices for Sensory Integration and the Discovery of
    Upward Direction...... *Clare Maxwell*   188

Towards the Development of a Conceptual View of the Body
    Construct as Aliveness in Movement...... *Zadok Ruben*   194

We are Evolved to Run......... *Robin John Simmons*   206

Curious about Experience – Moving – Noticing – Choosing
    Lucia Walker   209

Embodied Learning of Sensing Balance by Walking a Line
    Wolfgang Weiser   216

Natural Running...... *John Woodward*   220

PART FIVE
APPLICATIONS, NEW DIRECTIONS   229

'Too Loose Yet Too Tight'...... *Julie Barber*	230
Teaching to Trauma...... *Katherine H. Breen*	242
The Hyoid Matrix...... *Katherine H. Breen*	250
Mindful Recovery Practices...... *Becca Ferguson*	268
Taming to Touch...... *Caitlin Freeman*	275
An Introduction to Fascial Unwinding..... *Mika Hadar-Borthwick*	280
Eutokia: Optimal Position of Baby for Childbirth... *Ilana Machover*	283
Postural Rehabilitation...... *Elizabeth Reese*	289
STAT Research Group Panel...... *Julia Woodman, Lesley Glover, Kathleen Ballard, Korina Biggs, David Gibbens, Jane Clappison*	300
Alexander Technique and Burnout Prevention *Martina Süss and Christine Weixler*	308
The Art of Breathing...... *Jessica Wolf*	313
Notes from the Artist-in-Residence...... *Aisling Hedgecock*	317
Alphabetical Listing of Authors	320
Work Exchange pictures	322

Publisher's note
Pictures within papers are the copyright of the author unless otherwise specified.
   Where website addresses commence with 'www', insert 'http://' before.

10th International Congress Papers

Richard Brennan, Glenna Batson, Niall Kelly at the Opening Ceremony.

10th International Congress of the F. M. Alexander Technique

Empowering Humanity, Inspiring Science
9th–15th August 2015, Limerick, Ireland

The International Congress Spirit

In the spirit of the International Congresses we value the many approaches to the learning and teaching of Alexander's work. Registration for the Congress implies agreement to participate in this spirit of mutual respect and not to demean the person or work of other participants. We ask all those enrolling for their participation in fostering a supportive atmosphere where diversity is encouraged and respectful dialogue enjoyed.

Directors of the Congress
Richard Brennan
Niall Kelly
Glenna Batson

The Alexander Technique Congress Association (ATCA) organises International Congresses to further its purpose of enhancement, promotion, further development and deeper understanding of the F. M. Alexander Technique. For information about the next International Congress and to see photographs and feedback from the 2015 Congress, visit www.atcongress.com.

PART ONE

How We Work

International Panel: To Assess or Not to Assess? That is the Question.

Kathleen Ballard, Carol Boggs, Ed Bouchard, Terry Fitzgerald, Ann Rodiger and David Moore

A BRIEF HISTORICAL PERSPECTIVE ON STEPS TOWARDS REGULATION OF AT TEACHING AND OTHER COMPLEMENTARY HEALTHCARE DISCIPLINES IN THE UK
Kathleen Ballard

The early group of Alexander Technique (AT) teachers in London. We have no evidence on whether assessment methods interested the teachers trained by Alexander, but questions and doubts about teaching obviously did. In *A Time to Remember*, a diary kept by Walter Carrington in 1946, he implies a need for something more than the ability to use the Technique for his own benefit in order to succeed as one of Alexander's teaching assistants. References to the persistence Carrington required to discover the essence of the teaching method suggest that Alexander was still developing it then, along with ways to explain and describe it.

Patrick Macdonald is recorded on video saying that three years of training was found to be the minimum required for teacher competence. From the mid-century onward the lack of an explicit agreed curriculum, list of competences or an assessment procedure seems to have become an increasing source of concern among leading teachers and may have contributed to early rifts between them.

UK Progress toward voluntary regulation in Complementary Healthcare: 1950s to 2015. By the 1950s the UK government concluded that all trades and professions needed to raise their standards in order to increase and maintain national prosperity. A new system of work-based training awards – National Vocational Qualifications – was developed, with an emphasis on competence to perform the tasks required, rather than on book-learning and written exams.

By the late 1980s government attention focused on the Complementary and Alternative Medicine (CAM) sector. Prime Minister Thatcher announced that 'each CAM practice must get its own house in order'. Osteopathy, chiropractic, homeopathy, herbalism and acupuncture were considered first. Osteopathy and chiropractic chose statutory regulation through acts of parliament.

1997: **The University of Exeter, at the request of the Department of Health, publishes a Scoping Report by Budd and Mills.** This report on all

UK CAM practices and their various UK organisations included AT, and recommended that where several organisations represent a CAM discipline, these should be amalgamated into a single 'lead body'. In 1999 the report was revised.

About this time some STAT teachers agreed that AT teaching competences and a draft outline curriculum were needed. Drafts were prepared and considered at two meetings of STAT members. After lengthy debate the process stalled with no draft adopted.

1999: The Health Act 1999 becomes law. Chapter 8 states: '[This is] an act to . . . confer power to regulate any professions concerned (wholly or partly) with the physical or mental health of individuals; and for connected purposes.' Because this description clearly applies to the Alexander Technique teaching profession, AT teaching was now liable to UK regulation. The Act ended the historic right to practise, without regulation, a healthcare activity not included in orthodox medicine.

2000: The House of Lords Science and Technology Committee. Their report, *Complementary and Alternative Medicine,* was published. It refers to the AT as: 'A complementary therapy based on a theory that the way a person uses their body affects their general health. This technique encourages people to optimise their health by teaching them to stand, sit and move according to the body's "natural design and function". This is, in essence, a taught technique rather than a therapy.' The AT is one of 12 therapies for which voluntary regulation is considered appropriate.

2000–2008: The AT Voluntary Self-Regulation Group is formed. It included members from all four representative AT organisations in the UK, functioned under the guidance of a professional chairperson who was not an AT teacher, and received government funding.

Collaboration between the four organisations remains essential if they are to receive the necessary government support for the preparation or updating of National Occupational Standards, for AT teachers to be eligible to contribute to decision-making about practical implementation of voluntary-regulation principles, the constitution and structure of the proposed regulatory body – the Complementary and Natural Healthcare Council (CNHC) – and for teachers to join it.

2005: Publication of report *Development of Proposals for a Future Voluntary Regulatory Structure for Complementary Healthcare Professionals,* by Professor Julie Stone.

2006: Consultation on the Stone Report. At a meeting organised by the Foundation for Integrated Health for the 12 professions concerned, 68% of the 438 respondents approved the principle of establishing the CNHC as a 'federal', 'low cost' and 'light touch' regulatory body.

2008: The CNHC is established. It had initial government funding. AT teachers are entitled to join.

2000–2010: National Occupational Standards for AT teaching. These standards were prepared in collaboration with Skills for Health, revised and agreed. They contain both 'discipline specific' and 'generic' competence standards. Commitment to them is obligatory for membership of the CNHC. (https://tools.skillsforhealth.org.uk/competence/show/pdf/id/2800/).

2012: STAT Summit Meeting. Heads of Training, Moderators, Training Course Committee and Council met to consider the training curriculum. A draft version of a core curriculum was prepared in 2013 and is being tested at the time of writing (2015).

2015: STAT Assessment Panel. Presentations and discussions on student assessment take place at the Annual Conference and a report is issued (see also *Statnews* September 2015).

AT TEACHER COMPETENCY ASSESSMENT PROJECT (USA)
Carol Boggs, Ed Bouchard, Ann Rodiger

Competency is the demonstrated ability to do something with proficiency, ability, skill, accomplishment, and know-how, in this case teaching the Alexander Technique.

How do you know when you are observing a good AT lesson? How do you know when you are receiving a good AT lesson? How do you decide? What criteria do you use to make your decisions?

We are exploring a process to objectively demonstrate aspects of assessments already made by AT teachers, and to systematically document what AT teacher trainers consider sufficient teacher competency. We are constructing an assessment instrument following a course used in medical and scientific communities.[1,2,3] The method is highly regarded for bringing out the logic and shared expertise that exists amongst experts in a given field.[4,5,6] If successful, our discoveries will enhance our ability to communicate the logic that underlies AT teaching principles – facilitating further inquiries to bring the AT out of the shadows, on to the map, and into the 21st Century.

Professional assessment is becoming a requirement in many fields. In order for the AT to gain standing and credibility among other disciplines, as well as to secure a way to protect ourselves from restrictive regulatory legislation crafted by outsiders, a methodology for AT Teacher Competency Assessment is sorely needed.

We have been working on this project for three years and have created a website, presented workshops for three AmSAT ACGMs, had two weekend conferences with reports, held nearly weekly conference calls, and are now at the stage of looking at specifics.

While this project is an independent initiative, we hope that this project can become a joint venture that includes all interested AT teachers around the world. As Kathleen Ballard mentions, there is growing agreement about AT principles among teachers of different training course traditions as evidenced by the National Occupational Standards (NOS) agreement.

Our Mission
As teachers with our students and teacher trainers with our trainees, we constantly make implicit assessments. Our goal is to be able to be explicit about what we are doing as AT teachers. Assessment methodology can help trainers and trainees know what works and what doesn't work. Our mission is to:

1. Create means to assess competency in teaching AT principles and procedures.
2. Develop an assessment tool that can meet scientific validation criteria to accommodate various teaching styles and be adaptable to various types of lessons.
3. Communicate in a more explicit manner what we do as AT teachers.

Other professional fields have developed assessment protocols. The National Board of Medical Examiners, which was founded in 1915, pioneered competency assessment in US medicine and began a tradition of keeping assessment protocols up to date with developing test assessment technology.[7, 8] The Federation of State Massage Therapy Boards is adopting assessment protocols.[9, 10] Some US states are already requiring assessment methodologies developed by FSMTB for Massage Therapy licensure. Differentiating AT from Massage Therapy with a distinct and validated professional assessment methodology will contribute to maintaining AT autonomy.

The American Psychological Association has produced a relevant document.[11] These are some excerpts from it:

> Educational programs are expected to produce competence, professional credentialing bodies are expected to certify individuals as competent, policy makers applaud competence, and consumers increasingly demand it. (p. 3.)
>
> The assessment of competence fosters learning, evaluates progress, assists in determining the effectiveness of the curriculum and training program, advances the field, and protects the public. (p. 4.)
>
> Compelling methodologies for assessing competence must be developed to advance our education and training programs before standards can be imposed for certification within the profession. (p. 4.)

Methodology
Our team is systematically assembling specific features and constructs (concepts) of AT Teacher Competency from a number of sources, including certain AT texts related to assessment, and organised input from knowledgeable AT teachers jointly reviewing these texts at the annual AT Teacher Competency Assessment Conferences. A group consensus has formed about the specific features and constructs that are important for AT teacher competency. This collection of features and constructs represents the Curriculum Strands of an AT training course. Each of these strands is detailed

with items that are organised by levels of difficulty. Each item is then given an explicit rating scale. In this method of assessment we are developing a protocol to measure ability that will be used (a) to validate that the instrument is working to expectations and (b) to measure the levels of ability of AT teacher competency.

Next Steps
1. Continue to identify Curriculum Strands, and develop items with levels of difficulty.
2. Continue to talk to and collaborate with international colleagues.
3. Begin to build an Item Bank from which items will be selected to form instruments to be pilot-tested by Training Directors and trainees.
4. Analyse and collate the data collected from the pilot-tested instruments to discern reliability.
5. Plan for the AT Teacher Competency Assessment Conference 19-20 March, 2016 in NYC.
6. Strategise fundraising for professional assessment methodology input and support.

Researching assessment standards for sustainability in AT teacher education
Terry Fitzgerald

As a profession we are rightly proud of the scientific and artistic research conducted into the AT in the past century, and we boast about the recent evidence showing how it can help people with problems such as neck and low back pain. However, scarcely any similarly rigorous research has been conducted into AT teacher education, which is the foundation of the all the rest.[12,13] The late Dr Chris Stevens, in his 1988 STAT Alexander Memorial Lecture,[14] endorsed research into how AT teacher education practices might be enhanced through collective reflection. Our co-authored paper shows how teachers in the UK, the US and Australia are now adopting this perspective in the area of assessment standards for beginning AT teachers.

Now more than ever, we need to articulate the qualities expected of AT teachers: Alexander seems never to have written them down and his own graduates are no longer here to guide us. As well, 21st century educators are progressively incorporating professional training[15] theories and practices of holistic agency and personal responsibility that are familiar to Alexandrians, and researchers are questioning the value of attendance time as a measure of learning.[16] Organisations like the OECD now expect professions in advanced nations to adopt qualitative assessment standards,[17] and we can see this already happening in the education of school teachers[18] and medical practitioners.[19]

I argue here on behalf of research into models of assessment that reflect these professional expectations but may not be allowed by the AT Affiliated

Societies' (ATAS) current rules. The 2015 ATAS agreement says its first aim is 'Establishing and upholding common standards for the training and certification of Alexander teachers worldwide' (p. 3).[20] These standards are attendance-based and quantitative, and only implicitly refer to demonstrable competence. For our work to remain sustainable and our certifications internationally relevant, I believe we also need to collectively design explicit, qualitative assessment standards that ATAS (and other AT groups) will endorse.

In our AT teacher training we are broadly familiar with two models of qualitative assessment that could be adapted for our purposes. Summative assessment is assessment *of* learning that is already achieved and it involves testing or measuring a candidate's competence at specific milestones in their education, especially at graduation. Formative assessment is assessment *for* learning and is a process whereby teacher-assessors observe, review and give feedback to students, who continuously learn from these assessments and build on them as they progress towards and beyond their next stages.[21, 22] Developing explicit summative assessment standards to guide AT students, teachers and assessors would be a preliminary step towards formative assessment. Research will guide us towards the best ways of clarifying such standards for our particular form of professional education.

Ed Bouchard was suggesting twenty-five years ago that qualitative standards would be more useful than quantitative criteria for gauging the effectiveness of the various AT teaching courses and also give beginning teachers the recognition that they possess the 'requisite understanding and sensory ability to continue their study of the AT . . . and teach it to others'.[23] Bouchard also alerted us to the problem of *exclusion* inherent in the time-based model: 'Relying on strict, unyielding enforcement of the quantitative standard may end up excluding training courses that could indeed turn out qualified, even exceptional teachers.'

The attendance model excludes not only some courses, but also the many potential students and gifted teachers who are unable to attend courses because of time, cost, distance and other commitments, or because they prefer not to engage with the schools available. When a recent study shows that the median age of STAT teachers in the UK is 58 years,[24] how can we reasonably expect to sustain or build our profession while excluding potentially capable people? Furthermore, how much goodwill and emotional labour have been used up in the administration of these exclusions?

A possible approach to inclusion would be to embrace profession-wide, qualitative assessment standards for both structured and informal teaching environments. AT societies could then develop standards and supervise assessments, but not necessarily oversee schools. This would also encourage student responsibility. There will always be educators and students who prefer time-based school structures, and they should be free to have them. However, with standards accessible and assessors available, students could opt to construct their own apprenticeships by attending a school when it suits them, engaging a number of mentors, or combining these methods. Completion time would not be predetermined, nor would a school be required to accommodate each student's every need. Such a system might also generate a pool of consultants who are independent of schools and societies and whom students can engage for advice as they prepare for their assessments.

Many other scenarios become possible once we accept the idea of explicit assessment standards. This is where collective research into AT teacher education becomes important. With sufficient resolve among the various AT societies, we should be able to invest in an ongoing research program that ensures the sustainability of our work for generations to come.

Assessment processes – Alexander Technique Advanced Diploma
David Moore

In 1993 our training school established an Advanced Diploma of AT Teaching. This qualification is accredited under the Australian Qualifications Framework. It sits in the Vocational Education and Training system, whose qualifications are below those of the Higher Education System. This was not done out of any conviction that the government-mandated framework would add value to the training, but for the very expedient reason that it was the only way overseas students could get visas to study at the school.

There are other very concrete advantages having in place a clearly articulated competency-based assessment system that links into the existing national education system. Primarily, it allows for the type of qualification that bureaucrats can understand and may lead to greater access to professional involvement in the health and education systems. Other advantages for our students include exemption of their fees from the Australian Good and Services Tax, a 50% discount on public transport; means-tested access to a living allowance called Austudy, which effectively pays their fees; increased probability of funding from arts bodies; and recognition of competencies gained when applying to universities for jobs or further study (e.g. Master degrees).

The question arises: Does having the training embedded into this system impact negatively on the quality of the training? This is not our experience. The reason for this is that our course is written up in such a way that what is mandated are the competencies that trainees are required to achieve, rather than the manner in which they are achieved. Even so, we do stipulate a certain minimum time that trainees be engaged in study and practical activities.

It is worth noting that the VET system in Australia has been in constant crisis, with regular scandals about poor training and inadequate assessments. The problem has been that with an almost exclusive focus on assessment and the absence of specific requirements regarding the delivery of their courses, training organisations have diminished the teaching of their subjects while cutting costs in the competitive market place. The qualifications not tainted by the ongoing scandals are those of the traditional trades – plumbers, electricians, etc. A common factor in these types of training is that although competencies are assessed, trainees are also required to undergo several years of practical work as apprentices.

And although the ideologues of competency-based training don't like it, there are other courses within the VET system in Australia that do specify the minimum time for training. Among them is our Advanced Diploma of AT Training, which specifies a minimum of 1,600 hours over a minimum of three years, and the Aviation Training Package for pilot licences, which has minimum requirements for the amount of flying experience. Indeed, outside the VET system in Australia, the qualification standards for virtually all professions include a minimum amount of time for gaining practical experience within that profession.

I believe we should have in place clear guidelines and procedures for AT teaching that outline the minimum competencies against which graduates can be assessed and, in addition, we should maintain a minimum of 1,600 hours intensive training. However, I also believe the narrow focus on exactly how those hours are to be distributed is counter-productive to the interests of the profession because it limits access of highly desirable candidates to the training. It is my experience that these hours spread over four years of training instead of three could provide sufficient intensity to achieve the same or even a better result.

References
1. Bond, T. G., C. M. Fox, (2007). *Applying the Rasch Model: Fundamental Measurement in the Human Sciences* (2nd ed.). Lawrence Erlbaum Associates:Mahwah, NJ.
2. Wilson, M. (2005). *Constructing Measures: An Item Response Modeling Approach*. Routledge Academic: New York.
3. Wright, B. D., G. N. Masters (1982). *Rating Scale Analysis*. MESA Press: Chicago.
4. Lunz, M. E., B. D. Wright (1997). 'Latent Trait Models for Performance Examinations' in J. Rost & R. Langeheine (eds.), *Applications of Latent Trait and Latent Class Models in the Social Sciences*. Waxmann: Münster, Germany, pp. 80-84.
5. Masters, G. N. (1997). 'Where Has Rasch Measurement Proved Effective?' in *Rasch Measurement Transactions*, 11. 2, 568.
6. O'Neill, T., R. Castle, C. Mark (2006). 'Comparability of Practice Analysis Survey Results Across Modes of Administration' in *CLEAR Exam Review*, 17. 2, 9.
7. National Board of Medical Examiners (2015) (www.nbme.org/) [accessed 22 November 2015].
8. Hubbard, J. P., E. J. Levit (1985). *The National Board of Medical Examiners: The First Seventy Years: A Continuing Commitment to Excellence*. National Board of Medical Examiners: Philadelphia.
9. Tatum, D. S. (2007). *Job Task Analysis Survey Results*. Federation of State Massage Therapy Boards: Dallas, TX.
10. The Federation of State Massage Therapy Boards (FSMTB) and the Massage &

Bodywork Licensing Examination (MBLEx) (2015) (www.massage-exam.com/fsmtb-mblex.php) [accessed 22 November 2015].

11 The APA Task Force on the Assessment of Competence in Professional Psychology (2006) (www.apa.org/ed/resources/competence-report.aspx) [accessed 22 November 2015]

12 Gounaris, C., C. Tarnowski, C. Taylor, (2000). *Taking Time: Six Interviews with First Generation Teachers of the Alexander Technique on Alexander Teacher Training*. Novis Publications: Aarhus, Denmark.

13 Fitzgerald, T. (2007). *The Future of Alexander Technique Teacher Education*, EdD thesis, (www.researchgate.net/publication/228593007_The_future_of_Alexander_Technique_teacher_education_principles_practices_and_professionalism) [accessed 18 November 2015].

14 Stevens, C. (1988). 'Scientific Research and its Role in Teaching the Alexander Technique: Part 1 Kinds of Research and What We Can Learn from Them – The 1988 F. M. Alexander Memorial Lecture'. STAT: London.

15 Beckett, D., P. Hager (2002). *Life, Work and Learning: Practice in Postmodernity*. Routledge: London.

16 Silva, E., T. White, T. Toch (2015). *The Carnegie Unit: A Century-Old Standard in a Changing Education Landscape*. Carnegie Foundation for the Advancement of Teaching (http://www.carnegiefoundation.org/resources/publications/carnegie-unit/) [accessed 19 November 2015].

17 OECD, 'Assessment of Higher Education Learning Outcomes' (2012) (www.oecd.org/edu/ahelo) [accessed 18 November 2015].

18 European Commission (2005). *Common European Principles for Teacher Competences and Qualifications* (http://www.atee1.org/eu_policies_on_te) [accessed 18 November 2015].

19 O. ten Cate, (2014). 'What Is a 21st-Century Doctor? Rethinking the Significance of the Medical Degree' in *Academic Medicine*, 89. 7, pp. 966–969.

20 Alexander Technique Affiliated Societies (ATAS), (2015). *ATAS Agreement: May 2015*.

21 D. Boud & Associates, *Assessment 2020: Seven Propositions for Assessment Reform in Higher Education* (2010) (http://www.uts.edu.au/research-and-teaching/teaching-and-learning/assessment-futures/overview) [accessed 18 November 2015].

22 Masters, G. N. (2014). 'Assessment: Getting to the Essence', Centre for Assessment Reform and Innovation, *Designing the Future*, Issue 1. (http://www.acer.edu.au_files_uploads_Assessment_Getting_to_the_essence.pdf) [accessed 18 November 2015].

23 Bouchard, E. (1990). 'Toward Qualitative Standards', *NASTAT News*, issue 8.

24 Eldred, J., A. Hopton, J. Donnison, J. Woodman (2015). 'Teachers of the Alexander Technique in the UK and the People Who Take Their Lessons: A National Cross-sectional Survey' in *Complementary Therapies in Medicine*, 23, pp. 451–461.

Kathleen Ballard is a member of the STAT Research Group and regularly focuses on competency.

Carol Boggs, Ed Bouchard and Ann Rodiger and several AmSAT colleagues began discussing AT teacher competency in 2013 with a paper titled *Qualitative Standards Co-existing with Quantitative Requirements.*

Terry Fitzgerald researches ways of improving the traditional training model. David Moore heads an AUSTAT training course in Melbourne in which his graduates receive government recognition.

A Way of Practising the Alexander Technique through Linking Words (Guiding Orders or Direction) with Hands-on Experience

Anne Battye

> Where is the wisdom that we lost in knowledge?
> Where is the knowledge that we lost in information?
> T. S. *Eliot* – Chorus from '*The Rock*' (1938)

In these Continuous Learning sessions I wanted to look at the words F. M. Alexander gave us, and what they mean to us now as we apply them to our experience.

We can begin by looking at the two main principles of the Technique – inhibition in response to a stimulus and sending guiding orders or directing our attention to the release of muscle tension. We considered what is a stimulus, how do we inhibit responding to it, and what can happen next? In the space between the stimulus hitting our brains and our reaction lies the possibility of making a new decision to act, becoming aware of what we were going to do anyway and doing it consciously, or of making a decision not to react at that moment. In accessing that space we may discover something of our habit patterns that we are generally unaware of. We are finding a way of discovering our unknown patterns of behaviour – as a habit is, by definition, below the level of our consciously chosen behaviour.

In my training course Marjory Barlow always insisted that we say the words 'let the neck release to allow the head to go forward and up in such a way that the back can lengthen and widen and the knees release forwards and away' while our teachers used their hands to take our heads forward and up. In this way we learned to associate giving guiding orders with the sensory experiences that we received. No matter how competent we thought we were, it was deemed necessary that we continue to send the messages, using Alexander's words, while refusing to carry out or 'do' the orders.

The idea of keeping these 'primary orders' going 'all at once, one after another' confuses many of us. It is important to remember that the primary orders are inhibitory – in that they are designed to prevent misuse of the primary control. Once you can keep them in mind you may begin to add new and voluntary orders to perform an action whilst still maintaining the inhibitory directions, not stiffening the neck, pulling back the head, etc. Adding the direction 'knees to move forward and away' in order to find the chair or to go into 'monkey' is a case in point. Something has to happen so that you reach the chair, but that action must preclude shortening the neck or spine. Once you understand this principle, all other movements can be performed, maintaining a released neck, head and trunk while manoevering other parts of the body.

This is the point where our sensory perception clicks in – and, as F. M. found, it is usually inaccurate, not to say faulty. Generally we are used to 'feeling' out what we are doing, so if we try anything new it might appear to us to feel 'wrong'. But if we are asked to think through an action using Alexander's words, without 'doing' it, something really revolutionary happens. Refusing to react in the old way while continuing to inhibit our immediate responses, sending the messages to release excess muscle tension in the neck, head and back in order to decide on an action can take a lot of mental effort as well as a suspension of disbelief!

We experimented with many activities, from lying down, sitting in a chair, standing, walking, using the wall as a support for the back, going into a 'monkey' and up on to our toes. We added actions such as placing hands on the back of a chair, moving the chair while maintaining the opposition of the back and hands, all the time asking why we were doing this. My whole endeavour was to encourage people to question why we should work like this, what it means to 'work on oneself' and how we might practise these actions without disrupting the primary control. I think of these procedures as a blueprint for action in our everyday life and one of the questions I asked was: how many activities can you apply 'monkey' to? Not only 'monkey' but all the other activities we tried.

These experiments did not dismiss the information from our senses, but showed us that we might not always be able to trust them to give us accurate feedback. I paraphrased Alexander's saying that though one day you might be able to trust your senses, once you have learnt and can rely on sending the mental directions you will have a process that is much much finer. Marjory Barlow used to quote F. M.'s words – it is in her 1995 Memorial lecture to STAT. Not only is the new direction-sending mechanism quicker, but as our sensory perception has led us astray in the past, it is likely to mislead us in the future as we continue to form new habit patterns.

One approach we took was to look at use and misuse through the ages. I had brought along some pictures: of heads and necks, twisted bodies and beautiful stone carvings, and photographs of people at work for us to look at, in order to observe patterns of use and be able to comment on them. Looking at one, Pisanello's *St Eustace*, elicited an interesting discussion on horsemanship and how to maintain the neck–head–spine relationship in a horse as well as its rider. Van Gogh's drawings of peasants working were also useful, as were Honoré Daumier's almost caricature-like drawings of artists and critics.

Fig 1. One of the photographs we looked at in the workshop. Photograph by Anne Battye.

Fig. 2. Pisanello's *Vision of St. Eustace* (detail).[1]

Another activity was listening to sounds as we learn to fine-tune our hearing. Often when giving a lesson I find that suddenly my pupil's back will release, they give a huge sigh and their voice becomes clear and resonant. They love it! Once the back is working we can advance to song or speech. F. M. not only used the whispered 'ah' in his work but he encouraged his students to whisper all the vowels, diphthongs and then to add consonants in front of them, starting from the most open sound – ahh – in order to achieve a more flexible use of the voice. Practically everything we tried had its roots in what Marjory Barlow taught me and was in answer to the essential question of how Alexander learned to look after himself while he was teaching. We need to be able to practise working on ourselves, in order to maintain our own conscious awareness of what we are doing while we are working.

Finally, there was just time on the last day to touch on the most important link between our habits of use and our emotional states. Emotions themselves are like storms, they come, they overwhelm us and then, with a bit of luck, they pass through us. It is my experience that if a specific emotion, like anxiety or fear or depression, is repeated over a period of time it can lead to the creation of emotional states in the body. Then the body-construct may induce the emotion, which will lead to habits that can be really destructive, locking the person into an endless cycle of the body-shape producing the emotion and the emotion bringing on the pattern of misuse. Practising the Alexander Technique consciously can help to break these cycles. I gave a couple of examples from my own experience of working with deeply troubled pupils, encouraging them to repeat the verbal orders repetitively, before re-living the fearful occasion that had sparked their distress. Constantly returning to the framework of the lesson, by giving a stimulus, practising inhibition and sending the guiding orders, many times over, followed by action, or not, seemed to both calm and integrate my pupil.

When we work with people who have suffered trauma we may find that everything our pupils have ever experienced is locked in the musculature. This means that as we attempt to release hidden and long-forgotten tensions we should work very gently and with compassion. Not that we have to be psychotherapists, but it is as well to learn how be able to cope with the physical manifestation of damage released when we help to unlock frozen muscle tension! Being able to provide a safe environment in which to structure a lesson seems to be essential.

We have an amazing tool in the Alexander Technique – applying it helps to relieve pain, lessens discomfort, increases our ability to act and react appropriately in our environment, helps us to learn new skills, gives a boost to our creativity, allows us better to understand our emotional behaviour patterns while finding a wonderful sense of joy in the conscious use of ourselves! Its practice runs through the whole of life, but, like any practice, it does need to be applied rigorously.

1   Fig. 2 is from the Wikimedia Commons. The reproduction is part of a collection of reproductions compiled by The Yorck Project. The compilation copyright is held by Zenodot Verlagsgesellschaft mbH and licensed under the GNU Free Documentation License.

Anne Battye has been practising, teaching and living the Alexander Technique since qualifying with Marjory Barlow in 1964. She practises from home in the UK, is a visiting teacher on several training courses and is a STAT assessor and moderator.

Teachable Moments

An Exploratory Workshop

Pamela Blanc

This two-hour workshop had three points of focus:

1. Hermeneutical Reconstruction.
2. The Art of Teaching this Technique.
3. The Art of Learning this Technique.

1. HERMENEUTICAL RECONSTRUCTION

Hermeneutics is the science of interpretation.

Consider that we are interpreting what our teachers interpreted from their teachers' interpretation of what F. M. Alexander taught about his personal discoveries. We are teaching an interpretation of an interpretation.

Are we all teaching the same thing? Probably not – we are more likely teaching an interpretation of Alexander's work. In this workshop we will reconstruct our interpretations.

To explore what the individuals in the workshop thought their interpretation of Alexander's work was, each of them was asked to take out a piece of paper and pencil, do a whispered 'ah', and write down what they thought the *principles* of the Alexander Technique were. A few minutes were given for them to quietly consider the principles and write them down.

Next they were asked to turn the paper over and write down what they considered to be Alexander *procedures*. I suggested that for our purpose in this workshop, we define *procedures* as activities that F. M. Alexander did with his pupils to teach his principles.

When they completed writing their *principles* and *procedures* we listed them on the board for all to see. One side of the board had the heading, *principles;* the other side, *procedures*. Below are the lists the group came up with, in no particular order.

Principles	Procedures
Direction	Monkey
Inhibition	Whispered 'ah'
Use of self	Squat
Use affects functioning	Self-observation
Faulty sensory appreciation	Lunge
Respiratory re-education	Hands on back of the chair – Arms support the body
Unity of self	Chair work
Antagonistic action	Going up onto toes
Non-doing	Table work
Awareness	Thinking in activity
Observation	
Recognition of habit	
Endgaining vs. means-whereby	
Primary control	
Kinaesthetic re-education	

Then, the group spontaneously began naming other activities they apply the Technique to in lessons, and came up with the following:

Talking
Walking
Phone work
Writing
Spirals
Developmental movement
Dart work
Yo-yos – swingers
Riding – saddle work
Wall work
Practical application
Experimentation

The last two: Practical application and Experimentation obviously allow for all other activities. We understand that many of us are working with performers including, but not limited to, actors, singers, instrumentalists, and dancers.

2. The Art of Teaching this Technique

Along with reconstructing the interpretation of the basic principles and procedures of the Alexander Technique, I wanted to know if teachers were teaching the principles and if they were using the procedures to do so. My premise was that there is an art to teaching this Technique and that this art lies in the balance between

   i. giving the student an experience they can draw knowledge from; and
   ii. matching that experience with the understanding of *principle*.

I submitted to the group an opinion that perhaps sometimes there is too much emphasis on giving the student the experience, and trusting that he or she will gain their own understanding through it, without the need for explanation.

It's the old adage – do I want to feed them the fish, or do I want to teach them to fish? Sometimes I think there is too much 'feeding' going on and not enough teaching 'how to fish.' If we teach the *principles*, our students don't have to re-invent the wheel. Let's teach the *principles*. But then, I fall into the other chasm, of TEACHING; this is when I TEACH too much and don't trust or allow the student's experience to do the teaching.

On one end of the continuum is giving the experience and trusting the student will understand/come to embody the principle(s); on the other is explaining the principles without the experience. Where on this continuum do you typically land? Do you talk too much and do too little? Do you do too much and talk too little? Different students have different ways of learning.

I believe it is the understanding of the *principle experienced* that allows the student to have constructive conscious control of his or her self. Choice is the prize the student receives.

To explore our habits in teaching we paired up; one teacher being in the 'teacher' role, the other being the 'student'.

The instructions were that the 'student' was to choose a procedure from the list. The 'teacher' was to take the 'student' through the procedure and identify any particular principle as it surfaced. After 10 minutes they would change roles and the new 'student' would choose a different procedure. We repeated the experiment with a different partner and then gathered together to share our experiences.

Some said they realised in private practice they often did not identify what the *principles* were. But in a group class they tended to address the *principles* and explain them. They were more likely to give their private student the experience. They realised they rarely explained a principle, but rather trusted the student's experience to teach the principle for them.

The student isn't feeling freer, easier, lighter only because the teacher puts hands on him. He or she is feeling different because he engaged his thinking in directing, or inhibiting, or releasing his neck as he went into movement.

3. THE ART OF LEARNING THIS TECHNIQUE

We are aware that we want more people to know the value of the Alexander Technique. But, are we giving our students an anchor for their experience? Are we identifying the principles the Alexander Technique is based on? Why is it hard for our students to explain what they are learning? Are they learning in a way that they can understand? Are they relying on feelings? I encourage teachers to continue with our effective delicate hands-on work, assisting the student towards new experiences. However, we are not teaching experiences. We guide the student towards new experiences and we identify and clarify the principles. It is the working of the principles as the means-whereby that brings these experiences to life. If the student learns to work to principle, he can make his own constructive conscious choices and live his life with ease.

> Pamela Blanc (AmSAT) qualified in 1979 with Frank Ottiwell and Giora Pinkas in San Francisco. She is a Founding Director (1987) and Senior Faculty of The Alexander Training Institute of Los Angeles (ATI-LA) and is the Senior Teacher assisting on Jessica Wolf's Art of Breathing post-graduate courses offered to Alexander teachers internationally. Pamela has continued studying to enhance her own learning as well as consistently teaching the Technique for over thirty-six years both privately and in university music and theatre schools. Currently Pamela is teaching in the Music Conservatory, Chapman University, at ATI-LA, and in her private practice in Los Angeles.

I Could Not Feel so I Learnt to Touch

The Alexander Technique and Emotions

Richard Brennan

> The greatest weapon against stress is our ability to choose one thought over another.
>
> *William James*

In November 2013 I had a stroke – not a major one, but a stroke nevertheless. All my movements such as walking and bending were unaffected; physically it was only my facial and throat muscles that were actually changed. However, like many other people who have strokes I became much more emotional and started to be very conscious of some very strong emotional habits that I still held on to, despite the fact that I had been teaching the Technique for nearly 25 years. I had up to this point been completely unaware of them. For example I was no longer able to feel rushed or hurried by external circumstances – usually because of other people's needs or desires. In other words, for a few months I was simply unable to 'endgain' or be goal-oriented in any way. I also noticed that I was deeply touched by gestures of kindness and recoiled away from unfriendly actions or gestures by others. At this time I also noticed that people's words had a deeper effect on me than usual, especially those of Alexander; for example, the following quotes really resonated with me and I simply had a deeper experiential understanding of them:

The less you do, the better off you will be.

My brain is in my hands.

So, in our work, it is not a question of just relaxing the neck. That is the wrong point of view. The point is to stop doing with the neck what needs to be done with the arms, legs, etc.

The trouble is none of my pupils will believe that all they need to do is to think and that wish for the neck to be free will do the trick. . . .We are so brutalized by our belief in doing and muscular tension.

And the quote that spoke to me most of all was ironically one I don't remember ever having seen before – it was:

Six or seven places in my books I have made a remark which no one ever seems to remember, and that is that ends come by themselves . . . they cannot help but come by themselves.[1]

In fact, after the stroke I felt all my emotions were heightened, especially when it came to music. The music I was most drawn to was that of Leonard Cohen and while listening to his song 'Hallelujah' one day the line 'I could not feel, so I learnt to touch' jumped out at me in a clear and vivid way and seemed to resonate with something very deep within me. I realised that I had been taught from an early age to keep my emotions to myself, to be guarded, not to share my inner thoughts and feelings due to possible ridicule. So much so that I lost touch with what I was actually feeling and I realised that it was this condition of being anaesthetised that was perhaps the very reason why I started my training as an Alexander teacher in the first place – to be more connected to my fellow human beings. However, during my training I was shocked to see that people's emotions were yet again not accepted, in fact it was an unspoken rule that if one of the trainees felt emotional they would go to the bathroom until the feelings passed. I know that this kind of denial was not only present in my own training, but was common practice.

I have found that the common perception of the Alexander Technique, even among other Alexander teachers, is that it is an effective method when improving the way one physically uses oneself and can be of great help to those who suffer from back, neck or shoulder problems. Yet many teachers would shy away from helping those in emotional pain, saying that they had 'no training in that area'. I personally have found that while the Technique can obviously be very useful in helping people to sit, stand and move with greater ease, it can also be invaluable when applied to dealing with emotional habits as well – aspects such as improving self-confidence, the ability to listen to others and the ability to be really present, spontaneous and creative. What many people outside the Alexander community do not realise is that the Alexander Technique can also be extremely effective in combating the effects of stress or emotional pain, which can often be even more debilitating than suffering with physical pain. It would be useful if more Alexander teacher training programmes gave people the tools to deal with emotional habits such as anger, sadness or depression. For example applying inhibition while a person is having an emotional reaction would be very useful indeed. So it is not just a question of whether to express emotions or not, it is beneficial to try to gain conscious control when expressing emotions. In fact Aristotle summed it up well when he said: 'Anyone can get angry – that is easy. But to get angry with the right person, to the right degree, at the right time, for the right purpose and in the right way – this is difficult.' Even simply helping people to be more conscious of their emotional habits in a variety of every-day situations and not making them wrong can help a great deal. When a teacher has hands on a pupil who is having an emotional reaction it can be very valuable to just stay with the hands on, in a calm and comforting way. By being more conscious of, and changing, the way they react, many people can reduce stress levels in their bodies and their minds – in their whole selves.

PRACTICAL APPLICATION

During the workshop at the Congress we explored through observation the difference in muscle tension between various emotions, such as depression, sadness, anger, gratitude and happiness. For example, it was easy to see the contracted muscles during anger compared with the relaxed muscles during happiness. This quotation by William James says it all:

> What kind of an emotion of fear would be left if the feeling neither of quick-ened heart-beats nor of shallow breathing, neither of trembling lips nor of weakened limbs, neither of goose-flesh nor of visceral stirrings, were present, it is quite impossible for me to think. Can one fancy the state of rage and picture no ebullition in the chest, no flushing of the face, no dilatation of the nostrils, no clenching of the teeth, no impulse to vigorous action, but in their stead limp muscles, calm breathing, and a placid face?[2]

We also explored the differences between intuition and instinct and discussed Alexander's definition of each as laid out in *Conscious Control in Relation to Human Evolution in Civilization*:

> I have been often asked the difference between instinct and intuition. I define instinct as the result of the accumulated subconscious psychophysical experience of man at all stages of his development, which continue with us till we reach, singly or collectively, the stage of conscious control: while intuition is a result of the conscious reasoned psychophysical experiences during the process of our evolution.[3]

The second part of the workshop was more practical. The teachers were asked to work in the traditional way for about fifteen minutes, using traditional inhibition and directions and asking their partner to 'lengthen' and 'widen.' Afterwards, while staying with the same partner, they were asked to place their hands on with thoughts of kindness, caring, and support and asking the muscles to soften or ease rather than lengthen. At the end both the 'teacher' and the 'pupil' were asked to verbalise what the difference was and the feedback was that both felt more connected and more cared for. In the second exercise the person who was being worked on often felt more release and ease of movement after the session. It is well worth remembering that when you touch a person, you touch the whole person, the body, the mind, the spirit and the emotions – all at the same time.

It is important to realise that although a teacher has empathy and caring for their student they should not 'take on' the problems of their student or try to fix the problem. I think it is important for all Alexander Teachers to be familiar with the phenomena of 'transference' and 'projection'. 'Transference' is the unconscious redirection of feelings from one person to another, whereas 'projection' happens when the pupil defends him or herself against unpleasant impulses by *denying* their existence in him or her and *attributing* them to others. It is important to realise that whether or not a lesson has an 'emotional component', as teachers we need to remain conscious of ourselves during the process.

STRESS AND UNHAPPINESS

It is my opinion that Alexander teachers need to help people understand that changing how they react physically and mentally can have a profound effect on their emotional well-being. I believe that if we were to make the general public aware that people who practise the Technique often report that they feel happier and more at ease with themselves and others, we would be inundated with people wanting to know more. After my first lesson, which I took for a major back problem, I was amazed to feel as though I had been meditating for hours; I *felt* calm, light and serene even though I was still in some pain. I returned for my second lesson because of the way I felt, and not because the way I used myself had changed. As the stress level in my body dropped, I found that I was more able to cope with everyday problems as they arose; as the internal and external conflict was reduced, a more peaceful and harmonious way of living began to emerge. It was only after this that my back pain started to ease.

It is important to realise that Alexander's personal journey of self-discovery not only freed him from the causes of stress and anxiety, but led him to a place where he could help others to escape from their physical, mental and emotional habitual behaviour. He was convinced that external and internal irritations and pressures that occur at night as well as during the day cause many people a great deal of unhappiness in their lives. In *Constructive Conscious Control of the Individual* Alexander wrote:

> I shall now endeavour to show that the lack of real happiness manifested by the majority of adults of today is due to the fact that they are experiencing, not an improving, but a continually deteriorating use of their psychophysical selves. This is associated with those defects, imperfections, undesirable traits of character, disposition, temperament, etc., characteristic of imperfectly co-ordinated people struggling through life beset with certain maladjustments of the psychophysical organism, which are actually setting up conditions of irritation and pressure during both sleeping and waking hours. Whilst the maladjustments remain present, these malconditions increase day by day and week by week, and foster that unsatisfactory psychophysical state which we call 'unhappiness.' Small wonder that, under these conditions, the person concerned becomes more and more irritated and unhappy. Irritation is not compatible with happiness, yet the human creature has to employ this already irritated organism in all the psychophysical activities demanded by a civilized mode of life. It stands to reason that every effort made by the human creature whose organism is already in an irritated condition must tend to make the creature still more irritated, and, therefore, as time goes on, his chances of happiness diminish.[4]

Alexander developed his technique not only as a way of improving posture and physical health, but as a way of freeing mankind from his 'fixed prejudices' and 'erroneous concepts' which prevent us from being truly happy. His technique is based on the premise that there is an inseparable unity between the body, mind *and* emotions, and he firmly believed that mental stress will lead to muscle tension and eventually to emotional instability. He saw his technique as a journey of self-discovery and hoped that his experience

> may one day be recognised as a signpost directing the explorer to a country hitherto 'undiscovered', and one which offers unlimited opportunity for fruitful research to the patient and observant pioneer.

Oh, and by the way I also discovered that the Alexander Technique is a wonderful tool for helping stroke victims! An unexplored territory!

1   All the quotes that I came across are from www.alexandertechnique.com.
2   James, William (1890). *The Principles of Psychology*, chapter 25: The Emotions, https://ebooks.adelaide.edu.au/j/james/william/principles/chapter25.html.
3   Alexander, F. Matthias (1912). *Conscious Control in Relation to Human Evolution in Civilization.* Methuen: London, p. 47.
4   Alexander, F. Matthias (1923, 1946). *Constructive Conscious Control of the Individual.* Gollancz: London, p. 183.

Richard Brennan trained with Jeanne and Jorgen Haahr and Paul Collins between 1986 and 1989 and now is the director of the only Alexander teacher training college in Ireland (STAT and ISATT approved). He has written eight books on the Alexander Technique which have been translated into twelve languages and include: *The Alexander Technique Workbook, The Alexander Technique Manual, Change Your Posture – Change Your Life, Back in Balance* and *How to Breathe*. He travels internationally giving TV and radio interviews, running workshops and giving lectures. He is the co-founder and president of the Irish Society of Alexander Technique Teachers (ISATT) and was one of the Congress Directors in Limerick. His aim is to make the Alexander Technique accessible to as many people as possible.

www.alexander.ie

The Supreme Art of Education

Ted Dimon

Imagine, if you will, a classroom full of children. There is a teacher at the head of the room, and children engaged in various activities: drawing or making letters, playing games, socialising. These children are not 4 or 5, they are 10, 12, 14 – and they aren't just engaged in activities but paying attention to themselves in a way that has virtually never happened in a public school classroom. Their teacher is likewise concerned not just with what they are learning but with the quality of how they engage in their activities, because she (or he) has an awareness of the child's whole system and appreciates that it is the true foundation for whatever the child does. In short, the teacher cares as much about *how* the children do things as *what* they do, about the process of learning as much as the goals. This is a truly enlightened approach to education that takes into account the child's emotional, intellectual, and psychophysical development, encouraging the fullest development of the child and not simply focusing on end-goals and accomplishments.

I want to write about a classroom that focuses on the child in this way, because creating such an environment was dear to Alexander's heart and central to our work. And if our work is to be recognised in its full meaning, the future of the Alexander Technique must be not treatment, not therapy, not tension relief, but child development – a new vision of education and of the importance of Alexander's discoveries in the field of human development.

A NEW APPROACH TO CHILD DEVELOPMENT

It is, I think, rather obvious to Alexander teachers that the way the child uses him or herself is of fundamental importance to health, development, and learning. Here is this child, at perhaps pre-school age or in grade school, using him or herself in a way that is clearly harmful, and the entire educational process is not only unaware of this but actually encourages the behaviour. And because this is such an observable problem, we might think that merely demonstrating the issue to parents and teachers and showing them how we can address it in the classroom will solve the problem, establishing a new approach to education that focuses on the child's use.

But establishing our work in the classroom is not as simple as this, for several reasons. First of all, as a profession we are fairly certain that our approach is based on a fundamental discovery and a fundamental need – namely, the discovery of the 'primary control' and how to use ourselves more efficiently. But there are many other experts and methods out there that teach about lengthening the spine, body mechanics, and improved coordination, so what makes us right and them wrong? For at least two hundred years (and for probably much longer) people have known about the deterioration of posture and musculoskeletal health in children and have been trying to address the problem in some fashion, usually through body mechanics, deep breathing, and physical culture. Our approach is only one in a long line of approaches; what makes ours so important? The answer is that Alexander discovered something fundamental to child development, but we have yet to explain how this system works and whether it is scientifically demonstrable. How are we going to establish our work in the classroom if we can't scientifically validate the most fundamental physiological part of it, the part upon which our entire work is based?

Second, we can assert that children use themselves in a harmful way and that we are able to help them with this, but exactly how are we supposed to do this? When the teacher asks a child to learn, to take tests, or to learn a skill, he or she will ask the children to rely on their harmful use. Simply superimposing a knowledge of the primary control on the child's activities is not going to rectify this situation, if methods of learning and indeed the entire school system are based on the endgaining principle.

The third reason is the most important and subtle of all. Let's say that we can establish that the primary control works in a certain way and can convince educators, teachers and parents that our method addresses this fundamental aspect of development. What will they do with this information? I was once asked to teach kids in a school, but they had set aside time for the children to move about and didn't understand that the children's use was a matter of all their school activities, not just a form of movement training. This may seem like a small misunderstanding but it really isn't. If we represent – or allow our work to be represented – as a form of movement, nothing fundamental will change in how we educate children, because we will have done nothing to identify the psychophysical aspects of functioning that are so central to our work.

One thing this requires is new terminology, because it was immediately clear to me, when I began to teach in a university setting, that if I simply tried to introduce our work as someone's method, it would quickly be dismissed as just another in a long line of exercise and awareness methods rather than taken seriously as a integral part of child development (hence my use of the word 'neurodynamics' which, far from being a brand that I am promoting, is an attempt to advance serious inquiry into a crucial aspect of child development). The evolution of a field and acceptance of ideas should be based not on competition or branding but on intelligent inquiry into a real and serious subject.

1. The learning process and the means-whereby principle

One of the first elements we must look at, if we are to place the subject of use squarely in child development, is the means-whereby principle. Although theories of cognition and learning have advanced in recent decades, many children continue to struggle in school because the teaching of skills is based on crude ideas of drilling and correctness that remain much the same today as they were two hundred years ago. As Alexander showed, learning should focus not on external action and accomplishment but on mastery of oneself as 'the central instrumentality upon which all learning depends'. In addition to being eminently practical in helping children to overcome basic learning problems, such an approach leads to the fullest development of potential because blind habit is replaced with intelligent self-awareness, giving the child command over the self.

Perhaps the first thing we have to look at in helping children in this way is the process of breaking down a skill into discrete steps so that, instead of focusing on the end-goal we can master intermediate steps in the process of learning and, in this way, pay more attention to *how* we do things than to *what* we are doing. Even so simple a skill as swinging a baseball bat or tennis racket, if examined closely, can be broken down into at least five or six different elements; yet we are rarely given a chance to master these steps separately, or even realise that the different elements exist.

A second element of skill is what I call the 'receptive' component. If you have ever watched someone learning to hit a moving ball with a racket or bat, you know that the teacher's main preoccupation will be to show you how to swing the racket or bat properly as the basis for hitting the ball. But how can the student hit the ball if he or she doesn't first see it, or if the process of trying to swing the racket actually distracts the student from seeing it? This may seem obvious, yet how many of us have been given the opportunity, when learning a racket sport, to learn simply to see the ball first, as the basis for hitting it? Most skills are in fact comprised of a number of receptive components like this one, and if we want to perform effectively, we need to take the time to identify and to learn these elements or, in the case of children, be given help from a teacher who understands the elements and structures the learning environment in such a way that the child has a chance to master them.

The third element is coordination, which is by far the most complex element in learning a skill. Learning to swing a tennis racket may seem to be mainly about what you do with the racket – how you grip it, take it back, and so on. What most learners are usually unaware of is that, in order to swing a tennis racket, you must be able to perform a coordinated crouching or monkey position and to shift your weight; otherwise, you will be unable to transfer weight into the racket face or to properly coordinate the swinging action of the arm with the trunk. In this sense, swinging the racket is not actually about what you do with the racket but about what you do with your whole body, and if you are not well-coordinated, you will not be able to swing the racket properly.

All of these elements fall under the general category of focus on process, which raises an even more fundamental issue which I touched on earlier – the approaches to learning in schools. If the child is to learn based on attention to the process, then the methods on which all learning is based, both in and out of schools, must be conceived in kind. We can't teach kids to use themselves better without thinking about the endgaining assumptions underlying methods of learning, and without articulating a new and coherent theory of learning based on the means-whereby principle. If we don't do this, we will be working against the very principles that schools are based on and will end up working on children's posture, without establishing an intelligent process of learning – the true heart of our work.

2. How the motor–proprioceptive system works

The next thing we have to speak about when we look at children is the primary control. It is clear to all of us, I think, that the primary control is fundamental to our work and fundamental to child development, but what I think may not be as clear is how we represent this. Too often we speak about the primary control as a relationship of body parts that helps to organise movement so that, if a child is slumping or doing things badly, what we must do to help the child is to reorganise this relationship. But the most important thing about the primary control is not what we do to reorganise this relationship. The most important thing is to understand how it works, and this is an important distinction. Because as long as we speak about our work as a head–neck–back relationship that we work with as the basis for helping people, then we place ourselves in the realm of methods that fix things and not in the realm of science and knowledge.

To make this clearer, consider the example of Freud's contribution to our understanding of child psychology. When clinicians began to seriously study emotional problems in adults, Freud introduced the 'talking cure' as an innovative form of therapeutic treatment. If this was all he had done, however, he might have won respect from his peers for his ability as a clinician, but he would not have revolutionised the field of psychology. His greatest impact was the creation of a model of the mind that explained not simply how to treat illness but how development takes place in stages and why illness develops if these stages are not managed correctly. Forget about whether you agree with his model – that's not the point here. The point is that he placed the issue of emotional development in the sphere of science – or at least claimed to – and thus took it out of the realm of methods that fix something and tried instead to establish a new field of knowledge about how the human mind works and how to treat problems in this larger context.

This, as it happens, is precisely what Alexander did in his own field. He didn't just locate a harmful head–trunk pattern and determine how to assist the person by working with this pattern. He discovered a scientific principle of functioning that explains how the motor–proprioceptive system functions and how this system forms the foundation for everything the child does. What makes his work significant in this respect is his concept of *normal functioning*, not just the method he developed for helping children and adults. Alexander understood (among other things) how this system works and how to restore it, not just how to apply his re-educational method to children whose systems worked inefficiently. In the two courses I teach at Columbia Teachers College, I explain how this system works as a integral aspect of child development. It simply isn't enough to speak about the head–neck–back relationship as a helpful organising principle if we cannot articulate the subject matter behind it, the science and the theory. In fact, simply introducing a method will do the very opposite of establishing our work because it ends up placing us, not in child development but in the realm of ancillary methods, such as Pilates and physical therapy, which are designed to fix and help.

3. Psychophysical health and what this means

A third and really critical aspect of this problem, even more subtle than the working of the motor–proprioceptive system, is the psychophysical aspect of use, which of course is related to but not the same as the primary control. Let's say you are trying to teach a child to draw in a more coordinated way and adjust his musculoskeletal system so that he is more balanced in sitting and can now use his arms without unnecessary tension. You might expect that the child would now be able to perform the action in a more coordinated way, since the system, working more efficiently, is perfectly set up to allow the child to accomplish his end without difficulty. What happens instead is that, in response to the intention to draw, the child's muscular system seems to engage in the old way – that is, the harmful muscular activity is brought into play all over again. At this point, it becomes difficult to say whether the problem is in the faulty working of the muscular support system, which is clearly out of balance, or in the neural messages being sent to the muscles. Whatever the answer, we can only conclude that, because the activity is so complex, the instinctive working of the nervous system itself cannot be trusted to provide the correct guidance for the act, which must, accordingly, be taught to the child at a more conscious level. This bodily system, which is neurologically complex because of the proprioceptive elements that are essential to its organisation and control, is not simply *influenced* by the mind but is part of a total activity in which the mental and physical operate together as a total system in action.

An additional factor that must be mentioned is attention. We normally speak of attention as a mental function that is operating efficiently or inefficiently and that can be diagnosed and treated on its own. But attention is related to action and is a fundamental part of the holistic working of the system, as we can see in the case of infants, whose interest in things is directly connected with motor function. At this stage of development, a child's state of motor readiness and overall attention level are tightly coupled, operating as a complete and unitary system to produce an activity that can only be described as psychophysical.

Motor function plays a similarly critical role in the attention levels of school-age children performing more complex tasks. Many pre-school children take great pleasure in simple activities such as drawing because they are balanced and coordinated in their actions – neither completely engrossed and hurried on the one hand, or bored and desultory on the other. A child's ability to engage in such an activity represents a huge advance in complexity compared to the action of the infant. The infant, as we saw, acts intentionally but instinctively. In contrast, a child drawing is engaging in a purely voluntary act. He is painting because he enjoys it and chooses to do it; he can stop what he is doing to admire his work, or take a moment to think about what colours he may want to use and then resume drawing. In short, he can stop and think about what he is doing because there is no longer a fixed connection between his interest in what he is doing and his response in the form of painting. Yet his attention level is still an integral part of the activity and is linked with the actively-working motor system. If, for instance, this boy becomes worried about what he is doing and whether he is doing it well, he may begin to focus too intently on what he is doing and to use too much tension to perform the act, in which case he will no longer appear to be enjoying the process. At the other extreme, if his attention becomes dispersed, he will tend to slump and appear to perform in a desultory way. Just as in the infant, attention in the five year old still functions as part of the motor and behavioural systems, but in a way that is more complex and more easily disturbed. Precisely because his action is more cognitively complex, we tend to separate the act of attention from the total activity of which it is a part. Yet the disturbance in attention is not separate from the psychophysical system as a whole, and if we want to help the child to function in a more balanced way, we have to understand all the factors that enter into balanced action, including physical poise, motor control, response to stimuli, attention, and behaviour as a whole.

We have now identified three elements – the working of the motor–proprioceptive system, the functioning of the system as a behavioural whole, and the quality of attention – that constitute what I would call psychophysical health. Taken together, these elements form a new and comprehensive standard for understanding how the psychophysical system works in a balanced way as the basis for reliable development and learning. Because we lack a standard of psychophysical health in the developing child, we tend to ignore these factors until they reach clinically abnormal levels and fail to see that they are part of normal educational growth. Instead of treating children after the fact, we must develop a standard of psychophysical health in the developing child that places the burden of health not at the back end in the form of clinical treatment but at the front end where it belongs – in our understanding of normal development and learning.

THE DISCOVERY OF 'USE': A PSYCHOPHYSICAL APPROACH TO EDUCATION
I began by saying that if our work is going to be perceived as more than a glorified form of body therapy, we must articulate its profound importance in child development, and I hope I have now made clear why this is so. In the last century or so, we have made great strides in broadening our knowledge of child development, particularly in the areas of emotional and cognitive development. Two hundred years ago we had virtually no understanding of the importance of emotional development in the child; today we have quite sophisticated models describing how a child develops emotionally and for understanding cognitive development and its fundamental importance in learning. What we lack is an understanding of the child as an acting, moving organism, and without this, we have a disembodied, incomplete conception of development that, in spite of advances in the field, is still rather archaic in its lack of knowledge of the biological foundations of the functioning child. As such, the study of proprioception and motor control is not only worthy of our attention but essential to a complete model of health and assessment in the developing child, and to a model of learning based on a full understanding of the functioning self as the central agent in learning. This represents a truly enlightened conception of development, and if our work

is to develop properly, it cannot be placed in the therapeutic sphere because, in that context, it will inevitably be misunderstood and used largely for its benefits, not as a foundational part of child development. To be recognised in its full measure, to fulfill its promise as the revolutionary breakthrough that it is, we must place our work in the field of child development and as the foundation for a complete model of conscious development.

> This is an edited extract from Ted Dimon's longer article, 'The Supreme Art of Education', published in *The Alexander Journal* no. 25 (STAT, UK).

> Dr Theodore Dimon is the founder and director of the Dimon Institute and an adjunct professor in the Clinical Psychology Department at Columbia Teachers College. He received both masters and doctorate degrees in education from Harvard University and Alexander Technique teacher certification from Walter Carrington. He has written seven books: *The Undivided Self*; *Anatomy of the Moving Body*; *The Body in Motion*; *Your Body, Your Voice*; *The Elements of Skill*; *A New Model of Man's Conscious Development*, and *Neurodynamics: The Art of Mindfulness in Action*.

Miss Goldie's Understanding

'Come to Quiet; Give Consent, and the Right Thing Will Do Itself.'

Penelope Easten

This paper discusses the key principles of Miss Goldie's teaching on working on yourself as I understand it and as we explored in the workshop at the Congress. A second workshop took the principles into putting hands on, and won't be covered here. The quotes included are her teaching phrases to me – her phrases that burnt somehow into my brain, so that years later I can still hear them as they were spoken.

WHO WAS MISS GOLDIE? WHY DOES SHE MATTER?
Miss Goldie (1905-1997) first went to F. M. for lessons in 1927, then learnt to teach by apprenticeship, as all teachers did then. Froebel-trained (the alternative education method of the day, in some ways akin to Montessori) she was main teacher in Alexander's little school from 1929 until it folded in 1942. She was on the first training course (1931-34). When F. M. went to America during the war, she and four other teachers took the small school

there also. After they returned, F. M. and Goldie lived together, Goldie acting as F. M.'s housekeeper. She stayed closest to him to the end of his life and nursed him after his stroke, hearing his last thoughts on his discoveries. She loved him like a disciple, and he in turn was a great admirer of her work. She was with him when he died.

After he died, she kept largely separate from the rest of the profession, as she felt it had lost its way. She clearly considered herself the true guardian of the Technique, and attempted in her work to stay completely true to the principles by which F. M. discovered and evolved the Technique. Those of us lucky enough to be allowed to work with her, and with stamina to withstand the frequent insults, felt that through her one was taught to return to the essence of F. M.'s teachings. This old lady in Edwardian dress, including hat with hat-pin, who spoke always in measured, clear, perfectly-enunciated English, took one into a different, older world.

In workshops, I use games to enable participants to experience the qualities her teaching brought about, as I experienced it. She herself never used games, but worked with chair, and occasionally table, in the traditional way. The differences between her teaching and that of others were subtle but powerful, and difficult often to convey with words alone, as our words are often the same. The games have proved over many years now to be a fast, reliable way to shortcut to the experience.

OBSERVATION FIRST

Her work always contained observation. Fiercely precise, she was able to get one to see what one was doing, even though her remarks often sounded like insults! 'You have legs like bus-stops...' 'Now look at you! You are like a sack of potatoes, no! That would be insulting to the potatoes, because potatoes have life, and in this moment you have no life....' They were not intended as criticism, however, only as honest comment to help you to understand what you were doing. Then soft, almost murmuring, continual instruction: 'Now not your thing, not your thing with your head....' 'Come to quiet....'

So we began the workshop at the Congress with observation of how we engage in a simple task – looking for hidden objects round the room. Several participants noticed how easily they reverted to anxious or scattered thinking, endgaining, etc., and observers noted that the actions looked much more careful, even sleepy, than they might while doing such a task at home, or that small children might bring to the task. Miss Goldie might have remarked that they were either not conscious enough, or were over-involved with their actions. Continual consciousness in any task was a central theme: 'There is no switching off!'

MIND IN THE BRAIN, ATTENTION AND AWARENESS

We then embarked on discovering how to become conscious: by finding the place from where Miss Goldie wanted us to think. She often told me to bring my mind to my brain, rather than letting it be continually checking on myself. 'You are over-involved with your feelings!', 'How do you know what you are feeling?', she would demand.

She seemed to define 'mind' as the place from where one is thinking, which can move around the body (or be outside it). She contrasted it with the brain, which is a fixed organ, in the head. (I am aware there are other definitions of 'mind'; I will not discuss these here.) She wanted me to think from the top of my head, rather than from below the eyebrows, or at the neck. 'People forget they have all this area above the eyes and the neck.' She told me: 'At the end of his life, Mr Alexander told me he wished to God he'd never said "free the neck" – "All they can think about is their necks!"' Mind is different from attention. Attention is what one is thinking about. So as we will discover, attention and mind can be in the same place (the state of over-focusing on something, to the exclusion of all else), or they can be separate, so that you are aware of yourself as separate from the task.

When participants played with putting their mind in their foot, they could clearly perceive something moving downwards. When they then gave consent to wiggle their toes, they noticed that the sensation was definite, that they felt in control, but it felt tight. They were only aware of the foot, excluding the rest of the body. Their vision dimmed; there was pulling down and in; the world was lost to them. In contrast, with the mind in the brain and eyes seeing surroundings, they needed to trust that the message would reach the toes. Many found it hard initially to think of giving consent to wiggling toes without going down there. When they succeeded though, there were clear differences: the physical sensation was much less, but there was a sense of the foot integrated with the rest of the body, of greater freedom and lightness in the movement. The vision and connection with the world stayed clear. Miss Goldie often talked of trusting that the brain messages would get through.

But mind in brain does not shut us off from the body. Miss Goldie would talk of keeping the whole body alive, not switching off in the legs, for instance. We played with including awareness of each part of the body in turn, while maintaining the mind in the brain and eyes seeing out. Afterwards, participants observed a sense of lightness, wholeness. The awareness of the whole body then becomes a peripheral awareness akin to visual peripheral awareness, and similarly spatial in nature.

Vision and presence

Though Miss Goldie didn't talk about vision, I noticed that for me, her work brought about a quietening of my usually reactive eyes, and that depth perception came in, so the whole room would come quietly present. I have found that one can work this the other way round. Coming present to the whole room in this gentle 3D way in turn quietens the desire to over-involve with the body, although that too stays present. So we played with looking gently around, letting the eyes glide over what they saw, seeing spaces between objects, seeing detail across the space between self and object, seeing from the back of the head. Participants noticed a quieting of their whole being.

Inhibition, the key to real change

'Come to quiet' was Goldie's key phrase; for her, conscious inhibition was the key to change. Only when we let go of all desire to do an action will the brain stop preparing every muscle in the body to act in the old way, and we come to quiet. From this point true change can happen. Then we have a real choice whether to act or not, as we are not secretly committed (prepared) for the usual action. Only from this place of no preparation can the brain return to an earlier setting, even to blueprint, and re-find or configure integrated muscle patterns. Goldie called this 'making a discovery'; also 'going into the unknown'. But mostly, we do not come fully to that quiet; we pause, rather than stop.

Participants threw beanbags, initially to a partner, then to their other hand, letting each one drop, until they let go of ALL desire to catch the beanbag. Then we played with real choice to catch or not, checking we are still 'quiet throughout' – fully alive, not sleepy. From this quiet, alive place, participants could choose to give consent to catch. Then the hand moved as if by itself to catch the beanbag. The process was completely easy; coordination sorted itself.

Only a peripheral glimpse of the beanbag was needed to enable a catch. When 'quiet', the brain knows where all body parts are, and their spatial relationships. So we can understand Goldie's repeated instructions: 'Come to quiet, then give consent and let it happen' and 'Let the brain sort the task out.'

Putting it all together to rediscover the Technique

We set simple tasks, like walking to an object and picking it up. The first need always was to stop, with mind in the brain, seeing gently out to the task with depth perception.

To let go of all desire to do the task, we played 'No' games. This is the same game F. M. developed, and which he described in *The Use of the Self*,[1] in order to bring about a new way of reciting. Through this game he discovered how to bring about an entirely new way of doing any action. A series of instructions are given, then let go of. 'I will pick up the blue ball' – be aware of any slight preparation, such as leaning towards, starting to tense the hand. . . instead say 'no'. Let go of that idea. Completely. Instead, choose a new task, and repeat, changing tasks each time. 'I will pick up that green ball' – 'no'. 'I will walk to the chair' – 'no'. Sometimes we are only aware of preparation when we say no and it releases. By letting the brain begin preparing for the task, and then letting it go, repeating this with several tasks, eventually the brain gets tired of preparing and 'gives up'. Then we come to quiet, an alive place from which 'the brain is waiting out for the new instruction',[2] rather than guessing ahead. Participants noticed that bringing in depth perception, the sense of separation between self and object, helped them come to quiet much faster.

Only when there was NO desire to proceed, could we then give consent and let it happen. To let it happen without controlling it, feeling the way in it, checking the rightness of movement, being careful. . . Simply to see the object clearly and let ourselves follow the eyes and intent, as we stayed out of our own way. Then the Technique could be discovered afresh: participants who bent to pick something up found their bodies went naturally into monkey without any need to organise it, think about freeing the neck, etc. Walking was alive and full of intent, rather than sleepy or careful as observed in the first game of finding things. Hands reached in an alive way for an object and used appropriate strength for the task; the muscles acted responsively, not predictively, to the object's weight and size, and sensitivity of touch was vastly greater. Inhibition becomes a prelude to action, to letting life flow, rather than an end in itself which can damp us down.

Miss Goldie's anger

This was the nub of why Miss Goldie felt the Technique had lost its way. The protocol for teaching the Technique developed by Patrick Macdonald, Kitty Merrick (later Wielopolska) and Marjory Barlow, and later Walter Carrington,[3] and passed down in training courses, had turned Alexander's process around. F. M.'s original process was to come to quiet, and then in giving consent to let the body move, he discovered that the head led, the body followed, and the hand reached in a way that was secondary to the head neck back relationship. The teaching protocol then took these discoveries, and turned them round into a method: you free the neck, then let the head lead, the body follow etc, whereby we direct and organise our bodies into the prescribed movement. 'They [the training course teachers] have a theory: a set of fixed ideas which they like to impose on you – "practice". Whereas with F. M. it was the other way around: practice came first – discovery of the truth – and then the theory.'[4] 'Mr Alexander would make more discoveries making a cup of tea than most teachers make in their entire lives!' But most of us were never taught how.

Working on yourself in daily life

Participants in the workshop were keen to integrate this way of working on oneself into their daily lives. Miss Goldie suggested to me a way of doing this: to take a task a week, such as opening a door or brushing one's hair, and then every time you come to that task, to allow the time to stop and 'give yourself a lesson'. To come to quiet, with the four keys described here: playing 'No' games to STOP, rather than pause; bring mind to brain; maintaining awareness throughout the body; eyes seeing out to the task. Then to give consent, let the process happen, and see what happens next! Through this, you discover for yourself how the body moves, and how to make real choices. Also you build a new habit, not of how to do the task, but of coming conscious as you do that task, enabling one to be conscious more and more in life.

This then sets us up for working on others. 'People come to you to learn the quality of your life. If you have not been living your life well, then ten minutes lying down before a lesson is not going to sort it!'

THE FUTURE

Personally, I do not believe the teaching protocol developed by Macdonald et al has no value; up until recently it has been more accessible and communicable, and without it, probably none of us would be teaching today. But I now see our profession moving gently back to F. M.'s core technique. In the last decade particularly, we have begun to understand the real science behind what we do (which is beyond the scope of this paper), which the older generation were not able to give us. Alongside this understanding, fast ways of communicating the essence, such as these presented here, have been developed by several teachers.

In my own teaching practice, I use these games alongside chair and table work with all pupils. Coming to quiet, asking precise brain work from them, and observation and work on themselves between lessons, allows much faster change of their psychophysical patterns.

I believe this original way now needs to be incorporated into training courses and all teaching. Done with real understanding, rather than simply copying skills, it will both strengthen our technique and increase its accessibility to science, as we move further in time from F. M. himself.

1   Alexander, F. M. (1985, 1932). *The Use of the Self*. Gollancz: London.
2   Goldie's words to me, as are all the quotations here unless otherwise attributed.
3   Hunter, John (2013): *The First Training Course in 1931: a different perspective*. https://upwardthought.wordpress.com/2013/08/13/the-first-training-course-in-1931-a-different-perspective/
4   Goldie to Fiona Robb. Robb, Fiona (1999). *Not to 'Do'*. Camon Press: London.

Penelope Easten came to the Technique in 1983. After training with Misha Magidov in the North London Alexander School, she took lessons with Miss Goldie for four years. She has had busy teaching practices in London, then Sheffield, and for ten years now in the West of Ireland. She has been running courses on Miss Goldie's work in Ireland, UK and abroad for eleven years and her booklet 'Lessons with Miss Goldie' has sold worldwide. She is now writing a longer book on Miss Goldie and her work. She works extensively with natural breathing to bring the body fully present, alive and strong. With the Emotions Toolbox she has developed mind-body-centred ways of resolving emotional blocks and boundary issues that stop us coming quiet.

www.alexandertechniqueinfo.org

Slaying the Invisible Man

A Take on Alexander Consciousness

Henry Fagg

Why does the self often seem to 'disappear' when we are engaged in activity? In this workshop, I drew on some philosophical, scientific and experiential accounts in order to explore this phenomenon in relation to the Alexander Technique.

WHAT DO I MEAN BY A 'DISAPPEARING BODY'?
Writers of different backgrounds have described the way in which the body seems to 'disappear', 'vanish' or be 'absent' in activity. Below are three examples which help bring this curious aspect of our lives into focus:
When typing,

> I perch in a chair for hours suspending large portions of my corporeal existence in order to proceed with my specific task. This body is largely placed into background disappearance . . . (Drew Leder)[1]

When reaching for a glass,

> . . . all I experience is the look and taste of the wine as I drink it. I don't experience the various corrections made to the movements as my brain navigates my arm through the various obstacles on the table to reach the wine glass. I don't experience the change in the angles of my elbow or the feel of the glass on my fingertips as they adjust perfectly to the size of the stem. . . . As long as I stay in control I don't have to bother with the physical world of actions and sensations. (Chris Frith)[2]

When fetching a book from the bookcase,

> . . . if I were to formulate the content of my consciousness in this regard, it would not be in terms of operating or stretching muscles, bending or unbending limbs, turning or maintaining balance; it would not even be in terms of walking, reaching, standing, or sitting. Rather, in the context of an intentional project, if I were stopped and asked what I was doing, I would say something like, 'I'm getting a book'. All the bodily movement entailed in that action remains phenomenologically hidden behind that description. (Shaun Gallagher)[3]

PART 1. THE DISAPPEARING BODY AND IDEOMOTOR ACTION
In the first part of my workshop, I introduced ideomotor action and suggested it was related to the phenomenon of a disappearing body.

The ideomotor principle states that, over time and on an unconscious level, actions become associated with their sensory effects such that one need only think of the consequence of an action to initiate it. For example, over time, switching on a lamp becomes linked up in the brain with a particular sound, feel and visual effect. The ideomotor principle asserts that *idea* of the switched-on lamp (the 'ideo' in ideomotor) is then enough to initiate and control the action itself. William James first popularized this notion in the 19th century with his observation that 'we think the act, and it is done; and that is all that introspection tells us of the matter'.

Modern ideomotor theories[4] provide evidence that action can indeed be driven by 'end-state mental representations' in our brains such as a door opened, a button pressed or a field traversed. Since these representations are built on a lifetime of successfully completed actions, ideomotor acts are always controlled by what is known, or habitual, and they therefore take no account of the way the movement happens to be unfolding in real time. The similarity with Alexander's endgaining is striking.

I have argued elsewhere[5] that the 'experience' of an ideomotor act therefore amounts to very little sensorially. This is for two reasons. Firstly, because ideomotor acts are generated by representations stored in the brain, they do not require any ongoing sensory feedback during the actual movement. Secondly, because the brain accurately predicts the actual outcome in advance, ideomotor acts do not even require a conscious interest in their own result. It is only when something unexpected occurs (for example, if the switch on the lamp is broken) that we are returned to our senses in the 'here and now'. When caught up in an 'ideomotor attitude', our movements are for most of the time carried along by a mental projection of a predicted future. As such, our awareness of the self in activity all but disappears.

I believe Muriel Barbary captures a vivid sense of ideomotor action in her 2006 novel, *The Elegance of the Hedgehog:*

> Maman just went by in the direction of the front door, she's going out shopping and in fact she already is out, her movement anticipating itself. I don't really know how to explain it, but when we move, we are in a way de-structured by our movement toward something: we are both here and at the same time not here because we're already in the process of going elsewhere, if you see what I mean. To stop de-structuring yourself, you have to stop moving altogether. Either you move and you're no longer whole, or you're whole and you can't move.[6]

Part 2. Ideomotor action – the only way to act?
The narrator in Barbary's novel goes on to contrast the 'de-structured' movement above with the 'very fluid but above all very focused' movement exhibited by a New Zealand rugby player she watches on television:

> I got the impression that he was moving, yes, but by staying in one place. Crazy, no? Everyone was enthralled by him but no one seemed to know why. . . . That Maori player was like a tree, a great indestructible oak with deep roots and a powerful radiance – everyone could feel it. And yet you also got the impression that the great oak could fly, that it would be as quick as the wind, despite, or perhaps because of, its deep roots. . . . compact moments where a player became his own movement without having to fragment himself by heading *towards* . . . The commentators were sort of hungover but they couldn't hide the fact that they'd seen something really beautiful: a player who was running without moving, leaving everyone else behind him. And the others, who seemed by comparison to move with frenzied and awkward gestures, were incapable of catching up with him. . . . So I said to myself: There, I have managed to witness motionless movement in the world: is that something worth carrying on for?[7]

The second part of my workshop explored ways of acting which lie outside the ideomotor framework; ways of acting which arguably have much in common with Barbary's description above.

One of the features of ideomotor action is that it is under our *direct* control. In other words, one only needs to think of the result of the action and the action takes place – again, we may remember William James' notion that 'we think the act, and it is done'. Other ways of influencing our musculoskeletal system – such as Alexander's means-whereby or primary control – can be categorized as *indirect*. In the workshop, I suggested that a number of modern-day understandings from different fields of enquiry have similarities with the Alexander Technique because they too are concerned with the indirect control of human action. I explored six of them: James Gibson's *Affordances*, Hubert Dreyfus' *Skilled Coping*, Mihaly Csikszentmihalyi's *Flow*, Brian Bruya's *Natural Human Action*, Tim Ingold's *Correspondence*, and Victor Gurfinkel's *Postural Tone*.

As an example, perhaps the most well-known among these approaches is *Flow*, a way of moving which athletes seem to enter when performing at their peak, and described by the man who coined the term as the as 'the holistic sensation that people feel when they act with total involvement'.[8] With this in mind, a deeper understanding of Alexander's principles could be gained by a familiarity with some of the attributes of Flow; for instance, I have found the exploration of notions such as *action-awareness merging*, *unambiguous feedback* and *autotelicity* (doing something for its own sake) to be helpful. As with Alexander's own indirect procedures, Csikszentmihalyi is explicit about how Flow is only under *indirect* control, stating that 'It is not possible to make flow happen at will . . . and attempting to do so will only make the state more elusive. However, removing obstacles and providing facilitating conditions will increase its occurrence.'[9]

Along with the Alexander Technique, I believe that the six accounts of movement, skill and agency I explored in the second part of my workshop form a critique of ideomotor action. All of them have an affinity with so-called 'ecological' approaches to human action, and help to subvert or challenge the more dominant 'cognitive' explanations offered by neuroscientists.

And why might such approaches to action be necessarily *indirect*? It seems that acting in such ways requires the subject to relinquish full control and enter into a 'mutualist' relationship with the environment; or, as Rob Withagen and colleagues put it, 'intentions should not be understood as mental states that are insulated from the agent's body and the environment, and cause an animal to move . . . the animal–environment relation is the proper unit of analysis in understanding agency.'[10]

I give the full background to these accounts in my forthcoming article, 'Nine Modern Contexts for the Alexander Technique'.[11]

PART 3. A NEW TAKE ON ALEXANDER CONSCIOUSNESS: THE BODY SCHEMA
In the final section of the workshop I asked the question, 'What kind of consciousness for the Alexander Technique?'. In this, I argued that the six indirect approaches to action I described all rely on conscious access to the *body schema* which can be understood as *a holistic, three-dimensional map of the body which constantly tracks body parts in relation to each other and the environment.* Iain McGilchrist describes this map as being not just a picture, representation or sum of our bodily perceptions, but instead a 'living image, intimately linked to activity in the world – an essentially affective experience'.[12] It is for this reason that disturbances in the body schema are associated with profoundly distressing illnesses such as body dysmorphia and anorexia nervosa.

Although essential for all motor activity, it is often assumed that the body schema remains either unconscious or at best marginal to awareness, working in the background in order that we can successfully accomplish our everyday tasks. This is no doubt true for many people for whom an 'invisible body' is their default mode of being. It has been remarked upon by scientists in the following ways:

> Subjective awareness does not seem to be involved in 'how' actions are performed.[13]

> Actual sensory feedback has a remarkably limited role in the experience of action in neurologically healthy individuals.[14]

Obviously, the neural mechanisms underlying consciousness have more important things to do than controlling the low-level executive details of our actions. It may even seem optimal, in terms of neural economy, to assume that a movement unfolds as planned when it reaches its goal.[15]

Anyone familiar with Alexander Technique, or with other understandings of movement such as the six I explored in this workshop, would probably beg to differ with these views. In developing an alternative perspective, I have found the work of the contemporary French philosopher Dorothée Legrand useful, in particular her paper entitled 'Pre-reflective self-consciousness: on being bodily in the world'.[16]

Legrand maintains that the body schema is indeed conscious, and that it generates a type of 'performative awareness' which is particularly developed in dancers and other movement experts. For her, the subjective experience of the 'performative body' is distinct both from the 'invisible body' described above, but also from the experience of the 'opaque body'. This is where we use a 'spotlight' of attention to look at ourselves, such that our body and its parts are focused on as opaque objects which are clearly separate from their surroundings. In contrast, performative awareness does *not objectify* the body, is *pre-reflective*, and is concerned instead with *the whole self in relation to the world*. Despite its pre-reflective nature, Legrand argues that the performative body can nevertheless be brought to 'the front' of one's experience without turning it into 'a mere intentional object'.

As my title suggests, working with the body schema and performative awareness is likely to be a way to 'slay the invisible man'. Not only is it a probable foundation for the six indirect approaches to movement I explored in this workshop, but also for the application of the principles of the Alexander Technique. It has been said before that applying the Alexander Technique is akin to working on the body schema;[17] however, as far as I know, the Alexander Technique has not been explored before in relation to notions of the 'disappearing', 'opaque' or 'performative' body, or related in this way to ideomotor action or other indirect approaches to movement.

References
1   Leder, D. (1990). *The Absent Body*. University Press: Chicago, p. 29.
2   Frith, C. (2007). *Making up the mind: how the brain creates our mental world*. Blackwell: Oxford, p. 105.
3   Gallagher, S. (2005) *How the body shapes the mind*. University Press: Oxford, p. 33.
4   For example, Hommel, B., J. Müsseler, G. Aschersleben, W. Prinz (2001). 'The theory of event coding (TEC): A framework for perception and action planning' in *Behavioral and brain sciences* 24(5), pp. 849-937.
5   Fagg, H. (2015) 'The Alexander Technique as adaptive behaviour'. In C. Rennie,

T. Shoop & K. Thapen (eds.) *Connected perspectives: the Alexander Technique in context*, London: HITE.

6   Barbary, Muriel (2008). *The Elegance of the Hedgehog.* Trans. Alison Anderson. London: Gallic Publications. p. 36.

7   *Ibid.*

8   Csikszentmihalyi, M. (1975). *Beyond boredom and anxiety: experiencing flow in work and play.* Jossey Bass: San Francisco, p. 36.

9   Jackson, S., Csikszentmihalyi, M. (1999) *Flow in sports,* Human Kinetics: Champaign, IL, p. 138.

10   Withagen, R., de Poel, H., Araújo, D. and Pepping, G-J (2012) 'Affordances can invite behaviour: reconsidering the relationship between affordances and agency', *New ideas in psychology,* 30, 250-258, p. 255.

11   Fagg, H. (in press) 'Nine modern contexts for the Alexander Technique' in *The Alexander Journal,* issue 25, STAT.

12   McGilchrist, I. (2009). *The Master and his Emissary: The Divided Brain and the Making of the Western World.* Yale University Press: New Haven, p. 66.

13   Jeannerod, M. (2009) 'The sense of agency and its disturbances in schizophrenia: a reappraisal'. *Experimental Brain Research,* 192(3) pp. 527-32.

14   Fotopoulou, A. et al. (2008). 'The role of motor intention in motor awareness, an experimental study on anosognosia for hemiplegia' in *Brain,* 131(12), pp. 3432-42.

15   Desmurget, M. and Sirigu, A. (2009). 'A parietal-premotor network for movement intention and motor awareness'. *Trends in Cognitive Sciences* 13(10) pp. 411-9.

16   Legrand, D. (2007). 'Pre-reflective self-consciousness: on being bodily in the world', *Janus head,* 9(2), pp. 493-519.

17   See, for example, Blakeslee, S. and Blakeslee, M. (2007). *The body has a mind of its own.* Random House: New York, p. 37.

Henry Fagg trained in the Alexander Technique with Peter and Eleanor Ribeaux at the Centre for the Alexander Technique, London. He is also a musician with a background in English literature and comparative education. He has published research reflecting his diverse interests: the science and philosophy of the Alexander Technique, private tuition in the UK, and Mahatma Gandhi's holistic vision for educating India.

Lighten Up!

Chronic Endgaining, The Use of the Self, and Help for Well-Meaning People Who Try Too Hard

Diane Gaary

'My teachers tell me I try too hard, I think too much, and I am filled with tension. I just want to get it right. I've tried everything and nothing works. I guess I'm a really tense person.' As an Alexander teacher in the performing arts, when I hear this frustration from actors, singers, and instrumentalists, I know that once again I will be dealing with an old 'frien-emy', my nemesis – endgaining.

The problem with endgaining
If you've had the experience of working on something, and the harder you tried the worse it got, then you know what it's like to endgain. This paper will discuss endgaining as outlined by F. M. Alexander in *The Use of the Self*,[1] and offer strategies to address the problem of chronic endgaining.

Alexander defines 'a confirmed endgainer'[2] as someone whose 'habit is to work directly for his ends on the "trial and error" plan without giving due consideration to the means whereby those ends should be gained.'[3] Many of us are familiar with the unpleasant symptoms of working in this result-oriented fashion:

Symptoms of endgaining
- Increased muscular tension/force
- Result-oriented thinking
- Narrowed focus of attention
- Repetition of ineffective tactics to achieve the desired result
- Decreased coordination
- Decreased self-awareness
- Decreased creativity and choice
- Increased anxiety and frustration

Alexander writes, 'This habit of reacting too quickly to stimuli is always associated with sensory untrustworthiness, undue muscle tension and misdirection of energy.'[4] Endgaining leaves us tired and injury prone, and it doesn't allow us to effectively improve our skills or achieve the highest levels of skill. As Alexander put it, 'his very desire to "be right in gaining his end" defeated the end.'[5]

Why we endgain and why some people are prone to chronic endgaining
Endgaining is a response to a perceived need, with an unconscious belief that if we don't apply force, we won't get what we desire. Endgaining is an act of will in the face of fear that our needs won't be met. In this fearful state, we are less aware, we don't consider our options (the means whereby we could address our need), and in desperation we resort to muscular force.

Alexander wrote, 'Endgaining is a universal habit'[6] but some of us seem exceptionally prone to it. Those of us who are good at endgaining can endgain anything – even the Alexander Technique. 'This habit of "endgaining" is so ingrained that it will create a serious difficulty even when the teaching method is based on the "means-whereby principle".'[7] Since we can even endgain working on endgaining, it can be disheartening! It helps morale to recognise that although endgaining is frustrating and can keep us from excelling at the activities that matter to us, chronic endgaining is actually a reflection of some very useful personal qualities.

The typical personality of a chronic endgainer
- Caring enough to give 100% or more of one's self to achieve a goal
- Intelligent enough to identify useful goals
- Hardworking
- Giving enough to inconvenience themselves for a goal
- Passionate, dedicated, and committed
- Interested in quality to the point of being perfectionistic.

When viewed in this light, chronic endgainers seem to be a fairly attractive group of people who are intelligent, caring, giving, hardworking, dedicated, and passionately interested in quality. Society values these personality traits with encouraging phrases such as 'Try your hardest! Just do it! Be all that you can be! Apply yourself!' In the face of societal rewards, people who are prone to endgaining overuse these admirable personality qualities. These useful qualities help chronic endgainers achieve some success in their fields of endeavour, but the symptoms of endgaining frustratingly prevent them from achieving the very best results.

Using the Alexander Technique to develop a process-oriented approach to meeting our needs
Alexander Technique enthusiasts are experts on endgaining. In fact many of us came to the Technique because trying too hard caused us problems. Working to recognise and inhibit endgaining is a large part of Alexander teacher training. The Technique addresses endgaining through awareness, inhibition, direction, non-doing, and the means-whereby. Much has been written of these concepts, so here I will only mention how they relate to chronic endgaining.

Awareness

The Alexander Technique examines how we work with ourselves, which largely is how we think and relate to the world. Interrelatedness is at the core of our work. As we study the Technique, we become increasingly aware of how we habitually respond to people, situations, and inanimate objects. We also learn how we physically respond to our desires, needs, and thoughts. We discover that both external and internal stimuli are potential triggers for endgaining. Awareness of our bodies' responses to these stimuli is essential to having choice over those responses. A large part of studying the Alexander Technique involves identifying and working to inhibit our habitual responses to common and personal endgaining triggers.

Typical external/situational triggers
- Exercise
- Time pressures
- Large work loads
- Fatigue
- Performance activities
- Everyday activities that we find physically challenging.

Internal stimuli can be just as potent as external stimuli, because how we think affects how we function. Noticing thoughts that trigger endgaining (what I call 'toxic thoughts') can be invaluable in learning to change our endgaining habits.

Typical internal/mental triggers (toxic thoughts)
- I want to do it right
- I need to be good at this
- I've got to hurry
- I've got to be better than X
- I'm bad at this
- This is important
- This activity is difficult
- I really want them to like me and/or like my work
- For singers: I have to sound like X
- For actors: I have to be funny, to cry, be sexy, be angry, etc. . .
- I'm bored/hate what I'm doing and I just want to get it over with.

Even awareness of how we talk with ourselves about endgaining can determine how successful we are at changing our endgaining habit. Since endgaining is a state of mind, it helps to notice its opposite.

The opposite of endgaining
- Possessing the capacity to inhibit
- Experiencing an expansive field of awareness which is not fixed on any one subject, (rather like a camera with a flexible lens of focus)
- Employing a non-doing approach to working
- Using the means-whereby (focusing on the process rather than the result)
- Involving ourselves in the sensory experience of the present moment
- Exercising curiosity and exploring options
- Engaging humour (endgaining is funny – comedies are full of it)

Consciously encouraging curiosity and a positive attitude is helpful when working with chronic endgaining. Useful thoughts can be:

'Here I am endgaining again. I've done it before. I'll probably do it again. It's not the end of the world, but it's not helping me now. To help myself, I'm going to think: What do I need? What less can I do here? What are my options?' or,

'Oh, this situation is bad and I'm under a lot of pressure. Wait. Stop. I'm going to give myself time to calm myself down, think about what I need, and examine my choices', or,

'I always have the option of doing nothing. I can be in the state of non-doing possibility, until I can proceed in a non-doing manner.'

When we find ourselves in an endgaining moment, it also is helpful to recognise the fear component of endgaining and to treat oneself with compassion. Useful thoughts might be: 'What do I need here? Why might I not get what I need? Let me give myself a moment to inhibit and care for myself. Now, what means-whereby might help me get what I want?'

Since we often lack humour when we endgain, it is often productive to remind ourselves that using too much effort when we don't have to is funny: 'Look at me, here I am doing that silly thing that doesn't work again! I don't have to do that – I have better tools to get the job done.'

Inhibition
Awareness and inhibition support each other. Inhibition is a space of time in which we have opportunity to decrease muscular use, gather information about how we are reacting to a stimulus, and make choices about how we'd like to proceed. Inhibition gives us opportunities to notice cause and effect. Inhibition is also an opportunity to not engage in habits we have identified as disadvantageous. By calming our fear response, inhibition provides us with the ability to make choices. Alexander frequently stressed the importance of inhibition: 'All those who wish to change something in themselves must learn to make it a principle of life to inhibit their immediate reaction to any stimulus to gain a desired end',[8] and 'they must continue this inhibition whilst they employ the new direction of their use.'[9]

Lack of inhibition is the essential element of endgaining. Lack of inhibition creates a self-perpetuating cycle of overall misuse. Overuse of force leads to increased misuse, which decreases our inhibitory powers, and spurs us to use more force. Alexander wrote that people are more prone to endgaining if their use is compromised: 'In all the years that I have been teaching pupils whose use of themselves is wrong, I have never yet found any of them able to inhibit the desire to gain an end directly until this unsatisfactory use has been changed.'[10] In other words, endgaining and subsequent poor use can decrease our ability to inhibit: 'My failure to *continue to inhibit*, due to the habit of endgaining, was *the* obstacle to my employing the new "means-whereby".'[11] The encouraging message is that as we improve our use and increase our inhibitory skill, our tendency towards endgaining will diminish.

Direction and the means-whereby
Both direction and the means-whereby provide a process-oriented (non-endgaining) way of working. Direction helps us identify what would be going on in our bodies if all was operating well. Directing ourselves involves using neuro-muscular energy in useful ways. Using the means-whereby involves identifying the steps that will bring us towards our goals and using curiosity to immerse ourselves in those steps. The means-whereby is 'the principle inherent in the technique, namely, that the end for which they are working is of minor importance as compared with the way they direct the use of themselves for the gaining of that end.'[12] 'It is possible, by working to the principle of the "means-whereby" procedure, to strike at the very roots of the habit of endgaining which is so deeply embedded in our make-up.'[13] The problem is that it is possible to endgain direction and means-whereby, and this is why awareness and inhibition must be continuously present. Alexander only achieved success when his 'instinctive response to the stimulus to gain [his] original end was not only inhibited at the start, but remained inhibited right through, whilst [his] directions for the new use were being projected.'[14]

Issues that face chronic endgainers
Despite Alexander Technique training, some of us find ourselves with endgaining tendencies years after our training. We are chronic endgainers. Yet the Alexander Technique has not failed us. We need not get discouraged. Awareness, inhibition and direction are mental muscles that develop strength through use. By using these tools, we are developing a compassionately informed relationship with our bodies and ourselves. By noticing when we limit options by using too much force, we develop an awareness of our detrimental thoughts. By using the Alexander Technique, we discover how our bodies respond to our thoughts and we learn to think more clearly and effectively. The Technique challenges us to trust this process of working with the mind-body connection: 'My trust in my reasoning processes to bring me safely to my "end" must be a genuine trust, not a half-trust needing the

assurance of *feeling right* as well.'[15]

Learning to trust that working this way works better than endgaining can be challenging, since it involves being willing to exist in a state of possibility and choice. It is especially challenging to trust the effectiveness of this state of non-doing possibility when the initial experience of endgaining seductively feels powerful, energised, and full of accomplishment. Therefore, to change our endgaining habit we must recognise that endgaining is a state of mind and that improvement requires a change of attitude. To effectively rehabilitate our chronic endgaining tendencies, our beliefs must sincerely change to something such as, 'If I really want this to work, working with non-doing, awareness, inhibition, direction, means-whereby, and choice works better than any other way of working.' It is through practice that we learn to value the information gleaned from awareness, the opportunity for choice offered by the inhibitory pause, the guidance direction brings to our choices, and the freedom and creativity that result from working this way.

Conclusion

The Alexander Technique is not about achieving length and width, or up, or physical freedom, or vocal prowess, even though we welcome those benefits of the work. Endgaining is not something to be conquered; it is a universal tendency over which we have choice. Practising the Alexander Technique involves exercising our mental muscles to better work with ourselves. We will always have needs, desires, and fears, and sometimes they will be stronger than our mental muscles can handle. The tendency to endgain is always a possibility. But as we practise the Technique, our mental muscles get stronger and we are able to handle increasingly challenging stimuli. Our awareness becomes increasingly accurate, our powers to inhibit become stronger, and our ability to make choices and direct our activities becomes a more frequent part of daily life. As we practise the Technique we dedicate ourselves to becoming experts on using our thoughts and bodies to effectively work on our evolving selves. Those of us who practise the Alexander Technique are all recovering endgainers. With this recognition, we can make peace with our endgaining tendencies and come to the point where we can honestly say, 'I'm a recovering endgainer and I'm proud of it.'

References
1   Alexander, F. M. (1985, 1932). *The Use of the Self.* Gollancz: London.
2   Ibid., p. 57.
3   Ibid., p. 57.
4   Ibid., p. 74.
5   Ibid., p. 74.
6   Ibid., p. 74.
7   Ibid., p. 67.
8   Ibid., p. 105.
9   Ibid., p. 105.
10 Ibid., p. 66.
11 Ibid., p. 105. Italics are Alexander's.
12 Ibid., p. 111.
13 Ibid., p. 69.
14 Ibid., p. 47.
15 Ibid., p. 45.

Diane Gaary teaches speaking voice, dialects, and movement and has a particular interest in how body-use affects the speaking and singing voice. With a BA in Theatre and English from Smith College and an MFA in Acting from The University of Virginia, Diane has teacher certification from The American Society of the Alexander Technique (AMSAT) and the Lessac Institute for Voice and Body Training, as well as practitioner certification from the Feldenkrais Guild of North America®. She is on the faculty of Temple University and Arcadia University, teaches regularly at Westminster Choir College, and has taught classes and workshops at a number of universities and training centres. Diane teaches privately in Philadelphia. Her students have performed extensively on Broadway and in regional theatre, in film and television, and in major opera houses such as The Metropolitan Opera, The New York City Opera, and La Scala.

A 12 Step Programme for 21st Century Job Creation for Alexander Technique Teachers and Graduating Trainees

Monika Gross

INTRODUCTION

The goal of this programme, which I introduced in a workshop at the Congress, is to connect qualified Alexander Technique (AT) trainees and teachers to industry and population-specific jobs. It is a response to what I call the 'Alexander Technique Anonymous' syndrome:

> 'Hello. My name is Monika and I'm an Alexander Technique teacher.'
> 'Hello Monika. What's the Alexander Technique?'

Most professions mentor trainees into internships and ground-level job opportunities. Current AT training programmes sometimes offer professional development in starting a private practice, but do not often include curricula for training to work with specific industries or populations. Not all teachers are suited to entrepreneurship or managing a private practice. Some prefer salaried jobs and/or working in a communal setting.

Advances in neuroscience have lent scientific credibility to the processes behind AT and there is growing acceptance of innovative approaches in fields like education, business, and health and wellness. Building links with these areas of work in a strategic, organised way will lay the groundwork for employment opportunities for AT teachers into the future.

I believe the next decade is key. Enhancing credibility, creating demand, sorting out funding and delivery systems, designing job-training curricula for AT teachers, and introducing AT-principle-based continuing education programmes for other professionals must all happen concurrently or we will not be successful.

This initiative looks beyond our community of AT teachers to build new partnerships. Our students are underused as advocates. Also, many open-minded, forward-thinking professionals can help us bring our work to new industries and populations. Let's reach out to those who are eager to help. This initiative will be most successful if it is undertaken with a team approach that includes industry leaders, grant writers, media consultants and other professionals.

A primary motivation for this initiative is to make AT available to more socio-economically diverse populations than our current private-pay model allows. In addition, we will encourage more diversity in AT teachers if we work to ensure there will be a job with a living wage at the end of their training.

If you are interested in supporting this initiative in any way, I welcome you to contact me.

Current Employment Snapshot

The vast majority of AT teachers use a private practice model. A recent independent study sponsored by the Complementary Medicine Evaluation Group, Department of Health Sciences, University of York with a grant from the National Institute for Health Research[1] found that essentially 100% of UK AT teachers are self-employed (95% self-employed and 5% not working). 87% offer lessons in homes or in privately rented rooms.

23% of teachers hold post-graduate degrees. 8% are also members of statutorily regulated healthcare professions such as psychotherapy, nursing and physiotherapy. Additional trainings include cranial-sacral therapy, yoga, Pilates and massage. 51% combine AT teaching with other non-AT work. AT teachers teach AT for an average of 8 hours per week.

Only 12% teach at performing arts colleges or in a National Health Service clinic, but these also identify as 'self-employed' meaning they do not hold full-time salaried positions and are probably coming in for workshops or as part-time adjuncts.

Only 3% of teachers work in corporate, office or workplace settings. 5% work in non-profit settings, but the study doesn't indicate whether they rent space, are brought in to do workshops, or started an AT non-profit.

23% work at AT training schools, making AT training programmes our largest, and essentially only, employers.

The median age of AT teachers in the UK is 58. 74% of UK AT teachers are women. Most are located in the south of England, in large urban areas.

As for our clients, only 3% come for neurological reasons, such as migraines, Parkinson's Disease or Multiple Sclerosis; only 5% for psychological reasons, such as acute stress, anxiety or depression; and only 2% for sport or other physical performance. Only 8% of clients come for performing arts reasons.

91% of people who take AT lessons pay for lessons privately. 4% receive lessons for 'free or barter'. Only 2% of lessons are paid for by employers or through a college, and only 1.4% through a private health insurance or the National Health Service.

The median age of AT clients is 48, although 76% of teachers say they do some work with clients under the age of 18. 66% of AT clients are women.

There was no information collected regarding ethnicity or economic status of either AT teachers or AT clients.

This is an excellent snapshot of our profession. What is disturbing is that we are attracting such a tiny percentage of the general population to

AT – only people who can pay out of pocket and only as individuals – and we have essentially no institutional employment. We have not located funding and delivery systems to help pay for or subsidise lessons, such as non-profits, employers, educational institutions, athletics programmes, governments or trade organisations. We are not creating AT-focused non-profit models. And we are working in isolation, in private settings with little professional interaction with – or visibility to – the public.

If the median age of our teachers is 58, we are not attracting young professionals to AT as a career choice. Interestingly, AT teachers are mostly women, and women have historically earned less money than men and are more likely to work part time.

Our clients come to us mainly with musculoskeletal issues. We are not working with healthy children, adolescents and young adults and their teachers, parents and caregivers in institutional settings to help preserve poise before it's disturbed, but rather are engaging with adults much later, usually with a crisis as their entry point. We are not regularly employed where we are uniquely qualified to be of service, as in populations with neurological conditions or anxiety issues, or in sports and athletics.

Even within the performing arts community – where one would think we would have a stronghold – we are losing ground. Performing artists make up only 8% of our clients and performing arts training programmes are not seeking us for salaried employment.

In fact, there doesn't seem to be anyone hiring Alexander Technique professionals! Anyone entering 'Alexander Technique Teacher' for an online job search service will quickly find this to be true.

THE 12 STEP PROGRAMME

The current method for AT principles to reach a chosen population is for an AT teacher to attract private paying clients, one-to-one or in workshops, or to approach an institution such as a school or business as an individual.

The initiative I propose takes a centralised team approach, including non-AT professionals and consultants. It would result in the creation of jobs for AT teachers as well as the creation of continuing education programmes based on AT principles designed for the education of targeted industries. Payment is drawn from a mixture of sources: private-pay, employers, non-profits, government and non-governmental organisations and trade organisations. I plan to establish an independent non-profit organisation devoted to funding and implementing this initiative, which will follow the 12 step method outlined below. This will provide an infrastructure for supporting and coordinating existing efforts of members of the international Alexander community.

We start by identifying a target population: 'Who do we want to help?'
Example: 'Children, adolescents and young adults'. We then:

1. *Identify the industries that will connect us to the target population*
Industries with infrastructures in place and ongoing interactions with the target population.
Connecting Industries: Early Education, Primary, Secondary and Tertiary Schools, Day Care, Health and Wellness Systems, Summer Camps, Performing Arts Programmes, Juvenile Justice Systems, Sports.

2. *Locate AT teachers already working in a connecting industry with the target population*
AT teachers who have specific expertise with this target population or are working within one of these industries. They will often have additional qualifications that have given them industry credibility. They are a primary resource for initial guidance in navigating the process.
Connecting Industry: Primary Schools.
AT Teachers: Sue Merry and Esther Miltiadous from the Educare Small School in the UK.[2]

3. *Locate an Advocate/Translator*
A person with experience in those industries who also has personal experience or understanding of AT but who isn't an AT teacher. They essentially 'translate' between AT language and point of view and the language and point of view of the specific field or industry. They offer guidance throughout the process.
Advocate/Translator: Elementary school principal who has benefitted from AT lessons.[3]

4. *Identify the industry's perceived needs*
We often focus on needs that may not be actual concerns of a target population. We need to focus instead on the *perceived needs* that do concern the industry decision makers. We identify them with help from the Advocate/Translator and other industry professionals. If things go well and we get access to the target population, I hope to educate them later about needs they may not yet be aware of.
Perceived Needs
- Support children diagnosed with ADHD
- Improve test performance
- New games for recess and PE
- Reduction of aggressive behaviours.

5. *Research the industry's current solutions for their perceived needs (i.e. our 'competition')*
What other professionals are they using? What programmes are already in place? How much do they cost? How much time do they allow for them?

How effective have they been? How are they dissatisfied with their current solutions?

Perceived Need: Support children diagnosed with ADHD

Current Solutions:
- Assistant teachers
- Special education teachers
- Occupational therapists
- Pharmaceuticals
- Exercise/movement programs
- Mindfulness practices
- Therapeutic arts programs.

6. *Create an industry-focused 'AT Cultural Capital' credibility package*

To ensure a successful presentation, we will need to have a clear understanding of the industry's culture and language. What are their hierarchies? How do they interact? What are their basic beliefs? How is success measured? What will make AT credible to them? What makes AT the solution for their perceived needs? What do we offer that the 'competition' does not? Is there data to support our solution?

In general, the three *solutions* that AT offers are: 1) improved performance; 2) pain and injury management, recovery and prevention; and 3) performance anxiety or stress management. The long-term *benefits* are enhanced self-perception, self-regulation, and critical problem-solving skills. I call these benefits collectively 'First Person Expertise'.[4]

Industry-focused 'AT Cultural Capital' credibility package for primary schools can include:
- Approval process for an AT teacher in that school system
- Implementation process for the chosen intervention
- Expected costs
- Potential funding sources for the intervention
- Demographics of the children
- Our specific AT-based solutions – presented in primary school professional language, not in AT professional language.

7. *Locate forward-thinking industry experts*

Open-minded people in the field, interested in innovation and curious about AT's potential. Good individuals to test the 'AT Cultural Capital' credibility package and to help identify the best people for Step 8.

Industry Expert: The Executive Director of a local city schools foundation.

8. *Identify the industry decision makers (i.e. 'The Gatekeepers')*

Decision makers who can approve a pilot project or create a job. We need to prove to them that AT is the best solution for their perceived needs – and we will probably not get a second chance.

Decision Makers: Local or State Board of Education to approve AT teachers in ongoing positions in local government-run schools.

9. *Locate funding sources and delivery systems*

An economic system and organisational structure to support each pilot project, internship or job.

'For profit' structures include our current private-pay self-employment model, but can include limited partnerships or incorporated entities with other teachers, such as 'AT clinics' that look like businesses the general public is already used to, or franchise-type models such as Shaw Method.[5]

'Non-profit' structures are underused. Partnering with non-profits or starting our own can bring AT principles to new populations and countries and can support the training of a more diverse teaching profession. An interesting model: US speech-language pathologists who are frustrated at the limited time they can spend with aphasia patients because of health insurance limitations, and knowing their clients can't afford private pay, have formed non-profit 'aphasia centers' offering inexpensive group classes and using local university speech pathology students as interns. After a few years, they received enough funding to realise their goal to offer subsidised one-to-one sessions for their clients.[6] Worker co-ops are also potential models. There are also interesting hybrid models linking for profit and non-profit entities.

'Pro bono' creates a professional context for us to offer services not 'for free' or as 'volunteers' but pro bono: 'for the public good'. Becca Ferguson has been teaching pro bono in a prison in Chicago[7] and Andrea Bruno in a Veterans Affairs hospital in New Jersey in its complementary medicine programme.[8] Their efforts become models for professional programmes to work with these populations.

I imagine that the majority of AT teachers are interested in making a living rather than a 'killing', and we can do so by blending for profit, non-profit and pro bono models.

'Delivery Systems' connect AT teachers to target populations. For 'Children', a day care center that brings in an AT trainee as an intern would be a delivery system. For 'Occupational Therapists', AT-based continuing education curricula designed for OTs and approved by the American Occupational Therapy Association would be a delivery system. Presentations and AT sponsorship booths at professional conferences are delivery systems to many target populations. Anikó Ball presented at the 2015 36th Australian Dental Congress in Brisbane, which had over 4,500 attendees.[9] Candace Cox presented at the 2013 World Parkinson's Congress in Montreal, which had close to 3,500 delegates from 64 countries.[10]

10. Locate AT Training Programme Directors interested in additional Industry and Population-specific Training

Working on solutions with training programme directors becomes a vital part of our professional development. How will we position industry and population-specific training? As additional elective hours in their training course? As a fourth year of graduate training? As post-graduate courses? As onsite trainings?

11. Design and implement industry-focused curricula for trainees and post-graduate trainings for AT teachers

Curricula created from information previously gathered, with input by experts in their respective fields and training programme directors. We can also connect trainees and teachers to existing industry-specific certification courses.

12. Final Goal: Connect industry-qualified trainees and teachers to internships and jobs

Currently the only internship-style option for most graduating trainees is as assistants in AT teacher training courses. At this final step, there will now be many interesting internships, as well as jobs for more experienced teachers. Working in day care centers could be internships for trainees. Assistant teachers in primary schools could be entry-level jobs for recent graduates. However, handling the design and implementation of AT principles for an entire public school system would require teachers with considerably more senior experience and training.

The final outcome must be job security. We do not want to waste all this hard work because a friendly principal, CEO or sheriff moves on to another school, corporation or district and those who remain don't recognise the value of an AT professional. We want our AT professionals to be ongoing, integrated, vital parts of an industry's culture.[11]

CONCLUSION

The German word *Zugunruhe* (pron. *tsuk' un roo he*), combining *Zug* (move, migration) and *Unruhe* (restlessness, anxiety), is a scientific term for migratory restlessness prior to a journey central to a species survival. In his 2010 book of the same name,[12] Jason McLennan, co-founder of the green building movement, explains how the serious realities of climate change adjust the timeline for environmental action:

> Nature provides us with wonderful examples of how not to get stuck in habitual patterns of behaviour, as change is necessary for survival. As a tree grows, it adjusts constantly to respond to external forces. . . In essence, the tree redefines its process and structure continuously at every moment because of ever-changing inputs. If only human-made systems were so elegant. . . .

Once we create a system our tendency is to fall in love with it! . . . [The system] becomes a signature – part of our identity – and then it blinds us. We begin to look for anything that justifies how our process is correct and ignore signs that it is not. . . Somehow, our movement must shed the weight of the paradigm of the last thirty years and take bolder action if we are to succeed . . . Our baby steps must now turn into giant leaps and our processes must accommodate this new pace and the urgency behind it.[13]

McLennan suggests that 'instead of despairing over a lack of progress towards change, reach out and find others who are also working to create change. Look for people in other disciplines and for ways to bring your ideas and expertise together. This collaboration will inspire you and keep you positive, grounded and moving forward. Seek common understandings and solutions and make the cornerstone of your vision one that is inclusive, synergistic and open-source.'[14]

We can certainly draw parallels to our own situation. I know I am not alone in these concerns. Do you feel as I do that we are in a period of *Zugunruhe* in the AT community? Do you sense that the time has come when we can end this puzzling, persistent 'Alexander Technique Anonymous' syndrome? I hope you will find inspiration in these models and join in this initiative. With persistence and a team approach, I believe we can prepare the way to be of true service in the 21st century.[15]

References

1. Eldred, J., Hopton, A., Donnison, E., Woodman J, MacPherson, H. Teachers of the Alexander Technique in the UK and the people who take their lessons: A national cross-sectional survey Complementary Therapies in Medicine (Volume 23, Issue 3, June 2015, Pages 451–461).for abstract: http://www.sciencedirect.com/science/article/pii/S0965229915000643. For full survey: http://tinyurl.com/oot6lhx
2. Educare Small School, 12 Cowleaze Road, Kingston Upon Thames, Surrey KT2 6DZ, UK. http://www.educaresmallschool.org.uk/
3. This is a US example. Outside the US, terms and structures will be different, but the basic process will be the same.
4. 'First Person Expertise' is a term I use for the practical ability AT principles teach to consciously and continuously perceive, interpret and navigate myself in my environment from moment-to-moment.
5. The Shaw Method, The Factory, 407 Hornsey Road, London N19 4DX, UK. http://www.shawmethod.com/.
6. A conversation with speech-language pathologist and aphasia specialist Molly Secrest of Westboro MA, 5 July 2015.
7. From panel presentation 13 August 2015 at 10th International Alexander Technique Congress in Limerick Ireland: Ferguson, Becca; Cranz, Galen; Freeman, Caitlin. 'Diffability vs. Disability: Reframing Personal Definitions of Self'.
8. From presentation 20 October 2015 at Alexander Technique International Annual

Conference in Philadelphia PA USA: Bruno, Andrea. 'Working with Veterans at a VA Hospital'.

9   Ball, Dr Aniko, 'Overcoming Back and Neck Pain in the Dental Surgery' and 'Well-Being and Ergonomics for the Dental Team' 36th Australian Dental Congress, Brisbane. http://www.adc2015.com/speaker/dr-aniko-ball/

10 Cox, Candace, 'Long Term Effects of Alexander Technique in Managing Motor Symptoms of Young Onset Parkinson's Disease' 2013 World Parkinson's Congress, Montreal. https://drive.google.com/file/d/0BzbY4ZvnzS0WRTZTTGxxdmN6TlU. http://themillatpipercreek.ca/parkinsons/

11 For examples, see this 2011 report published by the Spanish Foundation for the Prevention of Occupational Hazards, which gathered data from multiple onsite projects that used AT principle based solutions to improve worker health and safety: 'Alexander Technique: training for the self-management of workers to prevent musculoskeletal disorder' Foment Prevención de Riesgos Laborales. Data gathered by Mireia Mora i Griso with funding from Fundación para la prevención de Riesgos Laborales.http://www.vanschuylenburch.nl/Uploaded_Files/439_Research.pdf

12 McLennan, Jason F. (2010). *Zugunruhe: The Inner Migration to Profound Environmental Change.* Perfect Paperback.

13 Ibid, pp. 238-241.

14 Ibid, pp. 273-274.

15 Two appendices for this paper ('Current Employment Models for AT Teachers' and 'Sample Target Populations, Connecting Industries & Decision Makers') can be downloaded at: http://tinyurl.com/nvnob9w

Monika Gross has taught Alexander Technique, postural integrity and performance skills for over thirty years. She had her first Alexander lesson in 1976 at age 19, and was certified in 1985, training with Lydia Yohay (ACAT). She participated in the First and Second International Congresses in 1986 and 1988. Monika taught in New York City for 25 years and is now the co-owner of *Form Fitness & Function in Asheville NC*. She was on the faculty of the Hayes School of Music at Appalachian State University (2011-12). She is a professional theatre director, playwright and performer and holds a BFA from the University of North Carolina School of the Arts. In 2009, Monika, Belinda Mello and Lindsay Newitter co-founded *Studio AT Large*, where Alexander teachers and students provided information and free AT 'tastings' in a variety of indoor and outdoor locations in NYC, promoting awareness of AT to a broader population. She is a member of the Western North Carolina collaborative teacher consortium Alexander Teachers of the Mountain Region (ATMR).

formfitnessfunction.com
FormFitnessFunction@gmail.com

Getting out of Splendid Isolation

Thoughts on Why the Alexander Technique is not More Widely Known

Nicola Hanefeld

REASONS WHY ALEXANDER'S DISCOVERIES ARE NOT MAINSTREAM ARE CONSIDERED
  i. We are a community of expert practitioners able to impart the 'Alexander-experience' but without a coherent theory which can be empirically tested.
  ii. Our way of presenting the work amalgamates Alexander's discoveries with the practical method (AT) leading to an inaccessible vocabulary.
  iii. Linking back to Alexander hinders passage into mankind's general body of knowledge.
  iv. Our community does not have a culture of entrepreneurial thinking and naming benefits.
  v. Insufficient exchange with the scientific community, lack of recognition/public awareness.

Attending the 10th International Alexander Technique Congress in Limerick was deeply inspiring and in several ways a great eye-opener. Ted Dimon impressed me with his great knowledge and engaging, clear presentation. I have a long standing dissatisfaction with our cumbersome AT jargon which I think is one of the reasons for the lack of wider recognition of our work. After the sessions with Ted, the following startling realisations came to me: our fundamental mistake, an inherent fault in our communication with the outside world, is that in our presentation we mix Alexander's practical method (i.e. the lessons we offer) with what he found out. In the same instant, I felt certain that if our main theory received high-level scientific recognition and become better known, it would create a greater demand by the public for our practice which we call the Technique.

I see Alexander's discoveries (our theory) as:
- The central importance of a freely functioning primary control for well-being.
- That sensory appreciation often becomes faulty the older we get.
- That we are subject to the force of habit, which is detrimental to the optimal use of the self.

I see our practice, his 'technique', as the application of inhibition and direction in an activity in order to improve the quality of the primary control/use. I realised that this mingling of theory and practice comes from our training tradition which has historical roots in Alexander's practical nature. He was a hands-on man who was well able to demonstrate what he had worked out. That was also how he most effectively passed on his knowledge: through his hands. Musing on these insights, the question arose whether it might be our responsibility to re-start, to break with tradition in order to spread Alexander's discoveries and the practical benefits of psychophysical re-education more effectively. I suddenly saw how our habit of continually referring to our founder hinders the AT from becoming more widely known and acknowledged and from entering the general body of knowledge of mankind. I contacted Ted Dimon with my ideas and he responded, agreeing, saying he had been working on these points for many years.

My impression from talking with colleagues is that we share a common feeling that our work has not yet received the recognition it deserves. We are not as well known as yoga, mindfulness or even Pilates. I will not have to convince any reader of this article that what we have to offer for enhancing awareness, well-being and improving the process of education is anything short of sensational. However, we are a rather self-contained, insular community of adept practitioners competent at passing on the 'Alexander experience' without scientific validation backing up our work. The input from Michael Gelb's sessions was also in my mind: the puzzle fitted and I realised that we can only poorly sell what someone else discovered, but we *can* market a method that practically applies the benefits of a discovery. We put everything in one pot when communicating with the public and often put F. M. and his discoveries first. Who is interested in F. M.'s long road to discovery at the end of the 19th century when they are looking for a solution to their problems at the beginning of the 21st?

Here is an analogy to make my point clear: a humanoid alien visits the earth. It learns how to ride a bike and asks, impressed, 'Oh, how does that work? We don't have bikes, it would be a great thing to export to Planet X but having learnt how to do it, I would also like to understand how it works.' We explain about bicycle mechanics and dynamics, about self-stability, angular acceleration and rotary inertia. The alien gets an explanation about the ground contact line, about gyroscopic effects which are proportional to speed, about balanced and unbalanced weight of the rider, the upwards force of the ground on the front wheel arising from weight distribution. We tell the alien about gravity, the metal and plastic bikes are made of, explain how gears work and the physiology of movement which makes bike-riding possible.

This humanoid alien also gets to know the Alexander work. After several lessons it stands there, also impressed, with better alignment and poise, freer breathing, a happier expression, better mood and heightened awareness.

The alien says, 'I feel really good – how does *that* work?'

We answer, hesitantly, 'Well, we are not quite sure. We haven't actually got it scientifically verified, yet. . . ummm. . .'

The alien is surprised: 'But this is great stuff! Why aren't your scientists working on it?!' We say, looking bashfully to the ground, 'Well, they are not really interested and we don't know how to get them interested. . .'

You get my point.

Dimon calls the work Neurodynamics or simply psychophysical education, emphasising what we do, and not our founder. To quote Dimon:

> The subconscious working of the human organism and the possibility of raising its control to a conscious level is the most compelling discovery about education and human development ever made. We must do more than simply preserve the experience of 'going up' that Alexander gifted to us. We must endeavour to understand the deeper knowledge behind that experience and build on it for future generations.[1]

Understanding that deeper knowledge behind the experience would also remove the mystery around hands-on work. Of course teachers can become highly proficient at initiating release of over-tense muscles, aiding re-alignment in the earth's gravity field with all the additional benefits. But an inability to communicate what the working mechanism is leaves us floundering and in danger of landing in the esoteric and/or 'inexplicable' corner, or simply expounding unsubstantiated assumptions.

Most of these realisations of mine came from attending Ted's continuous learning sessions. Here was someone who had obviously intensely occupied himself with Alexander's discoveries, and not only on a practical level. He presented in a highly digestible manner – here was anatomy come alive, it was almost tangible how my Alexander concepts started re-organising while I listened. I asked myself why Ted is not better known and more acknowledged in our Alexander world. He has an immense body of experience and knowledge on offer and I recommend his books, which have the same clarity as his personal presentation. He puts the discovery of the primary control at the core, calling it the 'primary organising principle of how people adjust in gravity'. His explanation of the working of the primary control was lucid. It made sense for the first time in twenty-six years of teaching *why Homo sapiens* habitually tends to shorten his neck, especially in 'civilized' countries and why it is 'vulnerable to disruption'[2] (Dimon). Of course I knew about this organising principle as a practical fact, having learned to sense when it is working efficiently or less so. But I had only been trained to give the Alexander experience and show how someone can learn to do it for themselves via inhibiting and directing; my understanding of what I *actually* do and *how* I do this was thin, not to say non-existent.

I will not go into the details of Ted's understanding of the primary control here because it is beside the present point and can be read in his books. However, his bottom-line message is that we need more research into the primary control. Ted propagates Alexander's discoveries as being 'an advanced model of conscious awareness', saying that F. M. put 'science and mindfulness together and theory and practise too'. Yes! I have a vision: we become more professional, we do a collective re-start, an effective re-think regarding how we present ourselves and research interest will be generated as demand for lessons rises. We use the impulses from the Limerick Congress to flourish and evolve. This work should become a well known, widely available, highly effective aid to *Homo sapiens* taking an evolutionary step forward – empowerment through constructive conscious awareness in living.

Michael Gelb spoke in his plenary session about the principles and practices of entrepreneurial success for Alexander teachers. He quoted Peter Drucker[3] in his talk: 'The best way to manage the future is to create it.' Let's go out and do it.

More information on Ted Dimon's work can be found at: www.dimoninstitute.org.

Note

'Splendid isolation' was the foreign policy pursued by Great Britain during the late 19th century, a phrase coined by a Canadian politician regarding Britain's minimal involvement in European affairs.

1. http://dimoninstitute.org/the-conservatory/alexander-technique
2. Dimon, Theodore, Jr. (2011). *The Body in Motion: Its Evolution and Design.* North Atlantic Books: Berkeley, USA, first edition, p. 14.
3. Peter Drucker (1909-2005), an Austrian-born American management consultant has been described as 'the founder of modern management'. (Wikipedia)

Nicola Hanefeld trained in the 1980s with Yehuda Kupermann. She has had an Alexander company, SPEEK, since 2000, working specifically with clients with stress-related issues. Her only claim to fame in the Alexander world is that she was Congress photographer at the 6th International Congress in 1999 in Freiburg, her home town. Photos from the 6th Congress are at http://img4web.com/g/3ZWAP

www.speek.de
hanefeld@speek.de

Introduction to the Alexander Technique: Returning to Your Essential Nature

Anne Johnson

Returning to Your Essential Nature is a new type of Continuous Learning Session created for the 10th International Alexander Technique Congress in Limerick, Ireland. The purpose was to introduce the Alexander Technique to newcomers in the local community, as well as partners and guests of teachers attending the Congress. It was also open to trainees and teachers interested in new ways of presenting to groups.

Returning to your Essential Nature is based on the premise that the principles of the Alexander Technique are embedded in nature, and that our true nature is hidden beneath habits of interference.

The Continuous Learning Sessions explored the relationship between thoughts and the physical body, examining the way words, phrases and images influenced the quality of action. Participants were guided to release restrictive postures, embodying a greater sense of integration and well-being. The Sessions met on two mornings for two hours each and included individual hands-on turns in the group setting each day.

I will present two teaching structures from the Sessions that explore *breaking habits around time* and *breaking habits around choice*. Inspiration for these explorations comes from my experience with, and admiration for the group teaching of Meade Andrews.

The first exploration is the foundation for receiving hands-on work that follows. Participants are guided to shift their awareness into the present moment and be in a space of discovery about themselves and their environment. Their shared experience creates a sense of unity and safety for the group.

I have made notes for the reader about the principles within the explorations. I invite participants to make their own discoveries without *initially* naming Alexander's principles. I typically introduce specific Alexander terminology when someone has shared a personal experience that relates to what Alexander discovered. This empowers the student's own learning process.

The second exploration is used after presenting a stimulus-response game to introduce F. M.'s discoveries of primary control, use, misuse, inhibition and direction. To trigger misuse, I blew up a balloon to its maximum volume and pulled out a sharp pin. Everyone experienced a physical reaction of contracting at the thought of the balloon popping, even though I promised that I would not (this is an adaptation from the teaching of Lindsay Newitter). This helped identify the habit of contracting the neck and pulling the head back and down on the spine as a common reaction to stress and made relevant to Alexander's personal story of losing his voice.

We then looked at the importance of honouring the head, neck and back relationship and the freedom of our breathing. Using the visual aid of a miniature plastic skeleton, the group discovered where the head balances on the top of the spine and the points of contact of the feet to the floor. Participants were then guided to experience the foundational support of the ground itself, allowing a flow of direction up through the body to the head balancing on top of the spine. Individual hands-on turns, with the group observing, provided an additional qualitative experience of releasing unnecessary tension and connecting with a flow of direction upward and outward. Participants experienced freedom of breathing, a sense of feeling lighter, taller, and expansive; a first glimpse of returning to their essential nature.

Exploration One
The conscious use of time: Appreciating the 'rest notes'. Breaking habits around time.

- Quieting the nervous system
- Laying a foundation for awareness and inhibition
- Creating support for the means-whereby
- Waking up the sensory register

There are three parts to this exploration. In each part, we consciously establish a group intention about how we will use time. The session opens with everyone sitting in chairs arranged in a circle.

Imagine listening to your favorite piece of music. You know it by heart. Your body not only responds to each note being played, but also to the notes that are not being played – the rest notes. This space between the notes helps you hear and connect to the music.

Now imagine hearing the same piece of music without any of the rest notes. How does your body respond to that?

Do you have many rest notes dispersed into your typical day? The Alexander Technique helps you cultivate the skill of integrating more rest notes into the action notes.

1. 60-second pause with eyes closed
The group intention is to develop the skill of consciously shifting attention away from thoughts of the past and future to the present moment. We do this by waking up the connection with the body and all the senses. The present moment is where we learn and apply the Alexander Technique.

Close your eyes and let go of any expectations that you have about this workshop. Practise letting go of any thoughts that creep in about the past or the future and return to the present moment. Sense the contact you are making with the chair and your feet on the floor. Sense where your back, arms, hands and legs are making contact with the varied surfaces. Feel the movement of your breathing. Hear the changing sounds around you. Sense the light and dark or any colour coming through your eyelids. Pick up any hints of fragrance around you or lingering flavours in your mouth.

If your awareness veers off to thoughts in the past or future, be glad that you noticed, let it go and bring yourself back to the present as many times as you need. The more opportunities you have to shift into the present, the stronger this habit becomes.

Note: This skill is a foundation that will be used later in the session when noticing the habit of pulling the head back and down and consciously choosing to let it go.

2. 60-second pause with eyes open
The group intention is to have an ongoing conscious connection sensing your body and breathing as you connect with the environment.

Open your eyes to the room around you and discover all the various shades of red (or choose any colour). Begin to notice if you are holding your breath while you search. If you are, let it go and allow your breath to freely move again. It begins low and wide at the bottom of your ribs. Imagine the breath starting from there. Imagine that your whole back is a 'breathing landscape'. Continue discovering the colour in the room until the minute is over.

A variation of this exploration I use on the second day invites participants to discover different patterns in the room in the same manner.

3. Communication and use of time
The group intention is to practicse breaking the habit of rushing when communicating. The group agrees to add a five-count pause between each person after they share their experience. Participants are also invited to be aware of whether or not they are holding their breath.

Participants share two discoveries they made from the 60-second pauses. The teacher communicates the importance of each person having his or her unique experience. There are no right or wrong answers. Passing or saying, 'I don't know' are valid and acceptable responses. This helps to establish trust and a sense of safety while sharing with the group.

It is noted that it is perfectly fine if someone forgets to pause for five counts; the fact that they noticed shows it a skill they are developing. One person begins and when they finish sharing, the teacher says 'thank you' to let the person next in the circle know when to start the pause.

All three stages not only help shift to the present moment to connect more fully with oneself and the environment, but also to discover that habits of unnecessary tension can prevent a fuller, more present connection to oneself and environment.

Habits and observations discovered from the 60-second and five-count pauses included:

'I found it easier to relax with my eyes closed.'

'I calmed down when all I had to do was to connect with what was here.'

'I got anxious having to pay attention to everything.'

'It was easy to get pulled into the task of finding the colours or patterns and forget to notice what was going on in my body.' (Lead in for explaining endgaining)

'I noticed my neck was tense and I was holding my breath the whole time I was looking around.' (Interference with the primary control)

'When it was my turn to share, the 5-count pause helped me gather my thoughts. I could also absorb what people were saying more easily with the pause.' (Advantage of practising inhibition)

'Am I doing this right . . .is that a valid pattern I see? What if the red I see is really more orange . . .how many colours am I supposed to find?' (Awareness of habits of perfectionism and worrying about 'getting it right' when the task was to become aware of what was present in the room . . . without any rules. Discomfort with the unknown. Opportunity to propose the practice of being okay with 'not knowing'.)

After everyone has shared, I respond to the discoveries as they relate to cultivating a new awareness and acknowledge this is the first step in utilising the Alexander Technique.

Exploration Two
Developing awareness of habits of choosing
Discovering more of who we are through the world we choose to connect with

- Waking up the sensory register
- Observing stimulus–response patterns
- Recognizing habits of interference.

As a visual artist, I have found that the way I connect with images helps me see and understand myself more deeply.

I have created a way of using artwork to reveal qualities that speak to our psychophysical unity. I use this exploration in the later part of the session, after the students have experienced hands-on work and the qualitative differences associated with the use and misuse of the primary control.

To begin this exploration, I lay out over 100 art postcards that I have collected from museums and galleries and give this instruction:

1. *Without much thought, choose one image that attracts you and one image that repels you. After choosing your cards, take some time to identify two qualities you connect with from the card that attracts you and two qualities from the card that repels you. Reflect on how these qualities might relate to your life.*
2. *Going around the circle one at a time, show your cards and name the qualities*

that you discovered from each using the 5-count pause as practised before. Remember that you always have the option to pass if you do not want to share.
3. After everyone has shared, look at the card that attracts you and notice if your body responds to the image in any way. Consciously register and make note of this feeling in your body.

Then look at the card that repels you and notice if your body responds to that image in any way. Consciously register and make note of this feeling in your body.

Once again practise the 5-count pause as a group, going around the circle and sharing the sensations registered in your body.
4. Finally, look at the image that repels you, but with the feeling you had looking at the image that attracts you.

Share your experiences using the 5-count pause.

Examples of how participants described the cards that attracted/repelled them:
- calm & organised / disconnected & dishevelled
- light & playful / closed & dark
- connected & open / sharp & confined
- joyful & celebrative / muddy & agitated.

Participants' discoveries that came out of the card game included:
When looking at the cards that attracted them, they recognised the release and openness they felt earlier in the session during individual turns. When responding to the cards that repelled them, they recognised the contraction they experienced from the thought of the balloon popping.

Identifying the qualities from each card revealed a deeper connection to their values, desires, fears and judgements. These were some responses to how the qualities of each card related to their life:

'I am attracted to this card because it reminds me I want to be more playful and open in my life.'

'I am attracted to this card because of the mystery in it.'

'This card repels me because it reminds me how disconnected and dishevelled I feel in my life.'

'This card repels me because I absolutely hate the colour pink and therefore I don't want to take the time to really look at it.'

When looking at the image that repelled them, but choosing to physically connect with the feeling from the image that attracted them (e.g. connected & open), they were able to see details in the postcard that were not initially visible. They also found that they eventually began to like the card that had repelled them.

This exploration helps participants:
- Experience that they can perceive body reactions to images and thoughts and begin to link this new awareness to how they are using

their primary control.
- Observe habits of choosing what they value and how that can shape direction in their life.
- Observe habits of rejecting, shedding light on snap judgements and their impact on reality.
- Learn from the unique discoveries of each person in the group.

Anne Johnson (M. AmSAT) is a teacher of the Alexander Technique as well as a practising artist who holds a BFA in painting. For the last twenty years she has used Alexander's principles in the creative process, facilitating clearer, freer, and more dynamic personal expression for herself and her students. Anne believes the Alexander Technique is at the heart of all we do. Anne currently teaches the Alexander Technique at the Esther Boyer College of Music and Dance at Temple University, as well as in her private practice. She has given workshops integrating creativity with the Alexander Technique in the M.F.A. Creative Writing program at Rosemont College, in the Art Department at Swarthmore College and to Women in Design at the Graduate School of Design at Harvard University. She has also been a guest teacher in teacher training programs in Japan, Ireland and the United States.

Beyond Posture

Anthony Kingsley

> We fall upwards into the ocean of Life that supports us. It is the actionless act of vital surrender.

It was a truly wonderful congress, with so many teachers, students and friends coming together from all over the world to explore the Alexander Technique with open hearts and open minds.

I presented the Continuous Learning Sessions to a wide range of participants. Each day drew a different content and a different rhythm from me. I was constantly creating and co-creating my thoughts and responses in relation to the group.

Alexander principles are best transmitted in practice, in face-to-face and hands-to-person dialogue. As they say, 'You had to be there to get it!' Our meetings were alive and spontaneous. Alexander work is essentially relational.

And so, if any of the following ideas seem partial or confusing, I invite you to email me or better still, come and meet me in person.

I will try and offer a brief flavour of the themes we explored together at the Congress.

Choice and the myth of conscious inhibition

In our Alexander world, a lot of time and space is devoted to the idea that we need to inhibit our reactions and choose a better alternative. I suggest that it is impossible to choose to inhibit. By this I mean that we are in fact not capable of actively inhibiting our reactions to anything. Inhibition is not under our conscious volition. What actually happens in reality is that when a stimulus impacts on our organism, we either react to the stimulus, or not. There is simply no time to choose. Our neurological make-up does not offer this kind of option. Neural reactions take milliseconds, and the conscious brain can in no way intercede.

You may then enquire, 'But what about those moments when I do actually choose my response to a stimulus? Isn't that proof of my successful inhibition?' The answer is 'No!' When you find yourself in a condition of choice, this is proof that inhibition did its work. But you, i.e. your personal ego-driven self, did not do the choosing. At this critical moment, inhibition chose you! This experience seems closer to *grace* rather than *choice*.

It is more accurate to suggest that when things work well, inhibition needs to be present *before* the receipt of a stimulus. This idea runs contrary to the received wisdom that we are required to create space *between* the stimulus and the reaction. Once a stimulus has arrived, it is all too late to do anything! Your response at this point will be determined by all the hard work you have done previously. Essentially, our response to a stimulus is conditioned by our psychophysical state at the receipt of the stimulus, and not by what we think we can achieve afterwards.

It may help to see inhibition as a state or resource rather than an activity of choice. Inhibition is a noun and not a verb. It is a capacity for non-reaction in the face of life – the ability to keep engaged rather than becoming overwhelmed by 'emotional gusts'.[1] And this resource, rather like a muscle in the brain, can become stronger and more easily available as a result of practice and discipline. This is our work.

Giving directions

The idea of giving directions has confused generations. The way out of this maze is to ask ourselves, 'Who is the Director?' Do we really believe that the source of our directions resides in the neocortex, our relatively new brain? How can our limited brains comprehend the vastness of the flow of life, much less direct it consciously? It is much wiser, and more true, to know that we are directed *by* Nature rather than the other way around. This is the beautiful and powerful realisation that Alexander arrived at later in his life. In a Eureka moment, he commented to his class:

'By Jove I've got it. It's crystal clear! If only we stop doing the wrong, the right will do itself.'[2] (From a personal discussion with Miss Goldie, c. 1990.)

This shift in thinking requires an act of faith rather than effortful ambition.

If it is true that we are directed by Nature, then consciously sending the head forward and up makes no sense. And where is forward and up? It cannot exist geographically. It can't be a place, nor an angle, nor a sensation, and not even a relationship. In fact, the less we know about *forward and up* the better.

I have not come across anyone (including myself) who, when attempting to give directions or send orders, doesn't glaze over and perform some rather bizarre muscular contortions. As we explore the value of giving directions, we need to question how we are using ourselves when we are carrying out these instructions. In my experience, most people, when asked what they are doing while giving directions, will usually report that they are focusing on some postural part or parts, or visualising some energy movement, or trying to sense some uplift or stretch in the neck and spine. But all this can only lead to a harmful form of concentration and effort. Conversely, it may induce a form of self-paralysis that creates a deadening impact upon our vitality. Have you ever had a conversation with someone who was consciously directing themselves? It's not a nice experience. It feels like the person has vanished!

Our attempts at self-directing, self-stretching or self-releasing keep us safely removed from our true nature, and stuck in comfortable delusions. Nothing of real value actually changes. We end up making more effort than before or we collapse, and we kid ourselves that something transformational is taking place – that we have changed our habits. But we remain essentially the same and our real habits of thought are left unchallenged. And these habits maintain our status quo – detached from the vibrancy and urgency of our living and present experience. We can instead cultivate an attitude of attentive playfulness.

The most helpful element of the classic directions is the 'let' or 'allow', rather than the postural details that follow. This was a dramatic shift from Alexander's earlier request to 'put' the head forward and up.[3] I am sure we have all experienced moments when we are not at all concerned with the postural directions, and instead we find ourselves in an attitude of 'surrender', and of 'letting'. We are in the flow. If we chase after the butterfly, it will surely fly away, but if we move towards inner stillness, the butterfly might just alight on our shoulder. And in this sea of surrender, the postural patterns will normalise of their own accord.

I suspect that many excellent teachers know that their experience denies the classical version of inhibiting and directing. Thankfully, we may not always practise what we preach!

The idea that directions are simply a holding or framing in mind, or little wishes, or a kind of hopeful intention, is equally problematic. It shares the same fallacy that the mind should be occupied with some spatial or imaginative *content* of the head, neck and back, thinking *about* one's directions or some energy moving along the spine, an idea of 'up'. The moment we request our pupils to hold any particular *content* in mind, we are actually compromising their spontaneity and their ability to fully participate in the present moment.

The classical version of sending directions may at best serve as temporary and useful distraction, which can neutralise the dominance of a habit of thought – for example the universal habit of endgaining. But it can never be a strategy for living.

The real 'change in thinking' that Alexander was ultimately aiming for, and the real essence of 'thinking in activity', is not an increase in mental *content* and mental clutter, but rather a change in *quality* of thinking. *Content thinking* embodies mere ghosts in a machine, detached from the sphere of true relationship, whereas *quality thinking* offers the potential of a way of being in connection to the world.

Directions can be understood as the ongoing state of harmony or distortion that is present within each of us and at every moment. It is a vital force. We are for better or worse raising or lowering our standard of functioning as a result of this ever-present and ever-changing drama.

Alexander described the giving of directions as primarily preventative, that is to neutralise our unconscious reactions of mind-body distortion. This is *non-doing* in the fullest sense. For example, the direction 'stay back and up', is not simply a spatial demand. It is rather a description of a psychophysical attitude of *alert and relational non-merging* that we are supported in maintaining by the teacher, and increasingly in our everyday life.

On a simple neurological point, we activate muscle contractions from the motor cortex. There is no separate pathway for releasing messages of contraction. The relaxation of a muscle or group of muscles can only take place as a consequence of the stopping of the original signal activation, i.e. prevention and inhibition.

USE OF SELF AND POSITIONS OF MECHANICAL ADVANTAGE

The *monkey position* and the *lunge* are not examples of good use. They are at best 'positions of mechanical advantage'. In fact, Alexander first used the term 'positions of mechanical advantage' to refer to a range of positions, including what we know today as the *monkey position*. Going into a monkey when working on a pupil is no guarantee of good work. It might help. But, here is the point that Alexander was making: positions of advantage support and encourage good use, by minimising the impact of other demanding stimuli on the system.

Conversely, I could work with my shoulders up around my ears, which would be quite uncomfortable after a while, and certainly not an advantage. But I might also have rather good use at the same time. Similarly, I could compress my neck and pull my head into my spine for a short period. This certainly would not feel very nice, but it would not necessarily mean that I could not communicate good use both to myself and the person I am working with. I can demonstrate this experience to anyone who is willing to question the primacy of the neck, head and back.

The conscious *movement* of the head back and down is therefore not the real problem. Ultimately, Alexander was interested in the *reaction* of the nervous system that can be witnessed by the unconscious act of *throwing* or *snatching* the head back and down – a spasmodic movement.

It should be clear that our reactions to stimuli affect the organism as a whole. We are not only affected in parts of ourselves, even though we may develop specific problems. We react with our total psychophysical selves, and this includes our neurological, biochemical, muscular-skeletal, respiratory, digestive and psycho-emotional systems. And therefore, the inhibition of our reactions would affect the totality of our biological and emotional health and functioning.

Alexander himself, later on, was at pains to refute any idea that his Technique was about ergonomics, postures and procedures: 'It's not getting in and out of chairs even under the best of conditions that is any value: that is simply physical culture. . . .'[4]

He was very clear about his purpose: '. . .it is primarily a technique for the development of the control of human reaction.'[5]

In other words, improving our use is essentially our growing ability not to react to stimuli both from without and from within the organism.

In my experience, the separation of 'use' from 'positions of mechanical advantage' was a huge relief to me. Initially I found this departure very challenging. But I also experienced myself increasingly liberated from the straight-jackets of Alexanderishness.

THE PRIMARY CONTROL AND REACTIONS TO STIMULI

The primary control is *not* the head–neck–back relationship. These two things are not identical. In fact, the head–neck–back relationship is not even primary. It is simply one rather accurate barometer of our state of reaction to stimuli. And it lends itself beautifully to observation. But other barometers exist that are no more and no less primary.

The voice is an excellent barometer of our general psychophysical state. When we are disturbed, our voice will always betray us. Let's not forget that Alexander was inspired to navigate the territory of the psychophysical self as a result of his voice troubles.

The eyes are a wonderful and powerful reflection of the soul. They don't lie. The breath mirrors our inner world and so too our body language, including our facial and body gestures. The quality and communication of our touch reflects our mind-body state. Hence, the experience that our hands-on work will always deliver our truth. You give what you are. All these processes are what I would call 'parallel processes'. In other words, none of them are more primary than the others. They are simultaneous.

The primary aim of the Technique is to evolve the capacity to not react to stimuli. The head–neck–back is secondary to this evolving stillness. Miss Goldie, from whom I received a number of lessons over many years, understood this very well:

> So the head–neck–back is secondary – it comes out of the stopping. You don't need to know it, but it's useful to understand it. The practice is in the stopping...[6]

The primary control is the unknown and maybe unknowable self-righting mechanism that animates us all. If left alone and undisturbed, it acts as an ongoing harmonising constant in our lives.

The primary control can only be seen via its manifestations. It cannot be witnessed directly nor experienced as a sensation to remember. There is no anatomy of the primary control.

We fall upwards into the ocean of Life that supports us. It is the actionless act of vital surrender.

Applied conscious control – A recipe for disaster

But aren't we supposed to apply conscious control to our everyday activities? In *Man's Supreme Inheritance*,[7] Alexander did indicate that conscious control of the physical machinery and the parts involved was indeed a method for attaining physical perfection. When we follow this idea, we engage in self-reflection and try to become conscious of how we perform our actions. But this can only lead to self-consciousness and over-control – the dreaded droid!

But by 1941, he refuted his earlier claim. It is no longer an applied method. I guess that by now, Alexander had recognised the pernicious danger of this type of mental manipulation:

> ... I use the term 'conscious control and guidance' to indicate primarily a plane to be reached rather than a method of reaching it.[8]

Now conscious control is a potential plane of existence, an evolved state. It offers mastery or control over human reaction. Like the non-attachment of Buddhism, it is the fruit of hard work and discipline.

Alexander's books and writings

Alexander's books and writings are nothing more and nothing less than a historical record, an evolution of the thought and practice of a determined investigator and passionate navigator of the human condition.

Alexander's four books are not the gospels and need not be treated with divine reverence, but rather critical and reasoned thinking. Many of our confusions in the Alexander world emerge from our tendency to view his writings as text books and signposts for our Alexander knowledge base.

We fail to see the evolution in *his* technique and understanding. So when we speak in Alexander's name or quote him, we need to be aware that he may have said something different beforehand or afterwards.

In his first book, *Man's Supreme Inheritance,* which was conceived before 1910, Alexander was particularly concerned with a position or positions of mechanical advantage. He saw his role as manipulating parts of the musculature and creating mechanical ease and improved functioning. The pupil's role was to 'order' these specific parts of the body under the guidance of the teacher as a prelude to the development of 'conscious control'.

Later in his evolution,[9] Alexander formulated his ideas of a 'primary control of use', which acts as a controlling mechanism of the total organism. This was his first attempt at a unifying principle, and it came to replace his earlier emphasis on positions of mechanical advantage.

And later still, he saw his work in terms of gaining control of human reactions to stimuli. But even then, he never really managed to abandon his earlier injunctions.

Ultimately, I am not concerned with whether my work conforms to a discrete period in Alexander's own evolution, but rather whether it is true. Blind conformity or slavish obedience to Alexander are the real betrayal of his own vision of constant re-evaluation if new facts come to light.

My favourite Alexander book is the one that he did not write, but I believe he would write today.

Fear reflexes and teaching

I am more and more convinced by Alexander's discovery that *learning can never take place when the fear reflexes are unduly excited.*[10] This truth has huge implications. It continues to inspire me more and more in my private teaching as well as in my training school. I sense that it is not fully embodied in the Alexander world.

We really do need to take seriously and consider how we engage with our students and pupils. I am clearly not at my best if I upset or frighten a pupil. And this includes making them feel wrong, stupid or judged. Does this happen in my practice? Yes, of course! I have been teaching for 30 years, but I am not always at my best. And when I fall short of my ideals, my teaching suffers. I need to accept and learn from moments when I fail my students and pupils, and I need to forgive myself. There is always an opportunity for repair and renewal, to make amends. I hope it is obvious that if I am unkind to myself, I am no use to anyone.

I make it clear to the pupil that they have no responsibility to succeed, and if things don't work so well, it is my failure rather than theirs.

I am not inclined today to use terms like 'misuse' or bad habits. There are really no such things as bad habits – harmful ones, maybe. They are best understood as necessary strategies for survival that may lessen when the person feels ready and supported. I do not inform a pupil that they are 'wrong'. I do not urge them to direct themselves 'better'. I do not request that a pupil needs to direct more or inhibit more or do less. I do not inform the pupil that they have a problem with their heads, necks or backs or any other part. Actually, I don't ask them to achieve anything. Any request to try and achieve will simply activate the fear reflexes, and reinforce the endgaining approach. This is the problem rather than the solution.

Today, almost the only request I make in a lesson is a movement request. I may ask a pupil to bend their knees, or look around the room, or breathe out, or take their heels into the ground, or stay back. These movement or non-movement requests are always understood, easily carried out and rarely evoke fear, anxiety, or confusion. Compare this to classic inhibition and direction requests:

'I want you to inhibit your reaction to the idea of sitting down, and instead I want you to stop, send your directions to your head neck and back, and then whilst continuing to send these directions to yourself, primarily, secondarily and so on, I want you to give yourself the opportunity of achieving your end using the means-whereby and not endgaining.'

This has to be a recipe for psychosis!

It is reported that one day Alexander was particularly excited and informed one of his assistants, 'Now I can give it to them if they want it or not.'[11] In other words, the essential harmony and vitality in the teacher will communicate something of value to the pupil. The non-doing, the stillness and the aliveness of the teacher is the real influence. This bypasses any self-request from the pupil.

The pupil is informed by this new experience and not by a request from within or from another to 'change'. Even the idea of change is a problem which can lead to a form of self-violence. Change, if it needs to happen is the fruit of not trying to change! What is called for is essentially an attitude of self-acceptance. My own ambitious agenda for self-change may not conform to organic and natural time which has its own wisdom and unknown ways.

This is why touch is such an essential element in Alexander communication. The beauty of touch is its directness. It is unmediated by interpretation, fantasy, imagination and analytic conceptualisations.

WITHOUT MEMORY, DESIRE AND UNDERSTANDING

The human individual is much more complex and ultimately more simple than we can imagine. To hold both the complexity and the simplicity in the palm of one's hand is truly a challenge. In this spirit, I would like to share a word from a teacher I never met, but who continues to inspire me – the psychoanalyst and philosopher Wilfred Bion. He urged his students to abandon or suspend 'memory, desire and understanding'.[12] He encouraged a discipline that fostered the ability to reside in the unknown.

There are echoes here of Keats' 'Negative Capability':

...that is when a man is capable of being in uncertainties, Mysteries, doubts, without any irritable reaching after fact and reason...[13]

Note Alexander's description of the necessity for 'an ever-increasing ability on the part of both teacher and pupil to pass from the known to the unknown.'[14]

We all want to hold on to something. And our pupils urge us to give them that very something to take away with them, to take home and practise or remember. It is of course human to wish to grasp after certainties, but it is sublime to hold the creative space of not knowing.

The Alexander relationship and emotional healing

The Alexander Technique can serve as a vehicle for emotional healing. And the Alexander teacher is a facilitator in this process. The use of the teacher and the use of the pupil both go into the mix. Use is infectious! In good teaching, the use of the teacher must influence the pupil more than the pupil influences the teacher. And like alchemy, when the conditions are ripe, out of the pot comes gold.

The mind-body self is indivisible, and therefore the impulse towards self-righting and growth is supported in the Alexander relationship. In the space between teacher and pupil lies the potential for processing emotional struggles and pain. How does this work?

First we must explore the function of habits of thought. Why do we find ourselves jumping into the future and away from ourselves? Why is the habit of endgaining so universal? Why is it so rare in our culture for someone to be able to remain in the present? These questions go to the heart of Alexander's so-called habits of misuse.

Under the influence of emotional disappointment and pain, the body reacts in various ways. In early childhood, we rarely have the resources to deal with too much pain. When the perceived threats to our psychological survival are sustained and strong, we develop certain strategies which include habitual postural patterns in order to defend against being overwhelmed by the experience. These patterns become fixed and get amplified as we react to the general stimuli of living. We become rigid in the face of danger, we hold our jaws against the urge to sob, we twist against anxiety, we straighten up against the fear of depression or collapse, and we compress ourselves to minimise too much excitement.

Our postural distortions and preferences are similar in kind to our behavioural and substance addictions. Our habitual patterns help us cope, and enable us to manage ourselves. They are our strategies for survival. They will remain and should remain until we feel safe enough to lessen them. The process of withdrawal can be quite uncomfortable.

It is a myth to assume that the action of the primary control naturally brings about a state of being which is nice, easy and pleasurable. Improving use is not a lollipop of instant gratification. Yes, it can sometimes feel this way. But in this same territory of emptiness and ease lives our storehouse of memory and experience.

This is why the move towards freedom and quiet may elicit strong emotions and memories. Lying down work can be a powerful trigger. Minimising our familiar patterns of control can evoke anxiety of 'losing control'. Becoming less of a control freak may well feel threatening.

Deep within the undisturbed and undistracted self resides both terror and bliss, laughter and tears, sadness and joy. The teacher needs to support us in this space of raw and undiluted experience without doing anything about it; to contain it within the embrace of loving stillness. The teacher must have navigated his or her own internal world to a sufficient degree in order to hold the arising experience.

In this role, the teacher is a special kind of friend, and is engaged in a mutual dialogue. Martin Buber suggests that in a genuine 'I-Thou Relationship', healing through meeting is possible.[15] If the teacher can hold our hand as we are immersed in the pool of unresolved struggles, then this toxic substance can be transformed into meaningful nourishment. This food can in turn be a source for emotional growth. Healing is a product of digesting and processing experience.

Recent research in attachment theory has indicated a mechanism called 'limbic resonance'.[16] Similar to empathy, it suggests that the capacity for sharing deep emotional states arises from the limbic system of the brain. The powerful attunement and synchronising of two systems can lead to increased health and profound personality changes.

The Alexander Technique has the potential to enrich our lives. It can increase our capacity to tolerate and more fully participate in the tapestry of everyday life, with its mixture of heaven and hell.

A DISTANT HORIZON BECKONS

If there is truth in the Alexander Technique, then it will be shared by other universal truths. The Alexander Technique as passed on down the line of Alexander teachers, from Alexander to today, does not hold a monopoly of truth and may indeed hold a number of delusions. Feel free to expand your own horizons without the limitations of received wisdom. There is no holy writ and no holy legacy. You can tear down the carved idols of Alexander doctrine that do not conform to your direct and lived experience. Alexander himself saw the dangers of 'fixed ideas and prejudices'.

You can't be a timid disciple and a brave explorer at the same time.

And yet with all of this, I am deeply aware of how I am just touching the surface of a vast enterprise. I notice more and more acutely how often I am 'not here', but rather lost in the vortex of reactivity. It's tough for a perfectionist like me to accept the human, and not to aspire to the angelic. I sense that these constant reminders offer me the potential for deepening my self-compassion and hopefully my compassion for others.

Today, I feel more able to sing my broken Hallelujah.

References

1. Alexander, F. M. (1911). *Man's Supreme Inheritance.* Methuen: London.
2. From my personal conversation with Miss Goldie, c. 1990.
3. Alexander first used this new formula in *The Use of the Self* in 1932, but he does not indicate when he changed his formulation.
4. Alexander, F. M. (1995). *Articles and Lectures.* Mouritz: London.
5. Alexander, F. M. (2000). *The Universal Constant in Living.* Mouritz: London.
6. Robb, Fiona (1999). *Not to Do.* Camon Press: London, p. 5.
7. *Man's Supreme Inheritance*, op cit.
8. *The Universal Constant in Living*, op cit.
9. Alexander, F. M. (1985, 1932). *The Use of the Self.* Gollancz: London.
10. Alexander, F. M. (2004). *Constructive Conscious Control of the Individual.* Mouritz: London.
11. Walsh, Nanette (2004). 'Peggy Williams In Her Own Words' in *AmSAT News*, Spring 2004. Available at http://riversideinitiative.com/about-the-director/articles/ [last accessed 7 December 2015].
12. Bion, W. (1967). 'Notes on Memory & Desire' in *The Psychoanalytic Forum.*, vol. 2, no. 3.
13. Rollins, H. E. (ed.) (1958). *The Letters of John Keats.* Cambridge University Press: Cambridge, pp. 193-4.
14. *The Use of the Self*, op cit.
15. Buber, M. (1970). *I and Thou.* T & T Clark: Edinburgh.
16. Lewis, T., F. Armini, R. Lannon (2000). *A General Theory of Love* (Random House: London.

After training with Shmuel Nelkin in Israel, Anthony was invited to teach at Dr Barlow's and Marjory Barlow's Alexander Institute in 1987. He has been training teachers since 1989. In 2004, he opened the Alexander Teacher Training School in central London. Anthony is a qualified psychotherapist and is particularly passionate about the potential of the Alexander work for emotional healing. He has been privileged to have learned from Patrick Macdonald, Bill and Marjory Barlow, Miss Goldie and Walter Carrington. Today his teachers are his students and pupils as well as his two sons, aged five and three. Anthony is a keen supporter of Manchester United, and is the producer of the Alexander DVD *From Stress to Freedom*.

The Means-Whereby of Excellence

Continuing to Grow as a Teacher

Brooke Lieb

BACKGROUND
This article relates to my workshop 'Masterful Teaching: Emulating our role models, innovating our own methods'.

To emulate means 'to match or surpass (a person or achievement), typically by imitation'. If we observe our teaching, we will recognise phrases we repeat, placements of our hands, ways we work with our students in the chair and on the table that are what we were taught or a modification based on our experience.

In the workshop, I demonstrate a teaching tool I emulated from one or more of my teachers, and invite the group to pair up and exchange work trying this out. Then, in pairs, each teacher has a chance to demonstrate with their partner something they have carried on from their teachers. We gather afterwards to acknowledge who we are emulating, and how we are making these teaching tools our own.

An example of emulation in my teaching: I often place my hands around a student's upper arm during chair work, touching the attachments of the pectoral and latissimus dorsi muscles. I was shown this hand position by many of the faculty members at ACAT, and I use it consistently. I have developed specific language of my own to address how we can think so as not to pull down on our arms and shoulder girdle. This language gives my students a simple way to think about how to inhibit pulling down through the armpits.

To innovate means to 'make changes in something established, especially by introducing new methods, ideas, or products'. Marjory Barlow said 'F. M. used to say his brains were in his hands.'[1] My experience corroborates this. There are explanations I give, activities I take my students through, and hand placements I use in teaching that arose out of my experience. In the workshop, I share recent innovations in my approach to teaching and invite participants to pair up and share their innovations with each other. We gather afterwards to reflect on the spontaneous moments when we may say something or use our hands in a way we haven't before. If we are lucky, innovation happens during the workshop.

An example of innovation in my teaching: while my hands are on my student's head and neck, I use one of my bare feet on top of my student's foot to assist in redistributing her or his weight to facilitate balance, mobility in the ankle joint and more 'knees forward' movement while I guide her or him into and out of the chair. I can take someone in and out of the chair through this contact on her or his foot, without hands on, and still perceive the organisation through the student's head–neck–back.

Most Alexander Teachers are entrepreneurs by necessity, seeing clients in private practice and offering a service. Excellent teaching skills do not automatically mean one has the business acumen to fill a practice, and I encourage all teachers to work with business coaches and professionals who have the expertise to help us with our businesses. This paper will focus on professional development as it pertains to our excellence in teaching.

My experience has been that many of us tend to underestimate our skills and our effectiveness in helping our students to see positive benefits from lessons. The doubt is especially likely when we are newly certified teachers and have just embarked on our teaching careers. This lack of confidence may be a habit that pre-dates our introduction to Alexander Technique, but there can also be a subtle tendency among some of our community of teachers to foster self-doubt in an unproductive way. It is vital to understand the difference between rigour and observation of our own misuse as a path to improvement, and undermining criticism, whether it comes from the self or from outside.

Your experience of training sets the tone for your launch into the profession

My Story

I attended The American Center for the Alexander Technique (ACAT) in New York City from 1987-1989, and received my Teaching Certificate when I was 26. Faculty at that time included Judith Leibowitz, Debby Caplan, Barbara Kent, Pearl Ausubel and Sarnie Ogus, among others. I joined the faculty in 1992, was given my own classes as Senior Faculty starting in 1997, served as Associate Director of Training from 2006 to 2008, and have been Director of Training since September 2008.

ACAT had been training teachers for 20 years when I joined the training course, so I adopted the attitude, 'They know what they are doing, and if they say it takes three years to learn to teach, then I will just show up every day and not worry.' There was a large and diverse faculty (I was taught by six to eight different faculty members each week) and student body (approximately 30 trainees). I understood the principles of the Alexander Technique and recognised their presence in the different styles of my teacher-trainers. We were always working with the Alexander Technique, whether applying the principles to the traditional procedures, use of the voice, explorations of respiratory function, or the activities of daily living.

I experienced a supportive and productive atmosphere of mutual respect, learning, experimentation and fun. I had excellent working relationships with most everyone, and used the opportunity of differences in personality and understanding to work on myself, by remaining open to hearing other points of view without feeling obliged to agree, disagree or win someone over to my opinion. This attitude has served me well in life.

I experienced a range of emotions and moods as I went through training. I felt perfectly safe to cry, laugh, feel anger or whatever else came up while in class. My teachers were present with me in those moments, without judgement. They didn't delve into the material or try to conduct any therapy with me. Instead, we continued to apply awareness, inhibition and direction as I experienced whatever it was.

During my training, our faculty members shared their own ongoing journey of learning, discovery and continued rigour with themselves, as they guided us in building the foundation of teaching – one's own use on every level. We knew none of us had, or ever would have, perfect use, and that was not a worthy or achievable goal for any human being. The Alexander Technique was held as a resource for choice and empowerment in life, but never as a panacea. Our humanity was paramount to our teachers when they worked with us on the training course. They were much kinder to us than we were to ourselves in our expectations for how quickly we should learn and change, and our persistent desire to be right. In turn, we learned to adopt the same attitude towards our students: they are first and foremost a person, not a set of habits or misuse patterns to fix or change.

My daily reminder to myself over the three years was: 'I don't have to already know this today, I am just going to show up and meet each moment.' I was given thoughtful and specific assessments of my skills throughout the process, linked with the support and instruction to develop the areas I needed to. I was curious and interested in being able to see my own habitual patterns, and welcomed my teachers' insights into my own use. Faculty members shared their insights about my patterns of thinking, moving and behaving without judgement, as information meant to give me deeper access to my own possibilities for choice and change.

My time in training was clearly embedded in a large and diverse professional community at ACAT, which also has a teacher membership arm, so I knew I would be welcomed into that community upon graduation.

That being said, over the years, other students on our training course have had very different experiences from mine in the level of support, acceptance, encouragement and empowerment they felt during their time in training. This was the case for some of my own classmates. Some of the difficulties were a response to the teaching and communication style of the faculty members. Other difficulties resulted from individual personalities and life experiences from childhood on up: experiences in school; unique ways of learning, changing, taking in feedback and opinions about ourselves; and the level of tolerance each had for feeling wrong, confused or different.

I have also heard from many colleagues reflecting on what they experienced during their training (for better or worse), that with the passage of time, their feelings about it change and change again. Some memories become more emotionally charged, some less so.

REFLECT ON YOUR EXPERIENCE OF YOUR ALEXANDER TEACHER TRAINING
Take an inventory of your time in training. This is obviously going to be influenced by all you have experienced up to this moment. I recommend you revisit this process every couple of years or so. It can help you see the changes and growth you have undergone.

- What aspects of training worked well for you, matching your learning style and how you like to be supported as a student?
- What aspects of your training gave you skills you feel assured and confident about today?
- What aspects of your training gave you insight into your own sensibilities and what you value about the Alexander Technique?
- What aspects of your training were not as productive or relevant to your way of learning and your interest in applying the work?
- Are there any anecdotes, interactions or experiences that you still remember, including those that were positive for you and those that were not? These memories bear reviewing: they can provide you with insight into what you do and don't want to do as a teacher, as a person, and when deciding with whom you wish to study, exchange and learn.

POSTGRADUATE EXPERIENCES CONTINUE TO SHAPE YOUR SENSE OF YOURSELF AS A TEACHER
I have been lucky in developing mentors and choosing post-graduate training classes. My experience with the majority of my colleagues has been mutually respectful and receptive. Teachers with many more years of experience than me have literally placed themselves in my hands and been open to receive what I had to offer. That kind of generosity has nurtured my growth and confidence as a teacher.

When setting up an exchange with a colleague, I always ask ahead of time how they would like to proceed. We have the option to ask for feedback from one another, or to be in the role of student and receive our colleague's work without having to assess or critique. There are many ways to set up a peer-to-peer exchange. I have found the most successful exchange experiences came when each of us had been very clear about what kind of feedback we wanted and we could adjust and explore the feedback our colleague was offering in the moment.

I have had a few experiences with colleagues where their feedback and comments were not constructive, and I believe the intent was to undermine my confidence and disparage my training. I have been subject to and witness to comments along the lines of '. . .everyone from your training course misunderstands. . .[this or that concept or approach to the Technique]'. I tend not to take any of this to heart, having read most of the books by the first generation of teachers and seeing what they had to say about each other's understanding (or lack thereof) of the essence of the work.

One experience that stays with me happened after I had been teaching for about sixteen years. After having me work on him at a lesson that was part of a post-graduate program he was teaching, a colleague told me I didn't know what I was doing. Fortunately, I had already had enough experience teaching and had gotten feedback from respected peers and mentors about my skills, so this person's attempt to undermine my teaching failed. Rather, it spoke volumes about him.

The experience above opened my eyes to what I might encounter with other colleagues, and helped me develop my own code of conduct with regard to how I treat colleagues and what I will and won't tolerate from others. Because of it, I have had many frank conversations with colleagues over the years about their experiences, and heard of other stories similar to my own. I believe it's a small minority who behave this way, but the behaviour does exist. It is helpful to be prepared so you don't doubt yourself should this kind of thing happen to you.

Finding your path to excellence

It is useful to have a specific plan for your personal development as a teacher.

Lessons, peer-to-peer exchanges and workshops are an obvious component of your ongoing learning and support. Depending on where you are located, you may have access to lessons, exchange partners or workshops on a regular basis without much travel. If this is not the case, in addition to making a trip yourself to study, you can create an opportunity for teachers to come to your location. If you have colleagues nearby, you can include them in the study opportunities. If there are no other teachers in your area, you can organise workshops for the public, or for your client base, or suggest they have lessons as a way to have another perspective on their learning.

Take an inventory of what you have already learned, the skills you have developed, the successful and effective cases from your private practice, the feedback you have received from your clients, and assessments from your peers and teachers. The beauty of the Alexander Technique is that the longer you work with the concepts and principles, the more you discover and uncover. Learning is a lifelong process for us. As we age and change over time, our experience of how the work facilitates living continuously evolves.

If you find yourself growing bored with your work or your students, reflect on the level of endgaining or habit that may have crept into your teaching. Look beneath the boredom to see if you may be frustrated, at a plateau or missing the interaction of a peer or mentor. In my experience, when I am truly engaged in self-observation and experimentation, I am not bored. I may not be comfortable or fully satisfied with my state or what I am aware of, but I am definitely not bored.

Finding the most effective learning support for your continued growth: Know yourself and choose your teachers mindfully

Here are some questions to help you understand your own preferences for learning, and how to identify the teachers who will be effective for you:

- What have your best interactions with mentors and teachers been like?
- Who have you learned from most effectively?
- What do you know about what you need to feel engaged, open and receptive when you are learning?
- What kind of feedback do you thrive on?
- What kind of feedback is unproductive for you (you may feel the need to protect yourself, defend yourself or leave)?
- What is the kind of feedback you fear hearing, but could benefit by knowing?
- Which teachers challenge you to learn more?
- Which teachers help you recognise your strengths?
- Who can you mentor and support? This could be private students, peers, teachers-in-training or less experienced colleagues.
- What developments and growth do you want to experience in your own work?

In closing

My passion is training teachers and working with graduate teachers to refine their teaching on every level. I hope this piece is a useful resource for you to develop your means-whereby to continue to evolve and grow in your work on yourself and in your Alexander teaching. Please feel free to contact me with any questions or anecdotes about your journey.

1. Barlow, Marjory, Trevor Allan Davies (2002). *An Examined Life*. Mornum Time Press: San Francisco, p. 30.

N. Brooke Lieb, Director of Training at ACAT, qualified from ACAT in 1989, joined the faculty in 1992, and served as Associate Director of Training from 2006 to 2008. Brooke has been Guest Faculty at Vivien and Neil Schapera's Teacher Certification Program in Cincinnati and at Nancy Romita's AT Mid-Atlantic Teacher Training Apprenticeship. Brooke has presented at the AmSAT ACGM and at the 8th and 10th International Congresses in Lugano and Limerick. She has taught at C. W. Post College, St. Rose College, Kutztown University, Pace University, the Actors Institute, the National Theatre Conservatory at the Denver Center for the Performing Arts, Dennison University, and Wagner College. She trained under Judith Leibowitz, Deborah Caplan and Barbara Kent, and has done postgraduate studies with Barbara Kent, Vivien Schapera, Walter and Dilys Carrington, Glynn MacDonald, Ruth Murray, Alan Philps, Elisabeth and Lucia Walker, Missy Vineyard, Tommy Thompson, Pedro de Alcantara and John Nicholls among others. Brooke maintains a teaching practice in New York City, specialising in working with people dealing with pain, back injuries and scoliosis, and with performing artists.

Chair Work: What is It? Why Do It?

Tom Vasiliades

In the Alexander teaching community there have been discussions and varied opinions on chair work: It is a procedure! It is an activity! It is something 'traditional' teachers do! It is boring!

From all accounts, Alexander did chair work throughout his more than 60 years of teaching. All first generation teachers also used chair work in their teaching, even if not everyone did it throughout their teaching life. Today many teachers continue to use chair work and yet many teachers do not. How come?

One thought is that standing, sitting, and moving from one to the other is a common activity that all able-bodied people do. Working on the practice of inhibiting and directing, and improving sensory appreciation in this daily movement would be helpful – but that could also be said of any activity: walking, reaching for a book on a shelf, speaking, etc. So, why chair work?

It is important to look at what goes on in chair work to understand how it is uniquely beneficial and fundamental to studying and practising the Technique. If one pauses in the movement from sitting to standing or standing to sitting, one is in monkey. When in monkey the ankles, knees and hips are flexed, the weight of the head and torso are forward and there is a stretch demand on the head, neck back (HNB) organisation, indeed on the whole structure. The stretch demand is a pull on the musculature with an increase of tone needed in the muscles of the neck and back for postural support. How is that demand met? If it is met by shortening or stiffening the neck, pulling the head back and down, shortening and narrowing the back, then it would be a misuse that would include rigidity and negatively impact movement and breathing. However, if the neck is free, the head going forward and up and the back lengthening and widening, then there is an improved integrated use and a dynamic elasticity throughout the structure. There is a change of tone in the musculature and an elastic spread throughout. Here dynamic has two meanings: 1) characterised by constant change (not rigid) and 2) relating to forces; in this case the pulls of the HNB in one direction and the pull of the legs in the other direction in opposition to the HNB-antagonistic pulls. By organising the head–neck–back relationship, one creates, as Alexander states in *The Universal Constant of Living*, an 'integrated (normal) working of the postural mechanism'[1] – postural support, with postural support being the necessary work of an integrated HNB relationship for uprightness. As we know, more often than not there is more work done for uprightness than needed. Doing less, inhibiting and directing is part of the process for developing well-organised postural support by allowing the deep postural muscles to do their work, instead of including muscles whose primary action is for movement.

I would like to state that using chair work does not have a cultural bias against those cultures where chairs are rarely, if ever, used. In some cultures there are those who squat, and there are other cultures where sitting cross-legged on the floor is the common form of sitting. When a person is seated in a chair, the legs are working less than they would be in standing, a monkey or squatting. A difference between sitting in a chair with feet on the floor and sitting cross-legged is with the feet on the floor there is a sensory feedback of that contact that stimulates both the legs and the postural muscles that doesn't happen exactly in the same way when sitting cross-legged, although there is a stimulation of the postural muscles in both cases by the contact the pelvis makes with the surface we are sitting on. So, sitting in a chair with feet on the floor allows the legs to undo and organise the HNB that can be easier for many people.

As explained above, flexing and extending the legs while moving up and down in space – including going into a squat through to going up on the toes, which, interestingly, is a movement most children do within the first year – puts an increased demand of muscle tone on the HNB organisation for postural support. This does not occur in other activities where the leg movements do not take a person into and through a monkey. While chair work can be looked at in terms of movement, it is more to the point to look at it through the underlying postural support that will allow for freer movement, better breathing and improved performance of all activities. If we look at chair work only in terms of the movement occurring with more freedom or ease, then it is like any other movement and one could feel bored by doing the same movement over and over again. However, if we look at chair work and the demand it puts on postural support and the synergy with movement and breathing in a way that other activities don't, then the uniqueness of what chair work offers and creates becomes clear. It is within this framework that we should look at chair work and by extension the Technique.

In terms of hands-on work during chair work, I won't get into the particulars of where to put the hands. Suffice to say this will differ from student to student. In the workshop, participants put hands on the head, neck, head and neck, back, torso, legs and arms while working to organise the HNB within the framework stated above. Of course, the teacher will do that which she or he thinks will be helpful at any moment in the lesson; this is the art of teaching.

There may be students who will not be able to do chair work. Walter Carrington described lessons his mother, who was diagnosed with visceroptosis, took with Alexander. The early lessons were done with her mostly sitting in a chair. I gave lessons to a student who was paralyzed up to his mid-chest, who gained benefit from practising inhibiting and directing and improving his sensory appreciation – though, understandably, his HNB organisation did not improve. However, those who can do chair work would benefit more by doing chair work than not doing it.

In the larger context of the Technique, there is the belief that if one is working with the principles of inhibition, direction, faulty sensory appreciation and primary control, then we are teaching the Technique. While teaching to principle or an activity-based approach has value, the process in chair work, as discussed above, develops one's use and improves functioning in ways that other activities or movements do not.

In summary, the movement of getting in and out of the chair, going into monkey, and squatting, puts a stretch demand on postural support that does not happen in other activities. Activities such as walking, reaching for a book on a shelf, or speaking are not the same in terms of this demand. These activities and others will not bring about the HNB relationship to have an elastic spread in the way that chair work does due to the inherent demands of the activities. Therefore, the development of the HNB relationship is maximised through chair work. Excluding chair work or not doing it consistently enough minimses the student's fundamental development in the work.

1. Alexander, F. M. (2000, 1941). *The Universal Constant of Living*. Mouritz: London, p. 107–110.

Bibliography

Alexander, F. M. 2000 (1941). *The Universal Constant of Living*. Mouritz: London.

Barlow, Marjory and Carey, Seán (2011). *Alexander Technique: The Ground Rules*. Hite Limited: London.

Carrington, Walter H. M. and Carey, Seán (2001). *Personally Speaking*. Mouritz: London.

Carrington, Walter H. M. and Carey, Seán (1992). *Explaining the Alexander Technique*, The Sheildrake Press: London.

Cacciatore, T. W., O. S. Mian, A. Peters, and B. L. Day (2014). 'Neuromechanical Interference of Posture on Movement: Evidence from Alexander Technique Teachers Rising from a Chair' in *Journal of Neurophysiology* 112.

Nicholls, John (2011 and 2015). 'Explaining the Alexander Technique' Part 1-7, blog on the website http://www.johnnichollsat.com/blog/.

Nicholls, John (1987). 'The Use of the Chair In Teaching' in *The Alexander Review*.

Roberts, Tristan D. M. (1995). *Understanding Balance: The Mechanics of Posture and Locomotion*. Singular Pub Group.

Tom Vasiliades is the training director of Training Center for the Alexander Technique –NYC (TCAT-NYC). He teaches at the Juilliard School. He has taught at the New York University undergraduate drama and the New School for Drama MFA Program where he was Chair of Movement. He has taught the Technique for over 20 years across the United States in universities, doctor offices, health clubs and in private practice.

Practising Our Practice is Our Theory

Sharyn West

INTRODUCTION

In the workshop that is the subject of this report, I set out to explore what is unique to the Alexander Technique (AT), what is shared within the community of its teachers, and also to identify what AT shares with standpoints in formal and mainstream education. I want to offer terminology that indicates ways to unpack the types of ideas that can be found embedded in the learning and teaching of any discipline. Knowing one's ideology is an important professional skill as it provides a way of seeing what can enhance and/or impede inter-professional and inter-disciplinary understanding and collaboration.

Our profession identifies itself as education. With this in mind I argue that learners and teachers of Alexander Technique (AT) operate in a particular kind of theoretical approach. I argue that we are constantly engaged in what amounts to research-based observation about learning. Underlying the Technique is a distinct theory of learning. We practise psychophysical unity in the means whereby we use ourselves, applying principles such as psychophysical unity and the constant effect of use on functioning. Practising our practice is our theory.

In AT we choose attention to process over outcome. We teach how to intentionally deploy a reasoned and sustained means whereby unnoticed interference in the innate coordination of ourselves-as-organism can be brought to notice and closely observed. This attention to the operation of the organism-in-action is a defining characteristic of the methodology of the AT.

AT increasingly involves interactions with people from ever-widening circles of professional backgrounds and disciplines, accomplishments and cultural interests. It has a wide range of relevance and applications, with health benefits becoming established as evidence-based outcomes. My focus for the workshop was a response to this, with an interest in encouraging inter-professional and inter-disciplinary conversations. Taking part in these, I argue, are as necessary for developing our profession as publicity is for making a living from teaching. To be able to present a comprehensive and comprehensible account of the scope and nature of AT is becoming an important and necessary professional skill. In this regard there is little value in saying: 'It is difficult to explain – you must come for a lesson.'

1. PROCESS, STRUCTURE AND CONTENT

I combined textual research, short informal interviews and summaries of emerging themes from CPD workshops with work in our training school.[1]

The workshop had two one–hour sessions with a 15 minute break.

One objective was to place AT in the context of wider theoretical positions and in current and perennial education studies. I compared dominant philosophies of education and then compared experiential learning theories[2] to locate AT as educative practice and illustrate commonalities and differences.

Another objective was to invite critical reflection. I asked three questions, addressed through activities:

1. What, should you leave it out, would make what you do *not* the AT? (15 mins.)
2. Map the connections between principles and activities in your teaching. (15 mins.)
3. What activities do you offer pupils to explore between lessons? (15 mins.)

From my teaching practice (teacher trainees and pupils) I have learned that the sooner I can establish an interest in the operation of worldview in use of the self, the sooner I can begin to identify that the Alexander Technique amounts to a particular worldview. I can then show how the principles of AT can be practised. When I identify the fundamental principles of psychophysical unity and the influence of use on functioning, and describe AT as a method for the control of human reaction, I assert a worldview.

2. Professions, disciplines and conceptual frameworks

Although the term profession loosely indicates work that is paid for, a stricter definition indicates that requirements and qualifications are required, usually at a tertiary level, from recognised institutions and regulation by professional bodies. Traditional professions arose in specific disciplines (e.g. Astronomy, Physics, Music, Medicine). They use specific terminology, techniques and tools. The history of their growth and development trace contested and debated concepts and narratives about:

1. **axiological** elements – what is valued;
2. **ontological** elements – what is taken-for-granted, believed in or conveyed in terminology;
3. **epistemological** elements – what is worth knowing and how that comes to be known.

Taken together these elements shape disciplinal standpoints, shaping what is taught, learned and researched. Some or all of these elements can operate as assumptions. Expression of values (axiology), notions of reality (ontology) and ways of learning (epistemology) can be seen in the following examples of worldviews:

Positivism is the dominant philosophy of science wherein facts are discovered by strict adherence to scientific method. Valid knowledge (truth/certainty/facts) is objective and conforms to external reality. Facts are discovered through sensory experience, deduced by rational, logical and/or mathematical calculation and provide grounds for predicting outcomes.

Constructivism/Critical Realism are prominent post-positivist philosophies. They both emphasise the need for reflective assessment and critique of society, culture and belief. Knowledge is socially constructed. Formal and informal social and educational media transmit and reproduce specific social, cultural and historical interests which show what is considered to be valued and valuable. 'Reality' is infused with human ideas and is contextually and historically relative. It is therefore dynamic, subject to human intervention and other change factors.

3. EDUCATION AS DISCIPLINED THEORY AND PRACTICE

Philosophy of Education is a set of linked activities that:

- Examines definitions, goals and practices at a level called metatheory (e.g. axiology, epistemology and ontology).
- Contributes to other fields of applied philosophy (e.g. how they are taught).
- Sets out educational philosophies for specific purposes (e.g. policy formulation).
- Specifies what education *should* address and how education *should* be conducted.

These activities produce the type of normative philosophies of education described below.

Like all disciplines, education also involves histories and philosophies of differing approaches that have emerged over time. Notice how the axiologies[3] included in the following Normative Philosophies[4] shape how teaching happens and what it is about:

Perennialism focuses on purported universal truths that have withstood the test of time. Learning happens by reading and re-reading the Great Books to absorb the concepts contained in them and understand the proper activities they espouse. It is equally important to learn and know one's position and role.

Essentialism focuses on facts about objective reality. A core curriculum is conveyed through key skills.[5] There is an emphasis on tests and measurable standards. This is outcomes-driven education tasked with producing valuable members of society who meet the needs of the economy.

Progressivism emphasises free will and the ability to take responsibility for one's beliefs and actions. Experiences, interests, and needs of learners are drawn on to generate learning through exploration and discovery. Skills are cultivated at the level of the individual in order to enable agency and acceptance that culture and society present and cultivate different ways of seeing.

Social reconstructionist/critical theory share much of Progressivism's worldview but emphasise the role of structural inequality and social injustice directly so as to develop appreciation of collective action. Study and social action are integrated and directed towards individual and societal transformation.

The first two approaches are entirely teacher-centred philosophies. The latter two are learner-centred.

4. THE PERSON AS *THE* SITE OF LEARNING

Differences in educational practice relate to conceptions of the dynamics and mechanisms of learning. Active learning grown from the experience of the learner is a recent departure in theories of learning, denoting a shift of attention from curriculum to learner. Below I set out a brief historical account of developments in experiential learning theory.[6]

Behaviourism asserts that the nervous system provides mechanisms for learning. There is a shared conviction that mental activities such as thinking and motivation are unobservable and therefore not available to research. Some contemporary behaviourists entertain the role of subjective experience in learning. Key theorists in this school are Ivan Pavlov (1849–1936); J.B. Watson (1878–1958); B.F. Skinner (1904–1990).

The Cognitivist school originates in Jean Piaget's (1896–1980) theory of psychological development. His central notion is that children learn actively, creating new concepts out of existing concepts by attributing meaning to new experiences. Cognitive studies explore mental activities of recall, recognition, analysis and reflection as the operational faculties behind this process.

The Humanist approach emerges from the work of Carl Rogers (1902–1987). He developed a person-centred perspective asserting that (adult) persons learn best from experiences related, consciously or otherwise, to maintaining or enhancing their understanding of self and agency. Malcolm Knowles (1913–1997) developed this approach further distinguishing the adult as learner (andragogy) from child learning (pedagogy) and development.

Situationists emphasise the social context, and address how lifelong learning might best be facilitated to develop motivation because adult learners can become adaptable and self-directed if they are enabled to change what they think or change their perception of the environment of their experience. Key theorists in this school are Julian Rotter (1916–2014) Erik Erikson (1902–1994), Albert Bandura (b. 1925).[7]

Constructivist/Critical theorists also emphasise the social nature of learning but turn to historical and contextual specifics of the learner's situation. Critical reflection on self (relative to the social construction of knowledge and the construction of social knowledge) can trigger transformational learning. Jack Mezirow expresses the Situationist outlook and takes it further to state the Criticalist position as follows:

> ... interest in the way one's history and biography has expressed itself in the way one sees oneself, one's roles and social expectations. Emancipation is from libidinal, institutional or environmental forces which limit our options and rational control over our lives but have been taken for granted as beyond human control (a.k.a. 'reification'). Insights gained through critical self-awareness are emancipatory in the sense that at least one can recognise the correct reasons for his or her problems.[8]

AT shares various elements with all the above but does not dichotomise the psychophysical or the psycho-social dimensions of learning. AT asserts that:

- learning outcomes are observable in balanced and poised movement and in stillness. Learning follows stimulus and response patterning through the nervous system (Behaviourist);
- process orientation pursues life-long learning adjusted to mental, physical and age-related capabilities of the learner (Cognitivist/ Constructionist);
- holistic, learner-centred development relates to needs, experience and context (Humanist);
- reflective practice drives learning, develops self-regulation and allows self-direction (Social Situationist);
- socialised assumptions are obviated through reflection and so enable constructive choice (Constructivist/Criticalist).

5. AT AS RESEARCH PRACTICE

F. M. says AT is an example of the skill Dewey called 'thinking in activity'.[9] Dewey says:

> ... active, persistent, and careful consideration of any belief or supposed form of knowledge in the light of the grounds that support it and the further conclusions to which it tends (and) includes a conscious and voluntary effort to establish belief upon a firm basis of evidence and rationality.[10]

Minding the body extends the scope of consideration in AT, and has the benefit of making both embodied mind and ceaseless change available to intentional, directed learning because human reaction can be observed and, with will, directed towards desired outcomes. Learning and teaching become linked as research and make AT suitable for personal, social and institutional inquiry.

Tendencies within established (tertiary) disciplines have led to research being a professional pathway[11] within disciplines and professions. Practitioner research, however, potentially remains implicit in AT practice. Its methods: observation, reflection, analysis and experimentation are both a means and an outcome of its process. F. M. Alexander tasked those who would learn AT to do what he did in order to get what he got. This included drawing on case studies and publishing his findings. What Alexander did[12] provides a basic, albeit improvable, research model.

Action Research (AR) is a design widely adopted in educational and social research. By its methodology one problematic stage drives the next problematic stage, iterating insights and research actions that address the stimulus question, increasingly refining these until the matter that necessitated research activity at the outset has been addressed.[13] This is akin to Alexander's reported process, uses naturalistic methods of pause and reflection, observation, analysis and requires experimentation. These methods are taught in AT teacher training and are already a requisite standard for certification. AT requires no *necessary* departure into other disciplines to research our practice or identify the conditions for, or efficacy of its outcomes.

6. Practising our practice as research

Alexander[14] provided an account of what he did to discover a means whereby his theories in practice produced results that were observable and verifiably linked to ways of enacting specific principles. He cites cases, often referrals from doctors, for specific ailments. Gathering evidence through compiling these cases can elevate anecdotal observations into objective studies. One simple shift might be facilitated if professional bodies explored how a structured reporting protocol might draw on practitioner research from across the AT active community.

7. Outcomes

Locating AT as educational philosophy and articulating its learning theory for a collaborative skills workshop, I arrived at advocating research. AT practitioners know that the use of the self, by minding the body, enhances communicative action. I proposed, in addition, that inter-professional collaborative skill is enhanced by the ability to explicitly give account of the premises of one's practice and notions of valued and valuable knowledge regarding learning, teaching and research.

Questions about AT training have emerged during my write-up such that I can now envisage a project that can show what curricula, practices and ideologies are in operation in AT teacher training. My AR process will ask: 'What activities express what is being done to train AT Teachers?' and 'Where is this being done?' It might then be possible to capture a comprehensive, although only contemporaneous, account of what we do to produce and reproduce the Alexander Technique. From that, we can critically engage with and describe what we find to be expressed in AT teacher training so as to make explicit our axiology, ontology and epistemology and also inform training regulation and standard setting.

References
1. Alexander Technique Learning and Teaching Programs – Johannesburg.
2. These are approaches that share with AT the premise that learning happens at the learner's end and is generated in the learner's experience.
3. These are not exhaustive.
4. Education theory that says how education ought to be understood.
5. Reading, writing, articulation and, currently, computing are considered to be key skills and valued and valuable learning centres on mathematics and science.
6. A more comprehensive exploration of these schools of thought and the practices they advocate is set out in West, S. and Walker, L. (2015) 'Minds, Mirrors, Touch and Talk: The Alexander Technique as a strategy for learning from action and experience through reflective practice' in *Connected Perspectives: The AlexanderTechnique in Context*. Hite: London.
7. Bandura, now 89 years old continues to provide valuable transitions between behaviourism and cognitive psychology.
8. Mezirow, J. (1981). 'A Critical Theory of Adult learning' in *Adult Education*, vol. 32:1:5.
9. Alexander, F. M. (1932, 1985). *The Use of the Self: Its Continuous Direction in Relation to Diagnosis, Functioning and the Control of Reaction*. Victor Gollancz: London, p. 42.
10. Dewey, J. (1933). *How we Think: A Restatement of the Relation of Reflective Thinking to the Educative Process*. Heath: Lexington, MA,. p. 9.
11. Medical researcher, market researcher, educational researcher, etc.
12. As recounted in *The Use of the Self*, 'Chapter 1: Evolution of a Technique'. However, the rigour of Alexander's reported research is not sufficient to current standards of research practice.
13. The AR research cycle can be expressed as: act, re-evaluate/reflect, adjust, experiment, act, reflect, etc.
14. In *The Use of the Self*, op cit.

Sharyn West has taught at all levels of the schooling and education system. After gaining extensive experience as a school teacher she returned to university to gain further qualifications and moved on to teacher training in the late 70s. She has been a teacher trainer at tertiary level at various universities and colleges, in South Africa, England and Hong Kong and holds higher degrees from the Institute of Education in London (MA) and School for Policy studies, Bristol University (MPhil). She trained with Elisabeth Walker (Alexander Teachers Training Course, Oxford) and graduated in 1991. She is currently co-director of the Alexander Learning and Teaching Programmes in Johannesburg, South Africa. She has extensive experience of learning, teaching and researching progressive education methodologies based in the principles of the Alexander Technique.

PART TWO

Touch, Direction, Working on Ourselves and Others

The Brain, Body, and Touch

Sarah Barker

Alexander Technique (AT) is unique in two uses of touch for teaching: conscious self-reorganisation at the same moment as promoting similar reorganisation in the student, encouraged through touch[1] and cognitive redirection and re-patterning of coordination during physical activity. New research on touch and how the brain represents our own and others' bodies, sensations and actions can inform and enhance the AT teacher's use of touch in teaching. This paper describes three experiments in the use of touch, and I suggest links between research on touch and movement and teaching AT with touch, to broaden our understanding and develop greater sensitivity in teaching with touch.[2]

QUIETING AND CALMING TOUCH

> ... touch is ten times stronger than verbal or emotional contact, and it affects damn near everything we do. No other sense can arouse you like touch. We forget that touch is not only basic to our species, but the key to it.[3]

Gentle but firm touch can convey support and presence, without demands. Anyone might use this touch and most of us have either touched a friend or family member or been touched with the intention to calm and stop action, anxiety or excess effort. Studies show that this quality of touch can have positive health effects including decreased blood pressure, heart rate and cortisol levels, and increased oxytocin levels.[4] In her exploration of touch in the nurse-patient interaction, Catherine Green[5] cites Merleau-Ponty's[6] and Sokolowski's research,[7] suggesting two points: 1) That touch is necessary in the development of self; and 2) that tactile interaction affects both the person touching and the person touched. Green argues that the experience of being touched can significantly influence a person's outlook, sense of self, and ability to heal:

> First, tactile sensation allows the person to identify the various parts of their bodies as belonging to them – as 'my body'. Second, it allows for the constitution of the person as a self with the many layers of meaning that accrue to that self... Finally, touch is important for the constitution of other persons as being 'like' me, a key factor in intersubjectivity.

> She goes on to state that a person's Mental Body Representation (MBR,

which includes body image and body schema) will be developed, expanded or changed by tactile interactions.[8]

The AT teacher can touch in a quieting and calming way to arrest unconscious preparation and effort, or what Alexander called instinctive misdirection and wrong habitual use. Calming touch creates a pause for students, in which they can distinguish between their desire to 'do well' and their intention to follow a reasoned approach to changing their use.

Studies I conducted in an exercise science lab to test the hypothesis that lessons in AT would affect postural sway[9] provided unexpected insights. I realised that I could detect and move with the students' postural sway, and this allowed me to generate the quieting quality of touch. The teacher can become more fluid and responsive to the student's natural movement, before giving direction. When I work like this, students develop the ability to observe their own movement without judgement or reactive changing, as in other contemplative practices where one's own experience is simply observed.[10]

Experiment One: Following the postural sway

In all three experiments in this paper one person in a pair assumes the role of teacher, the other, that of student; they then reverse roles.

Standing behind the student, the teacher firmly and gently places hands on top of the student's shoulders. Through the hands, the teacher's awareness extends into the student's body's minute sway. The student also concentrates on their own sway, which is usually very subtle, relatively random, moving in any direction and curvilinear. The more flexible and mobile one is, the smaller the sway.[11]

The teacher observes the student's sway, then focuses on their own sway, and imposes that sway on the student. Next, the teacher matches their own sway to the student. Finally, both compare the teacher's sway to the student's, being aware of both and changing neither. The teacher and student discuss the effect of each variation.

Many students unconsciously feel that they should be immovable, rather than stable in their standing or sitting. I am sure most teachers have encountered students who think they are being put in a position they must keep. One effective way to correct this misapprehension and create more freedom is to pay attention to natural and necessary postural sway. It promotes a quiet and collected state in which the student can notice phenomena. Breathing becomes easier; spatial awareness increases. Students are not assessing progress, but are physically observant, calm, and in an easier state.

Mental body representation

Our ability to observe and the accuracy of our mental body representation (MBR, researchers' preferred term, which includes body image and body schema[12]) directly affects our understanding and interpretation of other's intentions and actions. There is scientific research on how the brain constructs a neuronal representation of the body (MBR) and how that representation functions in our understanding of others. This research can contribute to AT teachers' understanding of how and what they affect in their students. In particular, three areas of research have bearing on AT's use of touch to re-educate the sensory mechanism: mirror neurons, body mapping, and tool incorporation.

Mirror neurons and touch

Research on the mirror neuron system may provide useful information about how an AT teacher observes the postural sway and matches the student's body. In research on the mirror neuron system, Gallese and colleagues found strikingly similar patterns and occurrence of neural activity between people doing an action and those simply observing, as well as between those experiencing an emotion or a tactile sensation and those observing them. Observing, for the brain, is very close to actually experiencing. This phenomenon is at work in an AT lesson, and it happens for both student and teacher – our experiences start to 'overlap'. Neural networks activated while watching a person do something are also activated when one is touched.[13] Gallese's research shows that much cognitive activity focuses on using information from other people's actions, intentions, emotions, and sensations to develop and improve our own actions.[14] This evidence supports the practice used by many AT teachers of demonstrating improved use by moving from (for example) a downward collapse to lengthening and widening while the student touches them.

Body maps

Studies have identified a network of homunculi (or body maps) in the brain that corresponds to: 1) the whole of the body and the location and function of its parts; and 2) the extent of use and number of sense receptors of each area. There are several homunculi on the surface of the cortex and they are an integral part of the mental body representation (MBR). There are no known skin or muscle receptors that provide information about the size of our own body parts. 'Instead, this information is synthesized from multiple sensory sources, in this case vision in particular, and then stored internally as an MBR. Information about one's own body is then retrieved from the MBR to interpret current tactile inputs, and generate a perceptual representation of the object touching the skin.'[15]

Wilder Penfield drew an illustration of the homunculus showing specific parts of the body, for example the lips and fingertips, proportionally larger because of the preponderance of sensors in those areas.[16] An AT teacher can bring greater accuracy, clarity and even help in the neurological development of the homunculi and the MBR. Teachers touch to locate joints and bony prominences and in many cases they will ask the student to notice these locations. William and Barbara Conable developed a comprehensive approach to bringing these body maps to full consciousness.[17] Many AT teachers integrate this information into their lessons.

It follows from the information above that inaccuracies in the MBR will affect a person's interpretation of incoming stimuli such as touch. This is likely why correcting body mapping can be so effective in increasing a student's ability to follow prompts from the teacher's hands and to later retain that improvement in self-use. Not only does this information relate to the student's experience but it also points to effects that can influence our teaching and use of touch. The more accurate our own MBR is, the more accurate can be our interpretation of what we see and feel (through our touch) in our students' movement. Experiment Two can be used to increase accuracy of touch perception related to body mapping as well as correct and expand the MBR of both teacher and student.

EXPERIMENT TWO: LISTENING TO THE BODY
The teacher stands behind the student and places both hands on the student's neck and base of the head or shoulders. The student begins in an easy coordinated standing, then isolates a part of the body through holding, pressing down, lifting up, or collapsing. After each isolation the student returns to balance and ease in the whole body. With each change the teacher describes what the hands feel. As both gain clarity about what they are looking for, more subtle variations can be explored, refining the teacher's ability to read the body. Teachers learn to detect any difference, gradually becoming more specific in analysing where holding or downward pulling occurs. While using touch to sense movement, balance and restriction, the AT teacher can also expand the student's awareness. For example, the student's sensory appreciation improves if the teacher gently touches the student's neck and asks the student to notice the area, the touch, and include the neck in awareness of the whole body.

During lessons, the teacher, confident in an accurate assessment of the student, can guide the student's thinking with precision and delicacy. This is best done using an indirect approach to improving the student's self-awareness. For example, if the student is unconscious or tight in their middle back I will ask questions that can alert them to their own use. Rather than saying, 'You are tightening in your middle back,' I will ask, 'When you think of your whole torso how far down do you think it goes?' or 'Is this area of your body part of your awareness?' or 'Can you include this part of your spine in the whole of your torso?' Often I find the answers are complex or surprising and I make new discoveries about the student, investigating and testing new ways of proceeding.

INTERPRETING TOUCH
A 2008 literature review by Spence and Gallace highlights the need to include the brain's representation of spatial and visual stimuli when examining con-

sciousness of touch.[18] They gleaned five important insights:

1. Integration of various sensory inputs can occur prior to conscious access to information regarding touch.
2. Information from other senses can impair or enhance one's awareness of tactile experience.
3. Spatial processing and representation are key in interpretation of tactile events.
4. Conscious perception of touch isn't necessarily determined by the location of sensors in the skin, but may be related to locations in external space.
5. Activity in the main sensory area of the brain for processing touch (S1) does not necessarily lead to awareness of touch. Rather, consciousness and interpretation of touch are derived from the firing of a circuit comprised of several higher order processing areas around S1.[19]

These insights, taken together, illuminate the neurological phenomena at work in an AT teacher's tactile perception of tension or mobility in a student's body. Considering the five insights while conducting Experiment Two can expand perception of what one is doing, and of further possibilities. It is important to pay attention to all the ways the teacher is gathering information. When the teacher uses touch to analyse the student's movement, vision and spatial awareness must be included.

Tool use and MBR

Another recent discovery in cognitive neuroscience regarding body schema and body mapping has given me new ways to interpret and direct my hands-on use. Dr Atsushi Iriki's research in cognitive neuroscience demonstrates that using tools expands the body schema (the body map expressed in brain neuronal activity). Measuring activity in the posterior parietal lobe in macaque monkeys he found that when the monkey uses a tool, its neuron activity expands to include that tool.[20] That is, the perceptual field, which tells a person where the body begins and ends, extends into the tool, which is then incorporated into the body schema. Thus, when people hold an object, through the proprioceptive sensory mechanism, they fully sense the dimension and movement of the object, mapping the tool as part of themselves. When a teacher touches the student, it is possible that the student's body is mapped as an extension of the teacher's own body. Better yet, an accomplished AT teacher is mapping two bodies at once. This explains why, after extensive experience, a teacher can tell students where their thought includes or omits parts of the spine or whole body. This gives the teacher another perspective for responding to and directing the student's movement. The student may also be mapping the teacher's body, though perhaps unconsciously.

AT teacher trainer Susan Sinclair's invitation, 'When the teacher's hand touches you, touch it back with whatever area of your body is being touched', can transform the interaction between student and teacher from one of the student being 'corrected' or 'worked on' to a mutual exploration between teacher and student. Green's description of the multi-directional nature of touch (based on Husserl) provides insight into the nature of an AT teacher's experience of touch:

> Unlike the other senses, touch always has a duality to it that is crucial to its nature (Husserl, 1989). You can reflect on your hand touching your knee in three very different ways. First, your hand can be recognized as the touching instrument and your knee that which is being touched. Second, with merely a shift of attention, you can reverse that sensation. Your knee can be understood as the touching instrument and your hand becomes the thing touched. Finally, we can also understand the touching of our hand to our knee or our knee to our hand as simply that act 'through' which the sensation of touch occurs.[21]

Touching a student to change their use can be both *manipulative* (as when touching or moulding an object) and *affective* (the emotional and relational nature of interacting with another person and their physical identity). Field tells us that these two modes of touch may be taking place in two quite different systems:

> Not only different parts of the brain but different systems seem to differentiate affective from nonaffective touch. For example, a recent study suggested that affiliative or affectionate touch is transmitted via unmyelinated (non-insulated) nerve fibers (McGlone, Vallbo, Olausson, Loken, & Wessberg, 2007). In contrast, the discriminative aspects of touch were conveyed by fast-conducting myelinated (insulated) nerve fibers. Thus, these two systems seem to have different biophysical, electrophysiological, neurobiological and anatomical properties.[22]

EXPERIMENT THREE: VARIATIONS ON GIVING DIRECTION THROUGH TOUCH
The teacher places hands on the student to give direction to free the neck, allow the head to move forward and upward, and the back to widen. As the student follows the directions, the teacher attends to body mapping and tool extension. Three variations in focus are explored:

   a. The teacher directs their own body for improved coordination while consciously mapping their own body. When a teacher places hands on the student the teacher maps the student's whole body as if an extension of the teacher's. The teacher, through touch, can feel the student's feet contact the floor.

b. The teacher intentionally uses touch to direct the student's body into better coordination. The teacher imagines mapping the student's body separately from the teacher's. The teacher also mentally directs their own body.
c. Teachers direct their own bodies for improved coordination. The teacher touches the student's body lightly and gently to improve coordination and balance and thinks of manipulating the student's body as an object.

The most important discovery is that changing perspective or attitude alters the experience. Participants report consistent effects:

1. When the teacher directs him(her)self and thinks of the student's body as an extension of him(her)self (version a), the student tends to feel a sensation of ease, lightness with some vagueness.
2. In version b, when the teacher thinks of the student's body as separate, and intends to encourage better coordination in that separate body, the student tends to feel certainty of the direction including the whole body.
3. When the teacher directs him(her)self and thinks of manipulating the student's body as an object through light touch (c), the student experiences nice touch but no change in use, or even confusion about the message the teacher's hands give.

Conclusion

Frequently, new Alexander Technique teachers have questions about hands-on work, wondering what the effect of their touch is. Is it consonant with what they feel when another AT teacher touches them? Should they use more insistent direction? Is a light touch while they direct themselves enough? Where are the best positions to put hands on the student? Lulie Westfeldt reported that she and her fellow teacher trainees lacked hands-on training from F. M. Alexander and the group had to meet daily without F. M. to discover how to use their hands.[23] Some teacher trainings continue this approach, doing little to train the hands and rather focusing on personal self-use. Even with extensive hands-on training more can be discovered by working with colleagues in the ways described in this paper.

The field of Alexander Technique will benefit from examining the neuroscience of touch and seeking to understand its implications for our teaching techniques. As a profession, we need to find science partners to work with us in investigating the neurological mechanisms at work when we use touch in our unique manner. There are many further questions to be answered.

As I have begun leading explorations in touch with trainees and advanced teachers I have seen curiosity and delight in everyone as we take ourselves into the unknown, trying new ways and testing old ways of guiding with the hands. Underlying it all is the powerful relationship between our thinking and our quality of touch. We know that the brain quickly responds to new use by adapting and developing new neural pathways. With that in mind we can expand our manual ability to convey what Mr Alexander discovered by taking advantage of our plasticity, flexibility, and creative conscious control. Please contact me with your own thoughts and insights.

SOME QUESTIONS FOR EXPLORATION
- What could influence greater accuracy in our touch?
- What assists and what hinders a student's learning through touch?
- What is the mechanism that allows us to detect rigidity, expansion, etc. in our students?
- What is the mechanism at work when we guide the student's organisation toward greater mechanical advantage and improved balance control?
- Is it possible that the same expansion of self-image and schema that occurs when we pick up and manipulate a tool is occurring when we touch a student's body?
- Is this combined with the overlay that happens in the brain when we watch another person in action, or touch them while they move?
- Do my conscious and unconscious preconceptions about the dimensions of my own body and my student's body affect the accuracy of the information I receive or give?

References
1   Zahn, Rachel (2012). 'The Embodied Mind' in *The Congress Papers – Learning from Each Other.* STAT Books: London, pp. 39–63.
2   It is my belief that AT can be taught in a range of ways, including words, images and touch and is not only conveyed through touch. In this article I focus on touch.
3   Montagu, A. (1971). *Touching: The Human Significance of the Skin.* Columbia University Press: New York. Cited in T. Field, 'Touch for socioemotional and physical well-being: a review' in *Developmental Review*, 30 (2010), pp. 367–383 p. 374.
4   Field, op. cit.
5   Green, C. (2013). 'Philosophic reflections on the meaning of touch in nurse–patient interactions' in *Nursing Philosophy*, 14 pp. 242–253. All subsequent references to Green's writing are to this article.
6   Merleau-Ponty, M. (1964). *Signs.* Northwestern University Press: Chicago.
7   Sokolowski, R. (2008). *Phenomenology of the Human Person.* Cambridge University Press: Cambridge.
8   Body image means a system of (sometimes conscious) perceptions, attitudes, and beliefs pertaining to one's own body. Body schema means a nonconscious system of processes that constantly regulate posture and movement. (Definitions from Shaun Gallagher, 'Dynamic Models of Body Schematic Processes' in *Body image and body schema,* Helena De Preester & Veroniek Knockaert (eds.), John Benjamins

Publishing Company (2005) p. 234.

9 Postural sway is the subtle, natural movement of one's centre of gravity, even when one is standing still. We all have some degree of sway, and a certain amount is essential due to small perturbations within the body, for example breathing.

10 Farb, N., J. Daubenmier, C. J. Price, T. Gard, C. Kerr, B. D. Dunn, A. C. Klein, M. P. Paulus, W. E. Mehling (2015). 'Interoception, contemplative practice, and health' in *Front. Psychol.* 6:763. doi: 10.3389/fpsyg.2015.00763.

11 Stel, V. S., J. H. Smit, S. M. Pluijm, P. Lips (2003). 'Balance and mobility performance as treatable risk factor for recurrent falling in older persons' in *Journal of Clinical Epidemiology*, 56, pp. 659–668.

12 Serino, A., P. Haggard (2010). 'Touch and the body' in *Neuroscience and Biobehavioral Reviews* 34, pp. 224–236.

13 Gallese V. (2005). 'Embodied simulation: from neurons to phenomenal experience' in *Phenomenology and the Cognitive Sciences*, 4, pp. 23–48; Ishida, H., Nakajima, K., Inase, M., Murata, A., (2009) 'Shared Mapping of Own and Others' Bodies in Visuotactile Bimodal Area of Monkey Parietal Cortex' in *Journal of Cognitive Neuroscience* 22:1 pp. 83-96.

14 Gallese, V. (2009). 'Motor abstraction: a neuroscientific account of how action goals and intentions are mapped and understood' in *Psychological Research*, 73, pp. 486–498.

15 Serino and Haggard, op. cit.

16 Penfield, W., H. Jasper (1954). *Epilepsy and the Functional Anatomy of the Human Brain*. A. Churchill Ltd: London.

17 Conable, B., W. Conable (1995). *How to learn the Alexander Technique: A manual for students* (3rd ed.). Andover Press: Columbus, OH.

18 Spence, C., Gallace, A., (2008). 'Cognitive and Neural Correlates of "tactile consciousness": A multisensory perspective' in *Consciousness and Cognition* 17, pp. 370–407.

19 Ibid.

20 Blakeslee, S., M. Blakeslee (2008). *The Body Has A Mind Of Its Own*. Random House: New York.

21 Green, op. cit.

22 Field, op. cit.

23 Westfeldt, L. (1964). *F. Matthias Alexander: The Man and His Work*. George Allen & Unwin: London, pp. 84-88.

Sarah Barker is Professor of Theatre Performance at the University of South Carolina and has been teaching the Alexander Technique in universities and theatre companies for forty-one years. Sarah's book, *The Alexander Technique*, has been translated into six languages. Her introductory DVD, *Moving with Ease*, is also distributed in Japanese. She is an evaluating Sponsor of Alexander Technique International. She is often an invited guest teacher to Alexander Technique Teacher training schools throughout the world, leading explorations in touch with trainees and advanced teachers.

sabarker@sc.edu
facebook.com/movingwithease

Timing and Touch

Erik Bendix

One of my favorite stories about F. M. Alexander is about his collegial relation to a leading doctor working in Harley Street in London. The doctor was a specialist on heart and lung function, and happened to have an extremely wealthy patient who was barely able to breathe and perhaps on the verge of cardiac collapse. The doctor was at a loss for what to do. Given the client's wealth and prominence, the doctor felt his reputation was on the line unless he could offer the man relief in a hurry. So the doctor called F. M: 'Matty,' he said, 'Could you come down and look this chap over? I'm at my wits' end how to help him.' Just as F. M. arrived at the doctor's office, the phone rang. It was an urgent call that took the doctor out of his office for the next twenty or thirty minutes. As soon as F. M. was alone with the patient, he winked to the man and said 'Let's have some fun!'. By the time the doctor returned to reexamine his patient, all the man's symptoms were gone, and the room was full of laughter and lively conversation. The doctor was baffled at first, and then realised he was looking at the results of F. M.'s handiwork.

What I love about this story (beside the fact that the doctor called Alexander 'Matty'), is F. M.'s supreme skill and confidence in bringing about such dramatic change in such a short time. How many of us currently teaching what we call the Alexander Technique are capable of pulling off such a feat? Very few, I suspect, despite all our years of training and expertise. The story also illustrates that F. M. was no stranger to quickly and effectively addressing heart and lung function. If we are serious about passing on his technique, we need to ask what it would take to attain this level of skill.

The need to clarify our skills was brought home to me at the 2013 Embodied Mind conference in Gargonza, Italy, during which Alexander teachers were giving turns to experts on robotics, cognitive science and osteopathy. The scientists were rotating around to different Alexander teachers, sampling some of the variety of our work. As I gave a chair turn to one of the osteopaths, he turned to me and said 'You are the only Alexander teacher here paying attention to the timing of my breath.' Oh dear, I thought, what are the other Alexander teachers paying attention to? The question has stayed with me, and in 2015 it led me to teach a class in Limerick on 'Timing and Touch', about noticing biological rhythms as we teach.

The timing we use as teachers can be habitual and stereotyped, or it can be adaptable and free. We easily fall into ruts in our teaching, and many of our ruts have a characteristic speed. Some of us always flutter about our students like butterflies, others always move at the speed of pouring molasses. Too often, our differences in speed make our work incomprehensible to one another. It is as if we were broadcasting and receiving on different wavelengths. I hope we all want the flexibility to meet our different students at whatever speed or wavelength they happen to be on. Perhaps our flexibility of pace might then carry over into our ability to understand each other's pace of work.

Every human being encompasses a world of different speeds and rhythms within themselves, many of them variable in response to circumstance. The breath has an obvious ebb and flow which anyone can notice in themselves or discover by resting hands on another person's ribs or abdomen. On average, human adults inhale 12 to 20 times per minute. Heartbeat, at a much faster average adult rate of 60 to 100 beats per minute, is surprisingly difficult for many people to notice, and even harder to notice in its relation to the pace at which a person is breathing. But with practice, pulse too can be noticed (or ignored), just as a musician learns to selectively attend to polyrhythms in an orchestra or jazz ensemble. Part of what speaks to us in music may be the play of different rhythms that we recognise from our own experience of being alive.

Digestion moves much more slowly than either breath or pulse. How many Alexander teachers have had the experience of slowing down in a lesson only to begin hearing digestive gurgles coming from a student's belly? Could their digestive organs be responding to our slowing down to a pace more closely matched with their own? Digestion is not often addressed in Alexander lessons, but there are reasons to think it too was something F. M. paid attention to, if only by making more space for it to happen in. He wrote about 'viscerotopsis' in his books, an antiquated term meaning 'collapse of the organs', so he must have thought about it. A very simple question to explore in putting hands on a student's belly, for example, is whether the contents of the belly seem to be dragged down or are being allowed to rise. Because the organs work slowly, don't expect a quick answer here. If the organs respond, they will probably do so very slowly.

The digestive system clearly has direction. Food goes in one end and waste comes out the other, a generally downward direction of flow of the food and drink we ingest. But that is the stuff we take in. Our gastrointestinal tracts themselves don't flow downward unless they are in a state of collapse and malfunction. A healthy gut tube gives resistance to the downward flow of what it contains. In this way the gut tube can be understood to reach forward and up toward its sources of nourishment. Watch any enterprising toddler soon after it has learned to walk, and you will see a child in lovely upward poise looking for the next morsel put in its mouth! The orientation of its head is guided as much by the mouth and gullet as by sight or hearing. It makes sense that this fundamental orientation toward nourishment would organise us in an optimal way.

Not just organs but also fluids can have direction and speed. The various fluids that circulate within us move at different speeds depending on how close their vessels are to the heart pump and on how wide or narrow the channels are through which they flow. Some fluids pass through screens of filtration that retard their flow to a very slow and continuous floating pace, perhaps the way water might seep through the vegetation of a swamp. The cerebrospinal fluid that bathes and feeds our central nervous system moves at such a very slow pace, so slow and continuous as to seem timeless. Slowing our work down to that rate puts us in touch with the timing of direct nourishment to the nerves. This is in marked contrast to the up to 200 metre per second speed at which messages travel through the nerves themselves (no, even that quick speed is not anywhere close to the speed at which electricity travels through wires – nerves are cells, not wires). The very slow rate of cerebrospinal fluid flow is one that craniosacral therapists try to synchronise their work with when supporting the nervous system to regain its balance between activation and rest. That balance can be elusive for Alexander teachers, many of whom function well when using the Technique, but then have trouble sleeping. The parasympathetic nerves that would help them rest come out of the brain stem, so that area at the base of the skull would probably benefit from less fiddling and the allowing of more quiet.

The brain activity that we call thinking is something I would love to hear more thinking about in our community. Surely there is thinking that is cramped and forced and shot through with endgaining ('trying to think' seems an apt description of it), just as there is thinking that is unforced and a pleasure, as when an idea pops into my head without effort. Geniuses, Michael Gelb tells us, are the people who keep track of the ideas that just come to them. Surely this kind of freedom of thought is something we could be cultivating. Isn't how freely we think connected to how we are using our heads? Why aren't more of us teaching workshops on liberating our brains?

Some of our mentors had very interesting things to say about the timing of thought. 'Reasoning takes time', Walter Carrington used to say. I wonder what he would have said about the book published in 2011 by Nobel-laureate Daniel Kahneman, *Thinking Fast and Slow*, on the ways we take often irrational shortcuts in our thinking to conserve brain energy. I certainly find the process of giving myself directions very slow and prone to error. Despite decades of practice, I still frequently skip steps by mistake or get my directions out of proper sequence and then have to go back and start them over. It makes me feel like a perpetual beginner. I often liken the process to trying to teach movement to an alligator. The lesson needs to be repeated over and over and over. It seems to be addressing a rather dimly lit part of one's brain.

Marjory Barlow said her goal as an Alexander Technique teacher was to help her students keep pace with time. I ponder those words often. Am I getting ahead of myself? Am I dropping behind, or struggling to catch up? What is poise in relation to the ceaseless flow of time? How does poise translate into the timing of my touch? Does my touch keep pace with time?

Here are some ways to explore some of these themes in practice:

1. *Keeping your own pace:* With a partner or several people, walk around the space you are in and notice the pace you most easily fall into. After a while, start making your pace easier to notice by clapping your hands each time you step. Carry on clapping, but come face to face with someone else and see how hard it is to maintain your own pace while becoming more aware of someone's else's. Do you tend to synchronise?
2. *Moving from one touch to the next:* Rest your hands very slowly on a student, but move quickly each time you take them off to move to a new touch location. Now try the opposite: touch the student only lightly and quickly, but move very slowly from one location of touch to the next. What is the difference between these two paces of touch for the student? For you? Do you prefer one over the other?
3. *Noticing changes in a student's breath:* Rest your hands on a student and do nothing until the student's breath changes in some obvious way. When the student's breath starts to change, take your hands off and move your hands to a new location on the student. Then repeat this process. How often do you time your teaching this way? Why?
4. *Noticing connections between neck freedom and changes in-breath:* Notice whether your neck is free, particularly the upper part of your neck, and then keep noticing. Does attending to your neck in this way affect your own breath? Now keep attending to the freedom of your neck as you rest your hands on a student. Does attending to the freedom of your own neck correlate with changes you notice in the student's breath?
5. *Four things to attend to: neck, head, breath and pulse:* Now try attending to two things in yourself and two things in your student. In yourself, ask whether your neck is free and also whether your head is releasing forward and up in relation to your neck. In your student, ask what might be happening with their breath in relation to their heartbeat. This is quite a few things to attend to. You don't have to come up with any particular answer. Just keep asking the questions, and see what happens by that attention alone.
6. *Slowing to the pace of digestion:* Rest your hands around a student's belly and lower back and ask yourself how slowly their digestive organs might be working. Slow yourself at least to that pace and settle in for a long wait. Here your positions of mechanical advantage are very useful, since they allow you to sustain remaining patient without strain or struggle. If you manage to truly stop trying to get anywhere, you may notice the organs beginning to wake up or respond under your hands. They can rearrange and redirect themselves in response to your patience and quiet.

7. *Thinking fast and then stopping:* Try thinking really fast as you give a hands-on turn, perhaps by running through your directions quickly over and over. Then all at once just stop. Turn off your mental chatter entirely. What are these two experiences like for your student? What are the experiences like for you as a teacher? Try switching roles to experience this exploration from the other end.
8. *Letting nerves rest into the protective fat surrounding them:* Nerves are embedded in a matrix of fat-filled cells that insulate them. Some nerves are more protected than others depending on how well organised the fat layers are that surround them. It is possible this insulation system could be affected by our awareness of it. Try allowing all of your nerves to rest into what surrounds and insulates them. Recognising that our nerves have protection can allow the nerves to find more security, comfort and reassurance.

Erik Bendix (MA, M.AmSAT) trained with Frank Ottiwell, Joan and Alex Murray, and Walter Carrington. Erik assisted Vivien Mackie's work with musicians, assisted on Vivien and Neil Schapera's Cincinnati training for five years, helped represent the Technique at the 2012-13 Embodied Mind conferences in Paris and Gargonza, and taught Alexander Technique in Taiwan and at Pomona College in 2013-14. He is among few teachers trained in both Dart Procedures and Body-Mind Centering®, disciplines focused on movement development in infants. He trained in BMC® with Bonnie Bainbridge Cohen in the 1990s, created The Learning Curve workshops to explore scoliosis, and developed his own ski teaching method based on the Technique, which he has taught at many workshops. Trained as a philosopher at Oxford and Princeton, Erik is a published poet and is widely known as a folk dance teacher.

Tapping into the Well of Chi

Alexander Farkas

The universal energy known as *chi* has been a recognised phenomenon of Eastern thought for many centuries. It comes down to us through the disciplines of T'ai chi, Qi Gong and Aikido among others. In these modalities the flow of *chi* through the limbs and central core (spine) becomes palpable. A distinct movement is perceived and a buzz of vibrational energy can be felt in the hands and elsewhere.

While I have some limited experience in only one of these traditions, Qi Gong, the similarity in quality of the best experiences during a lesson in the Alexander Technique and the fluid movements of the Qi Gong seem unmistakably to share a common core. The hands of an Alexander teacher function in a manner that awakens a recognisable flow of internal movement which, once activated, may then continue, uninterruptedly, and become an actual bodily movement in space. Ideally there is no boundary separating that internal flow from the realised physical movement. In a complementary manner, the flowing quality of the Qi Gong movements have the ability to engender the internal flow of energy which provides a gradually growing momentum very closely resembling what we Alexander practitioners call *direction*. The Qi Gong movements by design take on a flow which makes it seem as if they are going by themselves, as if they are happening without our trying, as if a *doing* of a certain quality becomes a *non-doing*.

In particular, and ever so pertinent to our work as Alexander teachers, the Qi Gong movements all seem to have a focus on the hand. Simple movements of the hand, with the arm gently following, filling space in up-down, in-out, rotating all in a soft, almost floating, manner lead toward a growing sense of energy in the palms. It is quite possible then to experience a kind of buzz or tingling when the hands are held close to one another.

My favorite movement is the one known as *Cloud Hands*. One hand, held at eye level, floats outward as the body gently turn, the spine fluidly rotating, and the other hand, at the lower level of the abdomen, acts as the breeze that moves the cloud. At the end of the rotation the hands change levels and the body turns to the other side. Legs soften along with the turning body, knees obligingly become fluid, and the entire body, as one unit, takes on a quality of lightness and ease. It is tempting to continue this kind of movement, as it generates a quietness of mind as the musculature seems to melt and allow the *chi* to take over effortlessly.

Since many of us who have trained in the work of F. M. Alexander have at times been puzzled as to what Alexander actually meant by the words '*directing*' and '*direction*,' perhaps such a direct *chi* experience will bring some clarity to the seeming quandary. Before we are able to awaken *direction* in our students, we as teachers need to have a clear concept and sufficient specific experience to know and to recognise the quality of *direction* within ourselves. Only then can the use of our Alexander teaching hand activate the movement of the *chi* and bring it to full awareness in the student's mind and body. Ultimately, I think we will come to see that F. M.'s '*direction*' and unimpeded *chi* flow are one and the same.

It is at this point that the implementation of *non-doing* becomes essential. The only way that we can clearly draw forth the flow of energy, whether we call it *chi* or *direction,* is to use our teaching hand in a totally *non-doing* manner. Once we are able to do this, the hand becomes totally receptive and begins to both transmit the desired message to our student and also to draw, with a clear power of attraction, any area upon which our hand is resting. During the workshop, students, working in pairs, discovered this phenomenon by resting a hand on a partner's forearm and observing how a lightness and fluidity induced an ease of movement in both themselves and the other person. This is the effective communication we all hope to uncover in our teaching. The effectiveness of the **receptive** hand cannot be overestimated; it is the essence of our work.

Even more important is the fact that the *chi* can be activated in an indirect, non-doing manner. Since the receptive quality of the Alexander teaching hand has the ability to draw forth the *chi,* we are in the realm of teaching in a *non-doing* mode. By working in this way, we are discovering that *directing* happens but **not** by our trying to *do* something. This means of discovering activated energy solves the contradiction of **trying** to direct, which can easily become a 'doing,' as opposed to discovering the principle of 'non-doing.' The awakened *chi* produces the lengthening we hope to activate, found through the receptive state of 'non-doing.' Thus we achieve the perfect balance of '*directing*' and *non-doing.*

The rewards of working in this way, as elusive as it may seem, bring us such a lovely sense of lightness, freedom of movement and an optimistic frame of mind as to warrant following the path that leads to such better, healthier states of being. If we are aided in this search by exploring the ancient ways of *chi,* it can only be to our advantage to do so.

> Alexander Farkas completed his teacher training with Shoshana Kaminitz in 1998 and, having begun in 1991, holds the record for the longest period of Alexander study. He has had additional study with Patrick Macdonald, Margaret Goldie, and others. Trained originally as a musician, much of his teaching is in the application of the AT to instrumental and vocal performance. Alex is a frequent visitor to the UK and Europe where he is a guest at teacher training courses. He is currently on the faculty at the Bard College Conservatory of Music (US). A collection of his writings on the Alexander Technique will soon be appearing.

Thinking Hands and Thinking Hands Listening and Talking

Brita Forsstrom

THINKING HANDS
When I agreed to teach a Continuous Learning session at the Limerick Congress I had an idea of what I would do. However, when the day came to write the outline for the congress website, something happened. As I moved my hand to wipe up a spill on the floor a completely different topic popped into my head. It was almost completely formed in that instant. My topic would be 'Thinking Hands and Thinking Hands Talking and Listening'.

Of course a topic of hands is nothing unusual in the context of teaching the Alexander Technique. Despite the different approaches to teaching the Technique we all agree that hands are important. Most of us use hands-on touch in most of our teaching and I would say that even for those who don't use hands so much, they are an essential part of their own good use. I have spent my years as an Alexander teacher working on improving my overall use and my hands-on work; in my daily teaching practice, working with other teachers, at workshops for AT teachers, teaching on a training course and in the last couple of years running my own teacher training course.

As I worked with the initial idea for my topic I began to connect my own experiences over the years with further research and exploration. 'OK, so I'm thinking "hands". What do I know about the hand?' The hand is a prehensile, multi-fingered extremity at the end of our arms. I looked at the evolution of the human hand. How is it related to evolution of upright posture? How different are our hands from those of other primates?

It is still unclear exactly what made our ancestors develop upright posture and how it happened but there is a definite connection between the development of upright posture, the hand, brain size and language. As the brain got bigger, primates became more upright and the hand changed. Compared to chimpanzees our hand has shorter fingers and a longer robust thumb with stronger muscles. This has given us the ability to oppose the thumb with the fingers which allowed our ancestors to become toolmakers. The area in the brain for tool use and the area for language overlap, suggesting that the development of complexity of language went hand in hand with the complexity of hand use.

Although we don't know if the brain getting bigger led to more complex use of the hand, or rather if the use of the hand led to the brain getting bigger, there are suggestions by anthropologists that physical function of the hand may have been co-opted for mental functions in the course of evolution. Experimental work shows that gesture processing and language processing are interlinked in the brain. The gesturing hand links action to cognition and language and manipulates mental objects or problem solving. Iconic gestures affect the mental world, i.e. they change something in the mind.[1] Professor Daniel Hutto[2] has talked about how human manual activity drives the growth of intelligence.

I was excited when I came across Lambros Malafouris,[3] who also suggests that human manual activity drives the growth of intelligence. He writes: 'Stone tools are *not an accomplishment* of the hominin brain, they are *an opportunity* for the hominin brain – that is an opportunity for active material engagement.'

Was this what happened when I made a hand gesture to wipe something off the floor and had the inspiration for the topic? Maybe. It certainly fits with the importance of the hands in teaching, not just as the part of the whole of ourselves that make contact with the pupil, but the importance of developing the intelligent use of the hand itself.

What made the topic finally gel together was this statement by Henri Matisse in *Jazz*, a limited edition artist's book of colourful prints accompanied by Matisse's written thoughts:

> If I have confidence in my hand that draws, it is because as I was training it to serve me, I never allowed it to dominate my feeling. I very quickly sense when it is paraphrasing something, if there is any discord between us: between my hand and the 'je ne sais quoi' in myself which seems submissive to it.[4]
>
> The hand is only an extension of sensibility and intelligence. The more supple it is, the more obedient. The servant must not become the mistress.[4]

We only need to substitute the word 'draws' with 'teaches' and it could be written about our work.

THINKING HANDS LISTENING AND TALKING

> You think yourself and feel your pupil.
> *Walter Carrington in response to a question when visiting the ATA training course in 1983.*

Importance of touch
How do we use our hands to teach? We touch our pupils. We also use our eyes, and listen to the pupil, but I believe the specialised hands-on use in Alexander Technique teaching gives us a particularly efficient way of sensing what is going on in the pupil.

Research taking place in the past twenty years or so suggest that touch triggers release of oxytocin, a hormone which decreases stress-related responses.[5]

Premature babies have been shown to thrive if they have skin-to-skin contact with the parents.[6] A study in the 1970s[7] showed that library users gave more positive feedback about the library service they received if they had been 'accidently' touched lightly when served by the librarian. Interestingly, this effect occurred despite the fact that none of the students could remember having been touched by the librarian.

Light touch is detected by receptors in the skin. Touch receptors are not distributed evenly over the body. The fingertips may have as many as 100 per cm^2; the back of the hand fewer than 10 per cm^2. Jonathan Levav of Columbia University and Jennifer Argo of the University of Alberta[8] found, in a study of financial risk-taking, that a female experimenter's light, comforting pat on the shoulder increased feelings of security. However, this calming effect did not occur when individuals were touched by a male and was weaker when the touch consisted of a handshake. Their experiments suggested that subtle physical contact can be strongly influential in decision-making and the willingness to accept risk.

As Alexander Technique teachers we develop a special kind of touch and the implications of these studies are relevant to how we think of using our hands in teaching. We should also be conscious of the fact that there may be cultural, social or personal norms regarding the way our pupils will respond to being touched. Other factors that affect a person's experience of touch, and therefore their learning experience, are temperature, light, smell and sound. If a person is highly sensitive to smells, for example, they may feel uncomfortable, even unwell in the presence of strong scent, and so may not respond to touch in the same way as they would normally. A project called 'Rethinking our Senses' at the University of Glasgow's Centre for the Study of Perceptual Experience is looking at how modern cognitive neuroscience is challenging our understanding of sensory perception, recognising that studying the senses in isolation is misleading. For example, flavour experiences are also affected by the colour of the foods, their spatial arrangements and even the sounds that accompany them. Also, the sense of our bodies not only combines tactile and proprioceptive cues, but is also dependent on vision. These effects all demonstrate that multisensory interactions are the rule rather than the exception.

Hands as part of the whole of ourselves
Our hands in teaching are an expression of ourselves as a whole and the state of body/mind that we are in; our sensitivity, our intelligence. We use them as extensions of our whole selves to communicate with our pupils. By developing awareness of which parts of the hands are in touch with the pupil, how much we move our fingers, our hands, our arms or our whole body, we can learn to use only the kind of touch that is appropriate for a particular activity. We can ask ourselves if different ways of touching and moving give us more information, if different forms of touch convey greater clarity of

direction to our pupils, how our size in relation to the size of the pupil affects how we use our hands. How do we 'leave ourselves alone' and how do we 'leave our hands alone'?

DIFFERENT PARTS OF THE HANDS

Different parts of the hands are used for both sensing different things and communicating different messages when we teach.

The **fingertips,** for instance, have most sensation and a gentle fingertip contact can tell me a lot about the student in a very instantaneous way. They sense softness, yielding quality, hardness, temperature, 'aliveness', etc. They communicate light directional impulses.

The **long pads of the fingers** are useful for sensing things like movement of muscles and skin against bone, freedom or lack of freedom in smaller areas like the front of the chest, the ribcage and the neck and throat. They are also good for sensing muscle tone and elasticity in larger muscles and muscle groups, e.g. leg muscles, biceps, top of the shoulders, back of the neck. They communicate the impulse to release in localised areas.

The **heel of the hand** senses weight, balance, pushing, resisting, larger bony areas, e.g. top of the back (7th cervical), sacrum, pelvic crests, knees, feet, etc. It communicates movement, direction, connectedness.

The **palm of the hand** (the hollow, not the whole of the hand) is good for feeling shapes, e.g. knees, elbows, back of the head, heels, etc. It is particularly non-doing and soothing.

The **whole of the hand** is powerful for sensing, and communicating with, the whole person, or the whole of a large part of the body. It senses weight, balance, pushing, restriction, yielding, etc. but also the nervous reactions and state of the person's overall frame of mind and body.

Of course I would like to be clear that in the middle of teaching a lesson I don't consciously think: 'Here I will use the whole of the hand', or 'Now I will touch the pupil with the length of the fingers', or 'This time I will use only the heel of the hand'. It is rather that I have become aware that this is the contact that I'm making with the pupil, and also aware that these are the variations of a teacher's hands on me.

HANDS ON BACK OF THE CHAIR AND ULNAR DEVIATION

'Hands on the back of the chair' is probably the most useful procedure we have, not only for preparation of use of the hands, but also for working on ourselves as a whole. Of course not just for us as teachers but for our pupils as well – everyone uses their hands as an extension of themselves for better or for worse. Most people use their hands with too much tension and this tends to tighten the thumb grip particularly.

If you look at the upturned palm of your hand when relaxed and you draw a line along the inside of the knuckles and a line from the base to the tip of the thumb you probably find that they soon converge (figure 1). When

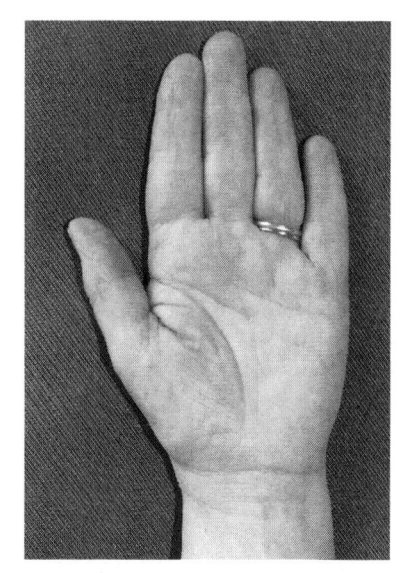

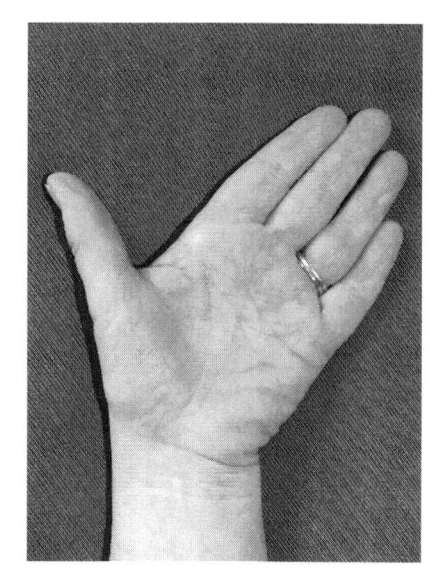

Fig. 1.

Fig. 2.

teaching we are looking for a more open hand, but if you attempt to open the hand by simply stretching the thumb out, the hand will become stiff and insensitive. Instead you will achieve the open free hand by tilting the palm of the hand sideways away from the thumb. This is what is meant by *ulnar deviation*; it is an anatomical term describing the hand deviating towards the ulnar bone of the forearm. It is of course important to remember not to pull the hand toward the ulnar, but to release and lengthen away from the radius.

You will now see that if you draw the same two lines they are much more parallel and you have a more open and supple hand (figure 2). In hands on the back of the chair the ulnar deviation is achieved by directing the wrists inwards towards each other. Why this is so important is that it allows the thumb pad to easily oppose the pads of the fingers without tension or gripping. It also assists in keeping the armpits free and widening across the chest and upper arms. Finally, the direction to 'pull to the elbow' which is a lengthening of the elbow back and away from the wrist, helps to get the back to widen and breathing to be free.

How we approach putting hands on our pupils is of primary importance. Leading with the heel of the hand, whatever part of the hand is being used, encourages ulnar deviation, which assists in a more open hand and helps to ensure that the initial contact is non-intrusive.

In the CL sessions at the Congress we explored these ideas in hands-on work with each other in different activities. We also worked with hands on the back of the chair and how to work with hands when in semi-supine.

Trainees and teachers often ask how important it is that we go into monkey before putting hands on. I don't think it is essential; what is essential is that we are thinking of our own use *before* we make hands-on contact. We need to be free to be able to go into monkey or lunge without disturbing the contact we make with our pupil. I call this being 'monkeyable'.

Our hands convey inhibition: an invitation to quiet listening, to not having to 'do' anything. They convey direction, a sense of self, of wholeness, of 'going up'. They do this because they are confident and thereby give the pupil the ability to trust in herself or himself. To develop this confidence in the hands-on contact we need to develop good use in ourselves. We need to be able to be in a 'good' monkey before we attempt to develop special hands-on skills.

> I want it to be very clearly understood that when I write of the arms, legs, hands and feet, etc., I always imply their co-ordinated use with the body as a co-ordinated support. (Alexander)[9]

References

1. Professor Sotaro Kita, verbally at 'The Anthropology of Hands', an interdisciplinary conference, University of Kent, June 2015, which I attended.
2. Also at 'The Anthropology of Hands' conference, also verbally and from my memory.
3. Malafouris, L., C. Gosden & K.A. Overmann (2014). 'Creativity, Cognition and Material Culture: An Introduction' in *Pragmatics & Cognition*, 22(1), pp. 1–4.
4. Matisse, Henry (1947). *Jazz*. Tériade: Paris.
5. Ågren et al., 1995; Stock & Uvnäs-Moberg, 1988; Uvnäs-Moberg, et al, 1993, cited in Alberto Gallace, Charles Spence (2010). 'The science of interpersonal touch: An overview' in *Neuroscience and Biobehavioral Reviews* 34, pp. 246–259.
6. Feldman, Ruth et. al. (2013). 'Maternal-Preterm Skin-to-Skin Contact Enhances Child Physiologic Organisation and Cognitive Control Across the First 10 Years of Life' in *Biological Psychiatry*, volume 75, issue 1, pp. 56-64.
7. Fischer et. al. (1976), cited in Zdravko Radman (2013). *The Hand, an Organ of the Mind: What the Manual Tells the Mental*. MIT Press: Cambridge, MA.
8. Levav & Argo (2010). 'Physical Contact and Financial Risk Taking' in *Psychological Science* vol. 21, no. 6, pp. 804-810.
9. Alexander, F. M. (1985, 1946, 1923) *Constructive Conscious Control of the Individual*. Gollancz: London.

> Brita Forsstrom has been running a private practice in London since qualifying in 1984 at ATA with Don Burton and Lizzie Atkinson, where she also taught for two years. She has extensive experience of group introductory teaching including at City Lit (in the Drama, Health and Movement Studies and Music Departments), gives workshops and consultations in the work place and has worked with choirs in Sweden and Singapore. Brita has been a Council member and Chair of STAT and served on STAT committees. She assisted on a training school in London for 12 years and since 2014 has run her own training course, City Alexander Technique School in central London. She is co-author of *The Alexander Technique for Pregnancy and Childbirth* (1995), contributed an article to *Connected Perspectives* (2015) and has written articles and features in magazines and newspapers.

Working on Oneself – Widening the Field

Dorothea Magonet

This workshop had two main elements: working on oneself, and what we might mean by the instruction 'keep your back back'. Using different activities in relation to the wall, we explored our stimulus-response patterns and investigated why the instruction 'back back' could be useful to develop an understanding of inhibition and oppositional directions. We playfully and indirectly used monkey, lunge and whispered 'ah' in different ways, and discovered how the oppositional span, which is achieved primarily through thinking your back backwards and up, can create energy with good use and a strong sense of directed self. We then took this experiment further and looked at how opposition is relevant for us in general and when teaching, and for the performer, especially the instrumental musician.

Preamble

Working on oneself is as important for the pupil as having lessons with a skilled teacher when learning the Alexander Technique. Making connections and applying inhibition and direction to all our activities is an essential part of the Alexander practitioner's everyday work. The underlying question of my Continuous Learning Sessions is: *How can the Alexander teacher assist the pupil in the process of owning the learning, so as to continue the work on their own?*

It is only when we actually start a movement or an activity that we have the possibility of finding out what we are really up to. Unfamiliar activities sometimes highlight our automatic reactions more starkly. Then we can discover something about our wish to endgain, our habitual movements, and how these are preceded by habitual thinking patterns, preconceptions, fears and desires, often secret and unnoticed. This then gives us a chance to recognise, to pause and rethink, direct and go renewed into activity, or exercise choice to do something different.

The most important element in this work is to take time. Firstly to be with what we discover, before reacting to what we feel by rushing into making a judgement and adjustment. Usually it is a difficult feeling or negative judgement, which propels us into doing/changing something (endgaining), with the best intention but often in an interfering manner. Respecting first what is and doing nothing about it 'just yet' gives us time to rethink and organise our system, which helps us to 'get out of our way' and let something new happen.

The activities described below are not to be thought of and practised as exercises – yet considered and reflective repetition is the mother of all learning.

Nothing is written in stone and ultimately everything is open to be explored in different ways. However, when we do so we also need to observe our motivations – are we following the path of least resistance, our well-travelled habitual movement patterns, or can we stay with something new, uncomfortable, unfamiliar, unknown and work with what we find in there?

We mostly worked in pairs, so one was the observer while the other performed the movement. Self-observation and peer observation are important learning tools, for us teachers as for our pupils.

How to use time

'I don't have enough time to do this work!' This is what I often hear. So, waiting for something to happen – even just waiting for all participants to arrive – provides an opportunity to work playfully on yourself; here are some practical tips:

- Standing – rock forwards and backwards in small movements from the ankles.
- Then, making a circle from the ankles, thinking of a long-handled brush on the top of your head, imagine making a coloured circle on the ceiling, a smaller one the other way round and so on until you come to a point.
- Sitting squarely towards the front of the chair, lean forward a little and back a little, thinking of your head–neck–back directions; think the back rim of your pelvis backwards as you come forward and let your sacrum take the full length and width of your back backwards when coming back.
- Continue as above – move forward from your hips while exhaling by blowing a feather (imaginary but could be real) – pause to 'smell the scent of a rose' – move back while blowing a feather, leaning very slightly back off balance – pause to inhale – move forward again – continue the movement for a number of times. Instead of blowing the feather you can use the whispered 'ah' or any vocalised sound. (Allow the **comfortable** length and rhythm of your breath to determine the speed and rhythm of your movement of moving forwards or backwards. Discover the dynamic expansiveness of your back and your front for the inhalation alternately.) *The movement breathes you and the breath moves you!*

Walking

Walking is a very useful learning tool. I use walking to start a workshop to bring everyone into the room, into themselves, into the group and into a rhythm. I use it in between tasks in order to change or neutralise the energy between activities. I use it myself to clear my thinking. Here are just some elements that informed our walking.

Start with walking – pausing – standing – walking – standing – become aware of how the space behind and in front of you opens up or shrinks when you walk – how the air moves around you – walk towards an object – see it – walk away – walk faster – walk slower – pause – remember the rhythm of the movement – start again in your own time – note the others in the group – observe the changes in yourself – walk to a wall – stand with back against the wall – observe your desires, irritations, frustrations – walk – pause – remember the rhythm of the movement (i.e. don't abruptly stop the movement when you pause, let it continue to reverberate) – start walking again in your own time – and so on.

MEETING THE WALL

This set of activities was developed with musicians in mind in particular, to help them make connections between 'hands-on' lessons and how to develop and enhance their own 'Alexander' thinking when they prepare to meet their instrument or prepare to sing. It aims to provide some ideas of how to work on themselves before or after practising and in preparation for performance. Of course taking time to do some lying down work is always recommended – a good rule of thumb is to practise for 30 minutes then lie down for 15. This gives the player time to absorb what has just been practised, to come back to themselves and to prepare for the next practising period.

The emphasis in the following movements is to understand what happens when we make contact with another object. What are our thinking habits that create the physical interferences? How can we work with our discoveries using inhibition and direction? How can we maintain a good constructive tension/energy/connection throughout our whole self, from head to feet and between, allowing our back to stay back when the palms of our hands make contact with the wall? How can we return to our length and width and most importantly also our depth? How can we tune our instrument – ourselves – to make a good tone?

The movements progress in a particular sequence. However, each section can be worked on separately and independently. We move from standing with the back against the wall, going on to tip-toes, to bending knees into monkey and back. Then, facing the wall, we place our hands against the wall. There is a progression of activities, which include a backward lunge, and the whispered 'ah'. The wall becomes your teacher, it provides feedback and opposition to your back, and staying back in your back is the physical manifestation of the inhibitory process.

I hope that the activities described below are explored in the spirit of research, as if in a laboratory, not certain but curious about the outcome, yet informed by Alexander's principles. Each movement requires precision and discipline in the execution, for a number of different reasons. This may or may not be apparent initially, but I hope that the rationale reveals itself to you as you work on each movement.

Working in pairs, one is the observer, giving verbal feedback when required.

BACK TO WALL, TOES AND MONKEY
- Stand with your back against the wall, not leaning but meeting and 'letting the wall be your friend' – find your contact – notice your thinking reaction – find your length and width and depth. (This is really about discovering your thinking habits and how to stay with what is, rather than feel you have to change something immediately – inhibition.)
- Rise up on your toes – back to feet flat on floor – bend knees – monkey – bring back to the wall and straighten. (Working with inhibition and direction in action: head leads, body follows, whether you go up or down.)
- Peel off the wall and walk, noticing your back in relation to walking forward – notice the space between your back and the wall you have left behind. (Discovering your supporting performance space, both within your back and beyond your back.)
- We followed this by going into *monkey in two stages* without the wall and then by a brief *semi-supine* session.

HANDS ON WALL – PRIMARY DIRECTIONS – PERIPHERAL DIRECTIONS
- Face the wall standing approximately a foot away from it – remembering the wall on your back from before – allow your eyes to be in soft focus.
- Place palms on the wall with fingertips about shoulder-height, slightly wider than shoulder-width. Explore the moment of anticipating the contact between your hands and the wall and what happens in this moment of meeting the wall – feedback from your observer is very useful here. Think of the opposition between the palms of your hands on the wall and your widening and lengthening back.
- Work with directing into length, width and depth from the central organisation between head–neck–back to the peripheral organisation of arms to hands to fingers – and back up to the centre from hands to arms to back; then from the back to legs to feet and floor – returning again through feet to legs to back, from back to arms to hands to wall and so on.
- Become aware of the space within you, between you and the wall along the inner circle of your arms and the outer circle of your arms and back – the opposition between your hands on the wall, your back and your feet. Enjoy your height, your width and your depth within this form.
- Remove hands from the wall – note what happens when you bring your hands and arms down?

The discoveries we made or difficulties we experienced during this activity opened up the issues around our thinking about where our shoulders should be or not be. We explored this further with the movements described below – 'Letting shoulders come home' and hands on back of the chair.

Backward lunge – opposition

Facing wall as before – feet close together – hands on the wall, fingertips shoulder-height and slightly wider than shoulder-width – step into a backward lunge with one foot – leading the movement of your foot and leg with thinking your back backwards and up.

Bring the back foot forward again and repeat the procedure with the other foot.

Leading on from this backward lunge we explored a *rhythmical forward lunge* away from the wall, letting the rhythm of the breath lead the movement.

Whispered 'ah' and backward lunge on wall – breathing and sound

Place your hands on the wall as above and step into the backward lunge, blow a feather away, smell the scent of a rose, and then whisper an 'ah'.

Step forward while blowing feathers and smelling roses and change legs and whisper another 'ah'.

You can also hum, or make a sound from 'mmh' to 'ng' to 'ah', or allow the whispered 'ah' to become a vocalised 'ah', or any other vowel.

Enjoy the span between hands, arms and feet, legs and head–neck–back and the resulting suspension of your ribcage, the freedom of your abdominal musculature as it responds to the rhythm of your breathing and vocalisations.

'Letting shoulders come home'

Over the years of teaching music students I have observed that many instrumentalists and singers (as well as pupils from all walks of life), have dearly held beliefs about where their shoulders should or should not be. These have been developed with much investment from early on during the musicians' formative lives. In most cases these thinking habits interfere severely with the free and full range of movement of shoulders and arms, hands and fingers, and with freedom of breathing.

In addition, many instruments require particular movement patterns of upper limbs and shoulders, which are practised diligently and repetitively, consciously and unconsciously, over many years, thus often leading to a limited range of movement of all joints and muscular involved. Just as it is important to be able to play full scales on the instrument in order to have the full range of the instrument available to use, equally, a good full range of movement is necessary to provide freedom for playing.

This series of movements could provide the pupil with the opportunity to re-discover the movement of the shoulder girdle and arms, hands and fingers in relation to the head, neck and back relationship, to understand what it means not to interfere with the shoulder girdle, thereby unlocking the respiratory mechanism and providing a supportive opposition in the torso when arms and hands have to move with dexterity, speed and strength.

Here, I have deliberately chosen instructions in images and phrases to stimulate the imagination and assist the gentle nature of the movement and to help break well-ingrained patterns.

Perform each movement first to discover what happens – especially also in one's thinking and feeling. Repeat the movements several times, then just remember the movement and the sensation. Keep it simple – less is more!

1. Shoulder girdle lift

Remember your length, width and depth, as you stand with feet shoulder width apart:
- imagine a hook and thread on the outer edge of your shoulders and shoulders being lifted gently from there;
- think of space opening up under shoulder joint in the arm pit and lengthening through the flanks of ribcage all the way from hip joints to shoulder joints (lengthening and widening);
- gently let shoulders return 'home' (let shoulders find their own place).

2. Forward curl

Opening the back especially between and around shoulder blades:
- let shoulders rise as above;
- let hands and arms gently turn inward with little finger leading the movement, so that back of hands face and touch each other;
- leading from head let the back become round;
- knees in a slight bend;
- eyes looking at little fingers;
- let arms, shoulders, back return 'home'.

3. Opening backwards

Opening the chest and shoulders:
- let shoulder rise again as above;
- gently let the thumbs turn arms outward;
- bring arms softly back and outward as you look up towards the top of the wall – be careful not to pull your head back and down!
- allowing mouth to open and knees to bend slightly;
- return gently back 'home'.

4. Lifting Arms
- imagine a hook and thread on upper side of wrists and someone pulling the arms towards the ceiling;
- let arms follow bending softly in the elbow;

- let the shoulders rise gently at the end, opening armpit and ribcage and space in waist;
- shoulders come home first;
- then let elbows and hands come back to original starting point.

Let the shoulders ride on the ribcage and on the breath!

It was a pleasure to work with everyone who came to these sessions. We pooled our insights, observations and discoveries and learned much from each other. Thank you.

> Dorothea Magonet completed her training in London in 1984. Since then she has worked full-time in private practice and with music students at the Royal Academy of Music. In the early 90s she organised the first two International Conferences on Teaching Alexander Technique in Music Conservatoires, which continue to take place every three years. From 1994 until 2004 she served on STAT Council. Dorothea teaches on the Shaw Method of Swimming training course and is now training to be an Art of Swimming teacher. She is the Main Assistant at the Westminster Alexander Teacher Training Course, London, and a STAT Moderator. She teaches in London and regularly runs workshops for performers in the UK, Estonia and Japan. She is also a practising and exhibiting visual artist.

Be Here Now

Or How I Use Spatial Awareness to Find This Quality and Affect my Primary Control

Penny O'Connor

This chose me as a subject to explore in my Alexander training and practice as I was a habitual mind-wanderer. Saying 'No' to un-wanted chitter chatter hasn't always worked for me. I was so non-present I didn't realise. I had a lot of things to let go of. Through the wizardry of David Gorman and Margaret Edis, my trainers, I discovered that I could pay attention. The mind quietened. Presence gathered, a shining jewel in the darkness of a busy mind. And these droplets of attention grew and continue to grow over the years. Without being present it is impossible to inhibit or direct oneself.

During our turns, David would ask me, 'Where is your attention?' More often than not it would be on a fixed point outside or an inner analysis, trying to feel something out, work something out, trying to get myself right – narrowed, effortful and habitual. 'Where was my attention?' As soon as I acknowledged it was in a fixed narrow state I could release myself to the outside world to free myself to respond to the external stimuli of the moment, rather than some pre-planned expectation or predictive text, based solely on past patterns of experience. If I was thinking outside of myself, then was it in the whole environment and space around me? Often not, often on the person I was putting hands on, or just an awareness of the space above me but not the space behind, on either side, the floor beneath my feet. And then when I had found a spatial three-dimensionality I would lock into it and be 'spaced out', not noticing the objects around me, and leading to the Alexandroid glaze and zombie movement. It took practice.

Spatial direction is what saved me. Before starting my training in the Alexander Technique (AT), as an actor I was rehearsing a scene from an Ibsen play, and the director asked us to consider that we were in an outside space – a lot of Ibsen's work contrasts the inner domains of the stifled 19th century Norwegian uprightness and the wild outside world of mountains, fjords and sea. I was amazed at the physiological effect that had on me. I was suddenly bigger, taller, easier in my movement. It was a glimpse of what I was to find and work with in my Alexander experiments.

During my training and beyond, when I was able to find a unified field of attention – being aware of myself, my surroundings and my action – I discovered that quality of ease, that sense of invisibility, and the absence of muscular effort, dis-ease and heaviness. The quality of effortless ease and wholeness was something other teachers had brought me to through traditional direction from different schools, but not something I could find for myself.

When someone says, 'Think of your directions', I think of the space around me. The space around me brings me to the moment, and to a unified field of attention. Frank Pierce Jones describes this well in *Freedom to Change*, in the appendix 'Learning How to Learn: an Operational Definition of the Alexander Technique'. I have called it my SEA of Consciousness: **S**elf **E**nvironment **A**ctivity, juggling those three attentions until they are one. It is firstly an inhibition of my habitual narrowed thinking and then a direction into widened attention and the *Now*. I was, I should say, also trained to think of neck free etc, so I cannot say that is not also associated with it, and comes along beside it, but if I am spatially aware, if I can take in consciously what I am seeing, hearing, sensing, then the traditional directions seem to happen on their own. It is our birth-right to be tall, wide and gorgeous!

Our brain has electrical activity that in the 1930s was loosely divided into four categories: Beta the aroused state, Alpha the resting state, Theta the dreaming state and Delta the deep undreaming consciousness.[1] Most of us are addicted to the endgaining attention that is narrowed, using a high Beta brain wave frequency. It is not that this attention is wrong, just that we are habituated to this and unable to switch it off. We may need this attention if we are (literally or metaphorically) running after prey, getting ready for the kill. But we forget to switch it off. 'Life isn't an emergency' as many gurus tell us. (I reckon I had been influenced by too many episodes of E.R.!)

Some years ago I was teaching a German social worker and tango dancer here in my outside terrace on Alonnisos. It has a beautiful view of sea and islands and is surrounded by plants, full of fragrance and sounds and life. The dancer had a pain in her foot that was interfering with her dancing, and she wanted to be rid of it. But what I was drawn to was her narrowed attention, visually and spatially, staring out to sea with a frown on her face. 'I didn't see the honeysuckle until you mentioned it!' Her face softened. I asked her to be aware of the space above her head, the space behind, on either side, the floor beneath her, and she grew taller. Within a couple of lessons, she was amazed to tell me that the pain in her foot had gone. When we think spatially, when the kill is over, we have eaten our fill and are relaxing on the pampas, we trigger the alpha rhythm of brain wave, which brings us to that 'relaxed alertness' or 'alert relaxation' that is optimal for learning and being at ease. Or a state of grace as I call it. We are not totally switched off, we are continuing to engage, but we have time to choose whether to take action or not. And our attention is spatially wide.

I play attention games with my M.A. drama students at Arts Educational Schools in London. Do you know Port and Starboard? It's a basic elimination game – one side of the room is port, the other starboard, and as I call one of them they all hurtle to that side. The last one there is out. If I call 'Hit the Decks!' they hurl themselves flat on the floor. After we have established a winner, I ask them where was their attention? Narrowed and endgaining of course. Then we play again with a different rule: the first one to arrive is out. They have to keep moving in the direction I call. I call 'Hit the Decks!' and a very slow trip through their version of monkey ensues. This time they are paying much more attention to their own movement, the means whereby they are getting to the floor. A little to the rest of their fellows, to see how the 'race' is going. The third time the rule changes again: they are not be the first nor the last . . . and that is when the attention pans out to the room and the others. They are 'up' and engaged and present.

So, here's an experiment for you:

Become aware of the space above you, the distance between you and the ceiling or the sky, the space behind you, the distance between you and the wall behind, the space on either side, the distance between you and the walls either side, the space in front of you, a panoramic vision of what is in front and the distance between you and the horizon. Become aware of the ground beneath you.

If it is possible, think of these spatial directions one after the other, all at the same time.

You may find this is already expanding your sense of self, so your head rises and your back lengthens and widens. It may bring you into contact more with the outside world so you see hear and sense consciously what is going on around you. This may take you out of your old postural fix, often governed by thinking inwardly. As we come into the world in this present moment we become more responsive and can change, letting go of held neuro-muscular patterns.

In the last five years I have been further influenced by Les Fehmi and Jim Robbins' book *The Open Focus Brain*, which includes a lot of exercises to encourage spatial thinking in the body. When I first read it, it struck me how I knew what they were writing about through my own education and experiments in Alexander Technique.

Here's another experiment you can use when sitting quietly or lying down in semi-supine. I call these internal spatial directions:

Think of the distance between the top of your head and the roof of your mouth; the distance between the front of your eye and the back of your head; the distance between your ears. Now it may be possible to become aware of the whole volume your head takes up in space, its three-dimensionality. You can work through the whole of your body's dimensions in this manner, adding incrementally to your awareness of self, so that by the end you have become aware of the whole three-dimensional space you are taking up from head to toe. Notice I am using the word 'distance' rather than 'length'. It creates a better notion of space since it is implying miles rather than inches. If you have closed your eyes in this 'space' trip through the body, open them again, and reassert the parameters of the room around you as well, so there's a three-dimensional you lying down with all this space around. I think this is a powerful way to direct our thinking in a non-doing way, as it is not asking us to even think of lengthening anything.

You can also think of the space between things: the space between your thumb and your index finger. The triangular space behind your knees, between your arms and your torso. Visual artists would say that we are paying attention to the 'negative space' – like drawing a chair by drawing the space between the legs, rather than focusing on the legs.

I will often ask a student to think of the distance between the top of her head and the ceiling, the back of her and the wall behind, and to simply notice how that distance changes as she sits and stands. As she pays attention to the changing parameters of the space as she move, her use changes.

Our attention is all. We habitually attend to the solid matter that we perceive as the self, which is only a fraction of what is. There is some debate but perhaps 99.999% of the atom is space.[2]

> Nothing exists except atoms and empty space; everything else is just opinion.[3]

One of my students who studies quantum mechanics told me that all the solid matter of the planet could fit into a space the size of an Oxo cube – but we would have imploded in on ourselves to do that and wouldn't exist to experience this anyway. . . but I get his point. So perhaps we are paying attention to the space that exists in us and around us. The gap between things. The gap between stimulus and response.

When I think of the space, I am asking my brain to pay attention to an apparent nothing. Perhaps that is why I can at last calm myself, leave my habits behind and be here now in my full stature.

Bibliography
Jones, Frank Pierce (1997). *Freedom to Change.* Mouritz: London.
Fehmi, Les, Jim Robbins (2007). *The Open-Focus Brain.* Shambhala: Boston.

1. http://www.brainandhealth.com/Brain-Waves.html.
2. http://physics.stackexchange.com/questions/126512/why-doesnt-matter-pass-through-other-matter-if-atoms-are-99-999-empty-space
3. Democritus (460 – 370 BC.).

Penny O'Connor has been teaching Alexander Technique since 1992. She has a private practice in London, teaches M.A. acting students at Arts Educational Schools London, assists at The Alexander Technique School Queens Park, and leads workshops and lessons on the Greek Island of Alonnisos every summer. She teaches internationally, runs a mentoring scheme for new AT teachers at ArtsEd and is part of the Performing Self team, a CPD project for AT teachers wanting to work within the performing arts. She practices Chi Kung, is learning folk fiddle and loves wild dancing and singing. In her past life she acted on stage, taught in secondary schools and wrote plays.

… PART THREE

Creativity and Performance

Making a Mark

The Physiology of Drawing and the Alexander Technique

Jane Brucker with Jeremy Wasser

As an artist and teacher of the Alexander Technique and a physiologist, we were curious to engage the participants at our workshop in an exploration of drawing as an activity that deepens awareness and provides an opportunity for direction and inhibition. We planned a series of drawing exercises and complementary physiological insights that provided a link to themes within the Congress and posed drawing as an exploratory activity. In this paper, we give an overview of our approach to 'Making a Mark'.

Exercise 1: We limited the workshop to three participants at each of four long tables. In front of each person was a stack of drawing papers and materials. The participants introduced themselves to others at the table by signing their name on the paper. This simple act of writing, using a traditional 'pen' grip was presented as the first 'drawing' exercise. Later, we would return to play with handwriting as an expressive activity.

Jeremy began by showing an image of the 26,000 year-old Pech-Merle cave paintings, representing mark-making as a fundamentally human activity. He reminded participants that in the opening address of the Congress, Michael Gelb presented the 'genius' thinking of Leonardo Da Vinci. Jeremy implied that not only can we learn to think like Leonardo, but we could also learn to draw like him.

From a physiological perspective, we are all using the same anatomical structures to see and to draw and these structures are connected to one another and integrated by our nervous systems in the same way. This is as true for the cave painter and Leonardo as for you and me.

In his book *The Natural Way to Draw*,[1] Kimon Nicolaides (1892-1938) remarked: 'Learning to draw is really a matter of learning to see – to see correctly – and that means a good deal more than merely looking with the eye.' We know this because a person can be neurologically blind – that is, can have perfectly functioning eyes, and a perfectly functioning retina, but if they are hit on the back of the head and damage the visual cortex, the region of the brain that receives and interprets the sensory input from the eyes, they cannot see. Likewise, artists learn to 'see' in a way that allows them to interpret information from the environment and translate this information into shape, colour, line, and value. Henri Matisse understood this perfectly. During an interview, Matisse was asked if when he was eating a tomato he perceived it differently because he was an artist. Matisse replied, 'No, when eating a tomato I see it the way anyone else would, but when I paint a tomato – then I see it differently.'

The job of our sensory receptors, wherever they are in the body, is to pick up information and transfer that information to the brain. They transduce (convert a physical signal into an electrical signal) the incoming information to a form that the body can interpret. This is an information-transfer system. Information comes from the environment and your brain uses that information to allow you to make sense of and manipulate the environment.

Handwriting is a kind of drawing practice and can be an example of this information–transfer; an idea in my mind of what I want to write becomes a physical mark, which may then affect the intentions in my mind as I continue with and modify the action. Handwriting is also a great way to understand drawing, hand–eye–tool coordination and use as a function of both habit and novelty. Our typical signature is a learned pattern that we practise. This pattern includes the way we hold the pen and the exact way we create the linear marks. Spacing and size of letters, pressure and fluidity of the pen on the paper and direction of the linear marks can all be observed. Changing one's signature can be achieved by deliberately altering these visual aspects. Participants were asked to notice the order of the letters, the shape of some letters, and anything interesting or distinguishing about the marks they made.

Exercise 1a: Each participant was asked to add three more signatures to their paper. They were asked not to change the letters or words (the name remained the same) but instead to vary the pressure, speed, spacing, and size of the marks.

In this exercise, students note that the meaning of the words made by the letters does not change but instead variation in visual elements creates expression. Participants saw that elements of their own writing were remarkably different from their neighbours, allowing them to see underlying tendencies in their own handling of the pencil and the line.

The nervous system is set up to receive and process information from the environment and then allow us to reach out and affect that environment. One may describe the system as having two parts – in physiological terms, two 'limbs':

- 'Afferent limb': Specific sensory receptors are being stimulated (photoreceptors for vision, pressure receptors for touch, and others). The signal travels towards the central nervous system (spinal cord and brain) via specific nerve cells (neurons) that physically (anatomically) terminate in specific regions of the cerebral cortex that are dedicated to that particular sensation (sensory modality). That is where you are actually 'experiencing' the stimulus.

- 'Efferent limb': The brain interprets the signals coming in and determines what you would like to do about them. A different region of the cortex (motor cortex) sends information via different neurons out of the brain and spinal cord to the 'effectors', for example, skeletal muscles, and you then manipulate the outside world.

Information only travels in one direction in any given nerve cell. The signal originates in the cell body and travels down the axon to the end of the cell. There it connects and communicates with the next nerve cell downstream. There is a physical gap between nerve cells, called the synapse. Information is transduced (transmitted) across that gap *chemically* (chemicals are released by the upstream nerve cell and bind to the downstream cell), whereas information travels down an individual neuron *electrically*.

Exercise 2: This exercise demonstrates this afferent and efferent concept. Participants used a landscape-format paper to create a series of vertical lines starting at the top and extending to the bottom in one long stroke. They drew a series of dark to light rows alternating with light to dark rows by changing and controlling the pressure they exerted on the pencil.

Exercise 2a: Once participants had filled the page, they were asked to repeat the exercise with their eyes closed.

Lastly, they described the difference between the eyes-open and eyes-closed versions, comparing both the drawings and their experiences.

This exercise demonstrates the concepts of magnitude and localization in the context of sensory physiology. What a neurophysiologist means by this is the ability of the nervous system to more or less precisely 'know' which sensory receptors are being stimulated in any given region of the body (in these exercises the fingers and finger tips). The more densely packed the receptors are in a given anatomical area (again think finger tips in a primate like a human), the smaller the 'receptive field' and the greater the precision with which the central nervous system locates the stimulus focus.

In the eyes-open exercise, each participant had input coming from two sensory modalities – vision and touch (pressure) and used both in deciding how they would draw the lines. In the eyes-shut version, they only had information from the pressure (touch) receptors in their fingers, but could still draw the lines as they wished.

In both exercises, efferent signals were sent to the muscles of the hand and fingers to control the pencil. Participants were manipulating the environment in the magnitude of their action (force exerted on the pencil) and localisation (where in space they chose to make the marks) and that information was constantly being fed back to the brain while drawing. This allowed participants to adjust how they applied the pencil to the paper to get the lines they wanted.

What is actually happening in this exercise reflects two kinds of 'localisation' phenomena. One is an expression of the artist's ability to make a mark where (and how) she wants on the paper or in three-dimensional space. The second is the physiological localisation described above.

We continued to discuss the relationship of the hand to the tool and the spatial experience of the page. A third signature exercise continued this idea and introduced the concept of proprioception.

To a physiologist, proprioception refers to the body's ability to sense and locate all of its parts in three-dimensional space, whether those parts can be seen (using the sensory modality of vision) or not. We have sensory receptors throughout the body but concentrated in the skeletal muscles, joints, and associated connective tissues that 'tell' the sensory cortex where our parts are at any given time.

Exercise 3: Participants reviewed Exercise 1 and 1a. Varied grips including the 'pen' grip were demonstrated. Each participant was asked to fill the rest of the page by holding the pencil and writing in as many ways as possible with several different grips, asking 'What do you notice?'

It is possible to 'map' our bodies on to the sensory cortex to illustrate how much of the brain is dedicated to interpreting sensory signals from a specific body part and on to the motor cortex to indicate how much is dedicated to 'controlling', via efferent signalling, a given body part. We ask the question: 'How much of our cortical brain area is dedicated to interpreting signals from a specific anatomical region?' We call these two maps 'sensory homunculus' and 'motor homunculus'.

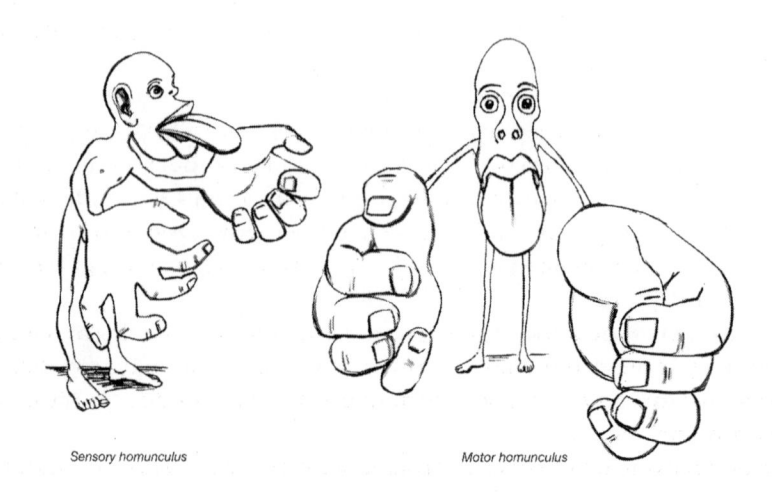

Sensory homunculus   Motor homunculus

The sensory homunculus in a primate, like us, illustrates how important signalling is from the fingers and hand (as well as the lips, tongue and genitalia). Our sensory receptors there are packed very densely and each one is responsible for only a very tiny area of say, a finger tip (small receptor fields). This allows our brain to differentiate very fine differences in where a signal is being applied (localisation in the physiological sense) and also how strong a signal is being applied to this spot (magnitude). Thus, the 'receptor fields' in the finger tips are very small. In contrast, the back has relatively few sensory receptors and the receptor fields are large. We do not have the ability to localise signals from the back very well although we do a good job assessing magnitude (you know it when you are touched lightly or punched hard from behind!).

The 'motor homunculus' illustrates how much of the motor cortex we dedicate to our fingers as well as to several other body areas (laryngeal muscles, muscles of the tongue). We are able to make very fine adjustments in the amount of force generated by these muscles and use them in very refined and sophisticated ways. The contrast between the size of the hand and fingers and that of the back and large leg muscles shows how the latter are not required to do any fine adjustments – they simply hold us up against the force of gravity (most of the time!).

Exercise 4: Participants were instructed to create a self-portrait using the information from the 'sensory homunculus'. Normally you would look in a mirror to create a self-portrait. But in this drawing, participants closed their eyes and I taught them to coordinate the pencil in their drawing hand with the movement of the opposite hand along the surface of the face, based on the emphasis of the 'sensory homunculus'. Starting with the lips, the most sensitive part of the face, students moved a finger slowly along the contour of the mouth, then explored the nose, eyelids and continued to explore the sensitivity of the face and head. Participants then had some minutes to explore aspects of the head or body they wished to follow on their own.

Exercise 5: This exercise explored the 'motor homunculus' by highlighting motor difference more specifically. Participants were asked to stand and use chalk, creating multiple lines to form a 6'- 8' diameter circular shape; duplicating the circle drawing several times on the page. Trying the same exercise with a square shape they were asked, 'Which was easier? Why?'

I introduced the circle as the universal human form. We all drew a circle at about age one to one and a half and continue to develop the circle as the basis for form, symbol and meaning throughout childhood. Most likely Leonardo drew one too!

When picking up the chalk, participants were asked to notice if they were

Clockwise from upper left hand corner: Exercise 1 and 1a, Exercise 2 (eyes open), Exercise 5, Enso, Exercise 4 (sensory face).

holding the chalk differently from how they held the pencil. Most were, and I pointed out the way they had adapted to a new tool. The new grip was the 'violin bow' grip used in gesture drawing. In this grip the chalk (or whatever one is drawing with) is held between the thumb and all four fingers. This grip changes control from the fingers to the wrist, elbow and shoulder. While we did not have time to learn gesture technique – often used to quickly capture the essence of a form – we did explore one important aspect of mark-making that was also part of the signature drawings – speed, or what Jeremy called 'velocity of muscle contraction'.

Exercise 5a: This exercise again explored the circle, but this time the outline was drawn multiple times and in layers to find a 'perfect' circle. They completed the exercise fast and slow using the violin bow grip. They were prompted to observe their 'use' and its impact on the form (often the circle will become 'pulled' or lopsided if the artist does not flow freely using the natural movement of the shoulder or wrist). They explored the impact of various positions (sitting, standing and monkey) on the fluidity, mark and appearance of the circle.

The last exercise introduced the meditative drawing practice from Japan, the *ensō*. The tables were cleared and only the black paper sheets remained. Each person stood and used the white chalk with a single sheet of black paper.

The *ensō* is a circular symbol often referred to as '*the Zen circle*'. The word itself simply translates as 'circle' in Japanese; however, it embodies emptiness or 'no-mind' and allows a person to be in the present moment. Participants were reminded to become more deeply aware, freeing the neck, and remembering their direction. I asked them to free the neck and fingers, hand, wrist and arm in order to retrace the circle.

An *ensō* begins in one place and ends with that one line. There is no redrawing. Instead of moving quickly, the line is contemplative, slow and fluid. Participants began by spending time observing themselves and attending to their breath. They were encouraged to follow the breath by beginning to move and draw after the out-breath. Inhibiting the need for a 'perfect' circle, they embraced the 'wabi-sabi' (beauty in the imperfect). Their mark was uniquely theirs.

Exercise 6: The final exercise asked each participant including Jeremy and myself to remain quiet, and allowed one person at a time to draw an *ensō*. After everyone had completed the *ensō* we gathered in a closing circle, each lifting their own *ensō* to create a circle of drawings that filled the room.

All illustrations are courtesy of Meghan Parker.

1   Nicolaides, Kimon (1941). *The Natural Way to Draw: A Working Plan for Art Study*. Houghton Mifflin: Boston.

Jane Brucker (MARA, MFA, AmSAT certified, ATI Los Angeles) is Professor in the Department of Art and Art History, Loyola Marymount University, Los Angeles. A practising artist, Jane uses sculptural objects and performance to engage the viewer through contemplation, movement and ritual activity. Her work has been exhibited at venues throughout the United States and in Nepal, France, Germany, Japan and the Czech Republic. In addition to her studio practice, she teaches at Loyola Marymount University where she incorporates Alexander Technique into teaching drawing to animators, designers and artists.

Jeremy Wasser (PhD) is Associate Professor of Physiology at the College of Veterinary Medicine at Texas A&M University where he also holds a position in the College of Medicine. His background includes training and research in biology, zoology, and physiology of human and non-human animals and he is a specialist in comparative physiology. As a singer and cantorial soloist, he has sung with several small companies as a baritone comprimario and for synagogues in Texas and Germany. He believes strongly in the marriage of arts and science and the value of a cross-disciplinary approach to the way animals function. Currently, he is working on a book on the history of physiology, focusing on the transformation of our understanding of how the body works from the magical to the scientific.

Embodied Stage Presence

Letting Go of Our Stories to Give Powerful Performances

Corinne Cassini

The shortest version of my story is, 'I love to play again!' How many of you can sincerely say this is true of you now, this moment? And yet, years ago you started to play and perform because you loved it, not because you dreaded it or got nervous... Then why and how do we stand in our own way? 'I love to play again' means I first enjoyed playing, and then something happened causing me not to anymore, and now I love playing again. How did this happen?

Storytelling with the Alexander principles is one of the ways I work with myself, musicians and other students to bring about freedom in general and, specifically, in playing. It's an opportunity for deep kinaesthetic listening, which is another way of saying awareness of use relative to an activity, in an environment where it is safe to fully experience any fears and nerves that arise. Our tension manifests itself precisely because we are unable or afraid to completely live through it and accept the experience of it. Storytelling in the support of the Alexander work and principles allows us to see, acknowledge, and then let go of these interferences in our playing.

Originally, I loved to play and perform, yet was not aware that simply loving playing allowed it to come naturally, nourishing in turn my love for the stage. My process in performing wasn't fully conscious. As life and experiences happened, the negative ones began to register more strongly, and those started to get in the way. These negative experiences coalesced into one interfering 'story'. I was then struggling to get back to the experience of simply being on stage playing, rather than 'doing a performance' and 'needing to do' other things to cope with and survive the experience. Looking at my stories in the way I will explain helped me come full circle.

The full story starts out with the most incredible performance. One of those times that we think can't happen again, where the light was just right, the temperature perfect, fingers agile, free movement throughout, ears open, eyes alert, total attentiveness, yet perfectly quiet and in the moment. I was sensing and aware of the room, the teachers listening, and I knew I was doing it and doing it well; I knew as I was playing that I was sounding the best I had ever played. A moment of total awareness (kinaesthesia, use, thoughts, emotions, etc. . . .) that I hadn't expected, yet I allowed myself to ride the wave. . . That performance stands out as an incredible learning experience.

It wasn't until later, when I was preparing for other performances that I started to get into trouble. I was endgaining, searching to reproduce that wonderful experience, attached to trying to make it happen again, whereas 'on that magic day', I hadn't been trying to do anything besides prepare for a performance and play. I was stuck because I was not giving myself the means, as I had previously done, to succeed after that peak performance. It took me some time to unravel this event, and it wasn't until Alexander training that I finally understood how crucial it was to let go of trying to reproduce a moment and learn to be in the moment just as I am.

I now know I was reacting to the experience of playing so easily and well. I was struggling and not enjoying playing because I was looking to recreate that incredible experience, which I *hadn't tried to create* in the first place. When 'the story happened' I was just going to play, nothing special, just another performance. Yet what became apparent later, was in my preparation for that performance, I had not endgained and actually moved through the learning process, gradually, step by step without much concern for the result, not suspecting this wonderful performance would be the result. So there was no way I was going to experience what I was looking for by only trying to recreate the performance (end result) without going through the methodical learning process (means-whereby). Now I needed to follow similar steps consciously.

Through letting go of trying to perform in that way, I finally let myself experience the loss of that natural state; and in that experience, I understood that hanging on to the experience was the interference itself. I needed to let each performance be its own event, focusing on *how* I prepared. I understood that very positive experiences can also cause us to react with narrowing, and can adversely impact our future experiences as much as the traumatic ones that we might more immediately think of when discussing stage anxiety. Preoccupation with a good experience, like preoccupation with a bad experience, means we are *reacting to our experience rather than just allowing ourselves to be with it.*

That peak performance was a moment when I was totally allowing myself to have the experience I was experiencing. Though I had never had an Alexander lesson yet, I was even then somewhat aware that this was happening, because I remember saying to myself, 'Wow, Corinne, this is incredible! You are having so much fun up here playing!' Later I understood that I was actually aware of those magic moments and allowing them to be without judging or evaluating – something I have now learned to allow into my experience.

Of course in the midst of traumatic situations we may not be able or be strong enough to allow ourselves to fully experience in real time what is actually happening. Or in some cases it may not be safe to do so. So going 'unconscious' might be what will allow the person to survive the situation at that given moment. According to Peter Levine and his somatic experiencing practices,[1] for the person who has gone into survival mode it is important that they address the experience as soon as possible when they are in a safe place or with professional support, to do this processing. In my classes and workshops I invite students and participants to choose a story that they feel was transformative, challenging or is recurring in their lives. By allowing them to choose I make sure they won't trigger anything they aren't ready to handle. In my private practice I may use story work on other issues besides performance trauma if my student brings it up by telling the story. Unfortunately, in both my personal and professional experiences I observe how we often miss the learning in our stories. We remain in these incomplete experiences that linger and initiate compensatory patterns of behavior. These patterns get stuck, becoming part of our use, which then permeates similar activities without our realising we are not fully living, only surviving.

For me, the initial step was to realise that simply doing the best I could in my preparation and letting go of being anyone or anything else than who I was at the moment became a moment of acceptance. I stopped trying and simply experienced what was happening, instead of reacting to what was happening. Later during a lesson with Tommy Thompson using story work to kinaesthetically register the performing experience and the interfering reactions I habitually had, I was able to shift the experience by transforming the story of my response to performing. A choice moment was born out of a clear awareness of two contrasting experiences: my past story and habitual reaction to the experience of playing, and a more spontaneous response based on the present moment's experience. I thus came back full circle to my initial love of playing and performing so that the story became: 'I love to play and perform!'

Exercise One

In the Congress workshop I led participants through this process of letting go of a fixed story from the past that repeats itself, to embrace a new story based on who we are today, in our present-moment experiences. We did this by telling and then retelling our stories to each other, in the safe setting of groups composed of a witness, a listener/Alexander teacher and a storyteller. The idea is to get started by reconnecting with, recreating, or slightly triggering the habitual reaction to an event by telling its story. This triggers the habitual reactions and interferences in our coordination we are looking to let go of, and gives us the opportunity to see them, register them kinaesthetically through a state of listening, assisted by hands-on, and experience the difference once we let go.

- To start off, the person in the role of the storyteller (S) tells their challenging story (the one they wish to let go of) while the listener (L) listens and the witness (W) listens/witnesses. When S is done, L comes behind S and puts hands on S for a couple moments (it need not be long) while S simply reflects silently on his/her story. L is putting 'listening hands' (like an Alexander teacher) on S to provide safety, presence, inhibition and a different perspective for S while s/he reflects on the story.
- While S receives hands-on support, s/he thinks of their story and what they have learned from it, especially relative to who they have become in their lives today. They consider how this story has impacted their lives and the direction of their lives.
- L then sits back down across from S and asks S to tell his/her story again, but now from the perspective of what was learned, allowing the information from the hands-on experience to permeate the story and response.
- Something happens here in the synergy between the 'listening hands', the thoughts and experiences of S, so that the second story is completely different. Usually it is shorter, simpler, less emotionally reactive, more compassionate, more universal in the sense that even someone who hasn't had that experience can relate to it and feel a human compassion towards what S is feeling and experiencing. There is also a clear reason for the story and the choices made at that point and later down the road.
- Bringing the hands on while the person is thinking of their story in the first stage allows them a moment of deep kinaesthetic listening, which is the moment in which they can *register the absence* of the habitual use associated with the experience. This brings them to touch their story not from who or where they were during the experience but who and where they are now, directing them to make different choices. So it is a highly inhibitive moment, where an experience is reorganised relative to who they are now, not to who they've been or who the story tells/told them to be.
- This deep kinaesthetic listening, which shines light on the habitual patterns, and then *the absence* of these same patterns, brings a person into responding in the present moment from an 'awareness born out of their experience' (Tommy Thompson's phrase) rather than out of habit. This is the inhibitive moment of self-observation or the moment of 'choiceless awareness' that Frank Pierce Jones writes about in *Freedom to Change*.
- This then directly leads the person into a moment of choice or action that is free of past experience. It's a new direction from a new perspective, a new beginning. This space of 'choiceless awareness' or 'freedom to choose' (F. P. Jones), is to me the creative space. We are

responding to our environment, to the circumstances present at our performance – the audience, the room, the acoustics. We are fully alive, and this in turn allows us to continuously check in with deep kinaesthetic listening, moving into awareness, thus completing the circle towards creative, free and spontaneous performances.
- W's role is to hold the space for the whole activity, providing added support and presence and feedback for both at the very end. W's role is important as an overall observer who will share at the close of the second telling of the story. W will first share what was observed during the whole activity, then S and L can share as well in conversation.
- Participants in this trio then switch roles until everyone has done each role once.

Moving forward and out of the storytelling experience with the lightness and freedom it provides, we are ready to acknowledge and embody our deepest qualities. As performers we are quick to criticise and find mistakes. This makes us much less in tune with the qualities that we might bring to our new experiences. It is important to have our qualities reflected back to us, so that we can see, recognise and embody them during our performances.

EXERCISE TWO
This activity is intimately related to the storytelling in its use of kinaesthetic listening.

- Two people form a pair and begin to exchange compliments. At first each person experiences reactions to what the other is saying. It is important to notice and observe these reactions which will be psychophysical and often include laughing, deflecting, rejecting, etc.
- In the second phase, the participants continue to exchange compliments, but now each time a compliment is given, the person receiving the compliment pauses and listens to where the compliment has landed. This is where they physically sense the kinaesthetic experience of the compliment. To acknowledge this, the person receiving the compliment touches themselves where they experienced the compliment.
- This moment is also a moment of deep kinaesthetic listening, and is crucial because sensing the compliment in their body allows the person to move from reaction to receiving, and finally to responding to the compliment from their present moment experience.
- Once the person has acknowledged through touching their own body on the area where they experienced the compliment or felt it land, they will speak a compliment back to their partner from where they received it. The exchange continues in this manner.

Both as a participant and an observing teacher, I have noticed how the simple gesture and space provided to receive the compliment allows for present-moment recognition of experience and awareness in relationship. The compliments are authentic and are received and given from and to the heart, even if participants have just met.

The workshop concluded with participants reporting that they felt more present, freer, more embodied, lighter and more deeply connected to themselves and to each other as a result of the two experiences of kinaesthetic listening. Many reported having experienced a whole new outlook on an old recurring story, that allowed them to finally move on from their definition of that moment. Several told me after the compliment activity, that they were able to acknowledge and give value to qualities they knew deep down they had but never truly or fully appreciated nor brought forth. To me this is what being alive and embodied in our experience means. It is essential to anyone's life and especially for a performer in creating moving and powerful performances that will touch their audiences. If we can be present and authentic with ourselves, using our refined kinaesthetic perceptions while applying inhibition and 'withholding definition' (Tommy Thompson) in relationship to others and the environment, then we can trust ourselves to let go and give all of what we have learned in our art back to the audience.

As a musician and an Alexander teacher I am deeply grateful for all my performing experiences, which challenged me to find ways to work with my senses, fears, false perceptions and judgements. This path has led me to an awareness of the experience I have just shared, which now guides my teaching and my work with musicians and performers. After practising these awareness activities, my students repeatedly report not only increase in freedom, physical and mental ease, but especially more happiness, spontaneity and connectedness with the music, their instrument, and the audience during performance.

1   *Somatic Experiencing®: Waking the Tiger* by Peter Levine, http://www.traumahealing.org

Corinne Cassini (AmSAT, ATI) teaches the Alexander Technique to Music majors at the Hayes School of Music at Appalachian State University and privately in Boone, North Carolina and in Angers, France. Following her three-year training in the Carrington tradition with Arie-Jan Hoorweg in the Netherlands she spent two additional years doing postgraduate work with and assisting Tommy Thompson, deepening her experience and understanding of the Alexander Technique as applied to performing artists. A professional cellist, she especially enjoys guiding performing artists both individually and in group settings. She enjoys travelling and giving workshops on performing and the Alexander work to varied audiences.

www.lightinbeing.com

The Use of Breathing and the Body Vowels

Agnès de Brunhoff

I began to practise the piano at the age of five, so music and instruments were always part of my being, my entire self. But it was only when I started to sing and work seriously at my voice that I had to stand to breathe better and discovered that I needed to activate my whole body. The surprise grew even more when I had my first Alexander Technique lessons about thirty years ago and realised that I had been practising piano, my first instrument, for a very long time but without my body being involved in my thinking, thinking only in the hands or shoulders.

I would like to share with you the journey of my research and observations in the most practical way possible. Below you can find an overview of the exercises and observations covered in my workshop at the 2015 International Congress. These can be read as theory but are primarily intended as practical guidelines to help you experience the various processes for yourself.

FIRST PRACTICAL EXERCISE: PEOPLE INTRODUCING THEMSELVES TO THE GROUP
We go around the group and I ask people in turn to stand and say a few words to introduce themselves. After a few people have spoken, we pause and reflect together. We make several observations – primarily we see that as soon as people know they have to speak in front of an audience, there is an emotional disturbance of their breathing. This is despite the fact that we are Alexander Technique teachers. We don't speak from our primary control and directions: the aim of telling our audience what we have to say disturbs our organisation (and the end gets in the way of our means-whereby).

After sharing these observations, the next few people begin to introduce themselves, followed by a pause for more reflection. This time, we see that the second group manage to take more time to organise themselves, thinking of their primary control and directions, but what they want to say still remains more important than how they use themselves while talking. It is clear that the tools we get from the Technique such as inhibition or calm breathing are not fully functioning.

In conclusion, we notice two things from this introductory exercise. First, how easily the natural flow or 'column' of air is interrupted. Second, that even with our knowledge as AT teachers we can't help being disturbed by the act of speaking and what we are saying.

In view of this fact, I suggest that maybe it is time to accept the fact that our *breathing is always going to be disturbed easily, at any time, by anything.* The emotional disturbance cannot be ignored, but if we accept it instead of fighting against it, maybe we can then work with it positively and establish good functioning with the appropriate tools.

The question is now: how can we change our attitude and functioning with regards to breath and voice? I suggest a good place to start is by using general work with the Alexander Technique. This develops a way of thinking and the proper muscular support we need to establish a reliable column of air. As always, the key is to think of dynamic energy along the spine starting from the primary control. Then, the breath can be added into this system. We can think of the in-breath joining the flow, from the primary control along the whole spine, right down to the perineum. After the in-breath, where the thought and breath reach as low as possible to the bottom of the spine, there is a moment of inhibition, a kind of suspension. This moment allows the movement to reverse, and the column of air is activated to go upwards, back along the spine, to produce a steady flow of air out of the mouth.[1]

Second practical exercise: Practising breathing without sound

1) Simply blowing out

We see that if you just hold up your fingers and gently blow towards them, you will feel a soft but tangible and dynamic airflow. Then take away your hand and repeat the exercise in exactly the same way. You might be tempted to push the breathing out horizontally, straight in front of you, as if you have to push the air to the other side of the room. The problem is that if you do this, you are likely to push your head forwards and down and tense your neck muscles, completely disturbing the primary control and also reducing the airflow. In order to avoid this, you can instead think of the airflow going vertically, like the continuation of the spine – not completely straight, but supple, with curves continuing above your head. Next you can practise the same thing once more but while going on your toes; check that your column of air remains free and doesn't change at all.

2) Inhibition and breathing

Here, you have a choice between three possible gestures: going on tiptoes, lifting up an arm, or breathing out. Allow the choice to happen rather than deciding actively. In this way, you realise that breathing can also be a neutral gesture as simple as any of the others which the body can produce.

3) Consciousness of regular breathing in other activities

Walking and breathing: walk through space at various speeds while allowing the column of air to remain calm. The in-breath should remain constant regardless of the speed you are walking. Remember that the breath goes right down to the perineum, and that you should aim for a passive 'letting in' of air, followed by a smooth, quiet, but active blowing out. The breath should stay constant, at the same rhythm, even if you change the movements within the body.

You can also change the speed or the length of the outbreath instead of your steps. For example, stand still and try breathing out for a shorter or longer time, and with more or less strength of air flow. If it helps, you can imagine candles of different sizes in front of you that you have to blow out. This exercise can really help us to decouple the breath from other habitual actions (like walking), and to decouple speed of breath from force of air flow – to be conscious of the fact that different actions in the body can happen independently of each other.

THIRD PRACTICAL EXERCISE: MAKING A SOUND
1) The 'BRRRRRR' sound with lips vibrating with a spiral of air
Do this first on one note, and then do the same thing on notes of music up or down as it comes. In the workshop, we noticed an immediate change of attitude here, because again we start focusing on the result. Once you start making a sound you begin to listen, try to control the voice, to do things right. Again we have to come back to the means-whereby and focus on our directions, to do the procedures one after the other and all at the same time.

2) The whispered 'ah'
First we practise 'the usual way' of doing this procedure as outlined by Walter Carrington in *Thinking Aloud*, in the chapter 'Whispered Ahs'[2]: imagining some light in the eyes, imagining you can smell a nice aroma, breathing in through the nose and exhaling on the 'ah'. Next we try my adaptation of the procedure. This arose thanks to my singing practice and my need to put together Alexander Technique principles with the deep breathing I experienced through voice work and singing. The difference here is that we start thinking before we breathe, already forming the shape of the ah-vowel as we breathe in. We continue to imagine the air coming in through the mouth (in the shape of the vowel), right down to the bottom of the spine and perineum.

In the workshop, we compared the two ways of doing the whispered 'ah'. With the second method (where we also breathe in on an 'ah' vowel), we notice that the air supports the sound, there are more and deeper resonances, and we make the space for the sound before we breathe in. Any tendency to push forward in the chest is also prevented. I don't go so far as to say this is a better way. I just notice through my research and teaching over many years (probably due to the evolution of the human body over the last century, and the loss of the use of a proper voice and pronunciation in society as a whole), that it is useful to practise having a large and deep in-breath and preparation for sound immediately on the way in. An important detail: in the second version, the in-breath is produced from a mixture of breathing through the nose and through the mouth. This prevents the danger either of lifting up the chest (if we breathe in only through the nose), or collapsing in the throat and ribcage (while breathing in only through the mouth).

3) Sound and whispered 'ah'

First we try to sing a rising second-interval on a long 'ah' vowel (singing one note, then the note above, and then the first note again, e.g. C/D/C or do/ré/do). While doing this, everybody checks in with themselves. We see that the moment the singing arrives, there is again an idea of sound and result, and the benefit of the whispered 'ah' is lost. Moreover, we reflect, the thinking is attracted forward in space and time to our desire to express something.

Second, we work with three possibilities, and between them always come back to the organisation of the primary control. We first whisper the sound, then start all over again and produce a spoken 'ah', then start over once again and produce a singing 'ah'. This time we notice that we can guide our sound to be the same as it is when produced naturally by the body and not with the aim of expressing something or producing a nice sound. This exercise can also be tried on an O vowel.

4) Rhythm and vowels

Now we say all the vowels one after each other: ah, eh, ee, oh, oo, first whispered, then spoken, then sung. To prevent the tendency to push the vowels out, or to pronounce them with active will or doing and not from the dynamic body coordination and non-doing, we work with a Brazilian rhythm, along with percussion instruments. While we pronounce the vowels, I suggest that if we can base our gesture on the natural 'bounce' we had as children, the vowels will change naturally instead of being changed by the tension of the face muscles we use for pronunciation. Many trained musicians have the habit of always pulling down to emphasise the first beat of a bar. By using percussion and movement we can avoid this tendency of emphasising one specific beat, and instead reconnect to the more continuous, natural 'bouncing' rhythm which children have, where all beats are equally important and constantly being renewed. When we did this in the workshop, we saw how the exercise quickly turned into a kind of game where everyone just enjoyed moving from one vowel to the next, with a lighter, dancing atmosphere.

Fourth practical exercise: Application to a text

Finally we take a written text, a paragraph from the start of *Alice in Wonderland*. The text is passed around the group and a number of people read aloud. Surprisingly, as soon as people are reading aloud, there is no presence, no tone, no 'incarnation' or embodiment. Just a minute ago, when we were singing with a rhythm, the voices were resonant, the faces full of great expression and the sounds natural. We have to ask ourselves, where has it all gone? Where is the use of the self now? By focusing on the result, the meaning, trying to read well, chewing the text with exaggerated movements of the jaw, we have again lost the voice functioning in the body.

To be able to speak the text clearly, it is essential to think the vowels first (for example, 'Hello how are you' becomes 'Eh-oh-ow-ah-oo'), before the words themselves, before the meaning, before the sound. This is the usual Alexander procedure. We start with inhibition, and allow the air to come in, and so to come out fluidly afterwards. Then amazingly, the focus on the vowels alone, and the practice of reading the text only in vowels, allows the reader to truly 'embody' the text and the meaning of the text. The voice gets its full resonances and the meaning of the text appears with the nice colour of the person's sound.

Two interesting points arose in reaction to questions asked at the end of the workshop. First, I explained that I feel the idea of 'dropping the jaw' is counterproductive. The muscles of the jaw are incredibly powerful and strong, in fact amongst the strongest in the body. (Just think how, in the circus, a trapeze artist can carry their partner just using their jaw muscles.) So we should never drop the jaw as this will lead us to pull down. If we think of the jaw being attached upwards in suspension with the skull, it can open wide without any forcing or pulling down. The jaw plays no part in the pronunciation of the vowels. We pronounce them through the activity of the breathing alone, and very small changes to the tongue or the chewing muscles near the cheek bones. This can be practised using the previous exercises with the change of vowels. For example if you pronounce 'ah-eh-ee-oh-oo', with practice you will discover that it is possible to actively change the vowels without moving the jaw at all. The vowels are formed on the inside of the mouth, through tiny, almost imperceptible movements of the tongue and throat, and you don't need any tension of the jaw, chin or lips.

The second question was about the 'attack in the throat' or glottal attack (for example, 'ach' in German, 'Arrête!' in French, an emphasised 'if' in English). In my opinion, the glottal attack is not useful when we are practising vowels. In these exercises, the sound should start from the breathing (in). If we use a glottal attack to start a vowel, this interrupts the breathing and encourages us to aim for the end of pronouncing a specific vowel. This does not mean that it is wrong to use a glottal stop, but it is not necessary, and moreover if you do this too much or in a brutal way it can damage the vocal chords. Moreover, if we regularly start a sound with a glottal attack, it may well show that we started with a specific plan to say something, forgetting about the more important aim, which is to stay connected to our primary control and the column of air which is the real source of the sound.

Finally, it was interesting to see that people trained to sing or speak may feel comfortable with these exercises but often they still focus on their voice and don't allow the production of the sound to come from the entire body. Their 'trained' sound can be clear and powerful when we listen to it, but it is not a full or 'holistic' sound. This was clear in the final exercise we did of reading aloud a text. We could hear that professional actors or singers could do this exercise with great skill and clear vowels and projection, but it was not connected to the whole body and thus to the listeners it sounded quite impersonal.

I hope that by reading about these exercises, and above all by experimenting with them yourself, you can experience just how much breathing and voice work are the most basic and primary applications of the Alexander Technique, and can lead us to expand and enjoy even more the extraordinary functioning of the human being.

1   I explain this idea further in my book *On Stage!* in the chapter entitled 'The Column of Air': A. de Brunhoff, (2013), *On Stage! Back to Yourself with the Alexander Technique*, published by Agnès de Brunhoff, Paris, pp. 76-81.
2   W. Carrington (1994) *Thinking Aloud*. Mornum Time Press, Berkeley, pp. 147-150.

Thanks to Joanna Britton for collaboration on revising the language and structure of this essay.

Agnès de Brunhoff is a singer, classical pianist and songwriter. She qualified as an Alexander Technique teacher in 1993, and since then has continued working both as a performer and as a teacher and trainer, including at the Guildhall School of Music and Drama in London, for the European Union Youth Orchestra, and at the Studio des Variétés school of performing arts in Paris. After 10 years in the opera department of the CNSMDP Paris conservatoire, where she ran the course: 'The body of the performer on stage', she now teaches Alexander Technique in all the departments of singers and instrumentalists. In 2008, she opened the CFT Alexander teacher training school in Paris. Through her coaching of a great variety of musicians, she continues her research into the dynamic relationship between the body, the voice and the principles of the Alexander Technique as applied to performance.

How the Congress 2015 Workshop: 'Seeds of Imagination: *Developing Creativity with the Alexander Technique*' became '*Developing Creativity in Teaching the Alexander Technique*'

Cathy Madden

This workshop was designed as an interactive report of my research at the University of Washington, using the Alexander Technique (AT) to train imagination skills for the Professional Actor Training Program. The exercises developed when I saw that these actors consistently lost coordination when playing imaginary circumstances. Further research suggested that their images, the building blocks of imagination, seemed limited to a two-dimensional world – perhaps from learning mostly through electronic media rather than life. The story of my original observations and subsequent hypothesis is covered in more detail in my article, 'Refurbishing Images in Actors and Others'.[1] I continue to develop ways to use AT to do what I initially called 'image rehab'. Now I think of it as retraining whole-self pathways to imagination – creativity-specific exercises in neuroplasticity:

> Plasticity, or neuroplasticity, is the lifelong ability of the brain to reorganise neural pathways based on new experiences. As we learn, we acquire new knowledge and skills through instruction or experience. In order to learn or memorize a fact or skill, there must be persistent functional changes in the brain that represent the new knowledge. The ability of the brain to change with learning is what is known as neuroplasticity. (Chudler 2013)[2]

The sequence of exercises begins with concrete sensory exploration and develops gradually into more and more complex metaphorical thinking.

> The primacy of real movement and engagement with concrete objects (environment) in childhood education is well researched. It is foundational to the metaphorical processes we need for creative expression. Fortunately, if these pathways are underdeveloped in adults, the Alexander Technique has proven a great aid in building skills for three-dimensional imaging. Since learning to coordinate continually insists on unity of thinking and moving – what we sometimes call 'minking and thoving' in the Professional Actor Training Program – we use the Alexander Technique intentionally to develop and strengthen the building blocks of the imagination. (Madden 2014, p. 285).[3]

The exercises rely on the AT's ability to coordinate the whole individual; they also draw from actor training exercises, studies in neuroscience, and nature.

DIMENSIONAL PRACTICES

At the Congress Workshop, the group learned a selection of these exercises. While they were designed for actor training, I believe they are relevant not only for actors, but also to anyone who grew up with or is currently using an abundance of electronic media. Over years of research, it has become clear that many people, not just actors, find themselves 'out of coordination' when searching for new ideas, or hoping for creativity. For discussion purposes, I am going to identify 4 levels of these AT- facilitated exercises for creativity:

- Level One: Retraining basic image-making skills.
- Level Two: Responding to imagined stimuli.
- Level Three: Linking images to each other.
- Level Four: Communicating the imagined world.

(Note: The designation of these image/imagination explorations into levels was developed for clarity in this paper. In practice at the University, we move seamlessly from one exploration to the next.)

Level One

These are AT-facilitated sensory awareness exercises. A simple example would be to use AT to pick up a cup of tea and ask yourself a series of sensory-based questions: 'How close is my hand to the cup when I feel the heat of the tea?'; 'Is there one part of my hand that receives the heat more than another?'; 'If I needed to describe the surface of this cup to someone who couldn't touch it, how would I describe it?'; 'Does the taste of the tea change as it is in my mouth?' etc. It is a detailed conscious sensory exploration of a concrete object.

The actors deliberately practise these explorations consistently over time in many variations. Ericsson, in a study of expert performance says: 'The core assumption of deliberate practice is that expert performance is acquired gradually and that effective improvement of performance requires the opportunity to find suitable training tasks that the performer can master sequentially.' (Ericsson 2006: 692).[4]

With this consistency, we are developing what I call studied rehearsed plans for whole-self three-dimensional omni-sensory response to concrete stimuli.

> Studied rehearsed plans are developed skills that serve the desired action. The primary studied rehearsed plan relates to the underlying coordination [i.e. using the Alexander Technique] – 'Ask myself to coordinate so that my head can move so that all of me can follow so that I can do what I am doing'.

The secondary studied rehearsed plans are those that include using the Alexander Technique for a specific skill or event. The primary studied rehearsed plan organises your underlying coordination so that the secondary studied rehearsed plans can carry out your performance plan. [. . .]Rather than a rote repetition, the Alexander Technique guarantees freshness every time.[5]

AT is the primary *studied rehearsed plan* and the secondary *studied rehearsed plan* is the sensory/image based exercise from Level One.

Level Two
We move from the concrete to the imaginative. Following Level One's example of using the AT to drink tea and ask questions, in Level Two you do the same thing *as if* you have a cup of tea. It looks like mimed action, and its intent is to use AT to respond to imaginary, rather than real, stimuli.

Level Three
Level Three uses AT to link three different images – sustaining your coordination in a metaphorical thinking process. Electronic media link images for us. My experience is that, due to the preponderance of electronic media, many people have not developed the skill to link images. As they try to do a skill they don't have (hence an impossible task), they tighten between head and spine. As they develop the new skill, AT helps them consciously associate 'cooperating' coordination with abstract thought.

In this practice the actor combines three different concrete stimuli in a one-sentence story (ideally without ands, ors or other connectives). An example of three images they might pick are: deer, gray, watermelon. A one-sentence 'story' could be: *The deer sniffed the watermelon that fell from the gray trash can.*

We have a lot of fun with this – it isn't always easy to get the three images in one story. Sometimes the one sentence story makes no sense, or is fantastical. Sometimes someone combines them in a way that causes a 'wow' in the room. Every option that comes out is ok – it isn't about the success of combining the three images, it is about the effort towards it. Some students can't do it all at first – even taking a year or two to succeed. Eventually linking happens.

Level Four
When we began to do the Level Four exercises in the Congress workshop the implications for AT teachers became clear. The form of this level is:

- use AT,
- ask people to be with you while you are with them,
- take three different images/ideas,
- combine the images into a one sentence story,
- and then invite your audience into the story as you say it.

In the workshop the participants organised themselves into groups of three or four to experiment. I walked from group to group clarifying, coaching, and teaching people how to use the AT in the process.

During this round, many experienced surprise as they realised that when they started to imagine ways to put the three ideas/images together, they immediately tightened between head and spine and were no longer inviting the other people to be with them as they had intended. The possibility of developing new thoughts from disparate ideas – while consciously communicating with someone else – was challenging their skills. For some, the task was almost inconceivable. It was a participant in the group who recognised that we were practising an essential tool for teaching:

<blockquote>
I use AT
So that I can omniserve my students
(I use omniserve rather than observe to acknowledge that I am using multiple senses to gather information.)
As I invite them to be with me while I am with them
So that I can gather information from many sources
(sources including AT, what I know about anatomy, what activity they are doing, the environment we are in, etc., etc.)
So that I can create a plan
(taking information from multiple sources, and through the lens of AT, create a plan – linking images/ideas – to respond to the students' needs, wants, desires)
So that I can invite the student to explore using the plan
(using AT for any of the many ways I might teach).
</blockquote>

Teaching requires the ability to link images in new ways. In an age in which many people have grown up with many forms of electronic media that link images for you, it is an unpractised and sometimes absent skill. My participants were experiencing what I have been experiencing in my own private teaching practice – *while the exercises were developed as part of an actor training need, they are useful for everyone, not just actors.*

In the Congress Workshop, we next moved on to one person doing this process in front of the whole group. The group offered three concrete images (for instance – table, cloud, cotton) – and the person standing in front of the group invited everyone to be with her as she created a one-sentence story combining the images. This is an essential acting skill, and also a group teaching skill. My intent in offering it in the workshop was, in part, so the whole group could see and discuss an exercise. The discussion took an unexpected turn.

Omniservational skills
When I learned to teach, my teacher, Marjorie Barstow (1899-1994) consist-

ently asked me to use words to describe how my student was moving and talking. It was the second skill she asked me to develop. The first was constructively using the AT so that I could look, listen, be with, walk, talk, etc. as I began to approach my student. Once I was clearly taking responsibility for my own coordination, she asked, 'What do you notice about your student?' This happened many many times – deliberate practice, a *studied rehearsed* plan for omniservation.

When I first talked with some AT teachers who did not have this omniservational skill in their training, I was surprised. The topic came up at the Congress Workshop as one of the participants was doing the Level Four exercise in front of the group. Each time she tightened between head and spine as she attempted the task, I asked her to pause, we figured out what was happening, and I offered a new constructive plan. Somewhere during the process, another participant asked, 'Did you really see that? What did you see?' With the participant's permission, I described in detail what I saw. Some people in the room were surprised at the level of detail in my description. (Note – one member of the group knows me well and affirmed my omniservational skills as well as helping to put my skills in context for those surprised by it.)

Since this skill is so foundational to my teaching process, I cannot imagine teaching without it. Where it serves me as a teacher is in what F. M. Alexander called 'analysing the conditions of use present' in which I omniserve my student as they coordinate to do what they are doing; these skills also help me evaluate the effectiveness of the new means-whereby.

Most of the rest of the Congress workshop time was spent in teaching this Level Four variation, as well as discussing the teaching process, deliberate practice in omniservation, and the necessity of directly integrating the AT process with omniservation, thinking, moving, etc.

A BRIEF LOOK AT THE NEXT LEVEL IN THE IMAGE/IMAGINATION SERIES
In the Congress workshop I offered a quick explanation of Level Five – 'The Forest' exploration. This exercise arose from blending ideas from three different fields – AT, acting, and biology. (It is an example of linking three images/ideas.) My daughter gave me a book – David Haskell's *The Forest Unseen: A Year's Watch in Nature*. In it, Haskell describes going into a forest near where he lives and picking one small place to visit many times over a the period of a year. When he visited, he noted what he saw each time and wrote essays in response to his visits. He says:

> The search for the universal within the infinitesimally small is a quiet theme playing through most cultures. [. . .] Can the whole forest be seen through a small contemplative window of leaves, rocks and water? I have tried to find the answer to this question, or the start of an answer, in a mandala made of old-growth forest in the hills of Tennessee. The forest mandala is a circle a

little over a meter across, the same size as the mandala that was created and swept away by the monks.[6]

As I read his book, I thought, this is what we need! We have been working with individual images/ideas – the next thing we need is an extended study of a whole world – a whole forest. Near the School of Drama, there is a wooded area that is specifically planted with native plants, and includes a large fallen log. It doesn't quite qualify as forest since there are pedestrian pathways, a road, a theatre, the School of Drama and the School of Business in clear view. Yet, it is a small patch of native forest.

We started going there as a class at least once a week to use AT to whole-self omniserve the space. I asked the students to visit it as much as possible, even if for only a few moments. Since they needed to walk by it at least twice every day, it was an easy assignment. And once a week, we would use AT to recreate the forest while inside the classroom. Weeks of consistent practice paid off. I was excited to omniserve my students moving dimensionally in space, sustaining a responsive coordination throughout. After one indoor re-creation, a student – whose images/imagination had consistently been tiny and two-dimensional – ran excitedly around the studio exclaiming 'they're big! They're big! They are not those puny images any more!' The increased range of expression in his acting since that day is a wonder to experience.

DIMENSIONAL TEACHING

The workshop participants discovered that the explorations I have been developing for actors would be useful for themselves as teachers as well as useful for their students. Most of us teach people who hurt from using their electronic devices. We have the possibility of consciously cooperating with our dimensionality as we use our very useful, though compact and virtually flat, tools. The payoff is not only in physical comfort – it supports creative, responsive thinking.

AT is vital for dimensional learning. The exercises I described would be useful in and of themselves, but AT's unique feature of consciously harnessing our psychophysical unity exponentially helps the image/imagination work. As I teach, I seek to repeatedly reinforce our whole-self-dimensionality. Stimuli from two-dimensional and small devices are abundant – we abundantly need to celebrate dimensionality.

References
1 *Direction Journal* (2005), vol. 3, no. 4, pp. 9-12.
2 Chudler, E. H. (2013), 'Neuroscience For Kids', http://faculty.washington.edu/chudler/neurok.html [Accessed 14 June, 2013].
3 Madden, C. (2014), *Integrated Alexander Technique Practice for Performing Artists: Onstage Synergy*, Chicago: Intellect.
4 Ericsson, K. A. (2006), 'The influence of experience and deliberate practice on

the development of superior expert performance', in K. Ericsson, N. Charness, P. Feltovish & R. Hoffman (eds.), *The Cambridge Handbook of Expertise and Expert Performance*, New York: Cambridge University Press, pp. 683–704.
5   Madden (2014), pp. 294, 295.
6   Haskell, D. (2012). *The Forest Unseen: A Year's Watch in Nature*. Penguin Books:New York, p. xii.

Bibliography

Chudler, E. H. (2013). 'Neuroscience For Kids', http://faculty.washington.edu/chudler/neurok.html (Accessed 14 June, 2013.)

Ericsson, K. A. (2006). 'The influence of experience and deliberate practice on the development of superior expert performance', in K. Ericsson, N. Charness, P. Feltovish & R. Hoffman (eds.), *The Cambridge Handbook of Expertise and Expert Performance*. Cambridge University Press: New York, pp. 683–704.

Haskell, D. (2012). *The Forest Unseen: A Year's Watch in Nature*. Penguin Books: New York.

Madden, C. (2005). 'Refurbishing images in actors and others', *Direction*, 3: 4, pp. 9–12.

Madden, C. (2014). *Integrated Alexander Technique Practice for Performing Artists: Onstage Synergy*. Intellect: Chicago.

Pearce, J. C. (1992). *Evolution's End: Claiming the Potential of Our Intelligence*. HarperCollins Publishers: New York.

Cathy Madden is Principal Lecturer of the University of Washington School of Drama, teaching for the Professional Actor Training Program. Her book, *Integrative Alexander Technique Practice for Performing Artists: Onstage Synergy* was published by Intellect in 2014. She is Director of the Alexander Technique Training and Performance Studio in Seattle, and a Creative Collaborator for Lucia Neare Theatrical Wonders. She has been a Keynote Speaker for the Alexander Technique Performing Arts Conference in Melbourne, and ATI meetings in Baltimore and Papenburg. She is a former chair of Alexander Technique International and currently chairs the Vision/Mission committee. She has been a Congress Teacher in Sydney, and both Lugano Congresses, and was a Topic Keynote Speaker for the Freiburg Congress. She regularly does workshops in Australia, Japan, and Europe for training schools and performing arts centers. Madden studied with Marjorie Barstow for twenty years and assisted her at workshops in the United States and Europe.

www.cathymadden.net

The Physicality of String Playing

Mechanical Advantage and Musical Freedom

Alun Thomas

The Alexander Technique provides an extraordinarily good basis for skillful string playing. Not only in terms of the mechanical aspects of instrumental skill that we might call 'physical', but also with the psychological and aesthetic aspects of making music: that of gaining *big ears* – learning to play with expanded awareness, flexibly and creatively, alongside other musicians. Unless a musician is planning a career solely as a string instrumentalist playing only one line without any accompaniment (!), sooner or later ensemble playing will be the main skill that he or she needs to hone. I believe that the more this skill develops, the more one enjoys making music.

In my work with musicians at Trinity Laban Conservatoire in London, I have developed games and explorations, clearly in the tradition of classic Alexander Technique (not confusing traditional pedagogy with a lack of modern relevance) though I have added many variations and extemporisations to make them meaningful to musicians at all levels of accomplishment. Most importantly, I have designed them to be usable by other Alexander teachers, who may not be well-versed in the details, small-muscle athleticism and many communicative tasks of the string player.[1]

I call these games 'Platforms for Expression'. They are not guaranteed to transform anyone's playing overnight, but they do offer a firm psychophysical foundation for creative development and a basis for further exploration.

There are two main aspects to these platforms, the *proximate* or *intimate present* – the personal environment and the larger, more encompassing *environmental perspective*. As musicians we need to be able to pay attention to ourselves and others without forgetting our primary purpose – to communicate. It's also important to be aware of general matters of musical style that are always in flux. There are many aspects to this. Firstly, in the intimate present, the choices we make based on our current levels of skill and self-knowledge, and secondly, the wider interactions that we have with audiences, performance spaces and other musicians, all the while making choices about matters of authenticity and composers' intentions.

In the workshop I presented several different games. These included balance games, paired activity games with a balloon, in order to explore: the basics of our relationship with gravity; the connections between the arms and the back; to explore our freedom to change in response to a change in direction from a partner; an exploration of what it might mean to listen with the hands – expressly, the possibility of listening without being explicitly verbal.

I also presented some variations on the well-known theme of mechanical advantage including a game called 'Being Pentapodal'.

I concluded the workshop with an informal, though highly rewarding discussion about the age-old issue of 'holding the violin'. While I have developed my own strategies for supporting the violin, there were others present in the workshop who had developed some very individual and unusual ideas. Tantalizingly, I thought that these might have some real value for further development, and/or could be used as a lateral 'provocation',[2] an indirect side-step, helping to shift the violinist's attention away from 'getting it right'. I have not presented these ideas here as a matter of courtesy,[3] but at the end of this essay I give a very brief overview of my own developments in this area.

Balancing on a drainpipe

As well as being fun, balancing on a drain pipe is an interesting and challenging activity that reveals some of our habits, the typical balance reactions of the body, and how we respond to forces and weights that challenge our effortless balance – for example, lifting a violin up into playing position, as well as coordinating the movements of the bow.

The tendency that many people have when they attempt to balance on a wobbly surface is to engage balance reactions to stop us toppling. Though balance reactions are reasonably well understood by physiologists, it is the *personal* information gleaned from our habitual response, and where we go from there that make such games so valuable. Many who attempted the perilous ride on the drainpipe realised that the same kind of balance responses were present (albeit in less easy to perceive form), when an instrument was lifted into playing position, even when on solid ground.

Many people seem to be frozen into an attitude of 'slipping on a banana skin slowly' when they play, with pelvis thrust forward (if only a very little) – rather than allowing information about size and weight to inspire easy adjustment: proper balance below the violin (and especially under the feet), and so on through the knees, hips and pelvis in the direction from the ground upwards. I would argue that any fine string playing can be seen to issue first from the feet!

In this game we are concerned with opposition from the ground up through the body, which has been described in various ways by some Alexander teachers, but is related to what physicists call the 'ground reaction force'. It resists the undue focus that I think many teachers put on the head–neck–back relationship. New students can more easily relate to the ground, and in learning to become aware of the subtle balance under the feet, many issues of instrumental support, however complex they might seem at first, become much easier to unpack.

The balloon game

The next game that we played explored *listening hands* – a kind of metaphor for musical flexibility. Musicians, and especially string players, tend to over-focus on the hands and arms to the exclusion of the rest of themselves and the wider spatial environment, forgetting that the arms and hands are really ambassadors of the back, and that we are always dynamically engaging with objects, living and inert.

Taking a single balloon between them, each player was invited to become either the leader or the follower as the balloon was moved in random ways. There are few instructions for this game, necessarily, as music (the subject 'proper') is essentially non-verbal, but involves listening, making decisions and reacting – all in an unbroken, hopefully seamless flow of intention, reaction and consciously willed action. The balloon game encourages this aspect of listening and responding to the ever-changing stimuli that a musician meets continuously.

The decision to vary such stimuli and to add new challenges to the paired dance with the balloon, such as walking on the spot or reciting times-tables was at the decision of the leading player. In this way the simplest of games can be extended ad infinitum to explore the possibilities of an ever more sensitive response.

It is always interesting to observe different groups playing this game. It's also instructive to the players to change partners and perceive the different neuromuscular 'signatures' that people display – just as they do when they play an instrument. As a game without any winners it is marvellously useful for students and teachers alike to witness endgaining and learn that by widening the field of attention, the arms become more responsive and one's general sense of space and time subtly expansive.

Being pentapodal

Recognising that our arms are truly messengers of the back, the next game explored our 'laterality', using ideas loosely derived from Raymond Dart's work. We can explore what happens to the elastic, tensegral[4] nature of our trunks and limbs, when a supportive strut (arm or leg) is removed whilst on all fours, but also with the head in contact with a wall or other oppositional surface. This is useful as a gauge for the interdependence of the arms, legs and back, and also provides insight into the essential holistic mechanism of our system. And, as a response to the rather amusing comment that I've heard, 'Musicians, they don't really have legs, do they?', the exercise is an attempt to invite a full acknowledgement that one's legs are to be included in any practice designed to improve manual skill!

For the second stage of the game the platform for support became another person's head, with each person on all fours in crawling position, head to head in delicate opposition. Using the response and unique feel of another person's direction it was interesting to explore being pentapodal[5] (five-pointed) while moving, *head leading* while pushing or being pushed in opposition.

There are many aspects to supporting our weight through the arms in the pentapodal position. Firstly, there is the useful activity of *dorsiflexion*[6] at the wrist. This can be helpful as a passive stretch for string players in particular, encouraging movements that are not habitual and helping to open and extend the range of movement of the joint, (perhaps counter intuitively) providing some help for people with strain and overuse injuries. The removal of the 'struts' – lifting up each limb in turn, and balancing on the arms/legs that remain is always fascinating. Learning that our system can absorb the changes in weight and balance involved, through elastic expansion rather than fixing, is very valuable for string players. This is especially important in establishing a more symmetrical distribution of body weight and in exploring the rotational aspects of the shoulder and their role in integrated playing.

Of particular interest to string players, following on from this use of opposition and change in weight bearing, is the nature of the interaction between bow and string. The quality of sound improves when the back is used as a lever and powerhouse, in the opposition between the two – so my bow and string don't just meet at the point where they touch in space, but also 'the long way round' – though my arm, back and my other arm holding the instrument. Good organisation between legs, back, neck, head and arms is crucial in allowing string players to produce sound at all dynamic levels with surprisingly little sense of effort.

THE BALLOON GAME *EN MASSE*

To conclude the scheduled part of the workshop we played a version of the balloon game, described above, which involved everyone present in a long, connected chain, pairing back to back and receiving a stimulus from the back of the next person, as their arms moved in response to their partner's movement.

In this way a sort of 'Mexican wave' was formed, with the intensity of the kinaesthetic 'signal' ebbing and flowing. The idea was to 'listen' to a kinaesthetic stimulus, and to respond. The response was not necessarily at the same 'volume' – a small movement could prompt either a small or a large one, being transformed by a creative and consciously determined response that would stimulate new responses in turn.

There are really no boundaries for this game, no turnings that are wrong, but it was clear to me as an observer that the creative range varied widely in the group with some 'players' enjoying the possibilities, and others more intimidated by over-focusing on the balloon itself.

SUPPORTING THE VIOLIN – SOME BRIEF REMARKS

The workshop concluded (as I hoped it might) with a long informal discussion about holding the violin. There were some interesting ideas from several people.

My own solutions to the contact of the violin with the body have taken the form of a collar-bone rest that I created nearly 15 years ago. Along with a chinrest I designed and had made that is more appropriately shaped and of a beneficial height, these solutions have provided further stimuli for exploration.

What is always interesting for me as an Alexander teacher and violinist is how my 'hardware' designs have changed over the years, but the principles of good use that underlie them are like a golden braid, which provides a true platform upon which to build both physical support and communication through teaching and music.

References and Notes

1. These may include leading and other rhythmic gestures with the bow, and in chamber music when to be a supportive voice and when to take a more active and primary role.
2. Edward de Bono coined this term to mean any intervention (provocative operation), however bizarre, that can give rise to new ideas and lead to more creative insights – and prove logical in hindsight.
3. Though see Bill Benham's (MSTAT) work on chinrests for very long-necked players: www.adjustablechinrests.co.uk
4. Tensegrity is a current view of the biomechanics of the body which is not built on Newtonian concepts. In this view we are not continuous compression structures but are tension dependent structures, a combination of tension and integrity – the soft tissues holding the skeleton up. The skeleton, in this sense, floats in the soft tissue-muscles and fascia. The integrity of the bodily structure lies in the balance of the tensional parts rather than the struts (bones).
5. Dart, Raymond (1996). *Skill and Poise.* STAT Books. Chapter on 'Postural Aspects of Malocclusion'. Pentapodal is a term meaning five-pointed. It is a primary crawling posture in which the forehead, elbows and knees bear the weight of the body. It is an excellent attitude in which to isolate partial movements of the limbs, jaw and face and to explore these movements as they connect to the total (poised) integrated pattern in the re-education of healthy upright bipedal posture and movement.
6. Dorsiflexion of the wrist refers to the extension of the wrist joint – as the hands are in the attitude of prayer.

Alun Thomas is Alexander Technique Coordinator at Trinity-Laban Conservatoire of Music in Greenwich, London. Alun has taught instrumentalists and singers at the Guildhall School of Music and given workshops widely, including for the orchestra of the Birmingham Royal Ballet. He has worked with actors including at the RSC. As a violinist he has played frequently with many orchestras in the UK, starting as a principal player in the Bournemouth Sinfonietta in the 1990s and including in the Royal Liverpool Philharmonic Orchestra, Northern Sinfonia, RPO and BBC Philharmonic, and as leader of the orchestra of London City Ballet. Most of his more recent work has been as a recitalist and chamber musician with his own group, Chamber Spectrum. He has a love of the solo sonatas by Bach and has given performances of the complete cycle. Alun believes his work is to rediscover the art of violin playing, harking back to an age when patience really was a virtue.

PART FOUR

Anatomy and Movement

Reasons for Thinking About Head and Support

Paul Norikazu Aoki

Reasons for thinking about the head
We need to think about our heads when we move. There are a number of reasons for this. Head position significantly affects the whole body's moment of force, because the head is located at the top of the body. If we place our heads in the correct position, the whole body's moment of force will be reduced. We are then able to reduce our muscular tension for body support.

For movement, thinking about the head helps us manage inertial force. Since the head is located at the top of the body, it experiences inertial force when the rest of the body moves. That means that the head tends to remain in place. If we do not allow for this, the head tilts slightly backwards because of the inertial force. We then need to pull the head to support it. In this case, both the front and back muscles of the neck are used excessively. This also involves the abdominal and back muscles excessively. If we anticipate and manage it (i.e. avoiding backward head tilt by using the longus capitis in advance), the head remains in a correct position. In this case, we do not use the front and back neck muscles as much. We are able to move using fewer muscles and with less muscular tension. We reduce functional limitations.

Another reason to think about the head is that we can then avoid backward head tilt against the pull of the sternocleidomastoid. Because the sternocleidomastoids cross over the spine and connect to the head's posterior side (rather than the head's anterior side), the head tilts backwards if the sternocleidomastoids pulls the head. The original pulling force is caused by the contraction of the abdominal muscles or of the sternocleidomastoids. It may also be caused by lower spine flexion (thoracic and lumbar spine) through thoracic anteversion. If the abdominal muscles contract, the thorax and the sternocleidomastoids (which also connect to the top of the thorax) are also pulled downward. The head is thus pulled through the sternocleidomastoids when the abdominal muscles contract.

We use abdominal muscles for most of our activities. We use them mainly for body support and activities requiring breathing such as speaking, singing, and playing wind instruments. Many people tend to hold their bodies too firmly and use their abdominal muscles excessively. In this case, both the thorax and the head are pulled strongly enough to be moved. Again, if we do not anticipate and prepare for this pull, the head tilts backwards and we require more force to support the head and body. We thus end up adding excess muscular tension. If we anticipate and manage it (i.e. support the head adequately), the head stays at a correct position and we are able to move or speak without adding excess muscular tension.

We can use the longus capitis to support the head (see figure). This muscle is located on the cervical spine's front surface and is attached to the cervical spine and the bottom of the occipital bone. Although this muscle would seem to be an effective antagonist to the pull of the sternocleidomastoids in order to maintain head position, this does not automatically occur. We need to use it voluntarily. What we need to do is support the head by turning our head forward or keeping the head from tilting backwards. This action corresponds to the direction 'head forward'. By giving the direction 'head forward', we thus are able to support the head against both inertial force and the pull of the sternocleidomastoids. We can maintain the head position and angle with minimum muscular tension in the neck.

It is actually difficult for us to detect our habitual responses to the pulling force on the head. Most of us are unaware of it. Most of us thus do not anticipate it and typically respond with excess muscular tension after the fact. Our movement quality will deteriorate and burden the body habitually and unknowingly. However, we can detect these responses and change them to better ones. To respond well, we need to manage head position and angle consciously from before the fact.

These are the reasons for thinking about the head in activities. It is about how we support our head and in turn how we support our body. It is about our attention and intention in supporting the body. Somehow, without knowing these bodily mechanisms and the physics behind them, Alexander understood our typical responses in the head and neck and discovered how to manage them. Directions such as 'think of the head forward and up' or 'think that the head leads the body' are examples. These are the kinesiological reasons why we need to think about the head.

I would like to add an alternative direction for the head. I think of the head in movement as 'move with my head.' I do not think 'the head leads the body' as a universal direction, for all times and actions. 'The head leads' helps when we move in upward directions like standing or jumping up. However, it may present the wrong image when we move our body forward as in walking. The head does not actually lead the body in walking. Although fish and four-footed animals seem to lead with their heads when they move forward, we human beings with our erect two-legged posture are different. The head and body move forward at the same time. It is enough for us to attend to the head and think 'move with the head'. This alternative concept works as a direction for the head in many different activities.

Reasons for thinking about the support

Some Alexander Technique teachers think about support parts – the parts of the body that contact the floor or other surface – while we move, in addition to the head direction. Here I describe how this works in the case of the standing position, where the support part will be the feet (or the bottoms

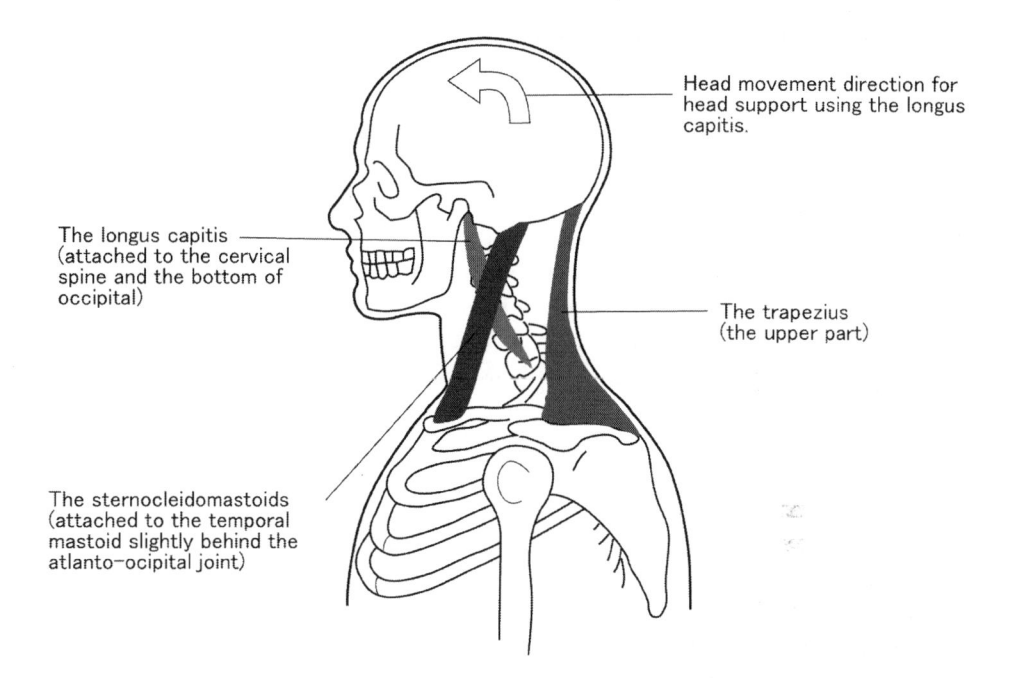

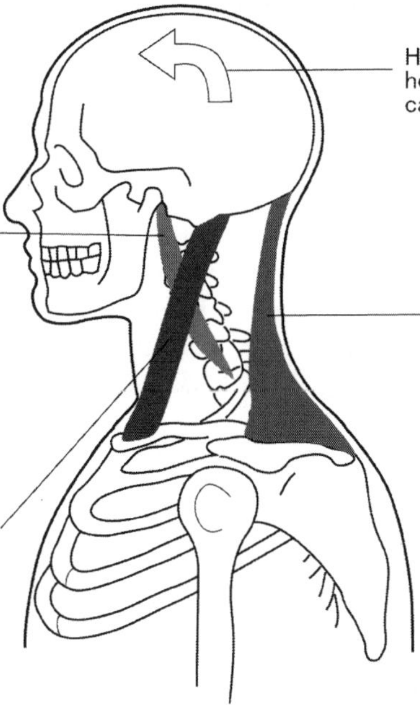
Head movement direction for head support using the longus capitis.
The longus capitis (attached to the cervical spine and the bottom of occipital)
The trapezius (the upper part)
The sternocleidomastoids (attached to the temporal mastoid slightly behind the atlanto-ocipital joint)

of the feet).

Thinking about the feet (or the bottoms of the feet) helps remind us where our body's centre of gravity should be. This works as a reference point for us to align the body's centre of gravity along the direction of a reaction force from the floor. We can thus minimise the moment of force (i.e. tilting less). Since less moment of force requires less muscular tension, we will have more opportunity for the position possible to release muscular tension for body support. We should think of not only the head but also the feet in an advantageous postural alignment.

Thinking about the feet also helps us use friction (the force generated in between floor and the feet) in order to stabilise the body during movement. We need to stabilise some parts of the body when we make movement (i.e. move the other parts of the body). Although most people think about their movement, they are not likely to think about their stabilisation of the body. In this case they will not be aware of friction force and use it fully, and they tend to stabilise the body too firmly with excess muscular tensions. They may use excess muscular tension in areas such as the hip joints, the abdomen, the back, and the neck. By intending to use this 'free' force of friction to stabilise the body, we save muscular contraction, another force source, for body support. As a result, we move with less muscular tension.

As I mentioned previously, many people tend to hold their bodies too firmly, with excess muscular tension in movement. This excess muscular tension is caused through our attempts to support the body. To release it, we need to change the pattern of supporting the body. Thinking about the support part – in standing, the bottoms of the feet – helps with this. In practice, I advise people to think 'place my body weight on my feet' or 'place the whole body on the feet.' We also should think of 'move while the feet stay still' in order to use friction force effectively. I call this 'anchoring' because it resembles the mechanism of an anchor, keeping the ship in one place by staying still at the sea's bottom, because of its heavy weight.

As for the order of these directions, I think about my feet (the support part) first. Then, I think about my head. The feet will be a reference point for the upward direction of the head. We will be surer to know the desirable direction of 'up' with a reference point. Without a reference point, people may put their heads slightly backwards with just the direction 'up'. We need to know at least two points to define a straight line (i.e. certain direction). Thus, it is better for us to have a reference point before we ask our head to do anything.

My interpretation as an advantageous way of supporting the body

We continually support our bodies, except when we lie down. However, we mostly do not think that we are doing it. We will succeed in supporting ourselves even if we do not think about it. In other words, we build and depend on an automatic programme in the brain (mainly the cerebellum) for managing support of the body, so that it can be done without thinking. This automatic programming in the brain is likely to make us support our bodies too firmly. Thus, we have unnecessary muscular tension and functional limitations in activities such as breathing, speech, and movement. In other words, this automatic programme is 'endgaining.' This means that the programme only targets goals such as 'the body is supported' or 'not falling down'. Effectiveness or efficiency in supporting the body is not considered. Even if we ignore its efficiency, we will still support our bodies and accomplish most of our daily activities. However, we end up with increasing bodily burdens and deteriorating movement quality, through use of this automatic programme. It will also be difficult for us to alleviate psychological strain through deteriorated breathing.

My interpretation of the AT is that it is a method of supporting our bodies more advantageously. This interpretation of the AT is not common among Alexander teachers. Some AT teachers may explain what we do as follows: 'We tend to pull our head down and back, adding excess muscular neck tension because of the startle or fight-or-flight response. Inhibiting these responses helps with good coordination and better functioning.' My interpretation is that excess muscular tension is rather caused by habitual way of supporting the body. Habitual muscular tension may be ignited by the startle response or fight-or-flight response, but I believe the pattern of the muscular tension originally comes from people's ways of supporting the body.

More details about the most advantageous way to support the body are explained in my online report 'An advantageous way of using our body' (http://www.alexlesson.com/?p=1409). The hypothetical mechanism of the primary control is also described in my online report 'What is the primary control?' (http://www.alexlesson.com/?p=1902).

Inevitably, we are supporting our bodies most of the time. Why not pay attention to it again? Why not try this new interpretation? It is worth testing.

Illustration courtesy of Paul Norikazu Aoki.

Paul Norikazu Aoki graduated from Body Chance (Jeremy Chance's training school in Japan) and has had a private practice at his own studio, Miwaza Lesson, in Tokyo since 2010. Before teaching the AT, he worked for Toyota Motor Corporation as a market researcher. He changed his career because of his experience of a cure for his chronic headaches through AT. He practises a unique approach to the AT, interpreting it predominantly as a method of voluntary postural control. He has taught AT at a private guitar school and to spa massage practitioners at Lush Japan.

www.alexlesson.com
paulaoki@alexlesson.com

Creativity in Motion

Korina Biggs

This workshop was designed to facilitate an easy, enjoyable way into creative movement and writing. The focus for this session was 'fluidity' as a reality and as a metaphor.

CONCEPTUAL INFLUENCES
The underpinning of the workshop came mainly from the writings of osteopath Bonnie Gintis (2007) on fluidity, as well as my ongoing practice and knowledge of the Alexander Technique. My premise was that as humans we are mainly composed of fluids and subject to fluid forces, and that we also have a conscious ability to direct our movement and attention.

THE PROCESS:
On the floor
We began on the floor with Alexander directions with the particular emphasis on allowing space and volume for our internal fluids to flow. Alexander refers to:

the harmful irritation caused by undue compression, the interference with the natural movement of the blood, of the lymph, and of the fluids contained in the organs of digestion and elimination.[1]

I then invited the group to have a sense of 'puddling out' on the ground and to gradually start moving whilst imagining oil in their joints, and encouraging their movements to come from a sense of allowing flow. I suggested rolling, imagining the floor was tilting, and gradually finding ways of traveling both up and down from the ground – finding ways, through directing ourselves, to fluidly unlock the sticking points. This was based on Gintis' statement that:

> By mimicking the movement of water it's possible to create a greater fluid resonance and experience the qualities one wishes to emulate. If we begin by 'roughing-in' fluid movement, the inherent fluidity comes into conscious resonance, and it is possible to create the conditions within your own system to more freely and creatively express the power of the inherent forces.[2]

Through the space
We then went into walking through the space, noticing if more awareness of external environment and of the other participants altered our sense of internal volume and sense of fluidity. I suggested allowing the floor to flow away under the feet and the air to flow past the whole body, especially the head, and to let the world move rather than getting stuck in the act of seeing.

Water and rocks
Continuing the theme of 'mimicking the movement of water', the next activity involved one person travelling across the room whilst two others gave resistance. Inspired by Gintis:

> If flowing water meets resistance, pressure builds up and its flow momentarily decreases. At a certain point, *depending on the situation*, the flow overcomes the resistance and it regains motion.[3] (My italics).

I demonstrated and explained that for the sake of the exploration, participants were encouraged to resist using 'head strategies' (for example diversionary tactics), and for all three of them not to push using tension or brute force. My aim was for them to explore what it felt like to find one's way forward by accessing a strong fluid sense of self. 'The situation', in this instance, was their conscious ability, through inhibiting and directing, to become malleable and fluid enough to journey forward whilst in contact with a living, moving environment.

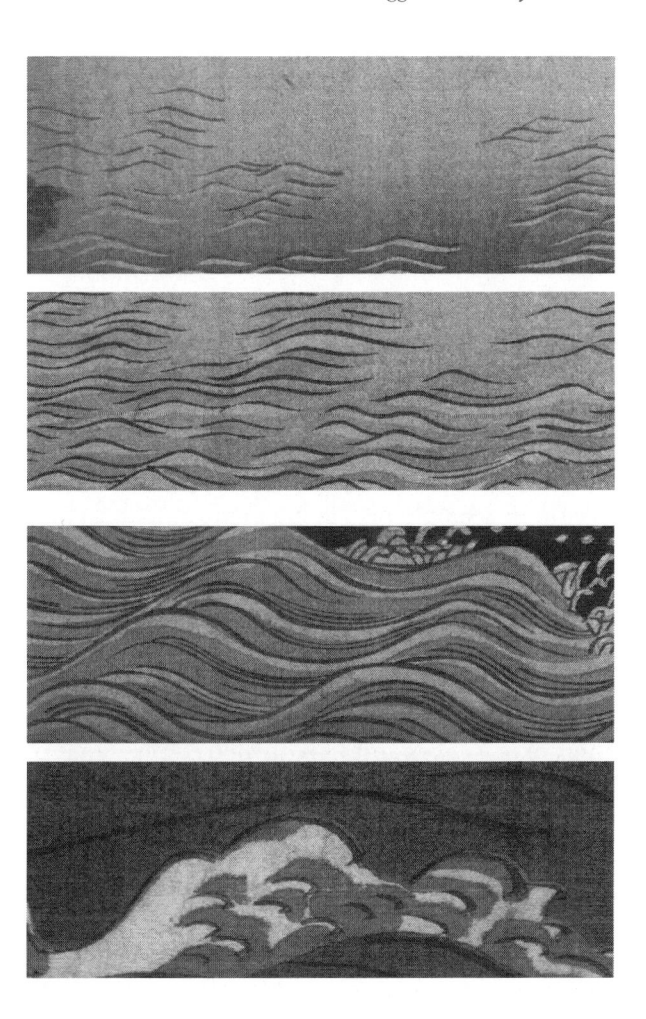

Writing

After this exploration I invited participants to go straight into writing or drawing. I encouraged them 'not to do', as in literally describe their experience, but rather to allow space in order for unexpected words or images to bubble to the surface. I suggested that, if they were using the lined Congress notepads, they didn't have to stay on the lines. The value of this practice is that non-habitual ways of using language often emerge from a self that is resonating from recent moving, relational experience. Images and stories that may have emerged and are continuing to emerge are given more clarity, and a moving experience that was ephemeral has been able to land on paper for future reflection. As Alexander teacher Miranda Tufnell puts it,

> Writing continues the imaginative journey begun in moving. . . giving us a means of dwelling upon and finding significance in what has occurred.[4]

She continues,

> By allowing words and images to spread out in response, we open up an imaginative field that plays upon and around what has occurred, writing as we might write a poem in order to touch deeper currents felt within the moving.[5]

Mover and containers
The next exploration was framed by Gintis' statement: 'Water and its movements cannot be isolated and separate from its environment'[6]; and her description of the 'fluid within the fluid... the nonmaterial quality that differentiates a living fluid in a biological system from an inert liquid in an inanimate container.'[7] One person, with eyes closed most of the time, was invited to move whilst the other two or three people were the 'containers'. Their role was to put hands on in a simple non-doing manner so as to provide a stimulus for the mover. The mover had the choice to move towards or away from the 'container', use it as something to push against, or simply register its presence. Plenty of time was allowed for each person to be the 'mover' and again time given to writing afterwards.

Closing circle
The group spoke about their experiences and were invited to read a bit of their writing. In this way shared and individual experiences were pooled and reflected upon.

In general
Each activity in the workshop was accompanied by music carefully chosen to ease and encourage participation in the explorations. An ongoing reminder from me was to occasionally pause and to wait and listen for the next impulse to move. I expressed it in terms of fluid motion finding form, and then finding the impulse to move again. As Walter Carrington said:

> It's not a matter of just not moving – that can lead to fixing or freezing – it's a matter of really leaving yourself alone and letting everything just happen and take over.[8]

References
1. Alexander, F. M. (1996, 1910). *Man's Supreme Inheritance.* Mouritz : London, p. 13.
2. Gintis, B. (2007). *Engaging the Movement of Life.* North Atlantic Books: California, p. 83.
3. Ibid, p. 82.
4. Tufnell, M. (2004). *A Widening Field.* Dance Books Ltd: UK, p. 63.
5. Ibid p. 63.
6. Gintis, op. cit., p. 81.
7. Ibid p. 106.

8   Carrington, W. (1994). *Thinking Aloud.* Mornum Time Press: California, p. 134.

Korina Biggs has been working as an Alexander teacher for fourteen years, and now also works as a somatic movement facilitator, having qualified with an MA in Dance and Somatic Well-being. She is part of the STAT 'Performing Self' team delivering CPD for Alexander teachers and has worked as a visiting tutor in drama colleges including The Lir, Dublin, and Rose Brufords and ALRA in London. She is a regular teacher for the Hampshire County Youth Orchestra. A founder member of Frantic Assembly physical theatre company, she remains fascinated by the application of the Alexander Technique to performance. She regularly enjoys various movement practices, is one of the founders of the collective 'Dancers In Landscape' and is a member of The Knowing Body Network. She belongs to the STAT Research Group and has recently had her research for her MA, which drew upon the Alexander Technique, published in the *Journal of Dance and Somatic Practices.*

Up off Your Ankles!

Joan Frost

Over the course of my thirty–plus years of teaching the Alexander Technique, I have observed time and again that students' lower legs seem dense and heavy unless they are specifically included in one's thinking and giving of directions. I used to describe the direction of 'knees forward and away' as forward and away from the hip-joints, and the 'away' as also meaning an absence of contracting the knees towards each other in sitting and in going from sitting to standing (and vice-versa). I now also include the lower legs in the wish of knees forward – a flow of direction up from the ankles in the direction of the knees. So, the direction of flow for the upper leg is from the hip joints toward the knees through one's three-dimensional upper leg, and the direction of flow for the lower leg is up from the ankles toward the knees through one's three-dimensional lower leg. These two flow directions, as they each approach the knee, arc out in the direction in which the knee would bend and continue to flow, approaching each other but never meeting (see drawings).

Working with a student on the table, if I go to put my hands under an outstretched lower leg and I find it dense and heavy, I ask my student to include her lower legs in her directions, as above. When I go to lift her leg to semi-supine, I wish the process to be a partnership where we are both participating actively with our thinking, rendering her leg almost weightless.

Fig. 1

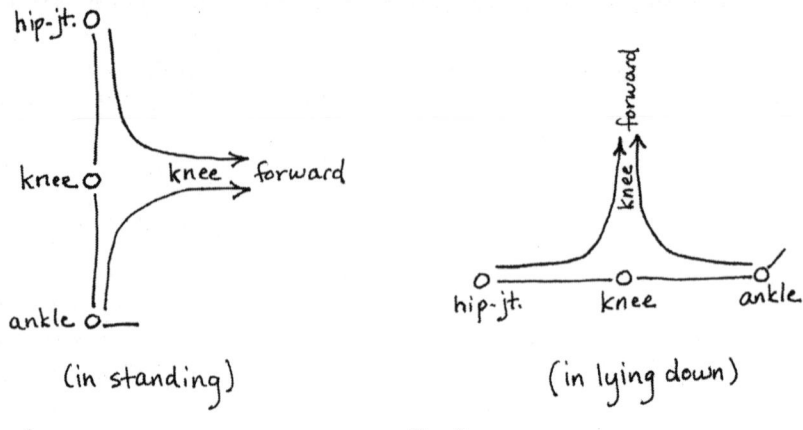

Fig. 2

In the Congress workshop, I had each participant lie on the floor and move his or her legs one at a time from outstretched to bent in semi-supine and then back down again. We practised having the direction wishes underpin the actual movement of our legs. In going from knee bent in semi-supine to leg outstretched, the knee-forward wish gets more challenging the straighter the leg gets. It's as the leg straightens that the knee forward wish is especially important. Similarly in walking, as I'll explain later in this paper.

I have found that, in unloading weight off a foot and in moving that foot, if there is a deficit in lower leg direction (upward flow from ankle towards knee), it's not uncommon for the top of the foot to contract, pulling the toes up. In the workshop, we went for a walk and returned to standing in front of our chairs in order to come to sitting. I was interested particularly in the last few steps. I often find that when one's steps are smaller, or turning is involved (turning to end up at the front of the chair), the coordination of knee forward, heel off the floor, toes last to leave and first to arrive in the next step of turning or adjusting, isn't clean. We explored this move in the class and took our time to find out what was actually happening with our foot/ankle coordination. (Were our ankles tightening and retracting our feet?) I had the class break into pairs so partners could observe each other and give feedback.

Many years ago, I was doing an exchange with a colleague, Kim Jessor, in the course of which she put both her hands around my lower leg, just below the belly of my calf. We both thought up repeatedly, and in a moment my leg spontaneously sprung up. It *wanted* to go. We switched roles and were able to repeat the experiment. Since that day, I have been doing that with my students. I place my hands around my student's lower leg, while they are sitting, right below the belly of the calf muscle and renew an 'up' wish. I ask my student to do the same. I do this hands-on move either from lunging alongside my student or from squatting in front of the leg I'm working on. If I begin to move my hands upward and my student's leg doesn't come with me, I stop moving my hands and ask them to renew their thinking. I'm looking for a kind of partnership where there's almost no physical effort on either of our parts. The work is mental.

In the Congress workshop, we practised the above with each other. First, we did a warm-up for lunging and squatting. It's important that the teacher finds a position that he can stay in for a bit of time without strain while his hands are on the student's lower leg and both parties are directing. I'm a big fan of props, and if lunging or squatting is difficult I recommend having a low stool or chair available for sitting on in front of the student's leg. Also, before the class worked on each other, I led them through a hands-on warm-up designed to undo any tendency to 'do'. The temptation on the teacher's part to endgain, to tighten to lift the student's leg, is huge. There is also the temptation to be a 'good student', which is often expressed in tightening the thigh muscles and/or the area behind the knee of the leg being worked on. If the leg is too light when I go to lift it, or the student is ahead of me, I inform her that she can do less. To check for tightness behind the knee, once I have the leg up with the foot clearing the floor, I move the leg forward a little bit, then back again (unbending the knee and bending it again). I demonstrated this in the workshop, then saw, as the participants were working on each other, that many were taking the leg all the way to straight. I don't recommend that. Just a move forward and back of up to six inches is sufficient.

We ended by working with walking. In walking, as the knee unbends in preparation to receive weight, the knee-forward (up off the ankle) wish is especially important. When the knee forward wish is functioning well in that cycle of the walking step, legs can feel as if they are like little bicycle wheels going around and around. I like to think of the head/torso as the carriage (directing up) and the legs as the wheels. Marjorie Barstow used to say: 'Be nice to the sidewalk.' Walking this way, the footfall is easier and one could imagine the supporting surface would be happier. Also, with lower leg direction, feet interact with the floor, but, as I mentioned above, they don't need to leave the floor by lifting the toes up. The class walked *without* including lower leg direction, then *with*, observing the effects of each through the entire system.

I like to say that ankles are often a forgotten joint. We can sense the contact of our feet with the floor, but above the soles of our feet, the next part of our body is the farthest from our brains and seems not to be as available to our consciousness unless we give some awareness to it. This workshop was designed to enlighten and enliven the ankle and lower leg part of our anatomy in the service of more freedom and availability of movement and better overall coordination.

Joan Frost has been teaching the Alexander Technique for the past 32 years, having been certified at the American Center for the Alexander Technique (ACAT) in New York City in 1983. She has been training teachers at ACAT since 1984 and was Director of Teacher Certification from 2001-2008. Joan has also been on the faculties of the Juilliard School, the New School, and has taught at Sarah Lawrence College. In addition to her classes at ACAT, Joan teaches at Spine Options, a medical facility in White Plains, New York, and has a private practice in Manhattan, in Connecticut and in Rockland County, New York.

Two Practices for Sensory Integration and the Discovery of Upward Direction

Clare Maxwell

I am delighted to be able to share here two practices that I taught in a workshop at the Congress.

The material introduced here can be very useful in teaching groups to develop sensory literacy outside frameworks of right and wrong. There is no movement form being learned and thus no standard to measure oneself by. These explorations are a wonderful preparation for constructively using movement forms such as sitting and standing from a chair, monkey, the Dart Procedures, or *any* movement form. By being willing to reconsider the meaning of terms like neck, head, torso, legs, and arms, and to investigate those meanings through somatic practices, I think we bring our Alexandrian 'thinking' into the present moment. We are then not teaching anatomy as a fixed set of truths, but as an inquiry.

This material emerged in response to my eight-year investigation of the Dart Procedures with Joan and Alex Murray and Marie Stroud. 'An Anatomist's Tribute to F. M. Alexander' from *Skill and Poise*[1] is particularly important to understand if you want to follow Dart's reasoning. I kept trying, and failing. Finally, being a dancer by trade, I just got down on the floor and began to explore the sequence of cranial and cervical nerves, one at a time, in my own body.

Raymond Dart proposes a physiological basis for the concept of unity of the self by emphasising the unity of our central nervous system (CNS) with skin, bone, and muscle cells as they develop in the womb. According to Dart, all four kinds of tissue arise from a singular segment of cells called a *somite*, of which we have 43 in total. For example, the cells that will eventually form the skull, brain, muscles, and nerves of the head all arise from the same group of 8 cranial somites.[2]

The CNS is comprised of the following:

1. The 12 cranial nerves (I have devised a practice for this, but it is too long to include here. I will send you a written or recorded version if requested.)[3]
2. The 31 pairs of spinal nerves that enervate the surface of our skin (*dermatomes*), as well as the muscles and tissues underneath the skin, with two significant exceptions (the face, supplied by the fifth cranial, or trigeminal nerve, and the skin of the ear canal, supplied by the 10th cranial, or vagus nerve).

In this report, I will describe ways to explore the dermatomes through mapping the skin, rather than the bones. Could the skin be a better method of mapping the self than bone? How would 'direction sending' be expressed at the level of skin? What are head, neck, arms, torso, and legs, when mapped at the level of skin?

ONE: EXPLORING THE DERMATOMES, SIMPLE FORM
Preparing
You are going to give your skin a sensory 'bath,' beginning at the soles of your feet, and ending at your head. It helps to have a nice, clean floor and something soft, like a pillow, sweater, or blanket that will feel pleasant to touch.

The tendency will be to use your hands to touch the rest of your body. That's perfectly fine, but I've noticed that movement and sensation from hands tends to override information from other parts of the body. A majority of our sensory and motor maps are dedicated to our hands. I want you to expand the experience of yourself outside this understandable sensory preference.

I suggest that you use different parts of yourself, such as a foot or an elbow *as if they were a hand* to explore surfaces, textures, temperature, and the environment, as well as sensations from inside your own body.

Practice 1
   Feet: Feel the bottoms, sides, and tops of your feet, all the nooks and crannies with your feet or hands. Feel the skin between your toes. Feel the skin that wraps around your ankle and heel. Where does the skin of your foot end and the skin of your lower leg begin?
   Legs: Feel the skin of the lower leg all around the bones, the skin covering your knee and kneecap, thigh, and upper leg. Use your foot and leg like hands to explore the floor around you. Where does the skin of your leg end and your torso begin?
   Torso: Feel the skin all around your groin, pelvis, belly, ribs, shoulder

blades, collarbones, and neck. Use the blanket, pillow, or your hands to feel your lumbar area where it arches off the floor. Explore bony and hard parts and soft and yielding parts. Where does the skin of torso end and the skin of arms begin?

Arms: Explore the folds of skin in your armpit. Use your upper arms as if they were hands to explore your own torso or the floor. Explore the creases of skin around your shoulder, upper arm, lower arm, wrist, hand, and fingers, folds of skin between fingers, thumb and palm. Where does the skin of the arms end and the skin of the torso begin?

Neck and head: Wrap your arms and hands around your neck to feel the contours of skin that pass over collarbones, throat, and neck. Rest your head and neck into the pillow or blanket to feel the contours of neck and head at the front, sides, and back. Feel all the contours of your face: lips, cheeks, eye sockets and eyelids, ears and ear canals, the inside of your nose. Where does the skin of neck end and the skin of head begin? Use your head like a hand to explore the surface of the floor.

End in a well-supported supine position and rest. How much of your internal movement (breathing, heartbeat, digestion) can be felt at the level of skin?

Two: Exploring the dermatomes, detailed mapping

Refer to a dermatome map to help you follow this exploration. For good maps of the dermatomes see Frank Netter's *Atlas of Human Anatomy*[4] or contact me and I'll be happy to send you my collection. Be aware that dermatomes vary significantly from person to person.[5] Many of the maps available conflict with one another.[6] Dermatome mapping is not a precise science and is constantly being revised!

I usually begin at the sacral end, from a sitting position with legs outstretched. I find going from bottom to top most conducive to getting people up off the floor at the end of the practice.

Use your hands to trace each dermatome pathway from one side of the body up to the spine, then down the other side of the body to its opposite end point, so that you experience left and right sides of the body as a single sensory unit. The connection of the dermatome to its section of the spine, be it a primary or secondary curve, is interesting to explore as well.

Practice 2

Sacral dermatomes (primary curve):

S1: Starts at the outside edge of the foot and little toe, goes behind the ankle bone and the outside of the back of the leg, over the outside of the sit bone and ends at the top of the sacrum.

S2: Goes from the big toe pad up under the arch of the foot, under the ankle bone, up the inside of the back of the leg, covers inside of the sit bone and the base of the sacrum, including the pelvic floor and sexual organs (you can suggest that people just sense the contact of their clothing on those parts!).

S3, 4, 5: These three dermatomes are all for the anus, each one a closer concentric ring around the opening from which waste is excreted.

Experiment with brushing or pushing the little toe side, or alternately the big toe pad, into the floor and observe how it sends your pelvis and tailbone away from the foot, or reach the foot away from pelvis.

Lumbar dermatomes (secondary curve):

L1: Goes over the very top of the pelvic rim, flows around in a spiral to the skin of the groin and inner, upper thigh.

L2: Goes over the pelvis, wrapping around to the middle inner thigh.

L3: Goes from the middle of the lumbar spine, wraps across the pelvis and greater trochanter, around the front of the leg to the inner knee and inner calf.

L4: Goes from the lower lumbar spine across the side of the pelvis and upper thigh, wraps around the kneecap and the top of the lower leg and foot, wraps underneath the big toe, and stops at the big toe pad.

L5: Goes from the base of the lumber spine across the bottom of the pelvis, down the side of the leg, around the lower leg, top of the foot and the middle three toes, under the foot, and wraps around the heel, covering the insertion of the achilles tendon into the calf muscle.

Explore flexing and releasing the heel and foot in relation to the lower leg. How does the action of releasing the heel bone follow in sequence through the leg, allowing it to flex on the torso? Does the lumbar spine move, during this flexing and releasing process? Does your lower back tighten when you flex? It doesn't have to.

Thoracic dermatomes (primary curve):

T12 – 1: Explore this section as a whole, following the flow of the skin from the thoracic spine down the ribs to the soft belly in front, all the way down to the groin, and all the way up the side of the body and inner arm to the little finger side of the wrist.

Rolling from side to front to other side, rest on the side of the arm and explore the relationship of inner arm and wrist to brush, reach, push, or pull to bring about the rolling motion.

Cervical dermatomes (secondary curve):

C8: Covers the pinky finger, ring finger, top and palm of hand related to those fingers, outside/underside of the arm and elbow, armpit, and middle of shoulder blade.

What happens when you lead with the little finger and outside of the lower arm as a weight-bearing surface? Explore brushing, pushing, and reaching motions starting from the little finger side of your arm.

C7: Covers the middle finger, index finger, and top and palm of the hand related to those two fingers; the rest of the back surface of arm and elbow, and the top edge of the shoulder blade.

    Explore using these two fingers to lead brushing, reaching, and pushing motions. How is it different from C8? What kind of motion sequences through to your shoulder blade? What kind of rotation occurs in your lower arm? Play with alternating between C8 and C7.

C6: Covers the thumb, webbing of thumb and palm, top of arm and very top of shoulder blade in the back.

    What is it like to lead from your thumb as you brush, push, reach, and grasp?

C5: Covers the inside of the wrist closest to the thumb, front/top of arm all the way up to the skin covering the front body and the collarbone where it meets the sternum.

C4, 3, and 2: All wrap around the neck from front to back above the collarbone, covering the voice box and the skin under the jaw, the very back of the jaw, all the way up the back of the neck, including the mastoid process of your skull and most of your ear, the back of the skull and occipital bone.

(C1: *has no sensory function* – controls only motor function of the sub-occipital muscles, which have no sensory input from outside the self.)

10th Cranial Nerve/Vagus: Enervates the skin of the inner ear and the skin covering the little cartilage flap that covers the opening of your ear.

5th Cranial Nerve/Trigeminal: Has three large branches. The third branch enervates the skin of your jaw and lower lip, and the strip of skin up the side of your cheek to high up on the parietal bone of your skull. The second branch enervates the skin of your upper lip, cheeks and nostrils, lower eyelid, and up the side of your skull to the temporal bone. The first branch enervates the top of your nose, the upper eyelid, and approximately two thirds of the front and top of your skull.

    Explore the skin of each separate branch – one for the jaw, one for the nose, and one for the eyes. Let your face lead and your body follow, as you begin to move up off the floor, gathering your limbs underneath your body and sitting, then standing, then walking.

The following ideas, observations, and questions have arisen as a result of these practices: Contact occurs at the level of skin, the boundary between self and other. The skin has many more sensory receptors than bone.[7] It conveys sensation from inside and outside the body to the brain. Is that why students move so much more easily under my hands after these practices?

- Upward direction emerges in response to contact with the ground, as well as from contact with the teacher. Contact, or 'yielding' is considered by somatic therapists to be the basis of all further developmental

movement patterns, as well as the first experience of communication between self and other.[8]
- Sometimes students do not move very much during this practice, but a sense of 'up' always emerges. Students report feeling supported, easy, and energised.
- Upward direction cannot be imposed on a person. I try to create a situation in which students realise that what is happening comes from inside them *in response to*, not *from* the teacher. If direction emerges, it is a sign not that we are 'right' but that the conditions are right at that moment, and that support has been perceived and is being used to carry out the wishes of the student.

Please email me if you have questions and comments, or would like to find out more about these practices.

References
1. Dart, Raymond (1996, 1970). *Skill and Poise*. STAT Books: London.
2. Dart, 'An Anatomists Tribute to F. M. Alexander', *Skill and Poise*, pp. 41, 47, 48.
3. Dart, 'An Anatomists Tribute to F. M. Alexander', *Skill and Poise*, pp. 36-37.
4. Netter, Frank (2011, 1989), *Atlas of Human Anatomy* 5th Ed., Saunders Elsevier: Philadelphia, plates 158, 159; upper limb details plates 401, 402.
5. Clin Anat. 2008 Jul; 21(5): 363-73. doi: 10.1002/ca.20636. An evidence-based approach to human dermatomes. Lee MW1, McPhee RW, Stringer MD. (found on Pubmed: http://www.ncbi.nlm.nih.gov/pubmed/18470936).
6. *J Orthop Sports Phys Ther.* 2011 Jun; 41(6): 427-34. doi: 10.2519/jospt.2011.3506. Epub 2011 May 31. Conflicting dermatome maps: educational and clinical implications. (http://www.ncbi.nlm.nih.gov/pubmed/21628826).
7. Purves D, Augustine GJ, Fitzpatrick D, et al., eds. *Neuroscience*. 2nd edition (2001). Sinauer Associates: Sunderland, MA. (http://www.ncbi.nlm.nih.gov/books/NBK11162/).
8. Frank, Ruella (2001). *Body of Awareness: A Somatic and Developmental Approach to Psychotherapy*. Gestalt Press: Cambridge, M. A.

Clare Maxwell first encountered the Alexander Technique in 1986. It changed the course of her life and career as a choreographer and dancer, and became the one thing that she was interested in teaching to others. She received her certificate to teach in 2000 from ACAT/NYC, and has completed further certification in The Art of Breathing with Jessica Wolf. Clare is inspired by many of her dance influences, especially the Dart Procedures as taught to her by Marie Stroud, Joan Murray, and Alex Murray. Clare has a private practice in New York City and is on the faculty of The William Esper Acting Studio and the dance organisation Movement Research. She has presented her work in the USA at the yearly AmSAT conferences, the Freedom to Act Conference in NYC, and in Russia at the LinkVostok Festival. Clare is passionate about improving the training processes of performing artists, therapists, and somatic practitioners.

claremax@mindspring.com

Towards the Development of a Conceptual View of the Body Construct as Aliveness in Movement

Zadok Ruben

INTRODUCTION[1]
'There really isn't a primary control as such. It becomes a something in the sphere of relativity,' Alexander wrote to Frank Pierce Jones in December 1945.[2] Alexander's statement could appear to contradict the main pillar of his life's work, as described in his four books. In my view, however, the statement represents Alexander's most important concept, a foundation of the Technique.

When I read Alexander's statement, I experienced a great relief. I could stop wrestling with questions about the nature of the 'primary control'. 'It becomes a something in the sphere of relativity' offered me a base towards understanding the nature of the body as a holistic construct; a construct where aliveness manifests in movement. Over the past seven years I have developed this view – that the primary control is about aliveness manifested in movement.

PERSONAL BACKGROUND
By the time I decided to train as an Alexander teacher, I had twenty-five years as a veterinary anatomical pathologist and a general toxicologist, investigating the harmful and beneficial effects of putative pharmaceuticals and other medications for human diseases. Investigating biological form-structure-function associated with health or dysfunction was the building block of my professional work. As for my own body, from age nine through my twenties, I had sustained several lower back/thigh injuries. Their effects built up with time and by about age fifty, it was clear that I was on my way to serious limitations in my movement. Despite the pain and the diagnosed spinal structural effects, I chose not to undergo spinal surgery. Instead, I pursued various mind-body methods, including the Alexander Technique. The outcome of these methods was a remarkable reclaim of my constructive proprioceptive-kinaesthetic behaviour – my self in use. (I prefer this phrase, self in use, to 'use of the self', based on my understanding of *The Universal Constant in Living*[3]). My reasoning behind this is that I see my 'self' as a subject that is active and in *use*, versus *using* my 'self' as an object.

While learning 'the Work', something was changing in my experience

– in the way I experienced being alive. As a scientist, it was important for me to seek clarity – to try to bridge the science I knew with what I felt was happening in me. After I graduated, my trainer, Martha Hansen-Fertman, offered me the opportunity to teach anatomy in her course, which I welcomed. How could I select and interpret from the vast amount of anatomical (and physiological/pathological) information so it was beneficial to the trainees? Martha advised me: 'Don't teach anatomy; teach *a conceptual understanding of anatomy*' – instead of teaching detailed body anatomy and nomenclature, the emphasis should be on the body as an integrated and living mechanism. This advice has guided me through the subsequent years of inquiry and teaching.[4] In the process, I have become an observer-witness of the body and its aliveness in movement. Additionally, my perception of nature has shifted, towards one that sees the relationship between aliveness and movement as holistically interrelated. Concurrently, the scientist in me has inquired whether my new observations were in line with the principles of Mr Alexander's writings.

PHYSICAL BACKGROUND AND TENSEGRITY

Three basic characteristics of mass (matter) are form, volume, and being composed of particles. The particles relate to one another during movement. Both mass form and volume are a manifestation of the particles' inter-relatedness at movement.

In the 1960s W. Buckminster Fuller proposed the term *Tensegrity* (tension integration or tensile integrity).[5, 6] He observed that for stability and shape, a body (mass) must have its firm, compressed particles ('building blocks')

Fig. 1. *Skwish*, an example of a tensegric construct. *Left*: volume and form are attained by the firm wooden rods that are separated from each other, while continuous connectivity is provided by the pliable elastic strings. Rolling the skwish will not alter its form or volume. Upon applying pressure, its form-volume will change (e.g., height will reduce). As long as the tensile-elasticity of the strings is retained, the form-volume will re-establish upon removal of the pressuring force. *Middle*: Collapse of the form and volume reduction is a result of reduction in tensile-elasticity of the pliable elastic strings.
Right: Re-establishing the volume and form by mechanical lifting.

Fig. 2. A geodesic dome – The Cinerama Dome Theatre on Sunset Boulevard (right in the left photograph) representing tensegric architecture principle as compared to the high rise 'vertical compression' building to its left, or The Empire State Building and its neighbour in construction in the right photograph [Internet public domain photos: www.waterandpower.org (left) and Wikipedia (right)].

separated from each other, while concurrently being continuously connected by tensile forces. This state of organisation he termed '*discontinuous compression–continuous tension*'. The *skwish* (fig. 1) is an example. The rods (struts) are an example of discontinuous compressed-firm parts, whereas the tensile strings (cables) represent continuous flexible elements. A classical example of an architectural tensegric construct is the geodesic dome (fig. 2a). Stability is achieved through the dynamic reciprocal relationship of its structural elements, which is different from that of a high-rise building (fig. 2b), where stability is based on fixed stacked layers, one on top of the other. The structural relatedness of the latter in Fuller's terminology is '*vertical compression*'. The sculptor Kenneth Snelsen, working with Fuller's concept, designed sculptures of dynamic tensegrity.[7]

TENSEGRITY, HUMAN BIO-STRUCTURAL CONSTRUCT AND MECHANOBIOLOGY

Fuller's principle of tensegrity can be well applied to the body construct of vertebrates including humans. The isolated bones (the 'firm struts') are continuously connected into an organic unity through tensile-softer structures such as muscles, tendons, ligaments, membranes and other fascia-tissues. The orthopaedic surgeon Dr Stephen Levin proposed the term bio-tensegrity.[8] Practitioners of Rolfing, massage and other somatic therapy methods have increasingly recognised the importance of the fascia in continually connecting the isolated bones into an organised musculoskeletal system (more accurately 'fascio-musculoskeletal' system).[9, 10, 11]

The concept of tensegrity has also been applied to the Alexander Technique.[12, 13] In my presentations, I devote a significant amount of time to tensegrity and the role of the fascia in the construct of the body.[4]

Biologists' interest in cellular form-structure-function relationships goes back to the late 19th century. The emphasis has been on chemical, biochemical and genetic processes. By the early 20th century, the Scottish zoologist Sir D'Arcy Wentworth Thompson offered fundamental observations on cell particles' movement and form during cell division.[14] Recently, advances have been made on the effect of physical stimuli on cellular form, structure, and function. This opened a new field of scientific inquiry known as mechanobiology or mechanotransduction. Dr Donald Ingber (pathologist and cell biologist at Harvard Medical School) demonstrated that the nature of cellular form-structure-function dynamics is consistent with Fuller's *tensegrity/ discontinuous compression-continuous tension*, and proposed his findings as the 'architecture of life'.[15] Further he proposed that advancements in mechanotransduction may lead to better understanding of processes associated with ostensibly unrelated diseases, and development of therapeutic remedies.[16] Importantly and congruent with the holistic nature of the Alexander Technique, Ingber has advocated a view of biology as an indivisible organisation and network.[17]

HOLISTIC-RELATIONAL BODY-CONSTRUCT, PROPRIOCEPTIVE-KINAESTHETIC BEHAVIOUR AND THE ALEXANDER TECHNIQUE

Around 2008, at the end of my teacher training, I experienced a distinct 'openness and release' of restrictions related to my lower back and thigh injuries. While studying Fuller's path and observations, and reflecting on what I was experiencing, I conceived the human body as a dynamic whole made of particles (parts) that are connected as an integrated constellation. Together with the mind, this constellation is congruent with aliveness that is manifested in movement. Further, it maintains a dynamic and stable relationship with its environment. Within this concept,[4] movement and dynamic stability are a composition of four affinities that occur concurrently ('interactively play') towards an organised dimension:

- Expansion (the particles disperse away from each other).
- Compaction (the particles move toward each other).
- Flexibility (achieving a flexible-elastic state).
- Tonicity (suitable tone for the desired function).

The inter-relatedness between the four affinities is mutual and perpetual – a dynamic process akin to 'an ongoing checks and equilibration'.

Such a simultaneous coordinative integration applies to all body parts regardless of their size and to the whole human body. It can be understood that the body parts are organised as a replica of living form–units, functioning in a relational–multidirectional suspensory vectorial equilibration with each other (*vector* denotes direction in space combined with force; *equilibration* refers to a continuous dynamic state where zero equilibrium does not 'exist'). By this, the proprioceptive-kinaesthetic use of the body (self in use) is integrated as a dynamic indivisible organism. A response to a stimulus in one part affects others and the whole. Further, this dynamic-tensegric suspensory equilibration among the body parts is essential to stability, movement, vigour, vitality, and an ongoing bipedal upright orientation with gravity. This dynamic holistic-relational view of the human body is in contrast to the common view of a 'firm-strong' erect body. This view of holding a vertical linear postural balance against gravity is more analogous to the high rise architectural model of *vertical compression*.

Upon reflecting on my conception further, I was delighted to find biological support from what Ingber had put forth based on cell research.

> ...the cell does not respond to mechanical stress like a 'balloon filled with molasses or jello'. Instead, the viscoelastic behavior of living cells results from collective mechanical interactions within the tense molecular cytoskeleton.
>
> Thus, forces that are applied to the entire organism (e.g., due to gravity or movement) or to individual tissues would be distributed to individual cells via their adhesions to the extracellular matrix support scaffolds.[17]

THE HEAD–NECK COMPLEX: AN EXAMPLE OF A MULTIDIRECTIONAL SUSPENSORY CONSTRUCT

For the following discussion I suggest viewing the head–neck complex as being divided at the base of the skull: above the bony cranium and its internal content (brain and associated tissues) and below, the neck–face complex. This partition is congruent with what Patrick Macdonald realised during the first teachers' training course – that the atlanto-occipital (AO) joint is pivotal to the head–neck relationship and balancing the head. Marjory Barlow emphasised the importance of Macdonald's anatomical clarification.[18] Macdonald writes,

> Dr Andrew Murdoch, a keen pupil and follower of Alexander, was at considerable pains to find anatomical terms of the fundamental truths of Alexander's discovery of a primary control of bodily behaviour. In conducting investigations at the Edinburgh School of Medicine, he noticed that there was a set of small muscles at the atlanto-occipital joint (where the neck meets the skull), and that no function had yet been ascribed by medical science.[19]

The Universal Constant in Living addresses Dr Murdoch's inquiry in more details:[20] the 'set of small muscles' are now well known as the sub-occipital

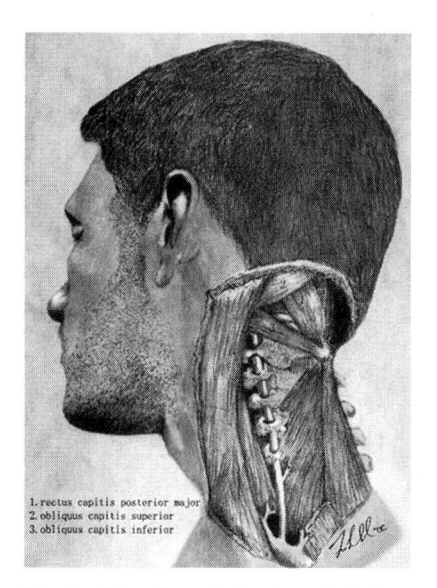

Fig. 3. The three left sub-occipital muscles connecting the skull to the atlas (1st cervical vertebra). (Internet public domain images: www.en.wikipedia.com).

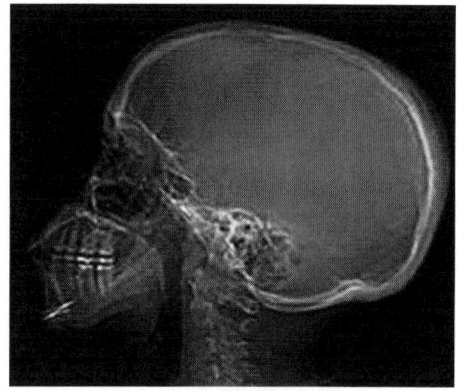

Fig. 4. Lateral x-radiograph view of the head and neck. The AO joint and the base of the skull are in a continuous up-frontward slant. The degree of the slant is somewhat exaggerated because the face is pointing up. (Internet public domain images: www.en.wikipedia.com).

muscles, also termed 'the sub-occipital triangle' (fig. 3). Since Macdonald's clarification, the AO joint and the sub-occipital muscles have become the focal anatomical 'staple' in the Alexander Technique community for pointing to the head–neck relationship.

However, this focus on the AO joint and the sub-occipital muscles did not make sense to me. I noticed through anatomical illustrations (fig. 4), that the base of the skull is slanted up toward the forehead (compared to the feet that spread parallel to the floor), that the AO joint itself is similarly slanted and that the center of gravity area at the base of the skull (roof of the nasopharynx) is virtually devoid of tissue support connecting with underlying organs. All this indicated to me that there is too much burden on the AO zone if it is the focal area for a dynamic suspensory head–neck relationship. Further observations led me to the hyoid (lingual) bone (fig. 5).

The hyoid bone is unique among other bones in the body. Its articulation with other bones is not via regular joints.[21] It is in a suspensory multidirectional connectivity: above, with the root of the tongue, mandible, chin, and skull (at two sites) and below, with the laryngeal cartilages, sternum, and shoulder blades. In addition, via additional intermediary tissue it reaches to

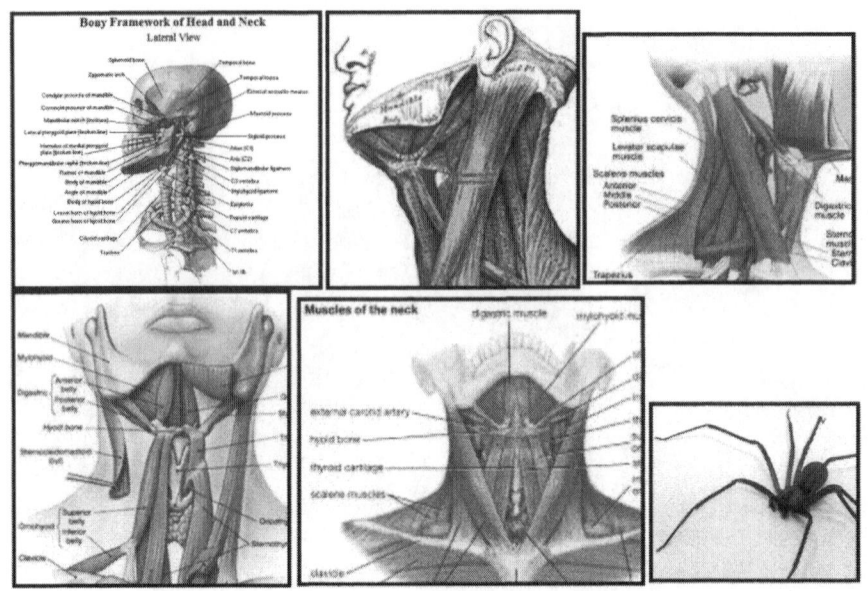

Fig. 5. Composite of anatomical illustrations to demonstrate the suspensory multidirectional connectivity of the hyoid bone and its analogy to a spider (Internet public domain images from top clockwise: www.googleimages.com, www.en.wikipedia.com, www.snipview.com, www.pinterest.com, www.britannca.com, www.wildmaryland.blogpost.com).

the soft palate, pharynx, and the base of the skull and AO joint area. Using the image of a spider as an analogy (fig. 5), the hyoid bone is the spider's body, and the multidirectional myofascial connections are the spider's legs. The spider's body manifests a suspensory organisation that allows elevation, lowering, forward, backward, right and left mobility. The crucial role of the hyoid bone–AO–cervical spine complex in the multidirectional suspensory construct compatible with 'neck free, head forward and up' became apparent.

By further studying the head–neck complex as a total construct, I noticed that the front face area is internally connected to the cervical spine–AO–hyoid bone complex via bony structures. Internal tissue connectivity among these structures is rather tight and inflexible. Yet, by experimenting on myself, I noticed that during intentional eye movements (while the rest of the face is 'stationary'), a reciprocal movement response occurs at the cervical spine–AO–hyoid bone complex. This movement was accompanied with a sense of openness that flowed to the entire internal head–neck complex and the whole body and upon my breathing. Following this experience, I could not find in my research any internal soft tissue connectivity that is associated with this continuous 'flow' (that is initiated at the extraocular muscle). Further, Thomas Myers' related discussion in *Anatomy Trains*[10], and what Peter Grunwald proposes in *Eyebody*,[22] together with the extensive scientific evidence for neural mediation[23] on the topic of the neck and extraocular

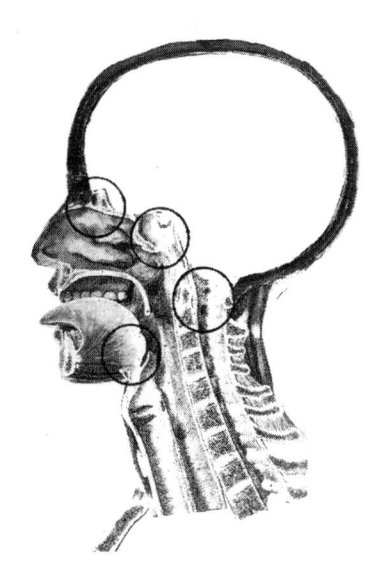

Fig. 6. The circles represent the four zones, counterclockwise from below: of the hyoid bone, AO joint-upper neck, sphenoid-pharyngeal tubercle, and behind the eyes. (Modified, from Internet public domain images, www.pinterst.com [from Bourgery J.M. and N. H.Jacob *Atlas of Human Anatomy and Surgery*; Jean-Marie Le Minor & Henri Sick, eds., Taschen-Barnes & Noble: New York]).

muscles, did not offer the answer I was seeking. I envisioned the base of the skull as a construct that is compatible with the concept of tensegrity, where the bones are separated from each other while continuously connected by a 'dense yet somewhat pliable' fibrous tissue. Later, I found a similar hypothesis from craniosacral osteopathy, referring to the role of the bony orbit but not addressing the participation of the extraocular muscles.[24]

I also considered the crucial role of two neighbouring structures in the base of the skull: 1) the pharyngeal tubercle (located at the top of the throat) and 2) the sphenoid bone (centrally located at the base of the skull). These, together with the nasopharynx located below, play a crucial role in bipedal uprightness, and air passage during breathing and vocalisation. The importance of the relationship of these anatomical structures is best exemplified in the practice of the whispered 'ah' and various other voice exercises.

Putting it all together, I suggest that the internal tensegric relationship among the four zones, those behind the eyes, the sphenoid-pharyngeal tubercle, the AO-upper cervical spine, and the hyoid bone, is crucial for the dynamic head–neck relationship (fig. 6). Support for this suggestion of hands-on teaching is illustrated in fig. 7.

The tensegric relationship between these four zones is attained by being in a dynamic state. Each of the four zones has a different quality of *discontinuous compression-continuous tension* (refer to commentary below). Together, they provide a tensegric construct through which the 'sphere of relativity' of the head–neck relationship occurs. In my view, the aforementioned dynamic organisation is the *means whereby* aliveness manifests in movement.

If we return to the notion of the 'flow', its initiation may start at any locale; the fundamental state is one that allows flow dissipation through the whole.

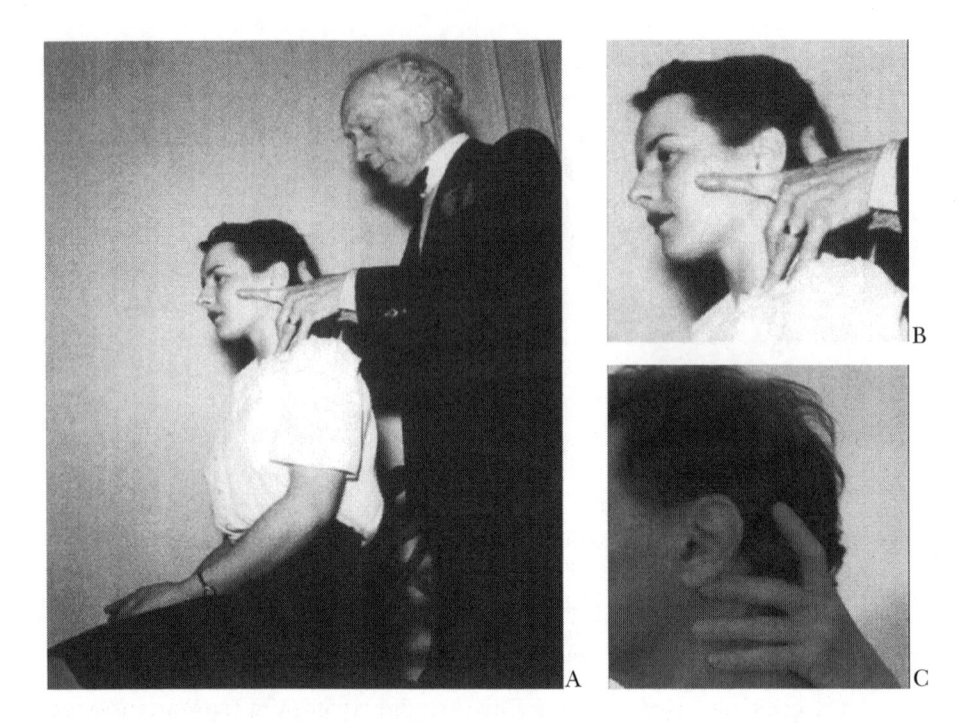

Fig. 7. Teachers in a process of enlivening the student's head–neck relationship via two different approaches. In as much as both approaches are effective, their comparison provides support for the aforementioned view. In A and B, Alexander's index finger is in contact parallel to the base of the skull and with the thumb supporting the occiput and the AO-upper neck zone; and the other fingers are at the lower neck and thoracic inlet. The contact by the teacher in C is limited to the occiput-AO zone-down to the mid neck zone. The approach depicted in A and B provides lesser mind-bio-physical effort (more 'energy' conservation) for the intended suspensory multidirectional vectorial equilibration of the head–neck relationship. In other words, by the approach depicted in A and B, there is less 'demand' on the hyoid bone and the AO-upper cervical zones than by the approach depicted in C. (Alexander's photo generously provided by Robert Britton.)

Macdonald[20] (in the chapter, 'Teaching the Technique') writes 'forward in Forward and Up is an unlocking device.' I am told that Jones had asked A. R. Alexander when working with a student, 'How will I know where to put my hands?' A. R. replied, 'Put them where they are needed.' If a 'lock' occurs in one particle, the blocking affect in flow dissipation modifies the whole (the exercise of 'group tensegrity'[1, 4] is an excellent example).

It is evident that when the tensegric movement initiates at the head–neck vicinity, a flow would dissipate throughout the whole body. Anatomically,

Myers[10] describes compatible myofascial connectivity with special reference to the *deep front line*. In addition, *body mapping*[25] is quite popular in teaching the Technique. In my view, regardless of the anatomical specifics, including the aforementioned four zones of the head–neck complex, the flow dissipation is multidirectional[4]. The movement of body particles is wave-like, curvilinear arcs and spirals, folding in and out, forming and bursting bubbles, etc. I draw support for this view from observing topography of muscles, bones, and other body structures; tongue, heart or intestinal movement; breathing cycles; animal movement including fish in the water; cells in culture; leaves in the wind; steam rising from boiling water; sea waves; etc.

Closing remarks

In the above mentioned letter to Jones[2], Alexander added (commas by ZR):

> The primary control of the use of ourselves in the activity of living, may be most accurately defined as that relationship of the head to the neck, and the head and neck to the body, at a given time, which makes for the integrated use of the mechanisms of the self as an indivisible whole.

This statement is a more specific definition than the abovementioned 'relativity', and complements it. I propose that the holistic-relational view of body construct presented herewith and elsewhere[4] are congruent with Alexander's combined statements, and could shed some light on 'it becomes a something in the sphere of relativity'.

In the context of Alexander Technique 'Work' (the lived experience), the views, interpretations and explanations, and the described living body construct, tensegric state, movement, flow, or proprioceptive-kinaesthetic organisation that are presented in this paper, cannot be achieved by 'doing'. In fact, any 'doingness' results in 'locks', interference effect on the dissipating flow and aliveness characteristic to the tensegric self in use. What allows aliveness and its manifestation in movement is the lived mind-bio-physical state of 'let', a lesser undue tension.

Commentary

The zone behind the eyes and its connection back to the AO joint, through the base of the skull, including the sphenoid-pharyngeal tubercle zone, is the most firm and 'rigid'. The zone of the hyoid bone and its above and below connectivity is the most soft and flexible. The softness-flexibility of the AO joint-upper cervical spine zone is somewhere in between.

> I would like to thank Martha Hansen-Fertman and Sarah Compton for reviewing the manuscript and suggesting valuable comments.

References and Notes

1. Parts of this paper were presented in a workshop (Holistic-Relational Anatomy and the Use of the Self: A Conceptual Presentation and Hands-On 'Work') with Tommy Thompson; 10th International Alexander Technique Congress, Limerick, Ireland 2015.
2. Alexander, F. M. (1945). Letter to Frank P Jones – unpublished.
3. Alexander, F. M. (2000). *The Universal Constant in Living*. Mouritz: London pp. xxxi-xxxii.
4. Ruben, Z. (2012). 'A view on a conceptual understanding of anatomy for facilitating a constructive kinaesthetic behavior (use of the self)' in *The Congress Papers: 9th International Congress of the F. M. Alexander Technique*. STAT Books: London, pp. 327-347.
5. Kenner, H. (1973). *Bucky: a Guided Tour of Buckminster Fuller*. William Morrow: New York.
6. Fuller, R.B. (1961). *Tensegrity*: http://www.rwgrayprojects.com/rbfnotes/fpapers/tensegrity.
7. Snelsen, K. http://kennethsnelsen.com
8. Levin, S. M. (1982). *Continuous tension, discontinuous compression: a model for biomechanical support of the body*: http://ati.net.com/articles/Levin.php (also, http://Biotensegrity.com).
9. Juan, D. (1998). *Job's Body: A Handbook of Bodywork*. Station Hill Press: Barrytown, NY.
10. Myers, T. W. (2001). *Anatomy Trains: Myofascial Meridians for Manual and Movement Therapists*. Churchill Livingstone: Edinburgh.
11. Schleip, R. (1998). 'Adventures in the Jungle of Neuro-myofascial Net' in *Rolf Lines*, vol. 26, no. 5, pp. 35–37.
12. Boggs, C. (2012). 'Biotensegrity and the Alexander Technique', *The Congress Papers: 9th International Congress of the F. M. Alexander Technique*. STAT Books: London, pp. 163-174.
13. Dietschy, D. (2011). Personal Communication: 9th International Congress of the F. M. Alexander Technique, Lugano, Switzerland, 7-13 August, 2011.
14. D'Arcy, W. T. (no date). *On Growth and Form*. (First paperback printed and manufactured in the USA).
15. Ingber, D. E. (Jan. 1998). 'The Architecture of Life' in *Scientific American*, pp. 48–57.
16. Ingber, D. E. (2003). 'Mechanobiology and Diseases of Mechanotransduction' in *Annals of Medicine*, vol. 35, pp. 1–14.
17. The Ingber Lab. (2001). http://www.children's hospital.org/research/Ingber/tensegrity.html
18. Davies, T. A. (2002). *Marjory Barlow and the Alexander Technique – An Examined Life*. Mornum Time Press: Berkley, California.
19. Macdonald, P. (1989). *The Alexander Technique As I See It*. Rahula Books: Brighton, Great Britain.
20. Alexander, F. M. (2000). *The Universal Constant in Living*. Mouritz: London, p 179, pp. 309-311.

21 Netter, F. H. (2004). *Atlas of Human Anatomy*. Icon Learning System, Teterboro, New Jersey, pp 25, 49, 55, 61, 64, 69.
22 Grunwald, P. (2004). *Eyebody: The Art of Integrating Eye, Brain and Body*. Eyebody Press in Association with Steele Roberts: New Zealand (English edition).
23 Sparks, D. L. (1991). 'The Neural Control of Orienting Eye and Head Movements' in *Motor Control: Concepts and Issues:* D. R. Humphrey and H.-J. Freund, eds. John Wiley & Sons Ltd.: Hoboken, New Jersey.
24 Cook, A. (2005). 'The SBS Revisited – The Mechanic of Cranial Motion'. *Journal of Bodywork and Movement Therapies*, vol. 9 (3), pp. 177-178.
25 Geham, S. 'Body Mapping': http://www.alexandertechnique.com/articles/body-map/

Zadok Ruben (ATI, ISTAT) trained with Martha Hansen-Fertman at the Philadelphia School for the Alexander Technique, and additionally studied with Alexander Technique training directors and senior teachers in the United States and Israel. In addition to a teaching practice, he is on the faculty at the School in Philadelphia and presents 'holistic-relational anatomy' at teachers training programmes and for other Alexander Technique groups worldwide. Zadok is a Doctor of Veterinary Medicine, PhD, certified as a veterinary anatomical pathologist and a general toxicologist with a specialty in research and development of pharmaceuticals and other medicines for human diseases. His Alexander Technique inquiry attends to the nature of aliveness and mind-bio-physical oneness in movement, as related to form-function dynamics in humans and animals. He has recovered from severe back injuries without surgical intervention.

zruben@patoximed.com

We are Evolved to Run...

The Art of Running – Workshop with Malcolm Balk and Robin John Simmons

Robin John Simmons

The context of these sessions was that humans are especially *evolved* to run. The sessions were divided into two sections each time. I began the sessions with a practical and explanatory session including lying down in semi-supine, rolling over into crawling, and demonstrating how crawling on hands and knees not only develops from homo-lateral (left knee moves forwards then left hand, then right knee moves forwards then right hand) to cross-pattern (left knee and right hand move forwards together, then right knee and right hand together) to develop and improve anyone's coordination, but also simultaneously enhances back muscle tone – all useful for running.

Following this I gave a brief description of the two running styles of modern-day hunter-gatherer tribes in South Africa. In both styles the aim of the tribe members is to get lunch, and both styles require running to achieve this goal. In one style the tribesmen look at the sky to notice any circling vultures. If they see this happening they run like mad to the area and chase away any animals that may be trying to feed on a recently dead carcass. They then grab the carcass. This is scavenging and requires speed running. The other style involves chasing an animal during the heat of the day and continually catching up with it, so it eventually is so exhausted it gives up running away. The tribesmen then easily kill it. This is called persistence hunting and requires a more long-distance style of running.

I then described how the double-spiral arrangement of voluntary musculature in our body, originally pointed out by Professor Raymond Dart, links the top of the back of the neck with the big toes. In this way it is clear that if while running you retain your Alexander directions, a healthy 'stretch' on the double-spiral is maintained, something akin to a well-organised spring, such that the 'up' consciousness links right through the whole body to the very pushing off point of the foot (the ball of the foot – big toe side) on every stride.

We then took the group outside and Malcolm taught how to run with the minimum effort and the least likelihood of injury. After some enjoyable warm-up routines Malcolm briefly filmed each participant as they ran. He would later be able to show in a frame-by-frame slow motion on the projector how each person was in actuality placing their feet in relation to the whole body in action. Despite people usually feeling that they were not over-striding Malcolm was able to demonstrate, using a clever app on his Ipad, that in fact

Robin John Simmons ~ We are Evolved to Run

each runner was placing their forward foot in front of their body on each stride, so that in effect their action was repeatedly causing a braking effect. It was obvious in the frame-by-frame film footage and simply undeniable. (What would Alexander himself have given to have this app at his disposal!)

Having demonstrated to everyone that their habitual style of running was tending to give them a disadvantage, Malcolm showed the group how to develop a whole-body springiness, using elastic energy, as stored in the tendons and connective tissue, rather than the usual employment of contractive muscular energy. Learning this springing style of running took a while to convey as it was new for everyone. Then Malcolm got everyone to change the foot-in-front stride error, shifting to the foot underneath or even a fraction behind. In this way one gets effortless propulsion in running.

The final stage was to ensure that the runners were not compromising their running by moving their arms in ways that would interfere with optimal action. We found that some runners repeatedly over-moved their right arm towards the left more than their left arm towards the right. This indicated an imbalance in the double-spiral muscle activity. In every case the runner was right-handed and this tends to support Dart's point that right-handed people have more hidden habits of twisting leftwards than they are aware of. Pointing out the imbalance gave these people the chance to alter their arm action. Also, by sending the elbow back and down as the moment of emphasis, in contrast to the emphasis being on the forward movement of the arm, the backward elbow action actually assisted in encouraging a general forward-and-up tendency of the whole body.

At the end the participants had the chance to 'put it all together'. As we only had four hours to impart so much teaching it was going to be a challenge to participants to accommodate all that knowledge straight away. Malcolm made it easier by suggesting that as the runners ran around the field he would whistle every 30 seconds to indicate they should focus on a new aspect of what they had learnt. After 10 minutes of this everyone was buzzing with enthusiasm for discovering so much that they could take away and practise.

We both enjoyed these sessions very much. People interested to follow-up on any aspect can contact either of us.

> Robin John Simmons has been teaching the Technique since he qualified from the Carringtons' school in 1971. He has run an approved teacher training school since 1982 (now in Zürich). In 2006 he was invited to Australia to give the keynote speech at the Australian AT Society AGM, and he gave eight differently themed workshops in Sydney. His interest in the Dart Procedures has led him to give regular workshops at Congresses and at his training school. He has recently self-published a study of the Dart Procedures in relation to the Alexander Technique called *The Evolution of Movement*.

Malcolm: malcolm.balk@gmail.com
Robin: info@alexander-technik-schweiz.com

Curious about Experience – Moving – Noticing – Choosing

Lucia Walker

This Continuous Learning workshop was an opportunity for me to continue to investigate my ongoing interest in cultivating curiosity, holistic self-awareness, refining proprioception, understanding levels of habitual or 'unconscious' response and clarifying the intention behind using touch in my teaching.

Currently I have a particular focus on how to learn, practise and share the skills necessary to be a teacher of the Alexander Technique. Observation, inhibition and direction are key in this process, along with re-educating sensory appreciation, including vision and proprioception. I am also interested in developing ways to support continually being interested in, and learning from our own experience, whatever that might be. Here I need to acknowledge the influence of the principles of Contact Improvisation and other studies in my path as a movement artist. These disciplines share with AT a fascination with how attention and awareness work, how we can address unconscious habit and physiological 'reflex', how we learn from our own perceptions and how we can consciously co-operate with and live more gracefully in our human design.

I set out to support three strands of learning in the workshop:

1. Deepening personal presence practice. This includes how to research our own experience.
2. Refining the use of touch in one-to-one teaching.
3. Consolidating some concepts around managing diversity of experience in groups.

This last is mainly to be covered by presenting clearly expressed studies or 'exercises' that everyone can participate in at their own level.

A group of around 25 met for two mornings in a spacious dance studio. A smooth wooden floor, large windows providing natural light and a long distance view contributed a very supportive environment to the investigation. Participants were reminded to notice different qualities in the room, and in the group, as well as in themselves. I chose to explore the same material with each Continuous Learning group. Lepkoff says:

> ... using my own powers of observation I can shift my perspective, have new perceptions, and free myself from my own conventional/habitual ways of seeing.[1]

Observation – Noticing

While we are still in stillness, sitting in a circle, I draw attention to various aspects of experience, particularly proprioception; the pressure by which we experience support, the knowing of how we are positioned (you could draw yourself), the movement discernible in stillness, the knowledge of head position, the lack of perception of the balancing movement of the head on the atlanto-occipital joint. Something about this conscious direction of attention to senses that usually function below the level of awareness seems to encourage a general quietening and enlivening and to support co-operation with our design and our situation. Frank Pierce Jones:

> It was only after I realised that attention can be expanded as well as narrowed that I began to note progress. In order to move to a conscious level in which I could be aware of both doing and not-doing (of the inhibitory as we as the excitatory part of the movement), I had to expand my attention so that it took in something of myself and something of the environment as well.[2]

Inhibition – Refraining from

I invite participants to do whatever they would like to 'get ready'. We practise our inhibitory capacity in several ways: by choosing not to habitually change position to get more comfortable, by refraining from the tension generated by 'trying' and by deciding not to directly affect the conditions we notice. In this way we can replace correction and labelling with curiosity and a wish to notice more. This may be familiar or new, but with the addition of a degree of awareness and curiosity about what they are choosing, practising, awakening. We also play with refraining from correcting or fixing things we notice that we are unhappy or uncomfortable with – these are often the first aspects of our experience we are aware of when we pause to notice. Fixing has the double meaning of making right and making permanent! We practise 'inhibiting' any tendency we express to 'put ourselves in the right state'. This opens up more curiosity about what else we can perceive. Alexander describes how important inhibition is:

> Inhibition is a human potentiality of utmost value in any attempt to make changes in the human self, and my experience has convinced me that it is the potentiality most in need of development.[3]

UNIFIED FIELD OF ATTENTION – FOCUSED AND PERIPHERAL VISION AND PROPRIOCEPTION

I like to acknowledge that for people who have done some theatre or movement training, to walk around a room with a group of people is a familiar activity; for others it might be quite strange. In response to the lack of 'end', people may tighten themselves in order to create some purpose. Even just the idea of 'becoming more aware' may stimulate tightening and effort. Once again the invitation is to notice if that happens, and to make the choice just to notice what you notice, and then to notice what you haven't noticed yet. Then begin to acknowledge the (probably unconscious) coordination that is allowing you to move amongst people without bumping into them and to enjoy the flow of your own choices of speed and direction at the same time as registering the patterns occurring in the whole. Enlivening the peripheral vision to the perception of the movement of the world as soon as we move supports a quality of fluidity. Then we experiment with walking towards a point of interest in the environment with the purpose of touching it and with closing our eyelids as soon as we have identified the goal. We notice how there may be satisfaction when we are accurate with the target and/or some irritation when we are not. We also acknowledge how the focused and peripheral vision are still functioning and serving each other when the eyelids are closed.

> The technique is a method for using kinaesthetic cues – the sensation of tension, effort, weight and the like – in order to organise one's field of awareness in a systematic way, so as to take in the whole of what one is doing instead of just a part.[4]

MOVING – FOLLOWING YOUR WHIM
DIRECTING ATTENTION – RESEARCHING YOUR SENSES

Most of our experience of movement involves wanting to achieve something – an everyday task, a more flexible body, a movement form or exercise, to be graceful, to be free of pain. . . I have found that there is a scope for new perception and observation if the focus of the movement is the investigation of sensory experience and the bringing of our proprioceptive sense into awareness. Usually starting from a place where balance is not an issue and the support of the floor is very tangible (lying or sitting) I invite moving and pausing *in order to* relish the perception of the movement. It is a little like doodling with different pens to ascertain their different colour and quality, or fiddling with an object to see what its properties are.

All and any observations are welcomed. I particularly invite people to monitor their level of interest or energy and notice making choices that support being present and involved. In other words if we feel ourselves becoming 'hypnotised', bored, distracted or anxious we can chose a different pace, a different movement, a different quality. The learning I offer here is that we can engage our will consciously and notice that even in exploratory movement or listening to a teacher's suggestions choice is always available to us. It helps me to refresh my attention when I remind myself that it is ALL new experience – *you've never been here doing this before and you'll never be again, so it's a pity to miss it.*

> Noticing what I am noticing is the easy part; noticing what I am not noticing is a crucial challenge. When my attention stops moving, my interpretation of what is happening becomes fixed, my vision becomes conventionalized, and so the questioning disappears. Perception follows attention. (Lepkoff, 2010.)[1]

I invite moving our attention to specific named aspects of experience for a few minutes at a time, choosing from an almost limitless range of possibilities: sound, the ground, mood, proprioception (position, tone, balance), vision (colour, angle/perspective, light and dark, shape, movement). We focus our attention in particular ways and also allow what arises in the peripheral attention, particularly any thoughts that suggest what we 'should' or 'should not' be doing/thinking/feeling and any new experiences, sought or unsought. We develop our personal exploration by finding out how the vision is affected by movements requiring a high degree of tone, or speed, or disorientation. I am impressed by how moving with this kind of attention and curiosity facilitates a deeper understanding of our design and how to consciously cooperate with it.

We are also able to cultivate the ability to observe ourselves and our reactions, both habitual and chosen, without judgement. A more compassionate witnessing presence, for ourselves and for others, takes some practice!

Touching and being touched

The person touching is encouraged to use their hands receptively rather than to influence, direct, motivate, teach or seek to give any particular input. This usually involves refraining from (inhibiting) learnt and practised ways of using the hands in relation to objects, instruments and other people. In the exploration, the 'toucher' has their eyelids closed; this seems to facilitate a more receptive sensing and helps to quieten the predictive visual brain. It also reveals some of the habits of looking and doing that we tend not to notice because of the speed and familiarity of how we use our eyes.

The mover has the opportunity to inhibit or refrain from the very usual response to move *for* their partner, to do something interesting, graceful or meaningful. They are invited, instead, to use their partner's touch to have themselves and their movement reflected back, to know where they are and to play with the ability to receive and be interested in visual information while being touched and having another aspect of proprioception expanded. I encourage all these activities to be performed without commentary or analysis, as I have found that talking can interfere with the possibility of observing something previously unnoticed. However there is plenty of animated exchange when the partners get to report the experiences of each role to each other. There is a quality of attention evoked in both roles and in the room that is most clearly described by some rather general terms: 'depth', 'three-dimensionality', lightness, presence. Smetacek and Mechsner describe the importance of proprioception in our perception of ourselves and the physical world:

Signals from this sensory orchestra [proprioceptors] are sent by afferent nerves through the spinal cord to the somatosensory, motor and parietal cortices of the brain *where they continuously feed and update dynamic sensory-motor maps of the body* [my emphasis].[5]

THE LINK TO TEACHING TOUCH
My objective here is to go back to a learnt and familiar activity so that any unconscious teaching habits might be revealed after the touch, vision and movement explorations. I suggest touching the partner as they perform an everyday activity, playing with the difference between eyelids open or closed, and then to give each other a short 'turn', whatever that means to each person. What do we need to add in and what can be left out? Any findings may open up the possibility of renewed clarity of choice and intention.

ARTICULATION – SHARING
As a teacher/facilitator of a group learning experience I find it very useful to hear something from each person. I ask participants to express one word or one sentence that identify a quality, a question, an insight, or a reflection from the two sessions or from their present state and offer that into the circle. I find it exciting how the process of learning from our own experience can be enriched in group explorations and open up further experimentation and learning.

I was touched and inspired by the level of engaged intention all the participants brought to the workshop. I personally experienced a satisfying integration of learning, teaching, practice and investigation, in an atmosphere of playfulness and mutual respect.

The employment of inhibition calls for the exercise of memory and awareness. . . . . In the process, both potentialities are developed and the scope of the use of both are gradually increased.[6]

Appendix

Included below is a list of contributions from the participants in the introductory circles for each workshop. 'Please say your name and a short sentence about your current interest/ongoing passion/motivation for being here. An articulation of what you are curious about helps set a constructive coordination towards achieving this.'

> Improvisation, seeing, talking, balance – what it is and what it isn't, different teaching styles, being here, the spiritual dimension of AT, leadership, curiosity and humour, inhibition, presence, boundaries, movement, using myself better, contemplative practice, movement, integration/wholeness/exchange, relationship to environment, movement, communication/thinking/seeing.

> Movement, more dimensions of the senses, input for own practice and training course, beauty and soul connection, from practice room to stage and from practice room to teaching, movement for actors/senses/presence/quality of movement, emotions through movement, finishing my training group, inhibition and staying with myself/relation to piano playing, sound and sound as touch, how to practise for myself, to be more comfortable with moving, how to actually change habits/identity/health/fixed ideas, movement/wholeness/working with actors, kayaking/movement/chronic illness, what is Alexander Technique and how to teach it, frustration of being lost and late, more integration between theatre and AT, relief of movement for a desk worker, movement and a calm place I can access when I want it, to deepen connection to self, being and interbeing, staying with self/being in a large space/the interconnection between movement and resistance.

> Deciding and the act of deciding, dance and AT connections, liveliness and creativity, AT directions in life, inhibition and moving, how to be an imperfect AT teacher, to move and play, movement, emotional and psychological aspects, curious about everything, different ways to explore, curiosity and play, be able to notice own moods and be present and centred, group work, creativity and play, been sitting way too much in last few days, touch base and see what's there, what am I saying to myself, how to be in this with a playful mind, recognising excitement and fear, how to be honest and express it to self, confusion generated by not understanding English, how to be kind to self and others, understanding layers of discomfort, spirit of playfulness.

Acknowledgements
All photographs by courtesy of Ralf Hiemisch.

References and Notes
1 Lepkoff, D. (2010). 'Writings'. http://www.daniellepkoff.com/index.php [last accessed 15/09/2015].
2 Jones, F. (1976). *Body Awareness in Action.* Schocken: New York, p. 9.
3 Alexander, F. M. (1941). *The Universal Constant in Living.* Gollancz: London, p. 93.
4 Jones, F. (1975). Talk given to Indiana University School of Music, http://www.alexandercenter.com/pa/musicjonesi.html [last accessed 15/09/2015].
5 Smetacek, V., F. Mechsner (2004). 'Making Sense' in *Nature* Nov 4, 432(7013): 21.
6 Alexander, op cit p. 93.

Embodied Learning of Sensing Balance by Walking a Line

Wolfgang Weiser

In my work I am interested in our ability to balance, our sense of balance, which we have access to at all times. Defining our ability to balance is complex, as it involves different sensory systems. The first system that is often mentioned is our vestibular system, which has its sense organs in the region of the inner ear where three semi-circular canals converge to regulate our equilibrium, involving directional information obtained by the position of the head. But we also need additional senses for our overall balance. One of the most important of these is our visual system which helps to give us reference to verticality of body and the motion of the head as well as spatial location relative to various objects around us. We also rely on our somatosensory system which includes the vital senses of proprioception and kinaesthesia, which involve relaying information to the joints and muscles by pressure and the vibratory senses. These senses also give us information about our spatial position and movement relative to the support surface, as well as movement and position of different body parts relative to each other. A lot of our balance activity is done automatically, but it is also within our voluntary control *(Ross and Wilson, 2011).*[1]

> Proprioception gives signals about body posture, balance, extremities and joints positions, muscle tension and movement. The systems sense organ is the balance organ and the organs in muscles, tendons and joints that are responsible for deep sensibility.[2]

Fig. 1.

When we do become aware of how we are balancing, for example by standing on our toes (figure 1), or just standing, closing our eyes and engaging our proprioception, we can make voluntary changes. We sometimes call it 'feeling', but it has nothing to do with local or cutaneous sensations. It applies to sensory nerves that serve the muscles, the tendons, the joints, and the middle ear and is in essence how Coghill explained the term 'proprioceptive'.[3] But our sense of balance involves other senses too. For example, our breathing affects our balance because the changes of the volume of air in our lungs changes the position and dimension of our trunk. Our hearing also gives us auditory information about how we interrelate in space. When working with balance, it seems appropriate to use an inclusive approach, by including all our senses, since they may be directly or indirectly engaged in our act of balance. To work in this way in individual lessons or in groups might be different from the way we learnt to teach in our training as teachers, but through my experience as performer and juggler I learned to be 'sharp' – attentive with all my senses. It is like being inclusive with everything at my disposal, to be able to sense what might be blocked or missing in someone else.

The balancing off the ground by tight-rope walking at the Congress in Limerick constituted a challenging investigation into how we use our sense of balance. Doing this particular balance activity we need to bear in mind that fear reflexes and endgaining also play an important part, as the stimulus is very strong. In fact, for some participants it is so strong that they reached their limits. As a teacher you have to be aware of this and to be responsible for handling whatever comes up in any situation. To explain in words how I do that can only be a poor attempt – describing just a small fraction of the total experienced interaction. When I lead students walking on the tight-rope (figure 2) the physical sensations and communication experienced is so rich and complex that these 30 seconds could fill a whole book. I believe that the moment of lived uncertainty, of gaining and losing, of decision for the next conscious step can be recognised in our wish to balance. My job is to be as responsive as possible, providing the student walking on the wire

Fig. 2. Fig. 3.

with sensory feedback and directive help in choosing the appropriate means whereby they can take the next step. I simply create a pause for them to choose the most appropriate act.

I perceive a very deep-rooted problem here: in attending to, or focusing on, the act of balance, students want to control the process by mastering body mechanics and creating technical models. But the task of an Alexander student is not to try to master specific acts. It is to improve the general use of our selves by investigation of our ability to balance in any given situation. We are not interested in the act of sitting and standing or getting out of the chair in itself, but with the sensory interplay or sensory appreciation that takes place during the act itself. Therefore it is always a completly different learning experience for each person when walking on the rope, as it is a completely different experience for everybody being guided in and out of a chair, because embodied learning is a somatic process and the outcome of a complex individual learning process related to our sense of balance. Walter Carrington's also confirmed this when he wrote:

> If the whole concept of upright balancing on two feet is called in question, it will be found that people's ideas and assumptions about it are extremely vague.
>
> Enquiry has established that whereas almost everyone will unhesitatingly claim that they know what balance is, the majority will freely admit that, for a number of reasons, their own performance is both poor and inadequate.[4]

As a balance educator and teacher of the Alexander Technique I work from my own experience and my evidence-based perception, and have realised that our sense of balance contains the ability to motivate our body to balance and move. In fact, our ability to balance constitutes a fundamental factor of life. Greek philosophers stated thousands of years ago that all movement involves continuous change in quality, quantity or position. I personally regard our sense of balance as a potential assessment of all continuous change regarding quality, quantity or position. Which simply means that our sense of balance reflects our potential to interrelate to the course of all events of our life. F. Matthias Alexander did not define balance to my knowledge, but instead used the word coordination, both in its conception and in its application, to convey the idea of balance in a general rather than a specific basis.[5]

In my work with movement one has therefore to accept all the components belonging to the conditions present. If we just focus on certain parts of ourselves, the neglected portion will be a trembling factor somewhere else. Isolation results in the disintegration of the whole and results in a dis-connection or a non-connection between inside and outside, space and materiality. One has to think of everything working all together and one after the other at the same time. In our modern life we do focus on targets and results as well as on virtual constructed tools and skills. At the same time we gradually seem to lose the physical skills that we need to perform in every present moment. The skill of engaging our sensory system in a meaningful directive activity is therefore essential to me. The activity might change, maybe we are just sitting or maybe we are engaged in a balancing act as we did in the workshop, balancing peacock feathers (figure 3). But the experience of walking on the string awaits me – the attentiveness, directedness and definition in space demanded at every present moment. This experience helps me to see the immense impact and meaning of the principles the Alexander Technique contains.

Acknowledgements
All photos are courtesy of Ralf Hiemisch.

References
1. Ross and Wilson (2011). *Anatomy and physiology in health and illness.* 11th edition. Churchill Livingstone: Edinburgh.
2. Nationalencyklopedin, 2015-02-07. http://www.ne.se/lang/rörelse/298119 [Visited: 14.10.2015] (my translation).
3. Westfeldt, Lulie (1964, 1986). *F. Matthias Alexander: The Man and His Work.* Centerline Press: California.
4. Quotations from Carrington, W. H. M. (1970). 'Balance as function of intelligence', The Sheldrake Press: London.
5. Alexander, F. M (1946). *Constructive Conscious Control of the Individual.* Chaterson Ltd: London.

Natural Running

John Woodward

INTRODUCTION
The Congress workshop began with a statement followed by an invitation.

The opening statement was a declaration that *I know nothing about the Alexander Technique or any of its key notions.*

The invitation was for participants *to regard themselves as a Force of Nature for the period of the workshop.*

In what way do the statement and the invitation interlink?

Regarding yourself as a Force of Nature is an open invitation to explore what you bring to the workshop from *the bottom up*. To accept such an invitation frees us all from any sense of *top-down* expert authority and certainty. With this in mind my intention is *not* to teach you how to apply the principles of the Alexander Technique in how you walk or run. The aim is to open up the tools for self-discovery that require no external authority. You are your own inner authority. I regard the community gathered together at the Limerick Alexander Technique Congress as a nation of Kings!

While the statement of renunciation might appear on the surface to be a form of career suicide, it might also be an invitation to let go of some of the certainties and orthodoxies of the Alexander Technique that I've been teaching for over 30 years. The statement that I made forms part of a personal exploration concerning how attached I may have become to my identity as an Alexander Technique teacher. My invitation for you to regard your self as a Force of Nature becomes an invitation to break free from another force: the Force of Habit. This includes letting go of identities, orthodoxies, traditions and certainties, clearing the way for us as equals, to explore uncertainties and the unknown.

THE NON-DOING POWER IN THE POINT-OF-NOT-QUITE-YET
We are wonderfully complex bundles of matter, information and energy that move through the space-time continuum. A raging torrent of matter, information and energy incessantly surges through us into the present moment like the river approaching a waterfall. The moment just before the water drops over the edge I refer to as *the point-of-not-quite-yet*. Mostly we move reactively through these points in space and time. The essential feature that changes this reactivity into creativity is the authenticity and genuineness of human presence. Such attention and presence demands the willingness and courage to stop clinging to identity and certainty.

Walking and lifting your foot from the floor
Here is a challenge to a very familiar and habitual certainty. As you walked here today to attend the workshop you lifted your foot from the support of the floor many hundreds of times. The capacity to achieve this is a certainty. Indeed it defines a walking stride as it does a running stride. In an average walking gait 80% of the gait cycle involves being on the support of one leg. This means that 80% of the time as you walked here you had one leg and foot lifted from the floor. When that 80% of time that you are on one leg moves to 100%, then your walk transitions into a run. The running step incorporates a flight phase during which you hop from one foot to the other foot. Whether walking or running you inevitably move through a-point-of-not-quite-yet: a moment just before your foot leaves floor. We usually do this with a top-down certainty that the mechanism of habit can make this move. Indeed if it did not happen we would cease to walk and we would shuffle along with the feet never leaving the ground!

Presencing the point-of-not-quite-yet
The Force of Nature invitation includes the process of simply being present for the moment just before your foot leaves the floor. Attend in this way, and if you can 'presence' that moment, then a familiar reactive top-down certainty can open up into a bottom–up process of questioning, of ascertaining and finding out. How do you lift your foot from the floor? The *point-of-not-quite-yet* opens into a world of infinite latent possibilities. Key among the infinity of choice points is the simple volitional choice **not** to move into that reactive, top-down certainty. You are sure and certain that you can achieve the end-goal of lifting your foot from the floor. By entering into that creative moment of suspension there is a further intriguing possibility that the way that you achieve this might be heavily conditioned by yet another unexamined top-down certainty: that the human foot is frail and in need of constant protection from a shoe!

We heard at the Limerick Conference of bio-mechanics experts who claim that the human spine is inadequate and cannot maintain an upright sitting posture. There are similar 'expertocrats' who state with authority that the human foot is insufficiently evolved and in need of support and protection. Both weighty top-down certainties fly in the face of the fact of our evolution!

A natural running warm-up
When I invite you to take off your shoes, you take your foot from out of somebody else's brain and ideas. Think for yourself. Challenge top-down authority. That pile of shoes might embody an idea that your foot is vulnerable, frail and insufficiently evolved and in need of protection.

I prefer another idea: *that the shoe you have just removed is a treasure chest.* The sock you peel away is a shroud that covers hidden treasure. When later we delve deeper into the treasure chest, we will bring to light an important 'string of pearls' that I refer to as *the foot knuckle, or the metatarso-phalangeal joint (MTPJ for short).*

This warm-up creates a complex and changing interweaving of rhythmic patterns as the foot is lifted from the floor while you are running or marking time on spot. We keep returning to the invitation to be present at the moment just before your foot leaves the ground. We use rhythm and chant, taking inspiration from natural runners in the more natural living cultures of the world.

We explore a kaleidoscopic variety of questions, including for example, what happens if you change a step on the spot to something that's more like an energetic stamp?

Whether stamping, running or marking time your attention is drawn to the way your foot drops to the floor directly underneath the centre of gravity of your body. When this happens it never occurs to anybody to land directly on the heel!

By the simple deft move of listening to the rhythmic sounds that your feet make you will connect your head to your feet.

A bottom-up process such as this warm-up is essentially playful. Rhythm and chant support the process. There is no judgement, and no right or wrong. The more presence you are able to bring to the moment just before your foot leaves the floor, the more you are able to challenge what it is that your foot is habitually just about do and the more fun will be generated. Be aware of the fun-robbing top-down tyranny of the norm. Just because everybody does something in the same way does not mean that the way that they do it is either natural or efficient.

From out of the openness to explore in the warm-up comes an intriguing possibility: maybe we all walk with the same heavily compensated gait. We all do it in the same way perhaps because we all share the same experience of adapting to the restrictions of a modern protective shoe.

The walk to run transition

You are invited to explore barefoot on the grass, how you transition from a walk to run. Young children are masters of the art! Observe how young kids effortlessly segue from walking to running. You might also notice how young children rarely mechanically repeat the same step over and over again. They demonstrate an astonishing variety. I have created a label for what happens when we eventually come to mechanically repeat the same step over and over again: I call it '*Trudgery*'. *How and why did we ever lose the enlivening variety of step that we had as young children?*

The demonstration of a natural stride

The natural stride looks and is remarkably light easy and simple. Over twenty-five years it has been refined to become economical and energy-efficient because it is passed through a non-doing prism. The lens separates the stride into a sequence of seven *moments-of-not-quite-yet*. Each of the seven phases generates a stand-alone *base-move* that forms the firm foundation upon which to build layer upon layer of challenge. The unique process is based on poised integrity. The neuro-systems that create poise and integrity do so *by the efficient management of weight organised by the ingenious use of opposing forces.* This extraordinary level of complexity requires the whole brain and not just the cortex!

A SUMMARY OF THE NATURAL STRIDE DEMONSTRATION: THE SEVEN PHASES

1. Aligned support over the back-foot.
2. Forward transfer of weight.
3. Pre-action, the preparation or lead up to change of support. (In this action the back foot rolls up lifting the heel.)
4. Change of support. (This completes the action by raising the foot off the floor as it moves from heel-to- rump.)
5. Forward lunge: in which the centre of gravity leads the hip joint and forward leg-swing.
6. Leg swing.
7. Foot-Fall/Propulsion.

Each segment processed through the non-doing lens or prism ensures that gravity is fully used to achieve the action wherever possible.

THE WALKING OR RUNNING STANCE

The natural stride begins in the running or walking stance. One foot is set about a foot's length ahead of the other. The feet are about hip-width apart and parallel to one another. Think of your head positioned in the walking and running stance in such a way that it aligns directly over the support of your back foot. From the head to heel length of this starting point you can then move into phase 2): You ease off the 'parking-brake'. This begins with a loosening around the head and neck as you start to move your weight forward. *You release into this move* because the body above the knee is arranged to be topple-heavy. Your topple-heavy head begins the process in a head-to-toe progression. It is like a toppling tower falling forward. This initiates phase 2) and phase 3) of the seven segments of the natural stride.

A KEY BASE MOVE

Phases 1), 2) and 3) create a base move which ends in a pose that you see in most statues in which:

- The weight is on the advancing leg.
- The rear leg is bent at the knee.
- The heel is raised and most of the foot has lifted from the floor.

The foot is poised on the ball of the foot preparatory to phase 4) that will complete the action that lifts the foot off the floor.

The key importance of the foot knuckle or MTPJ in the foot is explored. This easy, poised and simple non-doing base-move achieves the following:

- It allows the hip joint to remain centred as it swivels forward.
- It allows the knee to freely swing to catch up with the advancing knee without a push.
- It articulates the hinge of the ankle joint freely (dorsi-flexion).
- It engages the toes so that the forefoot becomes the broadest possible surface area as it spreads and lengthens out into a supportive rocker-like surface.

And all for virtually zero energy. And all very dependent on the free articulation of the foot-knuckle!

USING A GOLF BALL AND THE STEP TO FREE THE FULL KNUCKLE

A handy step and/or a golf-ball can be used to bring 'the string of pearls' that forms the MTPJ into the light of day. Placing the sharp edge of a step underneath this key joint while giving a clear instruction to lift and then lower the toes while straight is quite revealing. You can relay a direction but your toes may have no idea how to achieve this! The reason for this is that they are caught up in habitual flexion. Only when they break out of this habitual compensation can they begin to deliver the key articulation necessary for a natural stride.

The golf ball is particularly helpful in continuing to help to free each individual 'pearl' of the foot knuckle. At this stage we simply want to win back a freedom in a key joint that has become like a rusty hinge. There is much more to come as we build endurance, strength and agility on top of this freedom.

We emphasised how the action that lifts the toes straight into extension is so important because it is *the action that presents the front two prongs of the foot tripod*. The heel is of course the rear prong of the tripod. The conventional two-dimensions usually referred to as pronation and supination were demonstrated to be a part of a third spiral dimension. This magnificent double helically-opposed spiral works to wind and unwind the natural foot giving it an astonishing adaptability and also the rigidity necessary to support the big toe (first metatarsal) at that key poised point of propulsion.

PROCEDURE: THE WONDERFUL MASAI BOUNCE

In this wonderfully enlivening procedure we worked in pairs as the Masai warriors do, bouncing each other up and down into the air. We noticed how much that toe-lift added to the height of the bounce. We also emulated the extraordinary release of sounds that the Masai use as they bounce so powerfully.

Exploring the most efficient way to lift the foot from the floor

While there are an infinite number of compensated ways to lift the foot from the floor in order to walk or run, there is only one way that this can be achieved with maximum efficiency and ease. To penetrate through habitual compensated patterns requires the non-doing lens and full access to the brain's largely unused poise-creating systems. Then we can begin to experience the maximum efficiency and lightness and ease of a natural stride. This crucially requires the full functioning of the MTPJ or foot knuckle joint. A case can be made that *this MTPJ (and its key player the big toe) is of at least equal importance to the key muscles and joints at the top end of the support structure, at the head–neck junction*!

An introduction to the head-to-toe procedures

The base move is a building-block to a series of *head-to-toe procedures* that create a unique expansion of movement and fitness horizons formed upon a strong non-doing foundation. The aim of these progressions is to maintain integrity while progressively creating layer upon layer of challenge.

We began this process by using the base move to create not a forward step but a backward step. This unlocks various possibilities to strengthen the foot and to establish key head-to-toe connections between the dropping heel and the head easing forward and up. Much of this work draws upon *eccentric muscle contraction* in which joints and muscles are easing apart while working under what is often considerable load.

Foot competence 1: Breaking up the adhesions

This procedure is really 'layered-up' on top of the dropping heel procedure, where we worked the eccentric contraction through the calf and leg. There is an important difference here however, in that this procedure involves actively lifting the toes and maintaining a powerful toe lift, while pushing or driving the heel downwards. In the earlier procedure the heel was simply dropping, now it is been pushed downwards. This procedure works against the action that is lifting the toes. It is the toe-lift that fully forms the rocker-like surface of the toes. The toes at this stage are held stiff and quite rigid. It is this kind of strength and support from the fully supinated foot that enables the MTPJ to carry the weight of the body over its rocker-like surface with such ease. Powerfully driving the heel down while maintaining a toe-lift, will powerfully pull through the shin in front and through the calf muscles and tendons at the back. This may well create a 'burn' effect as various adhesions are broken up through this procedure.

FOOT COMPETENCE 2: THE FOOT ABCD
This procedure begins at the point in the previous procedure where the toes have lifted and the heel has been driven down. When the heel can contact the floor you then have full engagement of the three 'prongs' that constitute the foot tripod. The raised toes will push the fifth and particularly the first metatarsal into the ground. Joints 2, 3 and 4 in 'the string of pearls' that constitute the metatarsal joint are drawn up from the floor as to form the transverse arch. The foot maintains a flexible stiffness in this position. You then take a back step so that the foot with the toes raised is in front and you are ready to begin:

A. You lift the toes long and straight-up until the point that you feel the fifth metatarsal – the big toe joint – press into the ground.
B. In this phase you will raise the whole length of the foot while maintaining raised straight toes. The foot pivots back on the heel.
C. Here you lower the raised toes slowly back down to the same point that they were at the end of A) with the first metatarsal/big toe joint pushing into the ground. There is a slow, long lowering of your raised toes to the ground.
D. **In this phase there is a slow, long lowering and straightening of your toes while** *maintaining a focused attention to maintaining the height and full integrity of the medial arch.* **This phase develops the important capacity to lower the toes without collapsing that medial arch.**

RUNNING PROCEDURE: ELASTIC DRILL 1
In this drill we awaken a sense of the centre of gravity by positioning a belt so that it catches the top of the hipbones. Then the belt-buckle will be approximately where the centre of gravity of your body lies, 5 to 6 cm below the belly button. The great advantage of this configuration of elastic pull is that it will enable you to really slow down the phase 4) of the natural stride in which the centre of gravity fractionally leads and goes ahead of the action of the legs and hip. The elastic is really helpful in the process of easing out of an ingrained pattern associated with a shod gate: that is the tendency to stick the leg out in front in order to present the heel as the first point of contact. The elastic enables you to do it slowly enough for the brain to 'nail' a new pattern.

If you repeat the procedure a few times then, after the elastic is removed there will be that brief re-adaptation phase. What an extraordinary turnaround of the way in which your energies are being used! Instead of your own energies being used in putting the leg out in front, the re-patterned version of this forward movement uses gravity. The centre of gravity now initiates the movement of the legs as it eases forward! In this way you begin to experience a movement towards the freedom of a natural stride.

Running procedure: Elastic drill 2
In this procedure we use an ankle strap with the elastic attached to the front of the ankle. Now you go through the sequence of the natural stride and include the phase 4: you actually lift your foot off the floor. But now when you raise the foot the clever and adaptable proprioceptive sense has to work out how to achieve this, and at the same time counter the pull of the elastic. This will help to bring into your awareness the key muscles that pick the heel up on its efficient continued arc up towards the rump. The hamstring muscles that attach to the seat bones are the key players in this action. Once you're unhooked from the elastic and enter into the readjustment phase, you will appreciate how efficiently these muscles can work to organise the change of support phase in a really efficient natural stride.

The effect of the elastic drills is to make the running stride feel much more compact. A key change is the way it seems to work to tidy-up the running action. What is happening is now much more directly underneath you.

> John Woodward has a lifelong interest in human movement. After taking a degree in psychology he researched movement control at Nottingham University and afterwards played and taught guitar. John was taught by a second generation of teachers of the Alexander Technique at the Alexander Teaching Associates College in London and with Don Burton in the Lake District in the early 1980s. He qualified in 1985 and started a teaching practice before founding Bashful Alley teaching centre in Lancaster in 1989. For a number of years John has worked as an Alexander Technique Teacher for CancerCare in Lancaster. John also heads the Natural Running team, who teach courses on how to run more effectively, efficiently and with joy.

PART FIVE

Applications, New Directions

'Too Loose yet too Tight'

Working with Hypermobility

Julie Barber

Hypermobility – double jointedness – can be a great natural asset, giving a person enviably free joints with greater than average range of movement. However, for a minority, it can result in unpleasant symptoms including chronic pain, extreme tiredness, recurrent soft tissue injuries, digestive problems and cardiac and autonomic symptoms. When these symptoms occur alongside hypermobility (HM), it becomes a more complex condition known as Hypermobility Syndrome (HMS) or Joint Hypermobility Syndrome (JHS).

My daughter was diagnosed with HMS aged 13 after eight months of backaches and headaches that came and went, along with tummy upsets and increasing exhaustion. The diagnosis was a surprise to me – and to the AT teachers, osteopaths and doctors (including a consultant paediatrician) she had seen during this time. I'd never heard of HMS, though I knew of Ehlers-Danlos Syndrome – Hypermobility type. As I learnt more I realised that not only was I teaching a teenage pupil who also had HMS (but hadn't had a correct diagnosis despite seeing many rheumatologists), but also that about 50% of my pupils were HM to some extent. Talking with colleagues I realised that few had heard of HMS and most knew little about EDS-HM type. After further research I published an article on Hypermobility Syndrome in *STATNews* in January 2012.

The article led me to collaborate with Dr Philip Bull, a consultant rheumatologist, on his article on Alexander Technique for the *Hypermobility Syndromes Association Journal*.[1] Dr Bull finds AT valuable in helping his HMS patients recover and manage their condition. As HMS is often missed, my aim here is to bring AT teachers up to speed, so you can recognise and better understand this syndrome. It's possible that more of your pupils are hypermobile than you realise and I hope understanding more about the condition will inform your work with them. Also, HMS is a relatively new diagnosis and there is a lot of research going on into what helps recovery. The AT has so much to offer – this is a great opportunity for us.

What is hypermobility?

HM means that joints can be moved beyond the 'normal' range of movement. It is very common in the general population, affecting 20-30% of individuals to some degree either in isolated joints or widespread through the body,[2] affects three times more females than males, is more common in people of Asian and African descent than those of European heritage, and generally

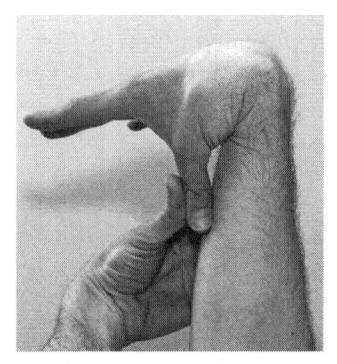

Fig. 1

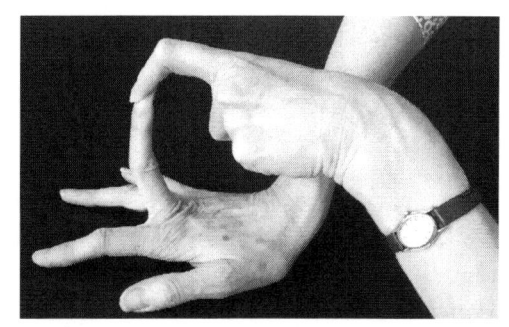

Fig. 2

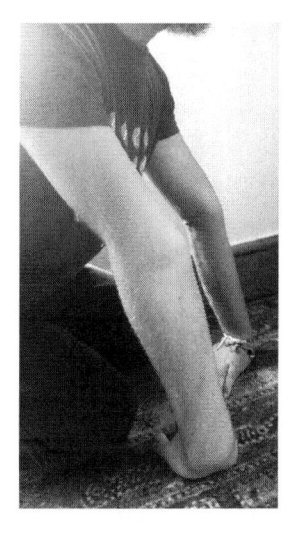

Fig. 3

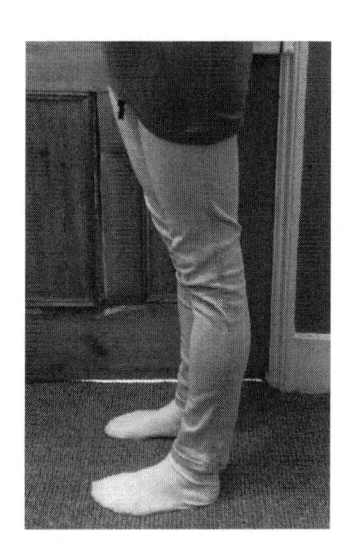

Fig. 4

Figs. 1–4. Alexander teachers and pupils demonstrating hypermobility.

diminishes with age. It is mostly inherited, though it can be acquired in certain joints through intense training (e.g. in ballet and gymnastics).

This looseness and flexibility gives a wonderful natural advantage to many sports people and performers. My daughter's first consultant reckoned that the top male tennis players are HM, it's easy to spot HM dancers and it's said that up to 40% of musicians are HM.[3]

When hypermobility causes pain, fatigue and injury it may signal an inherited connective tissue condition in which the body's collagen, in particular, is more elastic than normal. Collagen is the most common structural protein in the body – part of the myofascia alongside elastin, fibrillin, tenascin – and forms molecular cables that strengthen the ligaments and tendons, cartilage, bones, skin and internal organs (including lungs and gut). It provides structure to our bodies, protecting and supporting the softer tissues. You can see it in any cut of meat – the silvery material surrounding the individual muscle fibres and separating them into bundles, the 'sheath' surrounding the muscle itself, forming the tendon and merging with the bone. It gives the body its intrinsic toughness.[4] Hypermobile joints are lax because the collagen is looser and more fragile than normal, particularly in ligaments, tendons, joints and muscles. This makes 'the joints more mobile, sometimes unstable, thus more prone to injury'[5] and slower to heal.

Affected joints have a greater range of movement and appear 'double jointed' – as in swayback knees, TMJ (jaw) dysfunction, hypermobile elbows, shoulders, fingers, ankles, flat feet, etc. This instability can lead to pain and increased risks of subluxation (where a bone gets partially stuck at one end of the joint's range of movement) and even dislocation. Also to sprains, strains and injuries of the sudden traumatic type (such as ruptured tendons or torn ligaments) or from chronic overuse (such as tendonitis and bursitis, plantar fasciitis and carpal tunnel syndrome).

How is HMS diagnosed?

The classical medical test uses the Beighton score, which forms part of the Brighton Criteria.[6] A diagnosis of HMS is given when a person with one or more HM joints (not only those in the Beighton score), has pain, instability and soft tissue injury for more than 3 months (due only to the HM and not some other cause such as inflammatory illness). HMS people may actually appear stiff because their muscles are tight, so doctors will check for other symptoms including: 'growing pains' in children, scoliosis, gastrointestinal problems (IBS, reflux, bloating and pain), bladder and pelvic problems, 'velvet' skin that bruises, scars and forms stretch marks easily, headaches, anxiety states, depression, asthma, hernias, gynaecological problems, varicose veins, uterine and rectal prolapses. **It is important to note that HMS does not only affect joints – the skin and internal organs are also reliant on collagen**. As well as joint pain, some of these other problems may or may not be present.

HMS is also frequently linked with persistent, severe tiredness, poor proprioception and balance, fibromyalgia and autonomic dysfunction (discussed further below). Physical strength and endurance are quickly lost – 'if you don't use it you lose it'.

X-rays appear normal, as does soft tissue. Sufferers often look well and healthy, but have chronic aches and pains that come and go. Local anaesthetics can be less effective: HMS patients may need a larger dose.[7]

As we age we tend to stiffen, so sometimes it's useful to look back in time and ask questions, such as: have you ever had clicky joints? As a child could you do the splits or the crab? Were you clumsy or badly coordinated? Do you bruise easily? Do you have a close relative with any of these attributes?

BRIGHTON CRITERIA

Revised diagnostic criteria for hypermobility syndrome (HMS/JHS)

Major Criteria

1. A Beighton score of 4/9 (either currently or historically).
2. Arthralgia for longer than 3 months in four or more joints.

Minor Criteria

1. A Beighton score of 1, 2 or 3/9 (0, 1, 2 or 3 if aged 50+).
2. Arthralgia in 1-3 joints, or back pain or spondylosis, spondylolysis/spondylolisthesis.
3. Dislocation in more than one joint, or in one joint on more than one occasion.
4. Three or more soft tissue lesions (e.g. epicondylitis, tenosynovitis, bursitis).
5. Marfanoid habitus (tall, slim, arm span greater than height, upper segment: lower segment ration less than 0.89, arachnodactily).
6. Skin striae, hyperextensibility, thin skin or abnormal scarring.
7. Eye signs: drooping eyelids or myopia or antimongoloid slant.
8. Varicose veins or hernia or uterine/rectal prolapse.

The HMS/JHS is diagnosed in the presence of two major criteria, or one major and two minor criteria, or four minor criteria. Two minor criteria will suffice where there is an unequivocally affected first-degree relative.

BEIGHTON SCORE

Score 1 point for each hyper-extendable elbow, knee, thumb and finger; and 1 point for hands flat on the floor with straight legs. Maximum number: 9.

Fig. 5. The Beighton Score (above right) forms part of the Brighton Criteria (above left) used for HMS diagnosis.

Hypermobility can develop into HMS – the domino effect – following prolonged illness or injury in which there's loss of muscle tone, particularly when there's emotional stress or trauma. My daughter was initially diagnosed with a back injury (though she was unaware of any injury happening) and advised to rest. When the pains didn't stop but gradually increased she rested more, which led to her becoming further weakened and deconditioned until finally she was diagnosed with HMS eight months later. Before the 'injury' she was living a normal active life, but puberty was starting, and she'd had a difficult year transitioning to a new school.

HM IN CHILDHOOD

Hypermobile babies can be unwilling crawlers (preferring to 'bum shuffle') with delayed motor development, walking on tiptoes (which effectively splints their ankles), or in-toe or out-toe. (My daughter crawled, started walking at the normal time, but preferred to walk on tiptoe.)

HM children and adolescents: Knee pain is very common, and evidence points to HM's role in 'growing pains'. Handwriting and activities requiring fine motor coordination can be difficult. As puberty gets underway, testosterone stiffens joints so in boys the hypermobility often lessens. In girls it's the opposite: growth spurts combined with the start of menstruation may make the condition apparent. Progesterone relaxes collagen, reducing proprioception and affecting coordination. HM girls may be more prone to developing adolescent idiopathic scoliosis.[8] Many kids diagnosed with dyspraxia are also found to be HM and perhaps the two conditions should be considered to be within the same spectrum.[9] Holding fixed positions can be challenging and HM kids often fidget to relieve their pain and discomfort.

With age we all get stiffer, so joints generally become less flexible. However joint pain and other elements of HM may continue into later life. Most pupils I see are in this group.

HMS AND OTHER HEREDITARY DISORDERS OF THE CONNECTIVE TISSUES (HCTDs)

HMS appears in a number of specific hereditary connective tissue disorders, including Marfan's Syndrome, Osteogenesis Imperfecta, Stickler's Syndrome and the various types of Ehlers-Danlos Syndrome. There are genetic tests to diagnose some of these, but none have been found so far for HMS and EDS-hypermobility type. For recognition and management, HMS and EDS-H are now considered the same condition.[10]

HM/HMS Spectrum: People with lax joints fall along a broad spectrum: *most (90%) have no related symptoms*, some are only moderately affected with one or two of these symptoms, while the small minority at the far end with Marfan's Syndrome, or EDS classical or vascular types, may have potentially life threatening symptoms. Hypermobility has always been around, but in the 21st century it's increasingly leading to problems as children, young people and adults spend more time in sedentary pursuits, use their bodies less and subsequently lose physical tone.

HM/HMS Spectrum - Possible effects

Extreme Tiredness – Standing, walking and simple everyday tasks can be exhausting when muscles have to work extra hard to stabilise joints. Severe fatigue can persist despite rest or sleep[11] and be confused with Chronic Fatigue syndrome. It's important to have the right diagnosis as this will affect treatment.

Pain – usually comes from overstretched joints and chronically tightened muscles particularly towards the end of the day and after physical activity. Repetitive movements, or prolonged use of a hypermobile joint, can lead to pain, and fixed positions can be uncomfortable so people want to fidget and move around.

Injuries may cause acute localised pain but can progress to longer-term persistent, even severe, widespread pain, leading to possible centralised pain sensitisation, autonomic dysfunction and fibromyalgia. Chronic pain is debilitating, affecting one's life and ability to function, and can lead to *anxiety and depression*. There is no effective medication for this, though people may try increasingly strong painkillers. The best solution is to get help with managing the symptoms. Well-managed HMS will result in minimal pain.

Autonomic Dysfunction: The ANS (Autonomic Nervous System) is a highly specialised network of nerves that regulate many important systems, automatically adjusting functions in the body and compensating for change. It's the primary mechanism in control of the 'fight or flight' and 'rest and digest' reactions (sympathetic and parasympathetic) and the enteric (bowel).[12] Six out of ten patients seen in a HMS clinic describe some autonomic disturbance.[13] The commonest symptoms include dizziness and passing out following a change in posture, e.g. sitting from lying, standing from sitting (POTS); palpitations; bloating and pain in the bowel; fatigue, headaches, blurred vision, brain 'fog'.[14]

Proprioception, our inbuilt awareness of both movement and position in space, can be less sensitive and less reliable with HM. People describe themselves as 'clumsy' with poor coordination dating back to childhood. In a 'normal' joint capsule the brain knows exactly what has taken place as soon as we start to move. With extra laxity in the joint the proprioceptors won't fire until the joint has been stretched a bit further. Enhancing muscle tone and strength through exercise[15] has been shown to improve proprioception, as well as overall fitness and quality of life.

People with HM often lack the muscle tone necessary to maintain proper or 'neutral' postures and tend to 'hang' on their joints for stability, locking joints at one end of their range of movement to stabilise them – slouching or sitting bolt upright, habitually locking knees, standing with weight on one leg, resting on the outer edge of the feet. Over time this weakens the ligaments and tendons around the joint, as well as destabilising the rest of the body. With less reliable proprioception they don't realise they are doing this. *Learning how to be upright comfortably with minimum effort is very important.* However, maintaining a comfortably upright standing or sitting position for more than a few seconds can be challenging in the beginning as *'the postural muscles are unused to holding joints (the knee, pelvis and spine in particular) in a more neutral position, so endurance capabilities need to be built up slowly and gradually'.*[16]

I have noticed poor proprioception in many pupils who are clearly HM (and unaware of it) and are leading normal lives, though feeling poorly coordinated. People may be unaware of where certain body parts are. Understanding why this is gives me increased patience. For example, I recognised HMS in a young woman who was clearly very tight, in pain, suffering from RSI and exhausted all the time; she found it baffling and a bit offensive to be asked to 'let go' as she felt perfectly relaxed. Often I include AT procedures such as monkey, lunges, working against the wall and on the floor and using foam/air balance boards. I think contact with a hard surface aids proprioceptive feedback. The physiotherapy exercises recommended (and proven) to help restore proprioception and function – and reduce pain and instability – include work on all fours, sitting (often on Swiss balls), standing and being in semi-squat on balance boards.[17]

Pregnancy and Childbirth is often a completely normal experience for HM women and some individuals report feeling much better while pregnant. The general advice is to remain fit and active. However joint laxity increases so existing problems may be more noticeable and new joint pains or instability may arise, particularly in the lower back and pelvis. It's important to discuss the condition with the obstetrics team from early on in the pregnancy as there are complications associated with HMS such as premature rupture of the membranes, slow healing after tears or an episiotomy, pelvic floor problems and resistance to the effects of local anaesthetics (as mentioned earlier).[18]

Why is Hypermobility Syndrome missed?
For the majority of fit and physically active people hypermobility will present no problems, and even be a considerable asset. However, when HMS is clearly interfering with someone's ability to lead a normal, pain-free life (especially in a young person) it is crucial that they are seen by a specialist with knowledge of the condition (not all do). Without a correct diagnosis people are liable to become more sedentary and fearful, doing less and less in response to the pain and discomfort, initiating a downward spiral as happened with my daughter. Her recovery took 18 months and she is considered now to have well-managed HMS. A diagnosis gives people the information to understand what's going on so they can start on the road to recovery.

Specialist HMS clinics are few and far between.[19] A multi-disciplinary team offers physiotherapy (manual therapy, pain management, movement control, balance work, relaxation techniques), occupational therapy (help with sleep, pacing – see below – and aids), podiatry (for flat feet) and psychological (CBT) support (help with managing pain and fatigue, and the anxiety and depression that are often present).[20] The aim is to enable people to become physically fit and active, so they can lead a normal life. The young woman with RSI mentioned earlier was insomniac at night, then so exhausted she would sleep until the following lunchtime. When subsequently diagnosed with HMS she was advised to pace her daily activities until she recovered i.e. keep to very regular bedtime hours and allocate time each day for work, rest, exercise and fun. Within a few days of changing her routine her sleep improved, she felt better rested and her pain levels dropped significantly.

In a recent HMSA survey 52% of patients waited over 10 years to get a correct diagnosis.[21] People become frustrated, depressed and angry, having gone from one expert to the next with little improvement. Many healthcare professionals, including doctors and rheumatologists, are not sufficiently aware of HMS and overlook, or disregard, it. However, it's easy to spot once you can recognise the pattern of symptoms.

AT AND HM/HMS: A TEACHER'S PERSPECTIVE
- When someone is badly affected by HMS, AT is one part of a multi-disciplinary solution, alongside specialist medical and physiotherapy care, and possibly dietary changes (lactose or wheat intolerance?), acupuncture and gentle osteopathy (these last three are recommendations based on personal experience). With the right support and treatment, well-managed HMS will result in minimal pain or discomfort.
- It's very important to gradually introduce exercise to improve both strength and stamina so that well-toned muscles can take the place of lax ligaments, thereby protecting the joints and bony framework, and improving proprioception. As standing and walking become easier, people can move on to other physical activity they enjoy such as swimming, Pilates, cycling, tai chi or qigong. AT works best when the person has sufficient muscle tone to enable the directions to fully take effect and produce tangible benefits.
- An open, flexible collaboration between teacher and pupil helps build confidence in self-management. Encourage the pupil's nervous system to quieten so pain can diminish. Sometimes it can be difficult to gauge how free a HM pupil is. Don't think that their greater joint flexibility means that everything is necessarily free, as tension may be there as well (in their perception 'holding them together'). In our work, less is definitely more. People with HM are often highly sensitive and will not appreciate (nor benefit from) being 'taken apart' in a teacher's enthusiasm to encourage length and width.
- We can help pupils find stability and balance, reducing the strain on the body that leads to pain. As a pupil remarked: 'The AT drew my attention to my knees. By simply not locking them backwards my pain

levels significantly decreased.' However, be aware that being asked to **not** lock joints can feel confusing and scary to HM pupils.
- Learning how to release is very important and can alleviate pain. However, over-releasing, like over-stretching, can cause damage.
- 'Body map'[22] basic anatomy, so people understand their functional design better. Encourage mid-range movement to avoid joints locking.
- Allow pupils to move when they need to, and advise them not to hold positions for long periods without a break.

Sue Morgan, diagnosed with EDS-HM and Chronic Fatigue in 2009:

> About 6 months ago I was sitting in the theatre and suddenly thought, 'I haven't noticed my back!' For the first time in 40 years I wasn't constantly shifting position to try and get more comfortable.
>
> It has been a very slow process as by the time I was diagnosed with EDS-HM my muscles had become very weak and deconditioned. It was a real challenge to connect with them at all, but thinking in the AT way helped a lot. Even doing gentle physiotherapy exercise and slowly building up the repetitions would leave my muscles feeling stiff and tight (whilst looking very flexible). Most people would be advised to stretch at this point but if you are hypermobile it is so easy to overstretch. I now find releasing muscles using the Alexander Technique avoids this, and also makes my rehab exercises easier and more beneficial.
>
> Alexander has been an integral part of my continuing recovery. I feel more balanced, grounded and connected. My proprioception is more present and reliable, my neck feels more comfortable, I can breathe more easily and overall my pain has eased.[23]

Glenna Batson, Alexander teacher and physical therapist, comments:

> Alexander Technique teachers use their good use and their hands-on to imply directions, usually F. M. Alexander's primary directions, to redirect people away from states which cause the body to narrow, shrink, and collapse. For persons with HMS, however, it is important to ensure stability before directing the person outwards into mobility.

Batson continues,

> Physiotherapists use many hands-on techniques, based on neurophysiological principles of evoking localised reflex stability and mobility prior to full body action. One of these techniques is 'approximation' – a way of gently bringing joint surfaces closer together. Joint surface approximation happens naturally under usual circumstances of weight bearing, and evokes automatic neuromuscular reflex patterns that stabilise joints prior to movement. In HMS,

this automatic neuromuscular reflex patterning does not occur in a timely manner, leaving the person with little support for movement. If these persons are given primary directions too soon, they may not find ease of coordination, but rather experience more pain and sense of weakness. *Keeping in mind that the first direction is inward will help the AT teacher better understand the needs of the client with HMS.*[24]

Roxani-Eleni Garefalaki, an aeriaist, contortionist, and trainee Alexander teacher, provides an apt conclusion:

> If I have one thing to say about hypermobility this would be it: while normal people can be compared to strong bridges, hypermobile people are like bridges made of separate pieces of wood connected with rope. Thus everything that happens on this bridge will cause much more nervous stimulus, sensory information and movement. Feeling one integrated whole person can be tough when feeling so many details. [25]

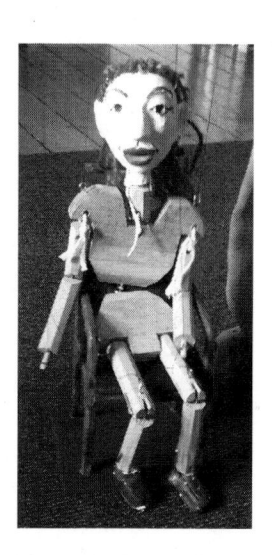

Fig. 6.

Sincere thanks to Dr Philip Bull for generously and patiently sharing his medical knowledge with me, Maddy Paxman and Ilia Daoussi for their editing and supportive skills, Glenna Batson for contributing, and Joe Friedman for his technical prowess.

Photos courtesy of Julie Barber, Maddy Paxman, Andy Smith, Sue Morgan, Roxani Eleni-Garefalaki. Figure 5 (Beighton score and Brighton Criteria) courtesy of HMSA (http://hypermobility.org/). Figure 6 courtesy of Young People's Puppet Theatre, photographed by Julie Barber.

References
1   Bull, P. (2015). 'The Alexander Technique' in *HMSA Journal*, 3 Spring, v.1.2 (www.stat.org.uk/press/alexander-technique-dr-philip-bull-hmsa-journal-spring-2015).
2   Hakim, A. J. 'Clinician's Guide to JHS', HMSA website http://hypermobility.org/help-advice/hypermobility-syndromes/jhseds-hm-clinicians-guide/ [posted 27 August 2013].
3   Dommerholt, Dr Jan (2011). 'CSF Ehlers-Danlos Syndrome Colloquium'. (https://vimeo.com/35766706).
4   Hakim, A. J. 'Latest News, Help & Advice, Welcome', HMSA website (www.hypermobility.org/help-advice/) [posted May 9 2015].
5   Grahame, R., N Hasson (2006). 'Hypermobility Syndrome'. Contact A Family website for families with disabled children, October 2006 (www.cafamily.org.uk/

medical-information/conditions/h/hypermobility-syndrome).

6   Grahame, R., H. A. Bird, A. L. Dolan, et al. (2000). 'The revised (Brighton 1998) criteria for the diagnosis of benign joint hypermobility syndrome' in *J Rheumatol*, 27, pp. 1777-1779.

7   Hakim, A. J., R. Grahame, P. Norris, et al. (2005). 'Local anaesthetic failure in joint hypermobility syndrome' in *J R Soc Med* 98 (2), pp. 84-85.

8   Binns, M. S. (1988). 'Joint Laxity in Idiopathic Adolescent Scoliosis' in *J Bone Joint Surg Am* 70-B3:420-422, .P. P. Perrin (2006). 'Why do idiopathic scoliosis patients participate more in gymnastics?' in *Scan J Med Sci Sports* 16(4), pp. 231-236.

9   Kirby, A., R. Davies (2007). 'Developmental Coordination Disorder and Joint Hypermobility Syndrome – overlapping disorders? Implications for research and clinical practice' in *Child Care Health Dev* 33(5), pp. 513-519. D. A. Sugden, A. Kirby, C. Dunford (2008). 'Children with developmental coordination disorder' in *Special Edition of International Journal of Disability, Development and Education*, 55(2), pp. 93-187.

10 Grahame, R. (1999). 'Joint hypermobility and genetic collagen disorders. Are they related?' *Arch Dis Child* 80, pp. 188-191. B. T. Tinkle, M. Lavallee, H. Levy, et al. (2009). 'Position Statement from the Professional Advisory Network of the Ehlers-Danlos National Foundation'.

11 Hakim, A. J. 'Fatigue'. HMSA website http://hypermobility.org/help-advice/fatigue/ [posted 10 June 2013].

12 Hakim, A. 'POTS, Hypotension, Fatigue and Upset Bowel, The Autonomic Nervous System and Hypermobility Syndromes', HMSA website http://hypermobility.org/help-advice/autonomic-problems/ [posted 9 June 2013].

13 As 10 (above).

14 HMSA (2014). 'The Hypermobile Child. A Guide for Schools', p. 11.

15 Ferrell, W. R., N. Tennant, R. D. Sturrock et al. (2004). 'Amelioration of symptoms by enhancement of proprioception in patients with joint hypermobility syndrome', *Arthritis Rheum* 50(11), pp. 3323-3328.

16 Keer, R., K. Butler (2010). 'Physiotherapy and occupational therapy in the hypermobile adult' in *Hypermobility, Fibromyalgia and Chronic Pain*. Churchill Elsevier: London, ch. 9, p. 152.

17 For more information on this I recommend reading section 2; 'Therapy' in *Hypermobility, Fibromyalgia and Chronic Pain* (ibid).

18 For more information read R Grahame and R Keer, '12.6 Pregnancy and the pelvis' in *Hypermobility, Fibromyalgia and Chronic Pain* (as 16, above). Also: A. Hakim, R. Keer, 'Pregnancy in JHS and EDS-HT', http://hypermobility.org/help-advice/pregnancy/ posted 1 October 2012.

19 See http://hypermobility.org/help-advice/hms-clinics/

20 The leading unit is at St John & Elizabeth Hospital, London (private). Full details on their website: (www.thehypermobilityunit.org.uk/).

21 Hakim, A. J. (2013). 'Clinician's Guide to JHS', HMSA website (http://hypermobility.org/help-advice/hypermobility-syndromes/jhseds-hm-clinicians-guide/) [posted 27 August 2013].

22 Conable, B., W Conable, 'Bodymap'(http://bodymap. org/main).
23 Bull, P. (2015). 'The Alexander Technique' in *HMSA Journal*, vol 3 Spring v.1.2, p. 33 (www.stat.org.uk/press/alexander-technique-dr-philip-bull-hmsa-journal-spring-2015).
24 Barber, J. (2012). 'Hypermobility Syndrome' in *Statnews*, January 2012, vol. 7, issue 7, pp. 28-29. (www.atfriends.org/Hypermobility.htm).
25 Email to Julie Barber, 16 May 2015.

Bibliography

Barber, J. (2012). 'Hypermobility Syndrome' in *Statnews*, January 2012, vol 7, issue 7 (http://www.atfriends.org/Hypermobility.htm).

Bull, P. (2015). 'The Alexander Technique' in *HMSA Journal*, vol 3, Spring 2015, v.1.2 (www.stat.org.uk/press/alexander-technique-dr-philip-bull-hmsa-journal-spring-2015).

Hakim, A., J. R. Keer, R. Grahame (2010). *Hypermobility, Fibromyalgia and Chronic Pain*. Churchill Livingstone Elsevier: London.

The Hypermobile Child. A Guide for Schools, Hypermobility Syndromes Association 2014 (available from the HMSA, see below).

Hypermobility Syndromes Association (HMSA) – www.hypermobility.org

Knight, I. (2011). *A Guide to Living with Hypermobility Syndrome, Bending without Breaking*. Singing Dragon: London.

Myers, T. W. (2001). *Anatomy Trains, Myofascial Meridians for Manual and Movement Therapists*. Churchill Livingstone Elsevier: London.

Smith, C., D Wicks (2015). 'Hypermobility in Heritable Disorders of Connective Tissue – An Overview. Basic Essentials for medical professionals and members wanting to learn about these conditions', *HMSA Journal* vol 3 Spring 2015 v.1.2.

Tinkle, B. T. (2010). *Joint Hypermobility Handbook: A Guide for the Issues & Management of Ehlers-Danlos Syndrome Hypermobility Type and the Hypermobility Syndrome*. Left Paw Press: USA.

Julie Barber (MSTAT) trained with Walter and Dilys Carrington at the Constructive Teaching Centre in London. After qualifying in 1993 she taught there for many years and assisted on the annual postgraduate summer school. She has taught individuals and groups in a variety of settings including the Department of Health, BP, drama schools, a residential home and 15 years at the BBC Club. She now teaches at the London Centre for Alexander Technique and Training (LCATT) and has a private practice in North London. She is a professional member of the Hypermobility Syndromes Association (HMSA) and regularly gives talks and workshops on HMS to Alexander teachers.

Teaching to Trauma

The Terror Trauma Response[SM]

Katherine H. Breen

If trauma is 'part of life', I've had a rich life. Traumas and injuries require therapies for recovery. Of all the therapies I've benefitted from, the Alexander Technique receives the credit for consistently bringing me back to 'true' and giving me back my full life on *multiple occasions*. Not only that, it has consistently gotten me *better* than I was pre-trauma or injury. How can that be?

Because I'm an Alexander teacher I observe myself in the act of living and this allows me to also observe myself in the act of trauma. Over time and many experiences, a pattern began to present itself. This pattern was not just identifiable in myself; I also discovered it in my traumatised students and loved ones, and I have come to think of it as the human *response* to the *stimulus* of trauma.

A traumatic experience can result from an external event such as an earthquake, or a 'physical' event such as a dislocated knee, an all body–mind event such as drowning, a diagnosis such as Parkinson's Disease, or an emotional event such as the fear of being hurt or the loss of a loved one. It can be produced by concussion, brain injury, whiplash and stroke. I would like to share my insights, from the inside out, for collegial consideration and feedback.

In this workshop, I sought to advance two hypotheses that, if true, could influence optimal care for brain injury and trauma:

One: The reflex pattern associated with severe trauma is not the startle reflex; it is a different response which I call the Terror Trauma Response[SM]. In this patterned response, the head goes back and down, the hyoid goes forward and up, the eyes roll up and back, and the shoulders roll back and down.

Two: I hypothesise that for some people the tongue and hyoid may stay elevated (and the head–neck held back and down), even after the situation has passed, and that this incomplete resolution negatively affects functioning of the entire head–neck–back–throat relationship and has a cascading effect system-wide. Not only that but it is a held pattern, easy to habitualise, primed and ready for deployment at the least provocation. It follows that many of the lasting malfunctions and undesirable symptoms associated with MTBI (mild traumatic brain injury), stroke, PTSD (post traumatic stress disorder) and post-concussion syndrome are not necessarily caused by a deficit in neural pathways or brain functioning, but may also result from interference of the head–neck–back–throat relationship[1] which in turn causes progressive disfunction in overall use and leads to the breakdown of specific parts.

The Terror Trauma Response

When I was a teenager I fell asleep while driving on a mountainous road and drove the car off a cliff. Years later, I almost drowned off the coast of California when thirty-foot 'sneaker' or 'rogue' waves appeared out of nowhere, crashed down on me, and carried me in a riptide out to sea.

Recently I was at a Goya exhibit at Boston's Museum of Fine Arts when I saw his painting *The Shipwreck* for the first time. I was transfixed. He had captured what I had experienced immediately after the accidents. Not only that, but what I saw was a deep, primitive-seeming pattern that I had observed time and again in my students who had been through deep trauma. I had always assumed that trauma would yield the startle pattern, but this other 'pattern' resonated deeply. I began looking at other pieces of art which depicted trauma (Picasso's *Guernica*, the famous Greek sculpture *Laocoön*, etc.) and saw the pattern repeatedly. It was obvious, intuitive. The head goes back and down, the eyes roll up and back, the shoulders roll back and down, the arms rotate externally (and may go up in the air or out in front to indicate 'Stop, I'm overwhelmed'). The vast majority of my students and I also experience that the tongue braces against the roof of the mouth; and the hyoid, the floating bone which anchors the tongue in the middle of the throat, goes forward and up. I call this pattern, which is not 'startle', the Terror Trauma Response.[2]

Different patterns of trauma and the sounds we make (or don't)

Different sounds – gasps, whimpers, wails, even silence – accompany different types of traumas and help differentiate and define nuances in the pattern.

Fig. 1. *The Shipwreck* by Francisco Goya, 1794, Bowes Museum, England.

I submit that the most powerful sound emitted in trauma is the terror scream. It has only happened to me once, and that was the time when I drove off the cliff. Like other sounds in trauma, the terror scream is a scream which you observe yourself doing, rather than consciously 'do'. I would describe it as coming from the very depths of the hollows. It is an eerie, otherworldly sound that comes at once from within and without, reverberating in a chilling, slow-motion silence. (You'll recognise it in a horror movie when the dead person rises.) I remember hearing the sound before I realised I was the one making it. I am years away from it now, but to reproduce it would require a rigid snap back of the head, snap up of the hyoid and snap down of the shoulders – all at once. How could it not stay with you? Knowing your terror scream fundamentally changes who you are.

Perhaps of equal power is the 'no sound' that can accompany extreme horror. This can happen when the trauma is 'unspeakable', or when a person's very identity is challenged as unacceptable. In these circumstances there was no outlet. Students of mine who experienced this kind of trauma report having lost their ability to speak, or find themselves with a gag, or a speech impediment, etc.

There is a moment in trauma when the experience peaks; it is the moment when the whole self, with all senses, is engaged in full throttle: eyes, ears, body, soul and voice work in tandem to contort and project (or prevent) sound at the climax; I consider this the *moment* of the terror trauma response.[3] When I work with students we often unravel their patterns, arriving at the remnants of the terror trauma response, and I now find it easily recognisable even in its more subtle forms. I hypothesise that this contortion sticks, unresolved, and creates a holding pattern embedded in the cellular/muscular memory of the throat, not unlike other holding patterns we create and learn to undo. By working in a deep way with the understanding of this particular pattern with our students, we can help them unravel and re-find neutral, and possibly the muscular and/or cellular memories and pathways disappear in the mix. I believe the Alexander Technique has helped me and my students in this way.

There are two points to consider in all of this in our teaching. The first is not to assume that you know the pattern, but instead to listen and observe the person in front of you as a unique individual. Do not assume existence of the pattern, or look for it. If there is time, patience and trust, it will present itself to you when the student is ready. If it doesn't, respect the silence. Don't be surprised if the student has an overlay of several patterns.

When I behold the pattern I find it important to hold it, and the student with it, in a pause as if I am swaddling a baby – but I am maximally strong, back and quiet in myself. I pause in the hold patiently and quietly with the person as they process. At a certain point, they find their natural way out of it and their system re-engages in all the right ways. At that point I 'catch the wave' with them and help lead them into length, width and 'forward and up'.

The second point is that in each of these cases the down and backward trajectory of the head appears to be accompanied by the forward and up trajectory of the hyoid.

THE CASE OF J.

In a first lesson I like to sit, listen and observe before putting hands on. It informs my teaching. I also use reflective listening to help establish trust. If the trauma response pattern presents itself as we talk, I notice it, and remember to expand my awareness to allow for it during the hands-on lesson if appropriate.

J, one of my newer students, came with breathing and swallowing difficulties. She happened to have had a videolaryngoscopy done six weeks before her first lesson with me. This particular student went through the terror trauma posture several times as she was telling her stories of trauma. Her lesson happened to be on the anniversary of the Boston Marathon bombing, which she described as one of the experiences that had deeply traumatised her. The precise *emotion* associated with the Marathon bombing for her, which came up in our conversation about the anniversary, was the same emotion that had surfaced in two of the other unrelated traumas she described, and her physical response was similar. I believe these experiences are retained in similar patterns in the self, and that by reworking the *association* of the emotion that is held in the response pattern, we appear to help students rid themselves of the retrigger – without having to relive the initial trauma. I did a normal table turn with her, paying attention to my own means-whereby, inhibition and direction (not focusing on the swallowing and breathing 'problem' for which she had come). In fact, work on her neck felt too invasive, so my work with her in that lesson was everywhere else; but all along I was describing relevant parts of the Hyoid Matrix to her[4] (as they related to her particular holding patterns) and asking her to think certain things as she unravelled. I spent a lot of time on her feet, because there is a way of working on the feet which I find provides good, unthreatening access to the Hyoid Matrix and the rest of the head–neck–back relationship. It was through her legs that she trembled a release from her whole self. I stayed with her until it stopped. Her lesson unfolded as described above and the internal musculature had a dramatic change. Unbeknown to me, her six-week follow up with her doctors was the next day. They were so surprised by her external changes, the change in her voice and her report of improvement, that they did a follow up videolaryngoscopy, which the doctor described as 'knock your socks off remarkable'.

To give the reader an idea of how I do this work: for example, during an intake conversation, a student may tell of a terror trauma experience in which they were hit by a car and nearly died. As teacher you may observe their body adopt the terror trauma response as they are telling the story. You see this with your eyes (their whole body stiffens and arches back, tightened

Before After

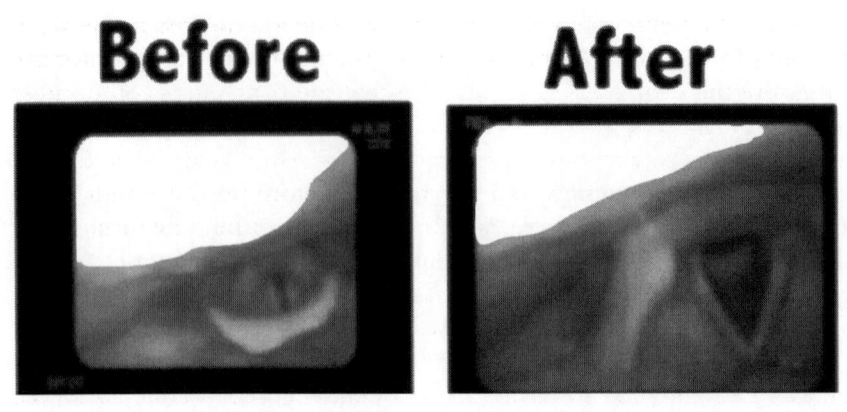

Fig. 2. Videolaryngoscopy courtesy of J. and Dr Jayme Dowdall MD Laryngologist, Co-director, BWH Voice Program, at Brigham and Women's Hospital, Instructor, Harvard Medical School – Otolaryngology faculty.

jaw, head back, hand often up, eyes may roll back), hear the tone of their voice with your ears but do nothing other than carry on the conversation and store what you observed as interesting information. Later during the hands-on portion of that, or a future, lesson the student may describe a much lesser event that happened to them but that would share significant traits and characteristics around the *emotion* of the first experience – perhaps a bicyclist suddenly skidding next to them on the same side – or simply a good friend surprising them from behind. At that same moment you might observe the previous terror trauma pattern as a very deep twist or a 'stop' deep in their body *and you are in that moment able to help them stop*, observe and undo the core internal holding pattern. I believe the throat and tongue may be the ultimate storage spot of retriggerable trauma.

It is extremely important to 'close' the student up after such a lesson before they go back out to the world. By this I mean, after such an event, make sure to spend time reintegrating all parts of them. Let them stay for a few extra minutes (schedule these students in a way which allows for that); follow their lead if they want to talk about it or not, don't pry, do allow strong compassion. Most will be smiling and have beautified expressions of gratitude and countenance at lesson end; you might feel exhausted. Take time for self.

WHAT HAPPENS IN A MILD TRAUMATIC BRAIN INJURY (MBTI)?
As mentioned in my essay on the Hyoid Matrix (also in these Congress Papers), I suffered a mild traumatic brain injury in January 2012, in what was probably my fifth concussion. In many MTBIs, doctors hypothesise, the brain is slammed against the other side of the skull, tearing neurons on the bottom of the brain as it crosses the craggy bottom of the skull. Maybe, but what if the mass of the brain never comes back to 'true'? After my injury, I

experienced that my brain was skewed to one side and twisted in the skull, and it felt like my body was spasmodically tightening to compensate for the off-kilter weight distribution. Could it be that the problem is confounded by poor use in addition to torn neurons? A good, quiet, slow and respectful Alexander lesson set me more 'right' and cognitive, physical and emotional functioning noticeably improved. If it were torn neurons, why would I have the ability to be better or worse? It seems to me torn would be torn, either connected, or not.

MINDING THE BODY TO MEND THE MIND: TEACHING STRATEGIES AND RAMIFICATIONS

I theorise that many of the lasting symptoms associated with brain injury, neural damage and/or PTSD may be aggravated by or even result from poor use of the head–neck–back relationship stemming compensatorily (and not directly) from the initial trauma. Many lasting symptoms do not begin until hours, days or even weeks after the initial injury. I hypothesise that what starts as a single 'trauma' event involving the brain initiates a series of events in the Hyoid Matrix in response to the first injury; these secondary and tertiary events become triggers in their own right, creating a successive series of challenges related to balance (physical and emotional), vision, fatigue and cognition, among other things. The feedback loop of these latter disturbances to the brain creates a troubling and self-reinforcing chain reaction. The brain is overwhelmed and can't think straight, inhibition is unavailable and direction is lost. However, by unwinding and allowing the head–neck–back and the Hyoid Matrix within the context of the head–neck–back to re-find 'true', the brain is itself re-educated. The correct neural pathways are re-found (or perhaps easier and more efficient new ones established). Balance (physical and emotional), un-distressed vision, hearing and cognition are returned, general functioning restored, fatigue diminished and the nervous system eased and reset.

The brain-injured student can't think well, or think about *how* to think. The student's brain doesn't have to be working well, however, for the teacher to positively engage it. By hands-on re-education of the functioning of parts within the context of the whole (working backwards to the brain), a skilled Alexander teacher can indirectly retrain and reawaken optimal conscious ability. That said, teaching a brain-injured student requires a dramatically quieter, slower, deeper and more nuanced approach. The MTBI and stroke student benefits from a teacher who thoughtfully moves the limbs incorporating inhibition, direction and reintegration with both the head–neck–back and the Hyoid Plexus, which activates ten of the twelve cranial nerves.[5] *Much less* is truly way more. I hypothesise that extremely slow, sensitive and quiet repetition of these externally directed movements, within the context of the whole, wakes up and comprehensively retrains all parts of the brain. The cranial nerves are distributed throughout the brain and, from my limited understanding of how recovery works, lighting up more of the brain at once will yield stronger results. The Hyoid system may be a goldmine in this regard, and begs to be further researched. Remarkably, the unified, psychophysical nature of the self allows the Technique to work counterintuitively: *the body is effectively re-educating the mind.* In my experience, in the early stages, the brain-injured student should have the eyes closed while the limbs are being gently moved like this, and be exposed to minimal auditory stimuli.

A traditional Alexander lesson indirectly reaches all 'parts' of the Hyoid system, and the indirect, comprehensive nature of our approach within this context may explain why the Technique is so successful. If the use of the body feeds back to and influences functioning of the brain (which is basic Alexander), it follows that maximum benefit from therapeutic cognitive, eye, balance or other exercises will be gained if done after an Alexander lesson (though only after the student has progressed far enough). This was my experience.

I hypothesise that a reset of the Hyoid system prior to part-specific therapeutic exercise for the brain (or body) amplifies and maximises benefit. In an ideal scenario, Alexander lessons would book-end other therapies, or become an integral part of them, or maybe even render them unnecessary. An expanded Alexander lesson may provide one-stop comprehensive therapy; a triple benefit in that fewer appointments reduce stress, are cost effective and allow brain patients more time for rest and healing. Finally, the educational component of the Alexander Technique, in which pupils develop the ability to observe and supersede counterproductive patterns in the act of their personal daily living, is invaluable; this skill set accelerates recovery. All of the above should be further researched and, I believe, implemented.

THE PROMISE OF HELP THROUGH THE HYOID – AND NON-ENDGAINING

On one day, after I had received an Alexander lesson for my concussion, I continued working on my own and I believe I was able to use the hyoid as a means of helping the mass of the brain float back to 'true'. Or perhaps the muscles just released and gave the sensation of movement of the mass. In any case, I no longer think my brain is off-centre and my misuse struggles are showing slow but sure improvements.

After this experience, it was difficult to not over-focus on the hyoid and its muscles. I tried to set it right. I spent hours. Weeks. Months. And got myself nowhere, worse than when I had started. But with my students, I was doing my best hands-on work ever. I share this as caution – just like all things Alexander, trying to 'feel it out' or 'fix it' quickly becomes over-focused on the part at the expense of the whole. If my insights are accurate, the best way to use the information is to stick to principle, work indirectly, pay attention to the means-whereby, don't endgain by trying to figure out where the hyoid should be, don't over-focus on the front at the expense of the back. Expand your awareness to include this as more of a deep knowledge and an academic backdrop when you come upon a 'stop'. Don't try to judge if you're correct; if you are, the student's system will usually tell you via tummy gurgles, a spontaneous breath, body trembles, eye movements, a sigh, etc. My students and I find this work to be deeper than the work we do when we 'free the neck' but, in our experience, one is not better than the other; both are valuable for different students at different times. I find it valuable to do both in a lesson. That said, I find it important to finish a lesson with a return of the hands to the Hyoid Matrix, giving closure to the lesson and integrating the changes. By this I mean: do put your hands on, in a way which imparts floating (not fixing), safety, closure and end. Also, while tablework is most appropriate initially, I find it important to spend at least a few minutes walking or doing chair work at the end, but solely for integrative (and not necessarily advancement) purposes.

If these hypotheses are correct, current practice for brain injury and trauma should incorporate Alexander Technique as a primary therapy and educational tool. The Alexander hands-on abilities within our 'total pattern integration' paradigm are second to none, and there is no greater tool we can give the recovering brain-injured person than the independent means to observe, inhibit and release patterns of 'misuse' which otherwise prevent advancement.

Notes
1. My inclusion of throat is intentional for clarity but this does not mean to imply that our general use of the term 'neck' is not inclusive of 'throat'; it clearly is.
2. 'The Startle Pattern is a "total reflex" that . . . is a stereotyped postural response to a sudden loud noise . . . . The two sets of neck muscles have contracted simultaneously, thrusting the head forward but keeping the Frankfort plane horizontal. The postural change does not stop with the head and neck. The shoulders are lifted and the arms extended, the chest is flattened, and the knees are flexed.' Using multiple-channel electromyography on eight subjects and sixty patterns, Jones and Kennedy (Jones & Kennedy 1951) captured this response and showed that 'the change, which is not instantaneous, begins in the head and neck, passing down the trunk and legs to be completed in about a half a second.' (*Body Awareness in Action*, Frank Pierce Jones, Schocken Books, New York 1979, p. 133.) Workshop participants wondered if it might be the Moro Reflex which is seen at birth and in the first months of life. This reflex is prompted by placing a baby face up on a soft surface and then gently lifting and releasing the head. 'The normal response is for the baby to open its eyes wide in a startled look. The baby's arms move sideways with the palms up and the thumbs flexed and may cry for a minute.' (National Institutes of Health, Moro reflex: MedlinePlus Medical Encyclopedia www.nlm.nih.gov.) This same NIH website defines the startle reflex as basically Moro but without the baby: 'The startle reflex is a brainstem reflectory reaction (reflex) that serves to protect the back of the neck (whole body startle) or the eye (eyeblink) and facilitates escape from sudden stimuli.' Although there appear to be slight

differences in definition (and name) of these different reflexes, the salient point here is that none of the descriptions describe the Terror Trauma Response.
3. Perhaps not so surprisingly, a trauma victim who doesn't produce this sound may experience gagging sensations or swallowing difficulties later in life.
4. See my essay 'The Hyoid Matrix', also in these Congress Papers.
5. I believe we will in time discover a full twelve out of twelve relationship. For more on this subject, please see my essay 'The Hyoid Matrix' in these Congress Papers.

Katherine H. Breen is the author of two papers in this anthology. Please see 'The Hyoid Matrix' for her biography and acknowledgements.

The Hyoid Matrix[SM]

Katherine H. Breen

In this workshop I sought to advance a theory that I believe may provide a means for researching, proving and explaining the effects of the Alexander Technique. The theory is a work in progress, and I submit it with hopes for collegial consideration, exploration, conversation and feedback. It is based on phenomena I have observed over the last twenty-one years concerning the tongue, the jaw and the hyoid bone and the complex matrix to which they belong within the head–neck–back relationship. I have named this web the Hyoid Matrix[SM].[1]

In this paper I will delve into a system that I believe is critical to human functioning and to understanding of the Alexander Technique – both why it works and how it works. Because of that I want to make it clear at the outset that I am not in any way implying that this system works in isolation. Quite the contrary, I believe the Hyoid Matrix influences and is influenced by every other part and system of the human being, and is just one part (albeit an important one) of the head–neck–back relationship.

The tongue, hyoid, and many other muscles in the head–neck–back–throat form a complex web with seemingly enormous reach. This web includes critical muscles, bones, organs, systems, arteries, nerves and early evolutionary arches of the head–neck–back, all of which appear to play a pivotal role in function and use. I have named the web the Hyoid Matrix, because I experience that it functions as a matrix of which the hyoid is the unifying feature and in which input determines output and vice-versa. I believe it would be a mistake to consider or treat any part of it as a sole entity. Any muscle, liga-

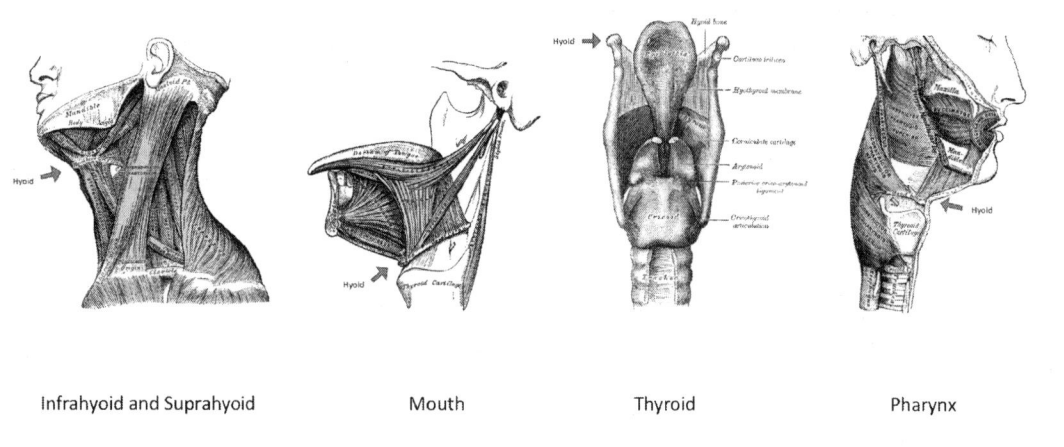

| Infrahyoid and Suprahyoid | Mouth | Thyroid | Pharynx |

Fig 1.   The various angles of the hyoid

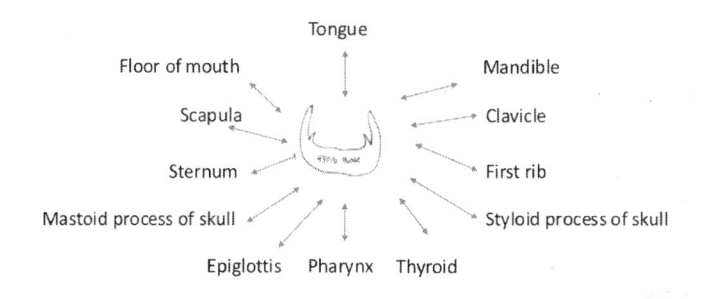

Fig 2.   The simple hyoid and connections.

ment, bone, membrane, fascia or nerve that connects to or affects the hyoid is included in my definition of the system.

I have experienced that the Hyoid Matrix is intimately involved in balance and emotional stability, and plays a role in determining the quality of auditory, visual and cognitive function as well as respiratory, digestive, and possibly even hormonal functioning. Although the Hyoid Matrix is just one piece of the overarching head–neck–back system at play, I hypothesise that better understanding of it may increase understanding of how and why the Alexander Technique works, aid in our ability to describe it, and be of help to many who suffer.

BACKGROUND

In January 2012 I had a devastating blow to the head (at the level of the ear, mastoid process and the occiput joint) which over the ensuing weeks spiralled quickly into life-altering challenges, such as an inability to turn over in bed,

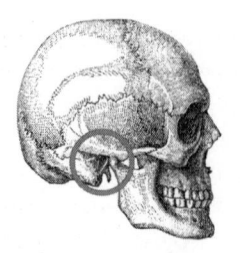

Fig 3. Location of injury.

a dysfunctional left arm, repeated falling, lack of audio inhibition, cognitive dysfunction/breakdown, extreme fear, disabling spasmodic back pain and a lag time between doing and seeing. As Alexander teachers know well, a hit to the ear at the level of the AO joint could be a devastating injury from a 'use' perspective. Most distressing of all my symptoms was that I couldn't 'do' Alexander, that which had always gotten me better. I couldn't even begin to free the neck; 'inhibition' was not available to me; I couldn't *think*. I was in spasm with no clue which way was 'up'. My internal compass and 'direction' were gone. Unresolved memories and injuries from earlier accidents were re-triggered and unprocessed former traumas crept into my thinking. I was diagnosed with a mild traumatic brain injury (MBTI). However, I was keenly aware that my area of injury was exactly the area that I had been focusing on so intently as an area of interest. In David Gorman's anatomy book *The Body Moveable*,[2] David had circled the very spot where I had been hit; his writing confirmed my self-observations about the consequences of my injury and why I was having such difficulty with my overall use.[3]

One day, after lying alone in a dark room for many hours, I remembered my teacher trainer Ed Avak telling me once that if you couldn't tell what you were doing, to try doing it more. The only thing I could notice was my tongue, because I could *feel* it shoved with great force on the roof of my mouth. As I proceeded to observe this phenomenon and wonder how the heck I was doing this with such force, what other muscles might be involved, etc. my tongue suddenly released, my hyoid dropped back and down, my head popped forward and up and a huge breath escaped which I heard sounding '*ahhhhhhhh*'. Alexander's whispered 'ah', one after the other and all at the same time without my doing a thing! Imagine my response! Could it be that Alexander's exercise was something that he experienced rather than created? I asked my concussion doctor what he knew about the hyoid. Not much, but he was intrigued and encouraged me to do my own explorations.

Doing nothing

One student continued to come to see me with the understanding that I couldn't teach or give a good stimulus. Our goal was for me to just put hands on and try to think of myself. We theorised it might help; and it seemed that her nervous system may have fed back positively to mine. My 'use' was abysmal. I couldn't free the neck, I was way forward of balance with knees locked, and I felt twisted in the brain stem. I couldn't do monkey, or even move around her body, but I was able to lay hands on her upright knees and notice my tongue down to my hyoid, and out to my shoulders. As I told her about my personal observations, and invited her to do the same, deep changes in long-standing, persistent holding patterns (that we had been chipping away at for many months) began to happen rather dramatically to both teacher and student. As other long-standing students began to come back, I did the same with similar results. For one of them the change was in the wrist, another the foot, a third, the groin, the shoulder and breath. As importantly, I noticed consistently that even though I couldn't free my neck, thinking of doing nothing with my tongue all the way to the hyoid bone, and thinking of doing nothing in the Hyoid Matrix so the hyoid could drop back and down, reliably and expediently sent my head forward and up (in a different way than freeing the neck) and ameliorated my concussion symptoms[4]. Freeing the hyoid resulted in sending the head forward and up, but freeing the neck to allow the head to go forward and up did not necessarily result in freeing the hyoid. After noticing this many, many times over a multi-year period, I began to incorporate it more consciously into my teaching, with powerful results. I was accessing a deeper place in my students and my hand placement was more and more reminiscent of what I had seen in photos of Alexander himself teaching.

THE IMPORTANCE OF THE HYOID MATRIX

I have come to consider the Hyoid Matrix as an important, strongly influential part of the head–neck–back relationship. In my experience thus far, without looking for it, holding patterns eventually find their root in the hyoid. In addition, as I hope to demonstrate via photographs (below), the placement of Alexander's hands and the ways in which we were taught in teacher training to use ourselves and our hands, as well as the principles upon which the Technique rests (non-endgaining, paying attention to the means-whereby, and the inability to separate mind from body) closely parallel the multifaceted working complexity of the Hyoid Matrix. For example, when we put hands under someone's jaw, our 'lengthening fingers' encourage the release down to hyoid while the pull to the wrist encourages the release of the jaw and the floor of the mouth. Similarly, hands on the base of the skull with fingers 'lengthening' on to the neck encourages release of stylohyoid and posterior digastric while the 'pull to the elbows' encourages the middle constrictor to release back. This influence on middle constrictor may create a quiet, more open space in the pharynx, aide in digestion, breathing and flow of blood and oxygen. When we place hands on base of skull from behind and under jaw in front, I experience an open passage in my students and a new balance. This happens best if the teacher is similarly balanced. Over-emphasis on parts comes at the expense of the whole, and intent to achieve an end result without attention to the means-whereby does not yield success. Finally, the whispered 'ah', as described above, positively engages and affects the entire Matrix. The reader may say, 'This is just the Alexander Technique' – exactly.

The difference in structure between the human hyoid bone and that of other mammals is attributed to our ability to speak. Speech was the issue at hand when Alexander made his discoveries, and speech was the register to which Alexander set standards and determined success or failure. All of his initial work and discoveries were conducted within this context.

Alexander first visited his doctor, before undertaking his own investigation: 'Is it not fair, then,' Alexander asked him, 'to conclude that it was *something I was doing that evening in using my voice that was the cause of the trouble?*'[5] [Emphasis Alexander's.]

After Alexander noticed that his speech improved when his head went forward and up and balanced freely on the top of the spine, he also noticed that he was unable to do this (despite his will) in the act of speaking because of the influence of the total pattern:

> The functioning of the organs of *speech* was influenced by my manner of using the whole torso, and that the pulling of the head back and down was not, as I had presumed, merely a misuse of the specific parts concerned, but one that was inseparably bound up with a misuse of other mechanisms which involved the act of shortening the stature.[6] [Emphasis mine.]

He says this quite clearly in the context of habits:

> For instance, as soon as any stimulus reached me to use my voice, and I tried in response to *do* the new thing which my conscious direction should bring about (such as putting the head forward and up) and *speak at the same time,* I found I immediately reverted to all my old habits of use (such as putting my head back, etc.).'[7] [Emphasis his.][8]

This is when he starts paying attention to 'habits of use' and the 'means-whereby'.

> Over and over again I had the experience that immediately the stimulus to *speak* came to me, I invariably responded by doing something according to my old habitual use *associated with the act of speaking.*' [Emphasis mine.]

Finally,

> After many disappointing experiences of this kind I decided to give up any attempt for the present to do anything to gain my end, and I came to see at last that if I was ever to be able to change my use and dominate my instinctive

direction, *it would be necessary for me to make the experience of receiving the stimulus to speak and of refusing to do anything immediately in response.* [Emphasis his.]

Alexander's discoveries came from noticing that the stimulus of *speech* resulted in a pull back and down of the head, a lift of the chest and a shortening and narrowing of the stature. I note that the back and down pattern of the head, the lift of the chest, shortening and narrowing of the stature also correlate with elevation of the hyoid bone. As I understand it, in refusing to *do* anything Alexander would have first and foremost been inhibiting extraneous activity in the Hyoid Matrix (in addition to other relevant systems and parts), and inhibition of the Hyoid Matrix would help the head stay forward and up.

Alexander's discoveries describe inhibition first of unnecessary activity in the area of the Hyoid Matrix (which is activated during speech). In fact, the directions he works out are quite specific:

1) inhibit any immediate response to the stimulus to *speak* the sentence,
2) project in their sequence the directions for the primary control which I had reasoned out as being best for the purpose of bringing about the new and improved use of myself in *speaking*, and
3) continue to project these directions until I believed I was sufficiently au fait with them to employ them for the purpose of gaining my end and *speaking* the sentence.[9] [Emphasis on all three points are mine.]

For these and other reasons, I have come to think of the Hyoid Matrix as a primary mechanism by which we may be able to study and explain the Alexander Technique.

Copyright 2015 © The Society of Teachers of the Alexander Technique, London.

Figs 4, 5, 6. F. M. Alexander teaching.

The placement of Alexander's hands
In these photographs (figs. 4–6), Alexander's fingers on the front of the neck are spread in ways which correlate with the Hyoid Matrix. They are in contact with the mastoid process, omohyoid, digastric, sternum, clavicle, and the hyoid. Through intention, we can also influence the Hyoid Matrix even when not in direct tactile contact – for example, we can be on the back, or ribs, or even feet (which of course, Alexander also did).

The Hyoid Matrix and trauma
Over the years I have followed one comprehensive holding pattern of the head–neck–back and then another with unexpected success in my students with back and other chronic pain; I was always amazed to discover that each thread had the hyoid in common with another. That said, it is only recently as I have been in recovery from a mild traumatic brain injury (MTBI) that I have begun to fully grasp the totality and reach of this network and its potential to retrain the brain.

Through working with the Matrix I have been able to gain some control over otherwise ungovernable multiple concussion symptoms, to positively influence my stamina and to advance my recovery. The effects have been so unexpected, and so compelling, that I have spent hours learning all I can about this area of the body.

What fascinates me about the Hyoid Matrix
To understand the Hyoid Matrix, we need to start with the unique attributes of the tongue and the hyoid bone to which it attaches.

The tongue
1. An individual's tongue is as unique as a fingerprint with no two alike.
2. Post-concussive/trauma students often report a change in the tongue – such as it is bigger, or pressed on the roof of the mouth.
3. The tongue is derived from three of the branchial arches. It is innervated by four of the cranial nerves and has taste, sensation and motor abilities.
4. The cranial nervous system innervating the tongue connects directly to the pons, in the brain stem, located just behind the back of the tongue. According to Norman Doidge,[10] the tongue is believed to house 48 sensory receptors which pass electrical signals to nerve fibres (of which there are 15,000–50,000 on the tip of the tongue alone), which create 'a huge information highway'. He writes: 'The brain-stem is where major nerves that enter and exit the brain converge. It is closely connected to the brain processing areas for movement, sensation, mood, cognition, and balance.'
5. The tongue is comprised of eight muscles, four extrinsic (attaching to

external structures) and four intrinsic. The extrinsic ones help form the floor of the mouth, descend from the soft palate and traverse over from the styloid process of the temporal bone.

6. Most muscles work as a team bound between two bones – one contracts as another lengthens. The tongue is not bound in this way; it is a free end. I experience it to be the best origin to initiate unwinding and resetting. Releasing the tongue of excess tension can positively impact functioning of parts even as far away as the groin, legs and feet.
7. For several years now my students and I have had good success stopping and reversing acute back pain through an exercise I developed which includes the tongue as a primary source. *It also appears to be true that noticing and releasing the tongue immediately post-trauma stops the trauma response from cascading effects.*
8. People who can't free the neck often can observe, and ultimately free, the tongue. For people in chronic pain, this is sometimes a necessary precursor to freeing the neck.
9. Observing tongue activity in a mirror illuminates how different thoughts ('release', 'lengthen', 'do nothing', etc) translate to action in one's own body. Since it is common for people in pain to 'do' the release (thus causing more problems), this practice can provide extremely valuable individualised information and feedback as to how to correctly inhibit.
10. I experience happy moments of normalcy when I am able to achieve a free and balanced interaction between the tongue, the eyes, the inner ear, and the skull on the spine. The tongue functions as a hydrostat[11] and interdigitates with fibres of other muscles in the mouth and throat; it enjoys a continuous muscular pathway to the pharynx, nasal passages and inner ear. In practice I also observe a linkage to the eyes. By expanding my hands-on awareness to consider and treat the eyes, ears, tongue and hyoid as an interdependent functioning unit, I experience an ability to subtly realign/recalibrate them. On many occasions now, this approach is repeatedly and consistently yielding immediately discernible improvement in function of all four. Headaches, foggy brain, eye strain, ringing in the ear, swallowing and breathing difficulties can all be helped by this expanded approach.

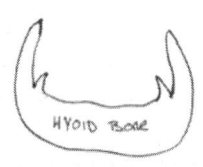

Fig 7. Hyoid bone.

What is the hyoid bone?
1. The hyoid is a small horseshoe-shaped bone to which the tongue is anchored. It is suspended by muscles and ligaments in the neck, just below the mandible at level C2/C3.
2. You can feel it on yourself with two fingers spread about two inches apart. Locate it at the very top of the neck, back from the chin. If you wiggle it, or yawn, or swallow, you will feel it move.
3. Its known function relates to swallowing, breathing and speaking.
4. While all mammals have a hyoid bone, the human hyoid is distinct in that it descends. This distinction is attributed to our ability to speak.
5. It is the only floating bone in the body (no bone-bone articulation) and attaches to the thyroid via the thyrohyoid membrane.
6. The hyoid bone lies in line with the skull's center of gravity, directly below the sella tursica. In my impaired state, it was very clear to me that *the hyoid bone served as a counterbalance to the skull*; in addition to speech, I hypothesise that its descent in humans may be related to upright posture. In my recovery, and with my students, its status determines quality of balance, as well as the turn of the head. It also seems to be an important proprioceptive register that works in tandem with the eyes, tongue and inner ear.
7. The hyoid is one of the smallest bones in the body, and the only bone without structural support from articulation with another bone, yet it houses *more attachments* than any other bone. Over twenty-four muscles, one membrane and five ligaments attach to it. Many of the origins of these muscles are in critical parts of the body: the mouth, the skull, the sternum, the scapula, the clavicle, the ribs, the pharynx, the thyroid, and the tongue.
8. In my experience, longstanding habits of misuse throughout the self seem to find their root in the hyoid bone.

Why is it important to consider the tongue and the hyoid as part of a matrix?

The tongue is anchored on the hyoid bone, which itself is suspended like a hammock via muscles and ligaments in the neck. The 'floating' hyoid bone has approximately thirty muscles, ligaments and membranes that connect to it and it is locus to a complex matrix which includes over a hundred muscles.[12] Some of the muscles function as pulleys and appear to affect base location, function and use of other muscles and organs.

For the Alexander teacher, the floating bone matrix allows expanded possibilities of influence through contact. For example, each shoulder-blade has an omohyoid linking it to the hyoid bone. Working from the hyoid down: the omohyoid inserts in the hyoid bone, descends down and threads through a fascial sling at the clavicle and first rib, does a 90-degree turn and finds its origin in the upper border of the scapula. Omohyoid appears to work as a pulley, and undue tension in it can be a root cause of hand, wrist and arm pain, thoracic outlet syndrome, and more. By teaching students to release omohyoid, we positively affect shoulder, arm and hand function as well as breathing and digestion. My students and I find the release of Omohyoid precedes and feeds into the release of trapezius and sternocleidomastoid. Because the hyoid floats, a directed hand on a student's right shoulder freeing right omohyoid up to hyoid can simultaneously influence the student's left shoulder, freeing left Omohyoid and thereby the left arm. Expanding our thinking to allow for this yields positive (and startling) results.

Alexander Teachers often say that the scapula essentially floats in muscle (even though it does articulate with the clavicle), and we sometimes describe the mandible (jaw) as a moveable fifth limb. Digastric is an interesting muscle in this regard. Like omohyoid, digastric is made up of two muscles joined in the middle by a tendon. The two muscles have different embryological origins and are innervated by different cranial nerves v and vii. Also like omohyoid, digastric functions as a pulley: it attaches at the mandible, is held onto hyoid by a fibrous loop, and has its origin in the mastoid notch located inside the temporal bone of the skull. I find it interesting to think of the implications of a pulley muscle originating from inside the skull to an external unstable structure! Some of digastric's fibres also interdigitate with sternocleidomastoid.

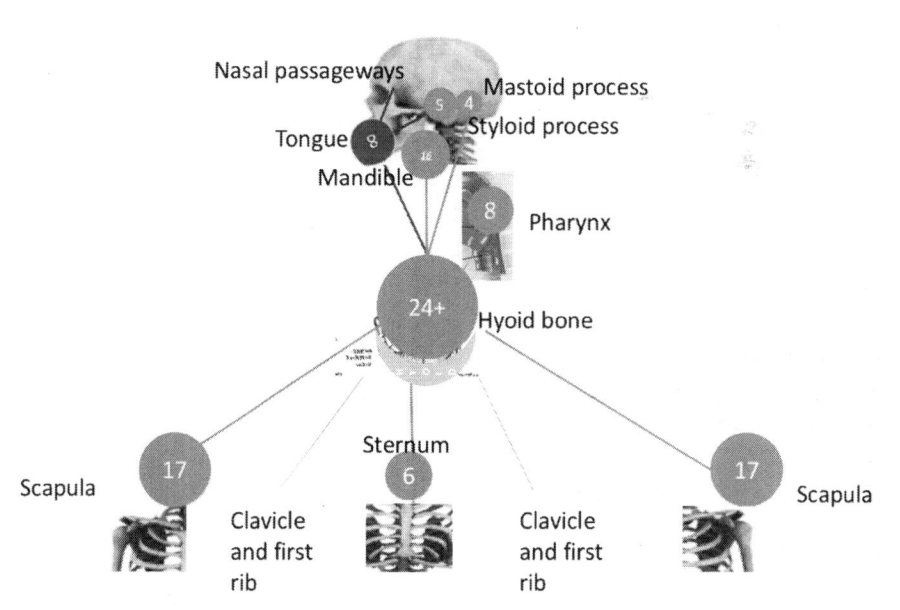

Fig 8. Graphic showing the number of direct lines of influence between the hyoid bone and other key parts of the body. This is not exhaustive – the hyoid also connects, for example, to the thyroid, the epiglottis, the clavicle and often the first rib and therefore the back. These lines of influence are primarily muscular, but also include ligaments, fascia and membranes.

The pharynx is a fibromuscular tube which holds the hyoid bone as part of its anterior structure and the spine supporting its posterior wall. The three primary muscles of the pharynx are of a circular nature (superior constrictor, middle constrictor and inferior constrictor), stacked one on top of the next, and share interlapping fibres along the top and bottom edges. Thus while only the middle constrictor connects to the hyoid bone, the passageway itself functions as an interconnected piece. This may be related to the open-channelled, unified passageway we are able to experience from head to foot.

The continuous interdigitating nature of the muscular and organ fibres in the Matrix may unify the five muscular layers of the body. Many of the muscles for example, lie upon, overlap and indeed, interdigitate, with more superficial, but critical, muscles which Alexander teachers will recognise as old friends: sternocleidomastoid, trapezius, the recti, scalenes, platysma and rhomboids for example. Others form an internal hydrostatic loop back to hyoid. For example, middle constrictor (which originates from hyoid) overlaps and interdigitates with the superior constrictor above it which overlaps and interdigitates with the stylohyoid muscles and ligaments originating in the skull, that traverse down to and terminate at hyoid.

If release of the musculature in the Matrix does in fact precede that of other, more superficial muscles found in the head–neck–back, it may be beneficial (and most accurate) to consider this Matrix as first among equals.

Fig. 6 shows how muscular, ligament and membrane attachments to the hyoid bone connect to bony structures providing origin to other principal muscles and organs. For example, seventeen muscles originate at each of the 'floating' scapulas. So hopefully the reader is beginning to be able to visualise how a floating bone as part of a pulley attached to other movable structures (that in turn serve as foundations for other muscles, organs and mechanisms) can have a primary, determining influence on equilibrium, orientation and function of other elements. In total, the Hyoid Matrix enjoys direct, interdependent, first-degree influence on over a hundred muscles.[13] The extent of this influence can perhaps be better appreciated in contextual relation to the entire body which houses between 640–840 muscles (depending on how they are counted). Direct influence of the Hyoid Matrix extends to over a sixth to an eighth of the muscles of the entire body!

Embryological development

The hyoid bone develops from the first three of the visceral/branchial arches. It is recognisable in the fifteenth day of embryologic development, mere hours after the embryo is first identifiable as an entity (fourteenth day).[15] According to *Gray's Anatomy*, by the end of the third embryologic week:

> In the nervous system the primary divisions of the brain are visible, and the primitive ocular and auditory vesicles are already formed. The primary circulation is established. The elementary canal presents a straight tube com-

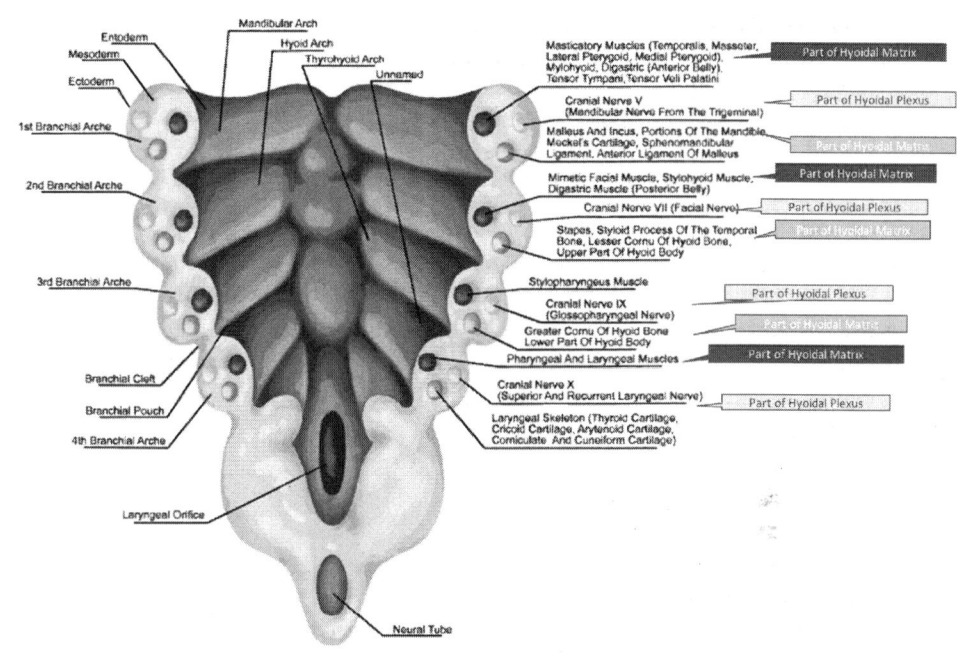

Fig. 9. Early weeks of embryologic development of the human as they relate to the Hyoid System.[14]

municating with the yolk sac. The branchial arches are formed. The limbs have appeared as short buds. The Wolffian bodies are visible.[16]

This is important because not only does the Hyoid System have a primal and integral relationship with other elemental parts of the human being, but this relationship develops in tandem throughout foetal development.

In his book *The Foundations of Human Well-Being, The Work of Professor Magnus and the F. Matthias Alexander Technique*, Walter Carrington explores Alexander's primary control, Coghill's mechanism of total integration, and Magnus' central control. He writes:

> According to Coghill, in the earlier stages of embryonic development, the behaviour of an organism takes the form of a 'total pattern of response': that is to say, in response to a stimulus either from within or without, the entire organism reacts as a whole. No single part, such as the head, neck, or limb, for instance, responds alone; but all the parts react together in a 'unitary pattern of action'. The form of this 'total pattern' is not merely accidental; it is determined by the structure of a definite nervous mechanism which Coghill has defined and which, he says, forms a 'clearly recognisable component of the nervous system'. This mechanism, described by him elsewhere as a 'growing organ' consists of an expanding chain of nerve-cells which grows throughout

the entire organism, linking up the various muscle-groups so that all the parts become 'integral factors in a primarily integrated whole'.[17]

I hypothesise that the Hyoid system (Matrix and Plexus) may be this mechanism.

THE HYOID PLEXUS

Ten of the twelve cranial nerves innervate what I am calling the Hyoid Plexus[SM]. The Hyoid Plexus nerves are those nerves that innervate any of the primary muscles involved in the Hyoid Matrix. Most of these are cranial nerves – primary nerves of the human system. Since our hands give a sophisticated, integrated, whole-patterned, stimulus to the muscles of the Matrix we are also giving this whole context stimulus to the various cranial nerve branches contained in the Hyoid Plexus and thereby simultaneously engaging multiple parts of the brain. When we engage our students in conscious awareness, I hypothesise that this influence is magnified. This may be why the Alexander Technique has such a simultaneous and comprehensive effect throughout the human system. The Plexus also seems to allow non-threatening access and re-education to what is experienced as a more primitive and vulnerable brain during a MBTI. Additionally, while the hyoid is housed in the neck, it is possible to work with it as part of the neck, or as part of the head. Perhaps this possibility is due to its origin and descent from the skull, perhaps due to the cranial nerve network and/or perhaps its derivation from the branchial arches. The indirect, respectful, non-manipulative and educational nature of the Alexander Technique, and the fact that all work is conducted within

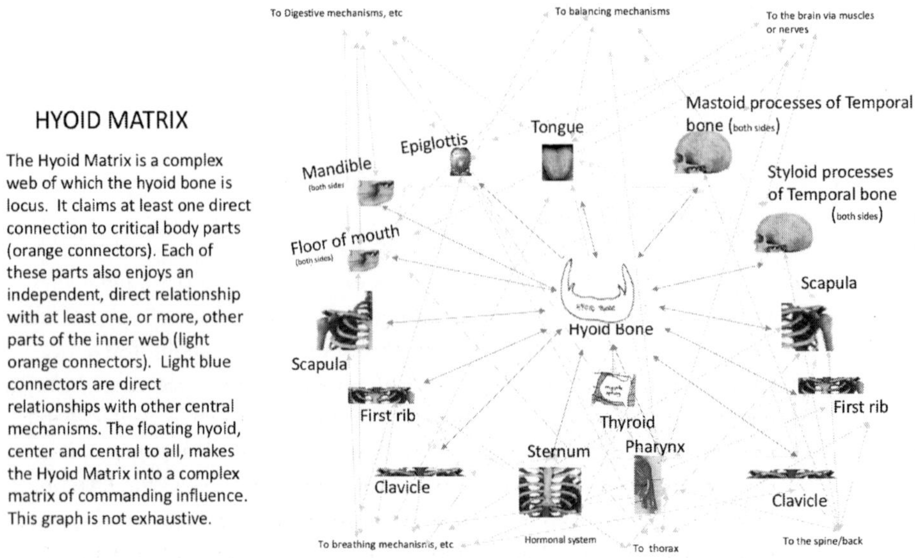

HYOID MATRIX

The Hyoid Matrix is a complex web of which the hyoid bone is locus. It claims at least one direct connection to critical body parts (orange connectors). Each of these parts also enjoys an independent, direct relationship with at least one, or more, other parts of the inner web (light orange connectors). Light blue connectors are direct relationships with other central mechanisms. The floating hyoid, center and central to all, makes the Hyoid Matrix into a complex matrix of commanding influence. This graph is not exhaustive.

Fig. 10. The Hyoid Matrix.

the context of the total pattern of integration, at all times, makes it uniquely and ideally suited for the sensitive nature of this work.

Related research

Over the years I have looked at what research I can find on the hyoid and the head–neck–back. Thus far I have not found any research to give pause or disprove my hypotheses; rather it has only served to further spur me forward. For example, studies involving abnormalities in the stylohyoid process point to disturbances in function of other parts of the human system. Hyoid Bone Syndrome is a rare, extremely painful condition causing radiating pain from the hyoid bone to about fourteen other sites (which I note correlate with the Hyoid Matrix). George Coghill's groundbreaking work on the total pattern theory focuses on the anterior (front) part of the neck of the Amblystoma, where the hyoid is located.[18] I have included a partial list of relevant research in the bibliography.

Significance

Current understanding of the Hyoid System appears to be divided into sections: the mouth, the thyroid, the infra-hyoid, the supra-hyoid and the pharynx, with little attention paid to how the interrelated system may influence the whole self. Most skeletons and anatomical drawings do not include the complexity of the hyoid bone.

Fig. 11. Three hyoids: adult, child and animal. As an adult my hyoid is descended; my daughter's is developing; the horse's is higher up than a human's, with its stylohyoid bone extending up between its eyes and ears. When this picture was taken I wasn't expecting to encounter a horse in the field, it scared us and my hand instinctively went to its hyoid matrix. Incidentally, my early experiments on the hyoid were with my dog, who would get a goofy, loving grin and settle right down at my feet.[19]

I believe that F.M. Alexander's primary discoveries may have been centered around this system. If these observations and hypotheses are correct, the Hyoid Matrix may provide a mechanism through which we can study, explain and promote the Alexander Technique. Disturbances in the Hyoid Matrix could explain many seemingly unrelated illnesses and symptoms currently perplexing medical professionals and resulting in human suffering. Greater understanding of this Matrix could fundamentally change how diagnoses are categorised and treated and give new hope to those suffering from debilitating neurological and other systemic conditions.

Figures

Figure 1: https://commons.m.wikimedia.org/wiki/Gray%27s_Anatomy_plates. Figures 1, 2, 6, 7, 8 and 9 that the drawing/composite graphic was rendered by the author using shutterstock images. Figures 4, 5 and 6 photographs Copyright 2015 © The Society of Teachers of the Alexander Technique, London.

References and Notes

1   Service Mark. The right of the author to control this phrase and name is asserted.
2   Gorman, David (1981). *The Body Moveable*. Ampersand Press: Canada.
3   'The relationship of the atlanto-occipital region to the head and neck. The area circled is the most important, the primary area to consider in dealing with the balance of the body as a whole. Here lie the semicircular canals detecting changes in the head's position, parts of the brainstem having to do with muscle tone, reflexes and balance, the fulcrum of the head on the neck (the atlanto-occipital joint), the hinge of the jaw, and the mastoid and styloid processes from which radiate multitudinous muscle and ligament connections. Thus there is an intimate relationship between this area and all of the surrounding structures; the tongue, jaw, hyoid bone, larynx, trachea, esophagus, clavicle, ribs, sternum and scapula; having to do with the processes of eating, reading, swallowing, talking, singing, seeing and hearing. It is easy to see how through these connections any undue tensions and imbalances will affect the balance of the head also, and how, if the head is not freely poised on the neck, these other structures can suffer too. Of course any release and freeing of one area will influence the state of others.' *The Body Moveable, Volume I: The Trunk and Head*, p. 167 David Gorman, 1981.
4   Foggy brain, eye strain and pain, headache, clogged hearing, disabling fatigue, etc.
5   Alexander, F. M. (1985, 1932). *The Use of the Self*. Centerline Press: Long Beach, USA, p. 8.
6   Ibid, p.13.
7   Ibid, p. 27.
8   I observe that the head goes back and down when the hyoid goes forward and up. I am not sure which happens first, but I think it's the hyoid. In some people, the hyoid goes forward and up with speech as an unnecessary habit. I hypothesise that in some people hyoid action not only correlates with, but overrides that of the head.
9   *The Use of the Self*, p. 33.

10 Doidge, Norman (2015). *The Brain's Way of Healing*. Allen Lane: London, ch.7.
11 'A muscular hydrostat is a biological structure found in animals. It is used to manipulate items (including food) or to move its host about and consists mainly of muscles with no skeletal support.' (Wikipedia, accessed 7 December 2015) A good way to understand a hydrostat is to think of the limb of an octopus.
12 Attachments to the Hyoid bone: genio-hyoid (2x), genio-hyo-glossus (2x), hyoglossus (2x), chondro-glossus (2x), mylo-hyoid (2x), stylo-hyoid (2x), aponeurosis of digastric (2x), sterno-hyoid (2x), thyro-hyoid, omo-hyoid (2x), hyo-glottis (2x), middle pharyngeal constrictor (2x), inferior lingualis (on occasion), crico-hyoid (when present), levatore glandulae thyrpoideae (1 when present) and the thyrohyoidean membrane. Ligaments include: hyo-epiglottic (1), thyro-hyoid (2), and stylo-hyoid (2). In sum: 23–26 muscles, one membrane and 5 ligaments. The above muscles, in turn, are in direct relation with another 74+ muscles (*Gray's Anatomy*), giving a direct sphere of influence over more than 100 muscles (in incomplete analysis). Fascia also, of course, plays a critical role.
13 This doesn't even take into account fascia, ligaments, tendons, and critical organs such as the diaphragm, whose functioning is determined in part by location and function of the scapula, clavicle and first rib. The opposite is also true of course; improving use and function of the diaphragmatic partners will feed positively back to the Hyoid Matrix. Included within this Matrix (and not covered in this paper) are critical nerves (vagus, phrenic, craneal, etc), lymph glands, ligaments, arteries, mucous membranes, fascia, organs and more.
14 Image courtesy of www.shutterstock.com. Arrowed captions on right are mine.
15 Gray, Henry (1977). *Gray's Anatomy*. Crown Publishers, pp. 958, 324, 123, 980.
16 Ibid p. 1215.
17 Carrington, Walter (1994). *The Foundations of Human Well-Being. The Work of Professor Magnus and the F. Matthias Alexander Technique*. STAT Books: London, pp. 16-17.
18 'That the early development of behavior is it the expansion of an integrated total pattern has been demonstrated in amphibians, reptiles, birds and mammals. As an example I use the salamander (Amblystoma punctatum, Cope), which has been the subject of my investigations. In this animal the earliest movement occurs in the anterior end of the body next to the head. As the individual grows older, the muscular contractions, still beginning in this region, extend farther and farther tailward until the entire trunk and tail are involved in the movements. The contractions are from the start perfectly integrated. As appendages develop they, also, are involved in this integrated movement. For a definite period, discrete movement of the appendages is impossible though they move in perfect integration with the movement of the trunk. Even the first coordinated walking movements are of this nature, those are also the first postural reactions of the limbs. It is only later that a stimulus upon a limb will, instead of exciting total action of trunk and limb, elicit discrete action of the limb only. But this discrete action, in so far as the movement of the limb itself is concerned, is exactly like that which was earlier performed as part of the total pattern.' 'The Biologic Basis of Conflict in Behavior' in *The Psychoanalytic Review*, Vol. 20, 1933, quoted in *The Foundations of Human Well-Being*,

The Work of Professor Magnus and the F. Matthias Alexander Technique, Walter H.M. Carrington (1994), STAT Books: London.

Bibliography
Alexander, F. M. (1985). *The Use of the Self*. Centerline Press: USA.
Carrington, Walter H.M. (1994). 'The Foundations of Human Well–Being. The Work of Professor Magnus and the F. Matthias Alexander Technique'. STAT Books: London.
Gorman, David (1981). *The Body Movable*. Ampersand Press: Canada.
Gray, Henry (1977). *Gray's Anatomy*. Crown Publishers.
Kapit and Winn (2002). *The Anatomy Colouring Book*. Benjamin Cummings: San Francisco.
Netter (1989). *The Atlas of Human Anatomy*. Ciba Pharmaceuticals Division.

Websites consulted: www.wikipedia.org; www.radiopaedia.org; www.dartmouth.edu; www.healthline.com; m.livescience.com; www.anatomyexpert.com; www.ncbi.nlm.nih.gov; emory.edu.

Relevant research
Behlfelt, Linder-Aronson, and Neander (1990). 'Posture of the head, the hyoid bone, and the tongue in children with and without enlarged tonsils' in *European Journal of Orthodontics* 12, pp. 458-467.
Colby and Gaudio (2011). 'Stylohyoid Complex Syndrome: A New Diagnostic Classification' in *Arch Otolaryngol Head and Neck Surg*, Vol 137.
Doidge, Norman, M.D. (2015). *The Brain's Way of Healing*.
Magoun, H. W., L. Marshall (2005). *American Neuroscience in the 20th century*.
Sutthiprapaporn, P. of Hiroshima University, Japan, (2008). 'Positional changes of oropharyngeal structures due to gravity in the upright and supine positions' in *Dentomaxillofacial Radiology*, Vol. 37, pp. 130-136.
Tallgren and Solow of Institute of Orthodontics, Royal Dental College, Copenhagen (1987). 'Hyoid bone position, facial morphology and head posture in adults' in *European Journal of Orthodontics*, 9 (1), pp. 1-8.

Acknowledgements
These papers have been over seven years in the making. There are many people I wish to thank: In memoriam to my teacher, Charlotte Coe Lemann, AmSAT, who overcame initial skepticism and said: 'that tongue and hyoid thing . . . I played with it. I may have been wrong, follow that.' The following people shared hours of their time, curiosity, wonder, and expertise. They also provided material and patient referrals. They fueled my passion and observations. I am deeply indebted to: Chantal Berna Renella, M.D. PhD, Massachusetts General Hospital (MGH) Center for Pain Medicine and Harvard Medical School; Raffaele Renella, M.D. PhD, Boston Children's Hospital and Harvard Medical School; Cynthia Koegler Ersland, Educator; Seth Herman, M.D. Instructor in Physical Medicine and Rehabilitation, Harvard Medical School and Co-Director of Brain Injury Medicine Fellowship, Spaulding Rehabilitation Hospital; Maribeth Kaptchuk, Lic Ac, Private practice;

Donald B. Levy, M.D. Assistant Clinical Professor of Medicine at Harvard Medical School and Medical Director of the Osher Center for Integrative Medicine at Brigham and Women's Hospital. To my students, who shared wonder and curiosity in observation and helped these hypothesis carry weight. Ruth Murray and Alan Philps have been so true to the principles that they ensure the way is not lost even as we explore frontiers; the 'truth' in their work always brings me home; I am so grateful to them for lessons, kindnesses and unwavering generosity, compassion and humor. Thanks to Mary Derbyshire, Rachel Gering-Hasthorpe, Elke Mastwijk, Elizabeth Reese and Missy Vineyard who refined my thinking within a context of camaraderie, wisdom, compassion and humour. This is what I want and need. To my family and dog, who are all my best friends, who have travelled this windy road with me, and who have selflessly given support, support and more support. These papers would be nowhere without the sacrifices you've made for me. Finally, deepest gratitude to my husband Tod, Maribeth, Lorie, Carolyn, John, Donny, Mom (posthumously) and Dad who caught us in our fall. I feel very lucky to have you in my life.

Katherine H. (Kitty) Breen took years of private Alexander lessons (with Charlotte Coe Lemann and Jerry Sontag) before completing teacher-training at The Center for the Alexander Technique with Ed and Linda Avak (1992). She is STAT and AmSat certified. Kitty further benefitted from a postgraduate fellowship at the Constructive Teaching Center with Dilys and Walter Carrington and Ruth Murray in London, England; as well as a multi-decade mentorship with Charlotte Coe Lemann, private lessons from Tommy Thompson and a post-graduate course that she created in Boston, Massachusetts featuring John Nicholls. Kitty is Founder/Director of the Alexander Back and Chronic Pain Center: home of the Educated Back™ (2003) and The Institute for the Re-educated Brain: home of The Hyoid Matrix™ (2015). She works in collaboration with Boston area hospitals and medical professionals and enjoys bringing the Technique to new health-related audiences. Kitty offers workshops for teachers, has presented her work at U.S. AGMs and the 2008 and 2015 International Congresses, and has authored several papers, including the chapter 'Teaching to Back Pain', published in the 2008 Congress Papers. Kitty holds a BA from Wesleyan University (1984) and a Masters in Management from Yale University's School of Management (1994). Kitty has over a decade of experience in education and programme-development in which she pioneered nationally recognised programmes.

Mindful Recovery Practices ^{SM}

Alexander Technique for Addiction and Co-Occurring Disorders

Becca Ferguson

At the Limerick Congress, Galen Cranz, Caitlin Freeman and I each made a twenty-minute presentation on the theme of 'Diffabilty vs. Disability: Reframing Personal Definitions of Self'.

As with all innovations, Alexander's discoveries invite further development, which remains true to the core practices of the Alexander Technique while exploring expanded applications. Galen, Caitlin and I have created personal, unique applications of Alexander's discoveries.

In our presentations, we each described how we had come to the Alexander Technique to deal with our own physical and neuropsychological conditions – conditions often diagnosed as disabilities. Galen has severe scoliosis, Caitlin has Autism Spectrum Disorder (ASD) and I have dealt with decades of Post Traumatic Stress Disorder (PTSD), anxiety, chronic pain, Attention Deficit Hyperactivity Disorder (ADHD) and addiction to alcohol and the prescription pain medication and tranquillisers prescribed to treat my conditions.

This essay is my overview of our discussion, with more information about my own story, and the Alexander Technique-based *Mindful Recovery Practices* that I've developed for those wishing to recover from addiction and co-occurring disorders such as trauma, anxiety and eating disorders.

Galen, Caitlin and I have each developed unique Alexander Technique paths, which use Alexander's discoveries to help us and others live with the 'defining elements' in our lives – specifically, the aspects of us that frequently get labeled as disabilities.

We have not submitted to the prevailing medical paradigms and treatments for our respective defining elements. Rather, we have each embraced our respective *different abilities* – or '*diffabilities*' – and used the Alexander Technique to empower, support and define life paths that enable us to live well as *differently abled* individuals.

The genesis of our Limerick presentation lies in my introduction to the Alexander Technique when I met Galen in Berkeley, California, some decades ago. As I grew to know Galen, I learned she had integrated the Alexander Technique into her journey with her severe scoliosis, which she'd chosen not to treat with Western Medicine protocols.

Galen's discipline, focus and passion in practising the Alexander Technique for her scoliosis created for me a compelling vison of the Alexander

Technique as an empowering, healing practice for life. Galen's work on herself provided an inner foundation and resilience, which helped her transcend the complex challenges of living with scoliosis.

Back in those early Berkeley days, Galen recommended the Alexander Technique for my neck and back pain and neuropathy – and also for the anxiety, panic attacks and other symptoms which were later diagnosed as Post Traumatic Stress Disorder (PTSD).

I was young and believed I could handle anything. I also did not understand what the Alexander Technique was, and lessons were expensive, so I did not pursue them.

Many years later, I see I wasn't ready to take that step into the Alexander Technique because I wasn't distressed or suffering enough to be willing to embrace change. I've learned since that 'pain is the messenger'. That is, we humans usually only embrace change when we are in severe enough pain – whether the pain is due to physical, mental, spiritual, emotional or other causes.

When nothing we've been doing works, when our pain finally gets our attention, only then do we become willing to stop doing things *our way* and try something new – even if we have no idea exactly what that new thing is, or if it can help us. Willingness is the key needed to make the first step into any significant change.

Like Galen, Caitlin Freeman is an Alexander Technique teacher who embraced change through her Alexander work. Caitlin's groundbreaking work grew out of her challenges as a gifted individual with Asperger's Syndrome, which was not diagnosed until she was an adult.

In 2012 I discovered Caitlin's website and her innovative Alexander Technique teaching practices for working with individuals on the Autistic Spectrum. Caitlin's website showed a discipline, focus and passion for using the Alexander Technique for Autism Spectrum Disorder issues in a manner comparable to Galen's Alexander Technique practice for scoliosis.

I was so impressed by Caitlin's site and the innovative practices she described for working with individuals on the Spectrum that I phoned her, and we've been in contact since.

Similar to Galen and Caitlin, my Alexander Technique journey has been based in a daily practice that enables me to live clean and sober with chronic pain, anxiety and PTSD symptoms.

A diving accident at age 13, in which I almost broke my neck and back, started me on the road to pain pill addiction. I was also treated for decades with tranquillisers for anxiety, panic attacks and other symptoms of Post Traumatic Stress Disorder (PTSD). As is often the case, I also used alcohol to self-medicate, and became an alcoholic as well as a prescription-drug addict.

I went through several stints of outpatient and residential treatment, regularly attended *Alcoholics Anonymous* (AA) meetings and worked on a 12 Step recovery programme. Nothing I tried provided me with the ability to build ongoing recovery because I was still in severe chronic pain and taking pain pills, as well as dealing with daily anxiety and ongoing trauma triggering, for which I took tranquillisers.

By my late thirties, I was in a cycle of chronic pain and dealing with PTSD and anxiety, while having periods of sobriety and relapse. Desperate for help, I started regular Alexander lessons with Charlotte Anderson.

During the time I was having lessons with Charlotte, I became inspired by a statement of Dr Wilfred Barlow, in his introduction to *The Use of the Self*: 'Alexander's work was and is concerned with the intimate management of our moment-to-moment perceptions of ourselves.'[1] Barlow's words helped me understand that developing mindful awareness is fundamental to the Alexander Technique. I realised that the Alexander Technique provided me with a profound, embodied mindfulness practice that calmed me and aided me in every aspect of my life.

Outside of my lessons with Charlotte, I integrated a new dimension of mindful awareness into my use of myself, and expanded my practice with the Alexander Technique into all daily activities, including when sitting in Alcoholics Anonymous (AA) meetings. Using inhibition and direction helped reduce my stress reactivity, pain and PTSD symptoms to the point that I was able to taper off pain pills and tranquillisers on my own.

When I was free of the pills that had shaped my life for decades, I went into a residential drug and alcohol treatment programme to stop drinking. Once I completed the treatment programme, I resumed my lessons with Charlotte, and deepened my daily '*Mindful Alexander Technique* (MAT)' practice – the name I coined for what I was doing

My MAT practice applied Alexander Technique basics of inhibiting and pausing my habitual reactions and behaviours. The pause created by inhibition gave me a moment to choose and re-direct into new, healthier actions, instead of acting out old habits and thoughts.

Over time, these MAT practices helped prevent relapse by improving my ability to self-regulate, and lowered my reactivity to stress, pain and constant trauma triggers. As I learned to redirect behaviours and emotions, I was able to build self-regulation and distress-tolerance skills that form the building blocks of recovery from addiction, and dealing daily with pain, anxiety and trauma triggering.

Lessons with Charlotte and my MAT practice proved complementary to my AA meetings and programme of recovery. After struggling through about twenty years of chronic relapse, practising the Alexander Technique in tandem with working a 12 Step programme has enabled me to be clean and sober since January of 2009.

The MAT practice has provided additional benefits that I observed in my second year of recovery:

1. My reactions to PTSD/trauma symptoms and triggering, anxiety and depression have become less severe. I'm no longer in a highly agitated, constant 'fight or flight' or 'startle' state, or as triggered from movements and noises. I'm calmer, more focused and respond differently to stress, anxiety and pain.
2. The Alexander Technique's unique weight-bearing movement practices have helped reduce my bone loss which was exacerbated by years of drinking and taking pain pills. I've since learned that bone loss and impaired bone health is a critical global health issue for alcoholics and drug addicts of all ages and genders. Studies show that chronic drug use – including heroin, marijuana, and opioids/opiates – adversely affects the bones, not only in terms of bone density. Unfortunately, impaired bone health is typically not addressed in conventional drug and alcohol treatment programmes. Further, the incidence of co-occurring disorders, such as eating disorders, is another cause for impaired bone health, particularly with women who begin drinking and using drugs as pre-teens or young adults.

Raising awareness of bone health issues caused by drug and alcohol use and co-occurring disorders is central to my work with teaching the Alexander Technique in chemical dependency treatment programmes.

My ongoing recovery and well-being with MAT inspired me to become an Alexander Technique teacher. I developed *'Mindful Recovery Practices'* (MRP) from MAT, to help others learn the Alexander Technique methods that saved my life.

Teaching Mindful Recovery Practices[SM] (MRP)

Since 2012, MRP has been taught in classes and workshops for drug and alcohol and co-occurring disorders treatment, as well as in two 'alternative sentencing programmes' for drug and alcohol offenders, including Chicago's Cook County Jail's Sheriff's Women's Justice Program.

MRP provides Behavioural Health clients with unique tools for managing stress and learning to self-regulate, which builds distress-tolerance, resilience and other skills needed for recovery, relapse prevention and treatment of co-occurring disorders such as trauma, anxiety and eating disorders.

My primary goal with MRP is to provide fun, easy Alexander Technique-based practices in 1-2 hour classes that provide clients of all ages and abilities – most of whom would never otherwise be exposed to the Alexander Technique – with immediate, positive benefits they can then replicate in their daily activities.

Working with a graphic designer, I've used my experience in marketing communications and technical writing to design and produce self-directed MRP practices in flyers and other teaching materials to give to clients to use on their own.

MRP helps clients discover new, healthier ways to live in their body, clean and sober. Even when clients are heavily medicated and/or in drug or alcohol withdrawal, the Case Managers and other professionals with whom I work have all observed that the MRP classes appear to rapidly help most clients with mood elevation and becoming calmer.

As the MRP class progresses, I observe hard-to-describe effects in most of the clients: they appear to 'be more in their body', more present and less anxious. When I gently inquire about my observations, most clients agree, and add that they're feeling good from trying MRP.

As a result of these positive emotional and physical effects, most clients understand within the context of only one class that MRP methods can help them with their ability to become more mindfully aware of themselves, and to relax and calm down, which will help them manage stress better and feel more in control of their body and recovery. The next step, of course, is folowing through with MRP practices on their own. Some clients readily do this; others do not.

Basic Alexander Technique practices are taught as the core of all MRP classes:

- Constructive Rest
- Standing
- Sitting
- Walking

Following is a list of **MRP 'Learning Outcomes'** that I must provide to administrators, in order to be approved to teach in the drug and alcohol treatment programmes where I work:

- Calming, mood elevation and self-soothing.
- Releasing muscle tension and reducing stress reactivity.
- Development of mindful awareness of body and thoughts.
- Building resilience, distress-tolerance and impulse control skills for stress management and relapse prevention.
- Pausing/changing habitual behaviors and reactions, and re-directing into new, healthier choices and behaviours.
- Fostering a compassionate, more gentle attitude towards ourselves.
- Learning unique weight-bearing movement practices for better bone health.

Teaching MRP in alcohol and drug treatment and corrections settings is fun, as well as challenging, and a privilege I never take for granted. Each group has a unique personality, and requires that I be present in a manner like no other situation in my life.

Regardless of the shifting human landscape of each group, the power of Alexander's work usually shows itself in subtle changes in clients such as calming, a smile, a little laughter, and more eye contact and engagement. These seemingly small changes are victories that provide the means-whereby to help pause and not 'pick up' a drug or drink, one moment or one day at a time, which is how recovery happens. These small changes also create hope, by creating the ability to make different, healthier choices.

One of my goals is to see MRP expand into widespread use in drug and alcohol treatment and corrections facilities worldwide. Another goal is to help promote the Alexander Technique in Integrative Medicine and Behavioural Health settings. To further this goal, I teach MRP and other practices I've developed to other Alexander Technique teachers, and share teaching materials such as class outlines and graphics.

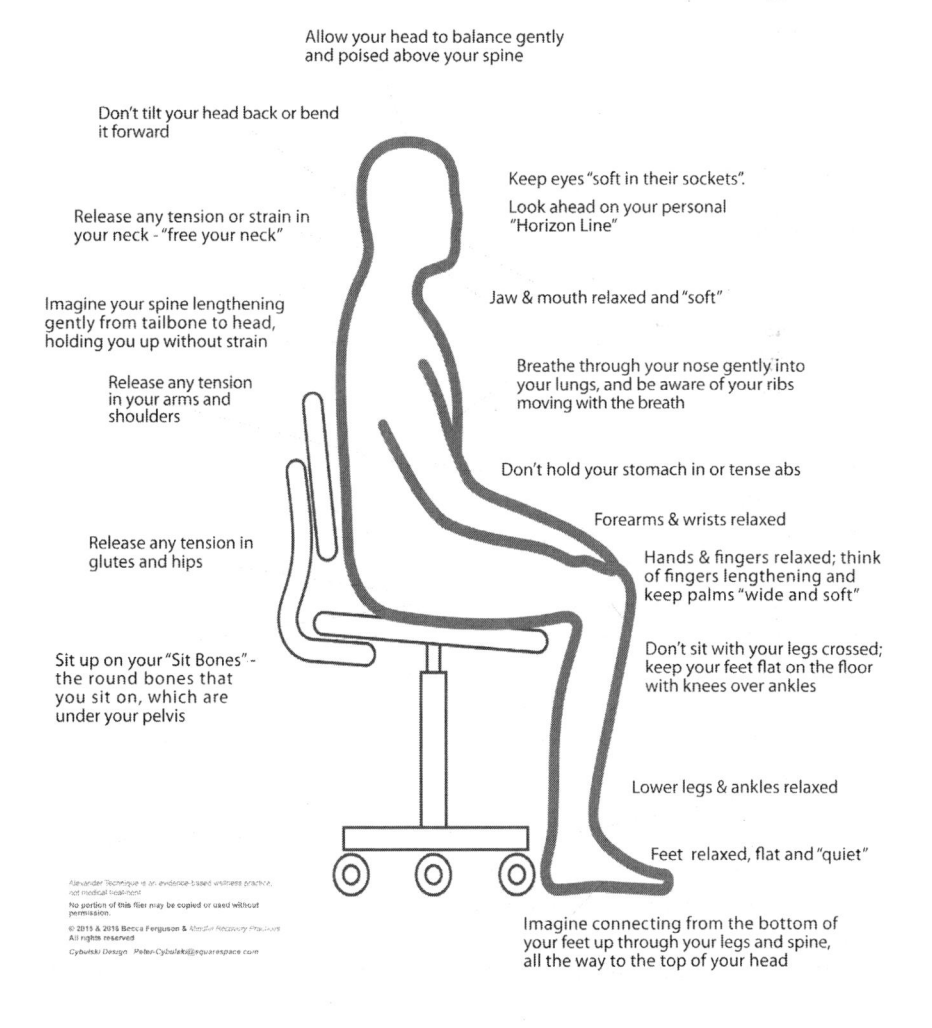

- Allow your head to balance gently and poised above your spine
- Don't tilt your head back or bend it forward
- Release any tension or strain in your neck - "free your neck"
- Keep eyes "soft in their sockets". Look ahead on your personal "Horizon Line"
- Imagine your spine lengthening gently from tailbone to head, holding you up without strain
- Jaw & mouth relaxed and "soft"
- Release any tension in your arms and shoulders
- Breathe through your nose gently into your lungs, and be aware of your ribs moving with the breath
- Don't hold your stomach in or tense abs
- Forearms & wrists relaxed
- Release any tension in glutes and hips
- Hands & fingers relaxed; think of fingers lengthening and keep palms "wide and soft"
- Sit up on your "Sit Bones" - the round bones that you sit on, which are under your pelvis
- Don't sit with your legs crossed; keep your feet flat on the floor with knees over ankles
- Lower legs & ankles relaxed
- Feet relaxed, flat and "quiet"
- Imagine connecting from the bottom of your feet up through your legs and spine, all the way to the top of your head

Alexander Technique is an evidence-based wellness practice, not medical treatment.
No portion of this flier may be copied or used without permission.
© 2015 & 2015 Becca Ferguson & Mindful Recovery Practices
All rights reserved
Cybulski Design Peter-Cybulski@squarespace.com

The Alexander Technique will always be an empowering daily practice for me, initially inspired years ago by Galen Cranz and more recently by Caitlin Freeman and other teachers around the world. I continue to explore the Alexander Technique and its many dimensions as one of the best innovations ever developed for living in a human body.

I push the boundaries of my own practice with ongoing challenges, particularly with trauma and pain issues. The Alexander Technique never fails me when I stay grounded in Alexander's principles.

To learn more about MRP and other Alexander Technique practices I've developed, please see my websites.

1   Barlow, Dr Wilfred (1985) 'Introduction' in F. M. Alexander (1985). *The Use of the Self*. Gollancz: London.

Becca Ferguson (M.AmSAT) graduated from *Alexander Technique Urbana*, directed by Rose Bronec. She has studied the Alexander Technique worldwide, including Peter Grunwald's Eyebody retreats in New Zealand. Becca teaches in Chicago, Urbana/Champaign and elsewhere. Areas of specialty include addiction, trauma, 'Sitting Disease', cancer survivor and patient wellness, bone health, and AT-based Mindful Labyrinth Walking. Becca teaches classes and workshops in hospital settings, drug/alcohol treatment and related alternative sentencing programmes. She is a guest lecturer on addiction and recovery at the University of Illinois, Urbana/Champaign. Certified as a Veriditas Labyrinth Facilitator, Becca teaches Alexander Technique Mindful Labyrinth Walking workshops for issues such as poor balance, trauma and anxiety. A graduate of the Rhode Island School of Design, Becca's artwork is in US corporate and private collections. Prior experience includes high tech marketing communications and training for start-up companies and corporations, publishers and utilities, including Simon & Schuster and Pacific Bell.

www.MindfulAT.com
MindfulAlexander@gmail.com

Taming to Touch

Alexander Technique for People with Autism Spectrum Disorder

Caitlin Freeman

I am an Alexander Technique teacher and I am also a person on the autism spectrum. Shortly after I graduated from my Alexander Technique training seven years ago, I began adapting the Alexander Technique as a sensory integration method to work with other autistic people. The Technique was essential in helping me learn how to manage the sensory overwhelm I experienced every day, and I knew that with a few modifications it would be similarly effective for other people all along the autism spectrum. After several years of teaching students on the spectrum and giving workshops on the Technique for autism support organisations, I decided to present my work at the 2013 AmSAT Annual Conference and General Meeting (ACGM) in Chicago, Illinois. It was there that I met Becca Ferguson and learned about her work applying the Alexander Technique to addiction-recovery and prevention. We took part in a panel discussion at the ACGM on integrating the Alexander Technique into fields that typically employ a Western medical approach. My work at the Chicago ACGM evolved into a book, *Autism and Alexander Technique*, which I presented at the 2014 ACGM in Long Beach, California. At the Limerick Congress, Becca, Galen Cranz and I shared our latest work in a panel discussion, 'Diffability vs Disability: Reframing Personal Definitions of Self.' In this presentation, we described the ways that our seeming disabilities have led us on a path of self-discovery and insight, and allowed us to make contributions that would not have been possible without our differences. This act of reframing my disability as a 'different ability' or 'diffability' is a skill that I gained from my training in Alexander Technique, and is something that I teach my students on the autism spectrum.

As a person on the spectrum, I have struggled with sensory issues all my life. My mother describes how when I was a child, she needed to 'tame me to touch like a wild animal'. When people touched me, it felt like an electrical burning sensation. My parents learned that I could tolerate deep pressure, and I gradually grew accustomed to their touch. Unfortunately, everyone else's touch was still so uncomfortable that as a child I developed an extreme aversion to any type of physical contact. Even hugs were painful. I desperately wanted to connect with people, but I felt like there was no way to bridge the barrier between myself and others.

Asperger's Syndrome first became an official diagnosis in 1994, and like many people with Asperger's who were born before this date, I grew up without any understanding of what was different about me. In fact, I was an adult before I received an official diagnosis. When I was a child, all I knew was that I was different and that something wasn't working, and that I needed help. But I didn't know what to do.

When I was a teenager, my parents encouraged me to try out for theatre productions, and I became part of the drama club at my high school. Theatre helped me socialise and connect with people in a safe environment. Acting allowed me to participate in scripted social interactions with known outcomes. I got to try on different characters and think about the world from other people's points of view. And actors tend to be a little different themselves, so for the most part they accepted my eccentricities.

I pursued theatre in college, and while I was there, I heard about the Alexander Technique, which was offered in the theatre department. Because the AT classes clashed with other things on my timetable, I wasn't able to study the Technique in college, but I met people who had taken the AT course and whose lives had been changed because of it.

After college I continued having difficulty with social and sensory issues, and for some reason I remembered the actors who had had such profound experiences with the Alexander Technique. I have a long-time friend of the family who is an Alexander Technique teacher, and I called her to ask about taking lessons. She told me about some of her experiences with the Technique, and encouraged me to find a teacher.

I was nervous about my first lesson because I knew that it would involve touch, and I didn't know if I would be able to handle the sensation. Contrary to my fears, however, my teacher's hands were calming instead of anxiety-provoking. I experienced a profound sense of peace even in my first lesson. I realised through the calm sensation I experienced in my lessons that my nervous system normally felt like it was on fire.

Soon I started to experience a deeply easeful state of mind and body that lasted for a few days after my lesson. I also noticed that it was becoming easier to interact with people without immediately becoming overwhelmed. My teacher also occasionally invited me to put my hands on her to demonstrate a point that she was making. This was profound because I had never experienced touching someone else in a way that wasn't fraught with anxiety and tension.

After several lessons, I decided that I wanted to train as an Alexander teacher, and so in 2005 I moved to Amherst, Massachusetts to train with Missy Vineyard. My lessons with Missy produced an even greater sense of calm. They also helped me develop my sense of spatial awareness, which I hadn't had much experience with before, perhaps because people on the autism spectrum often have deficiencies in the cerebellum, which is the primary brain area that processes balance and movement.[1] All of this made me feel even more at ease in the world.

As my nervous system calmed, my ability to interact socially improved even more. For the first time in my life I was able to make lasting connections with people without feeling like a nervous wreck, and without being exhausted afterwards.

We are all human beings who want to connect with each other, and this is also true of people on the autism spectrum. Autistic people desperately want and need to connect, but our nervous systems are often so overactive that we are overwhelmed past our ability to communicate.

After I graduated from Missy's training course, I decided to work with other autistic people to help them experience the same sense of calm and ease that I had found through practising the Technique.

For all its social drawbacks, autism has many gifts. We are critical thinkers, detail-oriented, and often have above average intelligence. If allowed to work to our potential, many autistic people become innovators who can change the world.

Temple Grandin is an autistic woman who became a change agent in the cattle industry, creating more humane cattle-processing plants that are used worldwide. The anxiety she feels as a result of her autism, combined with her genius for visual thinking, allowed her to empathise with prey animals like cattle and engineer humane processing plants that are designed to keep the animals calm.[2]

Many people speculate that some of the great scientific innovators of our age, such as Henry Cavendish and Albert Einstein, were also on the autism spectrum.[3] Henry Cavendish was a British natural philosopher of the 18th and early 19th centuries who is perhaps best known for discovering hydrogen. His notoriously shy demeanor combined with his scientific brilliance have led some psychologists such as Simon Baron-Cohen to retrospectively diagnose him with Autism Spectrum Disorder (ASD). As a child, Albert Einstein's delayed speech and difficulty with social skills were consistent with an autism diagnosis, and his genius with theoretical physics might be partly attributed to the out-of-the-box thinking that autistic individuals often possess.[4]

Due to the alternative wiring of their brains many autistic people can be brilliant and innovative. However, without intervention, many cannot function in society. Henry Cavendish, Albert Einstein and Temple Grandin all came from families of means and this afforded them good education and humane care, free from the institutionalised settings in which autistic people were and still are often placed. Nowadays institutions have largely given way to the warehousing of poorly funded special-education classrooms and sheltered workshops, and many families do not have access to interventions that would allow their autistic children to thrive.

An important part of this intervention is sensory integration, the process by which the nervous system learns to receive information from the senses and organise this data into a meaningful whole. When Temple Grandin was in college, she designed a 'squeeze machine,' modeled on the squeeze chutes used on ranches to keep cattle calm during inoculations. She identified that the deep pressure of the squeeze chute was calming to the animals, and that deep pressure would reduce her hypersensitivity as well.[5] She has said that without her squeeze machine, she would have been hindered by her overactive nervous system, and most likely would not have been able to achieve all that she has accomplished in her life.[6]

Autistic people often lack sensory integration in three important areas: touch, movement, and balance. When these three systems of tactile, proprioceptive, and vestibular input can be regulated, other systems are able to function more effectively, allowing people on the spectrum to develop language abilities and social skills, two of the areas in which they are frequently deficient. The squeeze machine that Temple Grandin developed was a sensory integration device, and it was effective because it helped her regulate tactile and proprioceptive input. Further, by lying face down in the device, it also allowed her to process new vestibular information. These beneficial effects may result from increased cerebellar activity, which helps regulate the senses of touch, movement, and balance.

Not unlike Grandin's squeeze machine, the Alexander Technique is a sensory integration method that regulates touch, movement, and balance. But even more effective than the squeeze machine, the Technique's noninvasive and calming touch combined with the mental principles of inhibition and direction can help people with ASD reduce their reaction to stimuli and learn conscious choice in their response to stress.

Alexander Technique teachers have a great deal to offer the growing autistic population[7] through the quality of our touch. Our hands-on work is more profound and sophisticated than the typical professionals that work with autistic people, such as occupational therapists and speech-language pathologists. Through a few modifications to our hands-on work and the language we use to describe the Technique, we have a great ability to help autistic people. The main changes teachers need to make are using a deeper touch when putting hands on, and using literal, non-metaphorical language to describe inhibition, direction, and Alexander's procedures. A 'light' touch, which is typically employed by AT teachers, can be startling to autistic people due to their hypersensitive nervous systems.[8] Further, due to the way that the autistic brain processes language, metaphor is difficult for many autistic people to understand. I have described these modifications in more detail in my book, *Autism and Alexander Technique*.[9]

With these few modifications, Alexander Technique teachers can help many autistic people find calm and ease in their nervous systems, so that they can take their seeming disability and turn it into a difference that has many advantages. This work has the potential to help the next Temple Grandin change not only her life, but the lives of countless others, as she learns to use the gifts of her autism.

1   Allen, Greg, Ph.D., and Eric Courchesne, Ph.D. (2003). 'Differential Effects of Developmental Cerebellar Abnormality on Cognitive and Motor Functions in the Cerebellum: An fMRI Study of Autism' in *The American Journal of Psychiatry*, Volume 160 Issue 2, February, pp. 262-273.
2   Grandin, Temple (2006). *Animals in Translation: Using the Mysteries of Autism to Decode Animal Behavior*. New York: Harcourt.
3   James, Ioan, FRS. (2003). 'Singular scientists' in *J R Soc Med*. Jan; 96(1): pp. 36–39.
4   Ibid.
5   Grandin, Temple (1992). 'Calming Effects of Deep Touch Pressure in Patients with Autistic Disorder, College Students, and Animals' in *Journal of Child and Adolescent Psychopharmacology*. Mary Ann Liebert, Inc., Spring 2 (1). pp. 63–72.
6   Grandin, Temple (1995). *Thinking in Pictures and Other Reports from My Life with Autism*. New York: Doubleday.
7   It is difficult at this time to determine whether autism is increasing primarily due to increased diagnosis/self-diagnosis, or whether there is a genuine increase of autism in the population. What we do know is that there is a growing number of people who identify as autistic or with ASD.
8   Grandin, Temple (1992). 'Calming Effects of Deep Touch Pressure in Patients with Autistic Disorder, College Students, and Animals' in *Journal of Child and Adolescent Psychopharmacology*. Mary Ann Liebert, Inc., Spring, 2 (1), pp. 63–72.
9   Freeman, Caitlin (2014). *Autism and Alexander Technique: Using the Alexander Technique to Help People on the Autism Spectrum*. CreateSpace Independent Publishing Platform.

Caitlin Freeman (M.AmSAT) is a professional autism service provider. She is also an individual with Autism Spectrum Disorder (ASD). In her private practice in Pittsburgh, PA, Caitlin uses the Alexander Technique to work with children, teenagers, and adults on the autism spectrum. Caitlin has been a featured presenter at the Autism Society of America and other autism support organisations, where she has lectured on the Alexander Technique as a method of sensory integration for people with ASD. She has presented her workshop, 'Autism and Alexander Technique,' at several AmSAT ACGMs. In 2014, she published a book based on her work, *Autism and Alexander Technique: Using the Alexander Technique to Help People on the Autism Spectrum*. For the past five years, Caitlin has been a faculty member in the Theatre Department at Point Park University's Conservatory of Performing Arts in Pittsburgh, where she taught the Alexander Technique. Caitlin received her BA from Sarah Lawrence College in vocal performance and theatre arts, and graduated from the Alexander Technique School New England (ATSNE), directed by Missy Vineyard. Caitlin's specialty is using the Alexander Technique, voice training, and theatre coaching to work with individuals on the autism spectrum.

www.alexandertechniqueguide.com

An Introduction to Fascial Unwinding

Mika Hadar-Borthwick

FASCIA
Fascia is the connective tissue that surrounds muscles, groups of muscles, blood vessels and nerves, binding those structures together. The fascia extends from the top of the head to the tip of the toes. Fascia can be seen as the organ linking all internal structures within the human frame, while separating its functioning units. It is responsible for the shape of our body, organising us into posture patterns.

'Fascia is the organ of posture.'[1] It takes time and work to change patterns within it, while at the same time it is constantly changing and adapting in response to demands placed on the individual's body and emotions.[2]

A PSYCHOPHYSICAL SYSTEM
The body's life is the life of sensations and emotions. The body feels real hunger, real joy in the sun or the snow . . . real anger, real sorrow, real tenderness, real warmth, real passion, real hate, real grief. All the emotions belong to the body and are only recognised by the mind.[3]

The fascia is like a library that stores the memory of our life events, both physically and psychologically. 'In the formation of a life impression, the membranes are the clay upon which the information is etched.'[4] In a case of trauma, this collagen-based soft-tissue gets stuck in patterns of stress, and bad use.

Psychophysical pioneers of the last century, like F. M. Alexander, Wilhelm Reich and Ida Rolf, pointed out that body and mind are a combined unit and affect each other.

Alexander wrote: 'the term psychophysical is used . . . throughout my works to indicate the impossibility of separating "physical" and "mental" operations in our conception of the working of the human organism.'[5] Ida Rolf was among the first to address how the body holds unresolved trauma in the tissues and how to restore balance: 'Go around the problem; get the system sufficiently resilient so that it is able to change, and it will change, it doesn't have to be forced. It's that forcing that you have to avoid at all costs.'[6]

According to Somatic Psychotherapy, chronic patterns of muscular tension can store negative emotions, thereby perpetuating the influence of those emotions on the individual personality. According to Reich we tend to hold unresolved emotional trauma in the tissues, thereby locking us into patterns of thinking and behaving.[7]

Self-corrective mechanism

When provided with the right conditions, fascia has its own inbuilt corrective mechanism to realign itself, release its traumatic contents, and correct bad habits of use.[8] As you give the body the space and attention to release itself from restrictions, from fascia–'pulls', it does just that – unwinds, moves spontaneously, finds its restrictions and releases. Fascial Unwinding is a very effective technique to assist this inbuilt mechanism to express itself.

What is Fascial Unwinding?

Fascial Unwinding is a therapy through which physical and emotional blocks, whatever their cause, can be released.

> Fascial unwinding provides a means of discovering and releasing the effects of traumas and tensions, be they recent or long-standing, thereby releasing restrictions which may be the deep rooted cause of pain. . . . It is a very gentle and non-invasive treatment process which involves responding sensitively to the body's demands, never forcing or imposing on the body tissues in any way. It is therefore generally painless (even in acutely painful conditions) and brings about a sense of ease, softness and relaxation, as well as the more profound therapeutic release of chronic underlying conditions.[9]

In Fascial Unwinding, the client undergoes a spontaneous reaction in response to the therapist's touch. Fascial Unwinding can be used to 'release' fascial restriction by encouraging the body or parts of the body to move without habitual restrictions.

The process of Facial Unwinding

I have been working with Fascial Unwinding for many years, often in conjunction with the Alexander Technique, sometimes as a system in its own right supported by the presence of direction and inhibition.

Fascial Unwinding (FU) requires a sustained active attention from the practitioner.

The person being worked with is invited to relax into an unconscious sensory space. Perhaps to close their eyes, and to rest their attention in a pleasant memory, or a quiet place. The practitioner is required to inhibit any 'doing' habits and to 'listen' and wait until a movement presents itself under their hands, sometimes hardly perceptible, allowing the person touched to open to their movements.

An FU practitioner will often start the practice by touching the person quietly, listening to the contact area, to the quality of the touched system and to any subtle movement that presents itself. Sometimes they will lift the person's arm, or another body part, support its weight, inhibit and wait, listening to the contact point and to any movement that presents itself. When a movement presents itself, the practitioner follows the movement, whether it is very subtle or very expressive. It is important to be open to surprises. These movements are unconscious. The practitioner just provides holding, listening, without any attempt to control the movement expressed, following the movement until it stops at a point of resistance, like a barrier. The arm, leg, or whatever is being held stops moving. The practitioner waits, staying there, witnessing until eventually the movement starts again, releasing the barrier, sometimes followed by an emotional expression. The movement is then followed to its conclusion where it comes back to rest. As the skill develops, one can transfer the listening to deeper tissues, joints, muscles and organs.

Fascial Unwinding and the Alexander Technique

Unlike the Alexander Technique, Fascial Unwinding is not an educational consciousness-building system. It is a trigger to an unconscious release. In fact, it requires a high level of inhibition and letting go of conscious control by the person being worked with, and by the practioner, allowing freedom of expression beyond the person's and practitioner's conscious control.

In FU the mindful process is *all* about inhibition, relying on the body's unconscious mechanism to know where it needs to go. The practitioner's means whereby in FU are **inhibition** and **listening,** supporting and following without any expectations, listening to one's own presence and poise, to the other person's system and movement, following that movement and allowing it to unfold.

Why Practise Fascial Unwinding?

I find FU to be a very useful, simple, yet profoundly change-evoking system. It is very compatible with the 'spirit' of the AT, with inhibition and 'non-endgaining'.

It is a great tool to use when the system is resistant to change, and when it has suffered physical or mental trauma. I find it a good companion to the AT when dealing with depression, chronic fatigue, persistent aches and pains. Alexander Technique is a teaching-therapeutic method; FU is a therapeutic method. One is all about being conscious, the other about opening to unconscious patterns. Both are catalysts for profound change.

1   Rolf, Ida P. (1990, 1978). *Rolfing and Physical Reality.* Healing Arts Press: Vermont, USA, p. 124.
2   See Ida Rolf op. cit. and Thomas Myers, https://www.anatomytrains.com/fascia/ [accessed 1 December 2015].
3   Lawrence, D. H. (1955). *Sex, Literature and Censorship.* London: William Heinemann, p. 232.
4   VanHowten, D. (1997). *Ayurveda and Life Impressions Bodywork: Seeking our Healing Memories.* Lotus Press: Wisconsin.
5   Alexander, F. M. (1955, 1923). *Constructive Conscious Control of the Individual.* Integral Press: Bexley, Kent, p. 2.

6   Rolf, op cit, p. 83
7   Reich, W. (1973). *The Function of the Orgasm.* Touchstone: New York, pp. 270–271.
8   Kern, M. (2001). *Wisdom in the Body: The Craniosacral Approach to Essential Health.* North Atlantic Books: Berkeley, California. Shea, M. J. (2007) *Biodynamic Craniosacral Therapy.* North Atlantic Books: Berkeley, California.
9   Attlee, Thomas 'Fascial Unwinding', http://www.ccst.co.uk/unwinding.html [accessed 1 December 2015].

Mika Hadar-Borthwick has worked as a healer and teacher for over twenty-five years. Through her work in teaching yoga, Alexander Technique, Cranio-Sacral Therapy and a variety of mind-body and healing systems, she has developed her unique style of teaching. She has taught and worked therapeutically in the UK, Italy, Estonia, Spain, Israel, Switzerland, India and Bali.

Eutokia: Optimal Position of Baby for Childbirth

Ilana Machover

Eutokia – Greek for 'happy childbirth' – is the name I have given to my work with pregnant women, applying the AT to pregnancy and childbirth.

I am delighted with the growing public awareness of the benefits that women can derive from the Alexander Technique (AT) during pregnancy and in childbirth. I feel very passionate about this, and think that more can be done to spread the word.

Medicalisation of childbirth has led to increased obstetric intervention – including use of drugs and caesarean section – some of it unnecessary or avoidable. Prospective parents are becoming aware of recent research on the immediate and long-term adverse consequences of such intervention for both mother and child. Many would like to avoid medical intervention and have a natural childbirth. As childbirth is an involuntary but quite painful process, the AT can help to make it proceed as nature intended. AT cannot eliminate pain but teach how to cope with it.

Positioning of baby
This workshop was devoted to the contribution of the AT to optimal positioning of the baby for childbirth.

One of the factors that increase the need for medical intervention is the malposition of the baby at the onset of the labour process. The optimal position of the baby at the onset of labour, known as occiput anterior (OA), is head down, neck flexed, and baby's back against the mother's left side. The most common malposition (much more common than breech) is the occiput posterior (OP): baby facing the mother's abdomen, with its back and head against her spine (see figure 1). If the baby remains in this position at

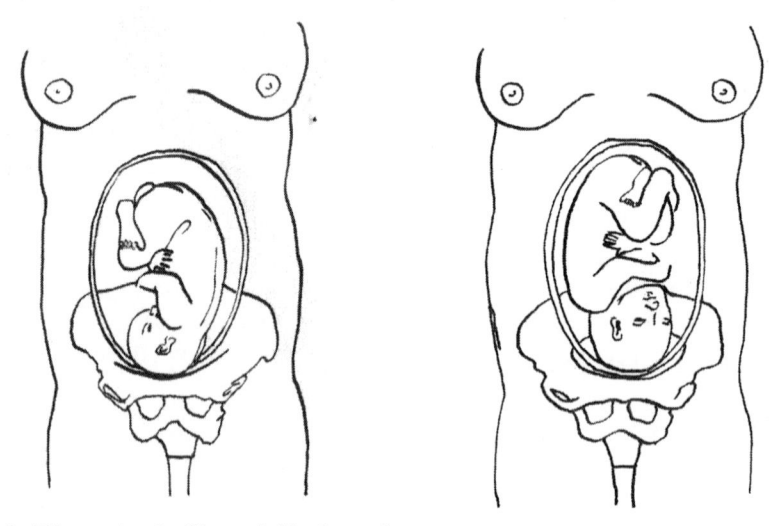

Fig. 1. (Illustration by Hannah Machover.)

the onset of birth, it may prolong labour (the baby needs to perform a much larger rotation) and cause complications (the baby's neck may be extended instead of flexed, so that the head does not present its smallest circumference to the pelvic outlet), increasing the probability of medical intervention.

OP position, whose frequency has been on the rise since the mid-1950s, often results from long-term poor use by the mother that persists during pregnancy. This in turn is partly attributable to current prevailing lifestyle (design of modern chairs and sofas, use of IT technology, growing trend for late motherhood).[1]

Learning the AT during pregnancy can help to prevent the OP position. But even if the baby does not rotate to OA before the onset of birth, there is no need to despair: the AT can still facilitate its rotation to OA during the first stage of labour, before the baby's head descends towards the birth canal. All the same, we have to accept that some babies won't rotate.

TEACHING THE MOVEMENTS

In my work with pregnant women I introduce them from the start to our AT procedures such as monkey, lunge, kneeling on all fours, crawling, and whispered 'ah'. I also use the chair and the gym ball. There is a detailed account of these movements in the *The Alexander Technique Birth Book* (ATBB), which I co-authored with Angela and Jonathan Drake. (Thanks to Rut Bordes, an AT teacher and doula from Barcelona, who assisted me in the workshop, a Spanish translation is due to appear next year.)

When a pregnant woman is in monkey or on all fours, her abdominal wall provides a sort of hammock for the baby, encouraging it to settle in the OA position. In addition, this is beneficial for the development of the baby: as pressure from the vena cava (the large vein that passes through the lower back) is released, the circulation of the blood that nourishes the baby is improved.

In this workshop we asked the participants to work in pairs while we guided them through a selection of movements, described below. Before each movement, we all paused to inhibit and direct.

Rotation during pregnancy
The following crawling movement may encourage the OP baby to rotate and assume the OA position.

- Move to kneeling on all fours.
- Rock gently forward and back.
- As you move backwards towards your heels, make sure that you have a meditation stool or a small pile of books on which you can sit without exerting excessive pressure on your ankles and knee joints. Now lean forward and support yourself on your hands and knees.
- Stay on all fours for a while and talk to baby; say that you are providing it with your abdominal wall as a hammock on which it can rest its back. Visualise the baby's movement rotating from right to left.
- Allow your head to lead, and move your left hand slightly forward, stroking the floor with the back of the hand. Direct your eyes to look at the fingertips of the moving left hand.
- While your head continues to lead, turn it to the right, looking backwards. Notice that your torso undulates to the left, so that your weight shifts onto the left hand and knee.
- Continue to lead with your head, your torso following forward, 'dragging' the right leg gently along the floor until your knee is approximately under the hip joint; then draw your right knee further forward (not too close to your right hand) to complete the step. Your head returns to look at the floor. Now your weight should be evenly distributed on all fours.
- Continue to crawl for a few steps, alternating right and left. From time to time pause, think about what you are doing, pay attention to your breathing, let your neck be free and keep your eyes lively, not strained.
- If you wish, move to rest by lying on your left side, and continue to

talk to baby and visualise its rotation.

You can see a video of one of my students doing this movement at: https://www.youtube.com/watch?v=sOR_PkRFcpg (or search for Alexander Technique, Pregnancy Crawling, Will Pinchin).
- Bring yourself to the cross pattern (right hand and left knee leading) and begin to crawl. (See figure 2.)

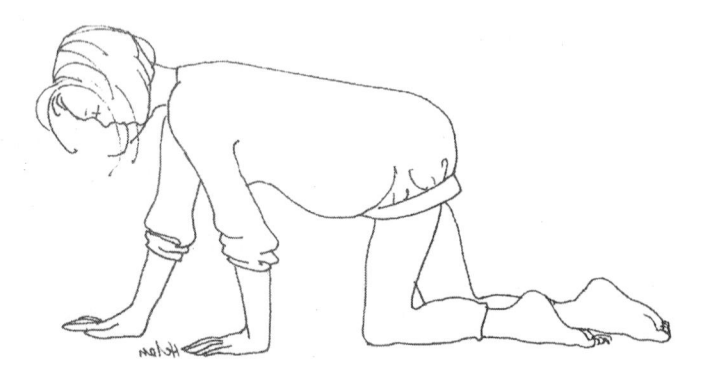

Fig. 2. (Illustration by Helen Chown.)

ROTATION DURING LABOUR

As I mentioned before, in case the baby is in OP at the onset of labour, we can still help it to rotate to OA. The most important thing is for the mother not to lie down (except for short rests, on her left side) but walk, stand in monkey, lunge, stand with one foot resting on a chair, or kneel. In the workshop we practised three movements in pairs. They are useful both during a contraction and in between contractions, when they may be meditative and restful.

Rotational lunge
- Stand with your right foot pointing forward and the left foot pointing away at an angle of about 60°, its heel at the instep of the right foot. Hold hands (your right hand) with your partner, facing each other mirror-like. Move together: it will help you find better balance.
- Let your right knee bend slightly and turn head, neck and torso to face in the same direction as your left foot. As you turn, take a step with your left foot, with the left knee bent, so that you get to a lunge, with your knee over the foot, and your weight on the bent left leg.
- Leading with your eyes, rotate your body to face forward, while gently unbending your left knee and bending your right knee, so that your weight now falls on your right leg. Make sure not to clench your toes.
- Alternate left and right, and vary the positioning of your partner.

One foot on a chair
- Stand facing the seat of a chair. Put one foot on its seat and lean your arms on its back for support and balance. Make sure you don't lock the other knee.
- Rotate your torso, with your head leading, over the hip joints.
- Your partner can participate by sitting on your foot and supporting you, or by standing behind you and hugging you while you move.

The pear movement
- Kneel on all fours.
- Move your torso slowly backwards and forwards, keeping your neck free and your back long, making sure that your lower back does not hollow and collapse. The pivots of your movements are the wrists, the knees and the hip joints; your elbows and shoulders should not be locked; the pelvis should not be tilted (either up-and-down or from side to side) but retains its normal alignment with the spine.
- Your torso remains roughly parallel to the floor.
- Rotate your torso, allowing your head to trace an oval in the same plane as your back. (The longer axis of the oval is an extension of the spine, and the shorter axis is parallel to the shoulder girdle.) Imagine: if you held a long pencil in your mouth, it would draw a pear-shape on the floor.
- A partner can participate by laying his/her hands on your back and moving with you.
- While moving, breathe out through a soft wet mouth and change the pace and direction (clockwise or anti-clockwise) of the movement. (See figure 3).

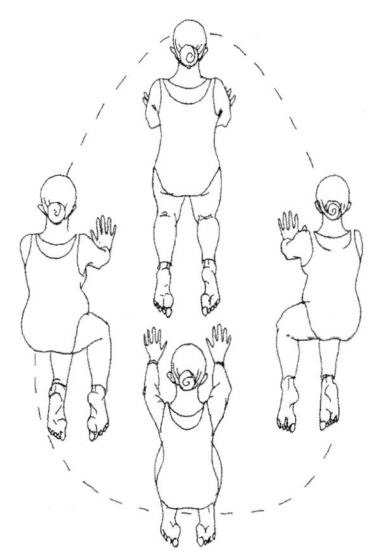

Fig. 3. (Illustration by Helen Chown.)

We encouraged the participants to be creative and transmit this attitude to their pregnant students.

During pregnancy, all these movements should be repeated several times a day. They are pleasurable if the mother applies the principles of the AT, most importantly inhibition and direction. When the mother's attention is directed to the movement she is only concerned with means-whereby, without endgaining. This repetition will ingrain the pattern of the movements in the mother's memory, ready to be applied during labour.

Note: The description of the pear movement here is copied from Ilana Machover & Angela and Jonathan Drake (2006). *The Alexander Technique Birth Book.* Mouritz: London. The crawl is copied from Ilana Machover, 'Turn, baby, Turn', *Midwives*, November, 1995.

1   This is argued in detail by the midwives Jean Sutton and Pauline Scott (1996). *Understanding and Teaching Optimal Foetal Positioning*, 2nd revised edition. Birth Concepts:Tauranga, New Zealand.

Ilana Machover is an Alexander Teacher and Head of Training of the Alexander Technique School, Queen's Park, London. She has taught Alexander Technique at the Royal Academy of Music since 1984, when the AT department there was established. She has published extensively and conducted many workshops on the AT. Ilana is a childbirth educator and doula and also runs special Eutokia workshops: training AT teachers to work with pregnant women and, if they wish, accompany them in childbirth as doulas. She is also a qualified teacher of Medau Rhythmic Movement.

http://homepage.ntlworld.com/ilana.m/
www.eutokiapartofeliz.com

Postural Rehabilitation

An Animal Model for Understanding Resilience, Stability and Embodiment

Elizabeth Reese
With contributions from Karen Gellman[1] and Judith Shoemaker.[2]

> First you must trust in yourself. Then you can also trust in the earth or gravity of a situation and because of that, you can uplift yourself. At that point, your discipline becomes delightful rather than being an ordeal or a great demand.
> When you ride a horse, balance comes not from freezing your legs to the saddle, but from learning to float with the movement of the horse as you ride. Each step is a dance, the rider's dance as well as the dance of the horse.
> Chogyam Trungpa Rinpoche in *Shambala: The Sacred Path of the Warrior*[3]

Postural Rehabilitation (PR) is an internationally recognised manual therapy method developed over the last twenty years by Judith M. Shoemaker, doctor of veterinary medicine, to help animals improve their postural organisation. In 2005, Shoemaker and her veterinary colleague Karen Gellman began to develop a continuing-education course for veterinarians seeking to learn the Postural Rehabilitation techniques. I had been giving workshops in dressage and the Alexander Technique (AT) for many years and was invited to give the students insight into their own postural habits. Most riders know that having a sense of one's balance and uprightness is essential for being able to clearly communicate with one's equine partner. It was proposed that the AT might enhance an equine practitioner's ability to communicate with the horse as well as to learn the Postural Rehab techniques. Together, the three of us developed a three-weekend course that was equal parts theoretical, clinical and experiential. We team-taught, each taking the lead in turn based on our own expertise, yet keeping an open dialogue between us to deepen our understanding of each other's perspective. Our common ground is our belief and understanding that optimal neutral posture (Normal Neutral Posture or NNP) exists for all animals, in which functionally balanced, stable support is achieved with minimal metabolic work and physical stress and that this NNP is essential for well-being.

Observing, studying and interacting with horses can give us great insight into the Alexander Technique. While there are some marked differences between a horse and a human, such as the orientation of the spine and the size of the frontal cortex, the similarities are sufficient to allow for comparison between equines and humans. The horse thinks, considers, problem solves and feels.[4]

Although their potential for complex movement patterns and conceptual thought is limited compared to humans (they are not, for instance, likely to spring into modern dance or write a novel) they are sentient beings, as capable as four or five year old children of understanding instruction, learning tasks and forming relationships. As prey animals, horses' senses are highly refined, which allows for quick responses to stimuli as well as for sensitive and attuned communication. Observing their movement patterns, their habitual stance, and their interactions can give insight into the relationship between primary control and physical functioning, emotional regulation and relationship, and allow for clear observations as to how postural stability, or instability, impacts the psychophysical whole.

What is posture?

Postural control is a complex integration of perception, emotion, cognition and relationship with gravity, as well as an internalised representation of 'upright' in our brains called 'body schema', which is fundamental to self organisation.[5] Posture is an emergent property of the complex neuromusculoskeletal system. It is a learned response which is influenced throughout life by environment and experience.[6] In other words, how we remain upright is the outcome of a complex interaction between all parts of us including our particular habits and history. We unconsciously manage, moment to moment, internal and external stimuli and, for better or worse, mostly remain upright as we move down the road.

The job of the postural control system is to produce consistently functional posture in relation to a dynamic, changing world.[7] Mechanically correct posture stabilises the musculoskeletal support system in reference to gravity and informs the locomotor control centres for stabilised dynamic function, which improves overall motor coordination, athletic performance and body confidence.

The mechanics and motor patterns involved with maintaining posture and movement are all in service to intention. The animal intends to drink water, and the neck, back and limbs all coordinate to solve whatever dynamic balance problem arises in accomplishing this intent. A human decides to pick up a cup and, again, there isn't a need to manage the specific coordination to accomplish this act. Intent organises both posture and locomotion, enabling the activities of life.[8]

Normal Neutral Posture (NNP)

In horses, a normal neutral posture is defined as the standing posture in a normal, sound horse at rest. Neutral stance balances and stabilises the body's centre of mass, allowing rapid, accurate movement when necessary.[9] NNP is the functional output of sensory and gravitational information, processed through the central nervous system, and is a prerequisite for wellness in all animals, including humans. The central nervous system regulates the activities of the mind and body as a complex system – an integrated, dynamic interaction of thought, nerves, muscles, bones, tendons, and ligaments, as well as visceral functions.

When horses are standing on level ground, all four cannon bones should be perpendicular to the ground (Figure 1 and 1a).[10] Having vertical limbs loads the body weight on to the bones and supporting ligaments, much like the legs of a table, and the vertical force strengthens bones, muscles and ligaments and stores potential energy for movement. Just as a table has stability in its structure, a horse in NNP does not need to use significant active

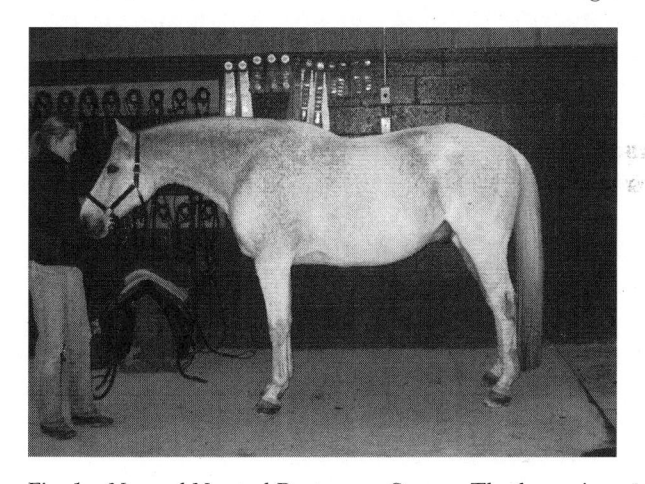

Fig. 1. Normal Neutral Posture or Stance. The horse is not 'placed' in this position. This is his normal stance, and the normal stance of all four legged creatures. *Photo credit: Postural Rehabilitation.*

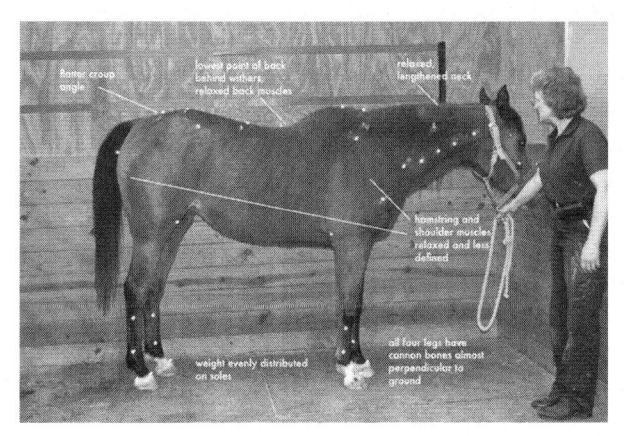

Fig. 1a. Normal Neutral Posture. (This is the same horse as in figure 2a without his winter coat.) *Photo credit: E. Reese.*

muscular force to maintain stance, saving metabolic energy for other functions. There is a moment of neutral posture in locomotion when, in a given stride, a leg is vertical to the ground and this is the moment of maximum weight bearing force that the bones have been strengthened for by standing in NNP.[11] NNP also organises the muscles of the back. In neutral stance, the superficial, movement-generating muscles along the back can be soft and relaxed since deeper postural muscles are providing the necessary support.

Abnormal Compensatory Postures (ACP)

ACP is a habitual stance where the mobilising muscles of the neck, back and limbs are recruited as stabilising muscles. Signs of ACP in a horse are: limbs not consistently perpendicular to the ground; an unwillingness to stand symmetrically; asymmetrical neck and head positions including eyes not held level; distorted spinal contour; performance problems; chronic or recurrent lameness with no known structural injury and chronic degenerative joint disease. The muscles in the underside of the neck and back are noticeably tight, the contour of the back is swayed, roached or laterally asymmetrical, there is rigidity at the occiput, and the hamstring and shoulder muscles are sore (figure 2 and figure 2a).

Numerous factors can result in ACP, including poor handling, diet, injury, illness, improper hoof balance, bad dental care, restricted exercise or living on inappropriate or unvaried ground surfaces. Abnormal Compensatory Posture creates chronic physical, physiologic and emotional stress, which effects long term health and behaviour.

Trauma

Traumatic experiences resulting from neglect, abuse, illness, disease, accident, can influence brain function, autonomic tone, learning abilities and postural stability. It is common to witness horses that appear to be on opposite extremes of the emotional spectrum: on one end, a hyper-reactive, highly emotional horse and, on the other, a horse that is physically unresponsive and that appears to be emotionally 'shut down'. This may be caused by long-term disruption of mind–body–emotion integration, parallel to that seen in human victims of illness, trauma, abuse, and neglect.[12]

The neuromuscular response to chronic stress is a perpetual 'cringe,' a defensive posture protecting the vital organs – the gut, the heart and the brainstem – by pulling the head down and back and drawing the limbs toward the body. As this stance becomes habitual, a person or animal loses the resilience and flexibility of their Normal Neutral Posture. We have observed that this physical imbalance results in less adaptability, which means having fewer choices in responding to the environment, causing increased stress, leading to more hyper-arousal. This cycle continues – until it doesn't. When there's nowhere to run to escape the stress, and no chance of getting away, the mind and emotions shut down into a dissociative state. A person in a dissociative

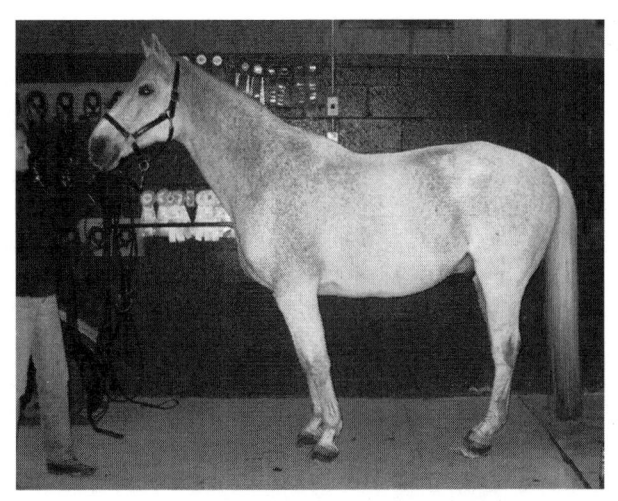

Fig. 2. Abnormal Compensatory Posture: a dysfunctional stance resulting from a myriad of experiences including injury, handling, relationship and environment. *Photo credit: Postural Rehabilitation.*

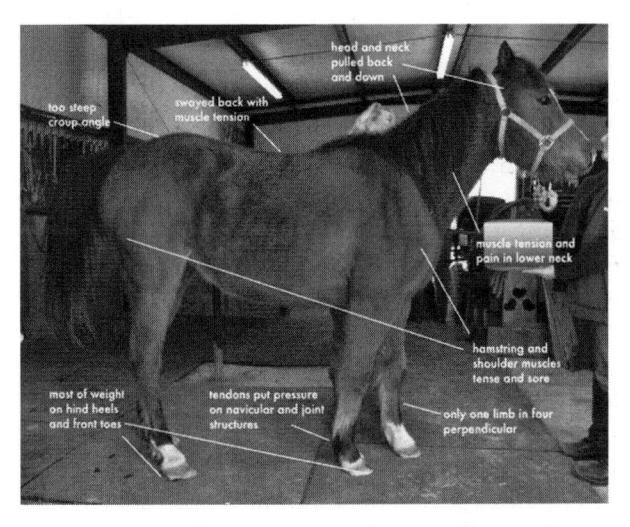

Fig. 2a. Abnormal Compensatory Posture. *Photo credit: E. Reese.*

state can appear functional, but is emotionally and psychically cut off from the experience of living, as if their life was happening to someone else and they were outside of it, watching. The dissociative state is rooted in the defeat response. When a threatening experience is beyond escaping, the body has a built-in response that, in essence, disconnects the mind and emotions from the current experience.[13] Physically, instead of a defensive stance, the body is more in a 'slump' or state of collapse. It is possible to fluctuate between hyper-vigilance and dissociative states.[14]

Once a stress response is established, it can be triggered by a similar stimulus, from any of the senses, that was associated with the initial experience: sight, touch, smell, sound, taste or feel. It is not a conscious response, in that there may be no immediate cognitive association with a memory. In these individuals, the brainstem, which mediates homeostasis and regulates alertness levels, is altered by the experience. The body, believing itself to be under extreme threat, increases the production of epinephrine, which activates the body to a physical state of high alert.[15]

We commonly see this displayed in ACP, in which domestic horses chronically show the high, hyper-alert head carriage and muscle tension associated with alarm and sympathetic nervous system stimulation due to poor handling, management or training. Continually activating the emergency adrenergic system through postural triggers when there is no danger can have long term health consequences: anxiety, gastric ulcers, adrenal exhaustion, and musculoskeletal overload.[16]

Current research in humans indicates that traumatic experiences, including disease, abuse or neglect, can result in deregulated emotional states that profoundly influence brain function, learning and autonomic tone.[17] Chaotic experiences create dysfunctional organisation, while repetitive activities can reshape the brain in patterned ways. Normal brainstem-diencephalon responses can be restored with patterned, repetitive somato-sensory activity.[18] Patients restored to normal neutral posture, often show behavioural changes indicating more effective emotional regulation.[19]

Finding a more stable, neutral posture can allow for an increase in overall resilience and adaptability. What we've witnessed in numerous horses is, when their postural stability is restored, they become less reactive, noticeably calmer, more responsive and easier to engage.

HORSE–HUMAN INTERACTION

Practising mindfulness – paying attention to oneself, one's thinking, one's environment and one's interactions – is epitomised in the horse-human interaction. When we engage with an animal, we are not just using our brains and muscles, but our full sensory system. Horses, as prey animals, are keenly aware of themselves in relationship to their surroundings and to each other. As herd animals, it is evolutionarily advantageous for them to 'tune in' to the movement and thought of their herd members. When you walk in stride with a horse, they often very quickly begin to follow your stride length, pace and cadence. Recent research suggests that when imitation is elicited in the motor cortex through mirror neurons, it is stimulating the recognition of a connection with another being (some researchers propose that this is the foundation of empathy.)[20] It is of great importance, therefore, to notice the quality and character of one's own movement and presence when with a horse, as the horse will respond it.

The care and treatment of horses has alternated between kindness and brutality for more than two thousand years. In this writer's experience, the many approaches to horse training seem to fall into two camps: teaching from a purely behaviourist model, versus teaching governed by the idea that horses are sentient beings capable of thoughts and feelings. How we understand and think of the abilities of the horse influences the interaction, the relationship and the outcome. Captain Etienne Beudant,[21] a French cavalry officer in the 1920s, stated:

> There are two ways of appealing to the moral nature of a horse: one, by terrifying him; the other, by speaking logically . . . to his intelligence.[22]

In his treatise, *Horse Training: Outdoor and High School*, Beudant continually stresses the importance of the rider/trainer attending to their own use – the quality of their movement, thoughts and intentions. His description of the horse–human dialogue could be a description of an Alexander lesson:

> It is calmness, calmness and nothing else, which converts disordered jerky gaits into smooth, flowing ones . . . a teacher must first get the confidence of his pupil, then evince kindness, gentleness and a will that, though calm, is inflexible. This is the immutable and sovereign law of teaching, whether the pupil be man or beast.[23]

Preceding Beudant at the Cadre Noir, the classical riding academy of France, General Alexis l'Hotte (1825–1904) defined the basic goals of training as teaching the horse to be *calm, forward and straight*.[24] *Calm* – because without calm there cannot be any clear communication; *forward* – referring to the horse's impulsive or energetic forces, moving unimpeded and without restriction; and *straight* – for the overall coordination and direction in the horse. Portuguese riding master Nuno Oliveira,[25] renowned for his work with the highly sensitive and intelligent Lusitano horses of Portugal, stated, 'If the rider communicates all the sensitivity he is capable of, then the horse will understand.'[26]

THE ALEXANDER TECHNIQUE AND POSTURAL REHABILITATION

One of the unique aspects of the AT is the skill of communicating neuromuscular changes to a student through touch. The hands-on work involves conscious awareness of one's own overall 'use' in relationship to others and the environment. Through intentional, directed touch, a teacher conveys changes to a student's neuromuscular patterns. The 'hands-on' work does not involve force or manipulation in the common use of the word, but there is a clear, skilled communication that comes from the teacher's whole psychophysical use. While research in mirror neurons points to neuromuscular responses from visually witnessing an action or hearing the voice of another being, experience suggests that a similar response may happen through touch.[27]

This communication through touch and through one's own quality of being is evident when working with horses. As with AT, effective change cannot be attained by the voluntary 'positioning' of a body part but is achieved through the synergistic connection between the horse and human. With horses, practitioners must pay attention to their own use – their stability, availability, presence and intention – to elicit significant postural changes in the animal. Problems in communication arise most often when a practitioner is unintentionally leaning, pulling or pushing the animal. Disturbing an animal's balance in this way requires it to prioritise its response to sensory information. If the animal needs to pay attention to its safety and uprightness, its sensitivity to the subtlety of communication from the practitioner is reduced. On his death bed, the influential horse master François Baucher[28] allegedly said, as he moved both hands forward and away from his torso to indicate a giving of the reins, '*This*, never that.'[29] Give, never pull. Learning to give, while staying connected, is a practice that continues to deepen throughout a practitioner's life. Some Alexander teachers descriptions of F. M. Alexander's hands in a lesson have been, 'soft as butter, strong as steel . . . hinting at great reserves of strength.'[30] This sounds very similar to Oliveira's description of the use of the hands while riding. 'The hand has to be a filter, not a cork or an open faucet.'[31]

To connect on the most effective level, one must engage a student's thinking, not just their physicality. Animals can be trained through the principles of classical behaviour conditioning, but to understand horses as thinking, sentient beings changes the relationship as well as the training outcomes. Alexander Technique and Postural Rehabilitation both employ the intelligence and intent of the practitioner-client dyad in partnership. While the Postural Rehabilitation approach employs several modalities, a key intervention is similar to the Alexander Technique in that the practitioner, with hands on assistance, asks the horse to release the compression in the occiput/atlas/axis, to release the neck from habitual compression, allowing a spring-like release through the entire spine. When a horse can maintain this direction, progressive demands are then made. Much like taking a student in and out of the chair, a horse is presented with a psychophysical problem to solve: How do I remain upright without tightening my neck and/or back? When the horse is able to maintain 'a free neck' while executing a movement, the right conditions are met for self-organisation to occur. The result, after calm, clear, progressive repetition, is the re-establishment of Normal Neutral Posture. In other words, accessing and improving the primary control results in a normal neutral posture.

CONCLUSION

Postural Rehabilitation and Alexander Technique both use conscious intention, repetition and progressively challenging demands to develop a more reliable sensory system. F.M. Alexander developed a criterion for determining whether the system was functioning well or not, the same criteria that equestrians have observed for hundreds of years:

> I have found a way by which we can judge whether the influence of our manner of use is affecting our general functioning adversely or otherwise, the criterion being whether or not this manner of use is interfering with the correct employment of primary control.[32]

When there is less interference with primary control, Normal Neutral Posture is the outcome. Chronic interference with primary control leads to Abnormal Compensatory Posture. Numerous factors including experience, environment, and relationship affect the postural system. When the system is not working well, the stress of working to stay upright takes physical and emotional energy which can lead to further misuse. Primary control is accessed through the brain, therefore positioning the body does not have the same effect as engaging the mind. With both horses and humans, we are not manipulating them to force change but teaching them to engage in the process of changing. Improvements in movement, emotional regulation and overall well-being are the result of improved Normal Neutral Posture. The 'correct employment of primary control' is the equivalent of stability, adaptability and resilience.

Acknowledgements

Teaching on the Postural Rehabilitation course has been one of the most enriching experiences of my life. I am indebted to both Karen Gellman and Judith Shoemaker for sharing their brilliance, their insights and their camaraderie over the past ten years of teaching together. Through our work, with all the vulnerability and courage team teaching requires, I have grown in my understanding, respect and love of both humans and horses.

References and Notes

1   Karen Gellman, PhD, DVM, is a PR practitioner, researcher and co-founder of the PR course.
2   Judith Shoemaker, DVM, is nationally recognised animal practitioner who developed the Postural Rehabilitation techniques over the last 30 years. She is co-founder of the PR course.
3   Trungpa, C. (1986). *Shambhala: The Sacred Path of the Warrior*. Shambhala Publications, p. 74.
4   Hangii, E. (2005). 'The Thinking Horse: Cognition and Perception Reviewed', in *AAEP Proceedings*, 51, p. 246.

5   Garfinkel, V. S. (1994). 'The Mechanisms of Postural Regulation in Man' in *Sov. Sci. Rev.F. Phys. General Biology.* 7, pp. 59-89.
6   Stuart, D.G. (2005). 'Integration of Posture and Movement: Contributions of Sherrington, Hess and Bernstein' in *Human Movement Science,* 24, pp. 621-643.
7   Roberts, T. D. M. (1967). *Neurophysiology of Postural Mechanisms.* Butterworth & Co: London, chapters 8-11.
8   Bressler, S. L. and J. A. S. Kelso (2001). 'Cortical coordination dynamics and cognition', *Trends in Cognitive Sciences,* 5, 1, pp. 26-36.
9   NNP also allows for normal compensatory posture. If I hurt my foot, I need to be able to stay off of it until it heals without risk of injury to the rest of me.
10 This is not to infer that a horse should be placed in a correct position. A horse stands for an average of 23 hours a day. He can sleep standing up, lying down only for deep REM sleep. Their four-legged stance is designed for this. When their resting posture is something other then NNP, it is cause for concern.
11 MacPhereson, J. M. (1988). 'Strategies that Simplify the Control of Quadrupedal Stance' in *Neurophysiology,* 60, 1, pp. 204-217.
12 Heller, L., A. LaPierre (2012). *Healing Developmental Trauma.* North Atlantic Books: Berkeley, USA.
13 Porges, S. W. (2004) 'Neuroception: A Subconscious System for Detecting Threats and Safety' in *Zero To Three,* 32, pp.19-24.
14 Perry, B. D. (2001) 'The Neurodevelopmental Impact of Violence in Childhood' in Schetky D & Benedek, E. (eds.) *Textbook of child and adolescent forensic psychiatry.* American Psychiatric Press, Inc: Washington, D.C., pp. 221-238.
15 Levine, P. (1997). *Waking the Tiger: Healing Trauma.* North Atlantic Books: Berkeley, USA.
16 Perry, B. (2006). *The Boy Who Was Raised as a Dog.* Basic Books: New York.
17 Levine, P. (2010) *In An Unspoken Voice: How the Body Releases Trauma and Restores Goodness.* North Atlantic Books: Berkeley, USA.
18 B. D. Perry '(2001) Op. Cit.
19 Levine, P. (1997). Op. Cit.
20 Kaplan, J. (2006). 'Getting a grip on other minds: Mirror neurons, intention, understanding and cognitive empathy' in *Social Neuroscience,* vol. 1, 3-4, pp.175-183.
21 E. Beudant (1883–1949) was a captain in the French calvary and a highly respected rider and writer. He believed in the versatility and ability of even the most ordinary of horses.
22 Beudant, E. (1931). *Horse Training: Outdoor and High School.* Charles Scribner's Sons: New York, p. 14.
23 Beudant, Op. Cit.
24 Alexis-Francois L'Hotte (1825–1904) was commandant of the French cavalry school and was a student of Francois Baucher. He is considered one of France's greatest riders.
25 Nuno Oliveira (1925–1989) was a Portuguese riding master known for his classical approach to riding. He is considered by many to be the most masterful horseman of the 20th century.

26 Oliveira, N., N., J. Sauvat (1990). *Horse and Rider: Annotated Sketches.* Editions Belin: Paris, p. 94.
27 Nicholls, J. (2014) Teacher of the Alexander Technique and trainer of AT teachers. Personal conversations.
28 Francois Baucher (1796–1873) methods continue to be debated today. His understanding of the head–neck relationship and the use of the hands to communicate forward energy to the horse (rather then the legs) is what is of interest to Alexander teachers.
29 Horse lore: the story goes that in his last days, Baucher said this to General L'Hotte and L'Hotte reported this in his memoirs.
30 Nicholls, J. (2014). Teacher of the Alexander Technique and trainer of AT teachers. Personal conversations.
31 Oliveira, N. (1980), *Oeuvres Completes.* Belin: Paris, France. Translation of quote from C. Stevens.
32 Alexander, F. M., E. Maisel. (ed.) (1995). *The Alexander Technique: The Essential Writings of F. Matthias Alexander.* Carol Publishing Group: New York, p.165.

Elizabeth Reese, cAmSAT, MEd, LMHC, began studying the Alexander Technique in 1981 with Margery Barstow and considered the work as a core part of her training as a choreographer/performer in NYC. Around 1987, she traded time at dance studios for more time at horse barns as she discovered the art of dressage, uniting her love of horses, dance and the Alexander Technique. She graduated from ACAT in 1994 and has continued to teach, ride and study both disciplines. Her work with both humans and horses suffering from trauma inspired her interest in the relationship of postural stability to emotional resilience. Elizabeth was a senior faculty member on John Nicholls' Alexander training course in NYC for ten years; one of the three core faculty and founders of Postural Rehabilitation, a continuing education course for veterinarians; and a therapist at Community Counselling and Mediation. She has taught workshops in Ireland, Denmark and throughout the United States. With the Postural Rehab team, she led a continuing education course for the Danish Veterinarian Chiropractic Association; was a keynote speaker at the Veterinarian Acupuncture Conference in Galway, Ireland and a featured presenter at the American Holistic Veterinary Association's national conference in Portland, Oregon. She maintains a private practice at her farm in Sugar Loaf, New York and in New York City.

STAT Research Group Panel

After ATEAM, ATLAS and Other Adventures in Alexander Research

Julia Woodman, Lesley Glover, Kathleen Ballard, Korina Biggs, David Gibbens, Jane Clappison

THE STAT RESEARCH GROUP

The STAT Research Group (SRG) was created by Erica Donnison in 2010, and consists of a small group of research-experienced UK-based teachers working on a voluntary basis. Originally called the STAT Scientific Research Group, it was renamed to reflect the diversity of type and areas of research.

The SRG's overall aim is to encourage and facilitate high quality research into all aspects of the Alexander Technique, its teaching and application, and explain the relevance to teachers. It is hoped that some will become interested in pursuing research themselves. In addition to the SRG, the SRG Network is an open, informal group of people with skills or interests in a particular area.

Although the SRG's role is primarily to enable and communicate research, rather than actually perform it, members have been active in several recent projects (see *Research update* below), including a survey of Alexander teaching in the UK.[1]

Since inception, the SRG has sought to use the Alexander research evidence base to increase public awareness and understanding of the Technique, and also to influence policy makers. For example, the SRG is a registered stakeholder with the UK National Institute for Health and Care Excellence (NICE), and has recently contributed to the scoping exercise for the next update of the back pain clinical guidelines. Similarly, research evidence has been submitted to NHS Choices and UK Advertising Standards with the dual aim of increasing their awareness of evidence that supports claims for the effectiveness of lessons, and improving their online statements about the Alexander Technique.

The SRG has created several initiatives aimed at communicating research to the Alexander profession and to outside audiences such as other health professionals and the general public. These include:

i. the web-based resource, Alexander Studies Online (see below);
ii. summaries of published research on the STAT website (www.stat.org.uk);

iii. an evidence-based review of the effectiveness of Alexander lessons for various health-related conditions;[2]
iv. articles on the Alexander Technique for various patient-support organisations;
v. the STAT skills directory (in process) to help teachers find colleagues with relevant experience.

The SRG has also built strong relationships with charities such as BackCare, and networked with public bodies such as the UK All-Party Parliamentary Group for Integrated Healthcare.

What is research?

In its widest sense, research is the process of identifying a question and seeking to answer it by gathering information, distilling it, synthesising it with existing knowledge, reflecting, drawing conclusions and disseminating findings. Research is a rigorous process, underpinned by explicit assumptions; it is a process of disciplined enquiry.

To date, research on the Technique has largely focused on exploring outcomes, including changes in function, physiology and individuals' self-reported experience after learning the Technique. Studies often focus on a particular condition. To move our understanding forward, we now need to broaden the scope of enquiry to include the processes of teaching, learning and applying the Technique, as well as the outcomes that result. We also need to employ a wider range of research methods that will enable us to increase our understanding of how change is brought about, develop a deeper theoretical understanding of the Technique and perhaps increase teaching efficacy.

All research methods reveal some things and conceal others. With this in mind it is necessary to think broadly so that a body of research literature can be developed which, when pieced together and considered alongside research from other fields, will provide a clearer understanding of the Technique and its sphere of influence. A variety of study types is needed, including experimental, survey, case study, interview, diary and mixed-method designs, along with a range of types of data, for example self-report, objective measures, neuroimaging, video and existing data such as narratives about the experience of learning the Technique.

Any kind of enquiry has to be ethical and adhere to ethical codes of conduct, incorporating fundamentals such as informed consent, avoidance of harm, and confidentiality. Studies must be justifiable and well-designed. To make significant progress, a critical mass of research is required to take us towards a more complete picture of the Alexander Technique.

The challenge is primarily one of resources: these include finance, numbers of individuals and structures/organisations willing to host and support our studies.

RESEARCH UPDATE

Although the Alexander Technique has been in existence for more than a hundred years and teachers and students alike are well aware of the power of learning and applying it in our daily lives, until recently there has been relatively little research on it. For example, a search of the Medline database (August 2015) for publications categorised as 'clinical trial' reveals less than 10 studies for 'Alexander Technique', in comparison with almost 4,000 on acupuncture and more than 500 on mindfulness. There is, however, room for optimism as research interest appears to be increasing, not just in quantity but also in quality and type. The breadth and depth of current research on the Alexander Technique is illustrated by the diversity of projects that SRG members are currently involved in, from large randomised, controlled trials to interview-based studies.

ATLAS

The ATLAS (Alexander Technique Lessons or Acupuncture Sessions) trial is a large, well-designed, well-conducted, randomised, controlled trial involving 517 people with chronic neck pain.[3, 4] It was funded by Arthritis Research UK and designed and managed by a large, University of York-based research team that included SRG members Julia Woodman and Kathleen Ballard.

Globally, neck pain is listed fourth out of 291 conditions in terms of length of time that pain and disability are suffered, and equal second, along with 'posture', as a reason for seeking Alexander lessons in the UK[1]. Medical practitioners and physiotherapists generally find chronic neck pain more difficult to deal with than chronic back pain and it is clear that self-care approaches are needed to alleviate the growing difficulties facing medical services worldwide.

The entry criteria for the ATLAS trial stipulated that participants should have suffered neck pain for at least 3 months, but it turned out that the average period was 6 years. The longest was 50 years! The severity of pain and associated disability was assessed by asking people to complete the Northwick Park Neck Pain Questionnaire, a self-report measure. Their score had to be at least 28% or higher. People with a serious condition already diagnosed were excluded. Those finally selected had an average age of 53, and 69% were female.

Participants were recruited by the University of York Trials Unit sending out 10,000 invitations to likely GP patients in York, Leeds, Sheffield and Manchester. Just over 1,000 replied and 517 met the entry criteria. They were randomly allocated to one of three groups: i) 20 one-to-one Alexander lessons alongside continuing usual GP-led care, ii) 12 acupuncture sessions of equivalent total length of time to the Alexander lessons alongside usual GP-led care, or iii) usual GP-led care alone. The usual GP-led care included any tests or NHS treatment needed. Each Alexander lesson was to include 30 minutes of actual teaching, so each appointment generally lasted longer to allow time for booking the next one etc, or for the initial consultation. Eighteen Alexander teachers participated; all belonged to STAT and provided evidence of a commitment to their continuing professional development. The teachers were asked, as a first priority, to enable participants to learn and apply the Alexander Technique, in line with the UK National Occupational Standards for Alexander teaching.[5] So, in other words, they should teach as usual and not be influenced by the fact of being part of a clinical trial and try to get the participants better by direct means. It was reassuring to find that teachers' log book data showed that in 94% of cases, they were able to teach in line with their usual practice. The acupuncture sessions included acupuncture theory-based lifestyle advice, most commonly related to exercise, relaxation, diet and rest.

The main findings of the trial were long-term benefits for people who attended Alexander lessons, or who received acupuncture.[4] Both groups experienced nearly a third less pain and associated disability (a 31% reduction for the Alexander group) at the end of the trial, 1 year later. This reduction was significantly greater than that experienced by the group who received usual GP-led care alone, and was large enough to be considered clinically relevant. The extent to which people believed in their ability to manage and reduce their pain ('self-efficacy') increased more in both the Alexander group and the acupuncture group than in the group that received usual care alone. Furthermore, this increase in self-efficacy was found to be associated with a greater reduction in pain and associated disability at 1 year. Other findings revealed an improvement, following Alexander lessons or acupuncture, in people's mental health at 1 year, as revealed by a self-report quality-of-life questionnaire. Finally, no safety issues related to the interventions were identified.[4]

Outcomes from an Alexander Technique pilot group for older people with a fear of falling

This small-scale pilot study was led by Lesley Glover and Jane Clappison, funded by Hull NHS Clinical Commissioning Group and undertaken in collaboration with the University of Hull and the support of STAT. It aimed to investigate the outcomes of a group Alexander Technique intervention for older adults with a fear of falling.

Eleven women and one man (aged 65–86 years) took part, and all completed the Alexander group intervention of 6 twice-weekly sessions followed by 6 weekly sessions each lasting 1½ hours. The sessions included: semi-supine, movement, explorations, discussion and/or feedback and some hands-on work. At the end, participants took part in focus group interviews and the following outcomes were identified (quotes are in italics).

Overall functioning was improved (e.g. *I feel that I'm sitting better; I can go and hang out the washing now without a walking stick*), and participants described different ways of being (e.g. *I feel more in contact with the ground somehow; Much calmer; It's taught me to . . . turn off the bits you don't need to use*). Fear was not removed but participants saw it as having a useful function (*You've still got that bit of apprehension there. . . . And I think if you didn't have, you'd forget to do it [Alexander Technique].*).

Participants described being more aware of themselves and their use, and of their surroundings (*I think a bit more about doing things. . .*). They seemed to have a change of attitude with an acceptance of limitations and a discovery that they had found new ways of doing things. (*I'm a bit slower . . ., but that's good; . . . if you can't do something there's always a second way of doing it.*) The combination of increased awareness and attitude change led to a sense of empowerment (*I never thought I could do that; I won't be rushed.*)

The outcomes suggest that the Alexander group intervention brought about positive changes for the individuals who took part. The changes that occurred extended beyond fear of falling to encompass a change in attitudes to ageing and allowed people the opportunity to find different ways of engaging with the world and others. The pilot study provides evidence to support further work in this area and is currently being written up for publication.[6]

Soma in the city
This research was completed by Korina Biggs as part of an MA in Dance and Somatic Well-being and is an example of a type of qualitative research in which the Alexander Technique was an influence. The basis of the research was: An interest in bridging the gulf between perceptual/movement practice informed by the Alexander Technique and being in a challenging urban environment.

Curiosity about how using digital technology can possibly create more, rather than less, connection to psychophysical self and environment.

An audio recording was developed ('a somatic podcast') and given to individuals. It consisted of verbal directions and suggestions, along with carefully chosen music.

There were six participants and research 'data' were drawn from the time shared together 'post-podcast'. This included movement, drawing, writing, and verbal description. Conclusions were drawn from themes extracted from the subjective experience of the individuals. The research methodology had a phenomenological approach influenced by humanistic psychologist Clark Moustakas' heuristic inquiry. This meant that the research was a creative and personal process of discovery revealing meaningful experience both in Korina and the participants. The development of content of the podcast involved her experimenting with language, music, timing both outdoors and in a studio. There were six participants who she worked with individually, and research 'data' were drawn from the time shared together after the participants had experienced listening and responding to the audio. This included encouraging them to either carry on moving, or to draw, write, or simply share their experience verbally. From these sharings, themes were drawn out that reflected the impact of the whole experience for the participants.[7]

Mobility and transport life-story study
Researchers from the Universities of Edinburgh and Manchester have been conducting in-depth interviews to find out how people's life experiences have been influenced by the Alexander Technique. The study is part of a much larger research project looking at mobility and transport in their broadest contexts, and recognises that people trained in the Technique have a particular expertise in mobility and movement. The larger study with members of the general public has identified certain common themes that have emerged from the interviews conducted. These themes included attitudes to ageing and trauma, and it was particularly notable how widespread trauma is as a feature of people's lives, whether from cancer, bereavement or other reasons. In-depth interviews have now also been conducted with fifteen Alexander teachers, trainee-teachers and students, and the themes emerging from the main group are being explored. Preliminary findings show a more positive attitude to ageing and a greater resilience to dealing with trauma among those with Alexander experience. While this finding may not be surprising to an Alexander audience, publications from the study will be valuable in helping to explain the benefits of the Technique to a wider audience of academics and the public. Moreover, the findings may help deepen our professional understanding of the ways in which applying the Technique can help people respond differently to life events.

ALEXANDER STUDIES ONLINE
ASO (www.alexanderstudies.org) was originally conceived within the SRG as the *International Alexander Research Forum*, intended to help develop a community of those with Alexander-related research interests all over the world, regardless of affiliation. But from the earliest days, we recognised that a website would give us the opportunity to support such a community with a range of resources, not just a forum. David Gibbens has led the whole initiative which includes: starting to build an online bibliographic database to document the many pieces of research into the Alexander Technique; republishing some important but hard-to-find contributions to Alexander theory; developing a 'universal index' of key Alexander writings; sketching out a model for developing autobiographical material; and designing processes for peer review for new work, to help us achieve the highest quality we can manage.

This is an ambitious project, but is conceived as a long-term endeavour. We do not expect immediate results but do want to ensure that whatever we do in the short term is to a high standard, building a solid base for the future. The Alexander Technique cannot flourish without a focus for disciplined enquiry, a willingness to ask challenging questions, pay appropriate regard to evidence and enter into a dialogue with the wider world of research. We hope that ASO will make a major contribution to this process.

LOOKING TO THE FUTURE

Based on the response of the Congress Panel audience, there is support among teachers for the idea of being involved in informal research, by writing up case studies describing the experiences of their students learning the Alexander Technique. These case studies could be collected on ASO as an online repository. If you are interested in this idea and/or have relevant experience or skills and would like to join the SRG Network, or if you are already conducting research, please do get in touch with one of the SRG Co-Chairs (Julia Woodman: alexander@woodman.eclipse.co.uk or Erica Donnison: erica.donnison@mac.com). For Alexander Studies Online please contact David Gibbens at: editor@alexanderstudies.org.

References

1. Eldred J., A. Hopton, E. Donnison, J. Woodman, H. MacPherson (2015). 'Teachers of the Alexander Technique in the UK and the people who take their lessons: A national cross-sectional survey' in *Complementary Therapies in Medicine* 23, pp. 451–461.
2. Woodman, J. P. and N. R. Moore (2012). 'Evidence for the effectiveness of Alexander Technique lessons in medical and health-related conditions: a systematic review' in *International Journal of Clinical Practice* 66:, pp. 98–112.
3. MacPherson, H., H. Tilbrook, S. Richmond, K. Atkin, K. Ballard, M. Bland, J. Eldred, H. N. Essex, A. Hopton, H. Lansdown, U. Muhammad, S. Parrott, D. Torgerson, A. Wenham, J. Woodman, I. Watt (2013). 'Alexander Technique Lessons, Acupuncture Sessions or usual care for patients with chronic neck pain (ATLAS): Study protocol for a randomised controlled trial' in *Trials*. 14:209. www.trialsjournal.com/content/14/1/209
4. MacPherson, H., H. Tilbrook, S. Richmond, J. Woodman, K. Ballard, K. Atkin, M. Bland, J. Eldred, H. Essex, C. Hewitt, A. Hopton, A. Keding, H. Lansdown, S. Parrott, D. Torgerson, A. Wenham, I. Watt (2015). 'Alexander Technique lessons or acupuncture sessions for persons with chronic neck pain: A randomized trial' in *Annals of Internal Medicine*. 163, pp. 653–62.
5. Skills for Health. National Occupational Standards for Alexander Technique Teaching. CNH3; Version 1 [Internet]. *National Occupational Standards* (2010). Available from: https://tools.skillsforhealth.org.uk/competence/show/pdf/id/2800
6. Glover, L, D. Kinsey, D. J. Clappison, J. Jomeen. 'I never thought I could do that…' Outcomes from an Alexander Technique pilot for older people with a fear of falling. In preparation.
7. Biggs, K. (2015). 'How does listening and responding to a 'somatic podcast' affect one's relationship to urban space?' in *Journal of Dance & Somatic Practices*. 7(1), p. 75.
8. Ballard, K. (2015). 'Ideomotor Principle. Was Alexander Correct?' in *Connected Perspectives, The Alexander Technique in Context*. Hite Ltd: London, pp. 49–71.

Julia Woodman BSc, PhD, MSTAT is Co-Chair of the STAT Research Group. She is a member of the trial management team for ATLAS (evaluating Alexander lessons for people with chronic neck pain), and is currently Visiting Research Fellow at the University of York. Julia's background is in clinical trials and medical writing but she is interested in all types of Alexander-related research. Julia has been teaching the Alexander Technique to individuals, groups and in business since 2006, having trained with Malcolm Williamson at the Manchester Alexander Technique Training School.

Kathleen Ballard BSc, PhD, MSTAT trained as a schoolteacher, later as a research scientist and became an Alexander teacher in 1984. Her questioning scientific approach has been applied to our training, teaching and professional practice. She is a core member of the STAT Research Group and author of a recent article on the ideomotor phenomenon[8] and the Alexander Technique. Formerly a member of several STAT study groups, Kathleen worked on descriptions of teacher competences and later played a key role on behalf of STAT in the development of National Occupational Standards for Alexander Technique teaching in the UK. These underpin the curriculum submitted to the Complementary and Natural Healthcare Council and help establish Alexander teaching on a more professional footing. Kathleen also served on the Voluntary Self Regulation Group that developed the initial guidelines for the constitution of the Complementary and Natural Healthcare Council.

Lesley Glover BSc, MSc, PhD, MSTAT is a core member of the STAT Research Group. She is a clinical psychologist and works part time as a senior lecturer in the Department of Psychological Health and Well-being at the University of Hull, UK. She trained as an Alexander Technique teacher with Lena Schibel-Mason at the York Alexander Technique School.

Korina Biggs Bsc Econ MA, MSTAT has been working as an Alexander teacher for 14 years, and now also works as a somatic movement facilitator, having qualified with an MA in Dance and Somatic Well-being. She is part of the STAT 'Performing Self' team delivering CPD for Alexander teachers and works in drama colleges including The Lir, Dublin and ALRA, London. She is a regular teacher for the Hampshire County Youth Orchestra. A founder member of Frantic Assembly physical theatre company, she is fascinated by the application of the Alexander Technique to performance. She regularly enjoys various movement practices, is one of the founders of the collective 'Dancers In Landscape', and is a member of The Knowing Body Network.

David Gibbens MSTAT is the project lead for Alexander Studies Online, having previously helped redevelop STAT's main website. David trained at Fellside with Don Burton, Joan Diamond, Michael Hardwicke and Jamie McDowell, qualifying in 1992. He has accumulated a wide range of experience across a range of industries and professions in strategic, management and project leadership roles.

Jane Clappison MCSP, MSTAT, MCSS works in private practice as an Alexander Technique Teacher and CranioSacral Therapist. She was one of the leaders of the small scale pilot study which looked at a group Alexander Technique intervention for older adults with a fear of falling (2015). Jane's previous work experience is eclectic, from owning a retail jewellery business to teaching dance and keep fit and latterly as a Chartered Physiotherapist in the NHS Pain Management field. Jane has been teaching the Alexander Technique to individuals, groups and businesses since 2013 having trained with Lena Schibel-Mason at the York Alexander Technique School.

Alexander Technique and Burnout Prevention

Martina Süss and Christine Weixler

Towards the end of our Alexander teacher training with Melissa Matson in Linz, Austria, we both found ourselves in very challenging life situations. Being friends, we regularly reflected on the stressful circumstances we were in. In doing this we realised how supportive the physical experience of lightness was, as we continuously renewed it during our Alexander training.

This led us to a series of questions and insights about the potential of the Alexander Technique to support a precise sense of how to maintain clear boundaries and look after ourselves while practising our professional activities. Spending a lot of time on her Alexander training, Christine's life as psychotherapist, mother and grandmother intensified in stressful ways. She worked more, still found time for her family, but had less spare time for herself. Martina, working on her PhD about body-oriented methods in counselling organisations – especially about the benefits of body-oriented work for holistic health and well-being – experienced something similar. Writing a doctoral thesis felt very hard; it led to excess muscle tension in her back and seemed not to allow a sense of well-being in her own body.

We faced different challenges but shared a similar basic experience: *being deeply involved in what we were doing disconnected us again and again from an easy use of self.* Coming back to our Alexander training, spending no time on solving our problems but 'only' working to find ways back to our well-made-ness and to a better use of self, we both found that our problem-solving capacities in everyday life increased.

We discovered that the combination of the intense group experience in our Alexander training, the regular peer exchange and our Individual Daily Alexander Practice[1] fostered a powerful and supportive process. The Alexander principles became more and more naturally available in challenging situations and helped us to in general feel lighter and be less exhausted in our lives.

As we realised that this combination of group training, peer exchange and individual daily practice proved extremely helpful and preventive of 'burnout' for us, we decided to share the experience and our insights with colleagues and clients. We designed our first seminar 'Helping Tires You Out – How You Can Wake up Refreshed' in 1999. This was the start of an inspiring journey through the fields of Alexander Technique, Client-Centred Therapy and Burnout Theory.

In the wide field of recent Burnout Theory there are a few shared basics. Our main point of reference is one of the pioneers in this field, the organisational psychologist Christina Maslach. She defines burnout as a subtle process of exhaustion in a person's professional activity:

Burnout is the index of the dislocation between what people are and what they have to do. It represents an erosion in values, dignity, spirit, and will – an erosion of the human soul.[2]

Maslach says the risk for burnout is high when you are in a working situation with chronic imbalance, that is, when you are in a situation in which the job demands more than you can give and provides less than you need.

What happens once you begin to burn out?

i. You become chronically exhausted.
ii. You become cynical and disconnected from your work.
iii. You feel more and more ineffective in doing your job.

Let's take a closer look at the dimensions of burnout that Maslach defines:[3]

1. *Exhaustion*: people feel overstrained, both emotionally and physically, and unable to recover. They experience a wide range of physical symptoms, such as pain from excess tension in back and neck, tightness of the chest, shallow breathing patterns, digestive problems, sleep problems, palpitations, etc. From an Alexander Technique perspective we can say that their stress patterns (habits) become chronic and show a harmful misuse of self.
2. *Cynicism*: With increasing exhaustion a second process starts: individuals develop a cold, distant attitude towards their work, their colleagues, clients, customers and themselves. They distance themselves from others and become increasingly disengaged and isolated.
3. *Ineffectiveness*: New projects feel overwhelming and the person loses confidence in their ability to work effectively. They feel a growing sense of inadequacy. As they lose their own self-confidence, others too experience doubts regarding the individual's competence.

Maslach found what we also experienced: once a person becomes aware of their exhaustion, they mostly fall back on the following **destructive strategies**:

1. *Endgaining:* A person suffering from work overload will often try to work harder and longer hours, and if there is still more work to do, they will work even harder and put in even more long hours – in the hope that relief will come at some point in the future. In the Alexander world we would say they increase endgaining.
2. *Reducing Inner Engagement:* The individual abandons their ideals and minimises their inner engagement. This is a two-fold process: when a person becomes despondent, they reduce their inner engagement with their work. This process weakens self-assurance and self-confidence as well as the ability to deal with challenging situations. This leaves them even more vulnerable to disappointment and exhaustion. In effect this strategy is an ineffective and potentially harmful attempt to protect oneself from disappointment and exhaustion. Having weak self-confidence and a negative attitude towards oneself, others and the work has a counter-productive effect: it damages the person's well-being even more and weakens the capacity to work effectively.

As a person is usually not aware of these processes, they spread gradually and continuously over time and lead to a **downward spiral** from which it is hard to recover.

For a long time it was thought that certain individuals had a stronger disposition towards burnout than others. When Christina Maslach and her research team conducted extensive research in companies, they discovered that burnout in individual workers says as much about the conditions of the job as it says about the particular workers to whom it happens. This was a big step towards the current state of academic discussion about burnout. There is now a general consensus that individual burnout and exhaustion is generated on three levels:

- the individual
- the organisation or system around the individual
- society.

Recent research suggests that everyone is at risk of experiencing burnout.[4] The causes for burnout lie in the person as well as in the surrounding organisational system, which is constantly influenced by the complexity of a rapidly changing society. It is still true, however, that the individual suffers from burnout, and the individual is the one who can take the first step out of the burnout process.

This is where Alexander Technique intersects with Burnout Theory. F. M. Alexander's insight that *how* we do something is more important than *what* we do offers a helpful exit to the desperate impasse experienced by those suffering from burnout.

In working with the participants of our seminars, we aim to provide an understanding of the burnout process and how to help, using basic Alexander concepts and Carl Rogers' idea of Unconditional Positive Regard. The core of the approach is a shift of awareness which moves a person from victimhood to choice.

What seems easy for an experienced Alexander Technique teacher is a long and challenging experiment for a burnout sufferer. What is it that allows a person to move into a **refreshing upward spiral** towards energy and vitality? What do they need to step out of the destructive downward spiral of exhaustion; what enables them to choose a **constructive strategy** in dealing with stress?

1. Our experience as Alexander teachers and Burnout Counsellors is that when a burnout client is invited to be aware of themselves, they usually have one of two experiences: either the person contacts pain and discomfort, or emptiness. Having uncomfortable or no sensations and no emotion is a very familiar state for a burnout client. To stay kind to ourselves is the big challenge at this point. Saying 'yes' to myself even when I don't like at all what I sense in my body is the first big step to coming back home to myself.

    A position of *unconditional positive regard* (UPR) for whatever we sense and feel in ourselves is helpful in facilitating awareness, inhibition and direction. UPR is one of the core conditions of Carl Rogers' Client-Centred Therapy[5] and a basic instrument of personal change in psychotherapy. In most Alexander lessons UPR is implicit and allows the pupil's process of change. *Naming it and making it explicit has proved to be very helpful in our work with Burnout clients.* It is the antidote to the unhelpful strategy of endgaining.

    Introducing UPR as a core condition for personal change helps individuals realise that a No to their habits never means a No to themselves. This insight is the first step towards the refreshing upward spiral.

    UPR is a non-doing, non-judging position, and underlines how and why Alexander Technique is such a constructive answer for people suffering from distress.

2. UPR is the basis for the second step in the upward spiral, which is experiencing and practising the **Alexander principles** of awareness, inhibition and direction in everyday life. This is one of the great gifts of the Alexander Technique. In our seminars we offer different settings in which participants can gain awareness of their physical and mental stress habits and practise letting go of these habits with the support of the Alexander principles. Once a person understands that

the important choice they can make is *how* they use themselves, rather than *what* they have to do, the door opens to step away from being a victim towards being in control of one's own life again. This is the step away from the downward strategy of reduced inner engagement and towards the upwards strategy of practising awareness, inhibition and direction; this enables the individual to stay in a lively contact with themselves while staying with others.

In our workshops we offer various exercises to consciously experience the physical and emotional effects of

- UPR
- Awareness, inhibition and direction
- Stress and habit
- Constructive use of the self

We also help people to transfer this experience into their everyday lives. We support them in finding a small individual daily practice they can cultivate at home to continuously nourish their ease and well-being.

We run our workshops mainly for those working in the Helping Professions, such as staff in hospitals, women's refuges, debt counsellors, etc. We do co-operate with Human Resource directors of the organisations we work with as we develop customised workshop programs. Depending on the needs of each organisation we offer workshops of varying length and structure. This meets the organisational requirements for professional development and training in the Helping Professions in Austria.

References and Notes

1 Individual Daily Practice: This idea was introduced by Melissa Matson in our Alexander training in 1997. We had to choose a small daily activity, like dishwashing, brushing teeth, etc. in which we would practise the Alexander principles of awareness, inhibition and direction.
2 Maslach, C. (2001). *The Truth About Burnout.* Jossey Bass: San Francisco, USA, p. 17.
3 Ibid p. 17 ff.
4 Burisch, M. (2014, 2013). *Das Burnout-Syndrom.* Springer Medizin Verlag: Heidelberg.
5 Rogers, C. (1995, 1961). *On Becoming a Person.* Houghton Mifflin: Boston.

Martina Süss originally studied Business Administration, with a special focus on Organisational Psychology, and later trained as a Dance Therapist and Brainspotting Trauma Therapist. Her ongoing interest in a psychosomatic and creative understanding of the self led to a fruitful cooperation with Melissa Matson, with whom she developed and organised an Alexander Technique training course in Linz, Austria from 1997 to 2007. She qualified as an Alexander teacher in 2003 and currently works as a Business Coach, Alexander Teacher and Body Therapist.

Christine Weixler has been a Person-Centred psychotherapist since 1992 and has been training psychotherapists since 1997. She trained as an Alexander Teacher with Melissa Matson 1997–2001 in Linz, Austria. Her ongoing practice and interest in Dance Improvisation, Authentic Movement and Trauma Therapy influences her work as an Alexander teacher, psychotherapist, supervisor and coach.

Christine and Martina have been investigating the connection between Alexander Technique, the Person-Centred Approach and Burnout Prevention for more than fifteen years.

The Art of Breathing

Jessica Wolf

Breathing is as essential to life as the beating of our hearts. Each person's breathing rhythm is unique; timing and effort vary from individual to individual. Although breathing is reflexive, we can influence its efficiency by the way we use our bodies. I have observed that faulty breathing patterns are most often the result of learned misconceptions about the respiratory system. When we put stress on our musculoskeletal systems, we negatively impact our breathing.

I developed *The Art of Breathing* by integrating the work of F. M. Alexander and Carl Stough. Stough became known as a pioneer in the field of respiratory science for his discoveries about the breath. He identified the inhalation phase as a reflex induced by the phrenic nerves. During the exhalation phase, he noted that the diaphragm and all the other coordinating muscles promote an equal turnover of air. This allows for the appropriate volume of air to enter and exit the body. Stough asserted that a well-balanced vocal system offers flexible resistance and stimulates the diaphragm during the exhalation. By using the voice, he could assess and develop coordination among the respiratory muscles for greater diaphragmatic movement. He termed this *breathing coordination.*

Central to my technique is the notion that you *never have to take a breath;* an easy exhale prompts an easy inhale. For my Congress presentation, I explored this concept in the context of common conditions that obstruct respiration and performance. As Alexander teachers, we often see students with asthma, acid reflux (GERD), smoking-related illnesses and mood disorders such as anxiety and depression. By exploring these pervasive issues, I demonstrated how understanding the breath and the anatomy of the respiratory system is vital for constructive change. I also shared practices I use to address some symptoms caused by each of these problems.

Asthma is a persistent inflammation that narrows the airways. I often observe asthmatic students 'gulping' for air, which leads to hyperventilation, a form of over-breathing. This constant raising and lowering of the ribcage on every breath comes at a cost. When asthmatics overuse accessory breathing muscles (chest, neck and shoulders), they throw the body out of balance. I help students sense when they stiffen the chest, and guide them to release their shoulders and move into their backs. I teach them to create harmony among all their respiratory muscles by exhaling the stale air from their lungs. Over time, as students improve their use, breathing becomes easier.

Gastroesophageal reflux disease (GERD) – more commonly known as 'acid reflux' or 'heartburn' – can cause stomach pain, constipation, and vocal fold irritation. The oesophagus is the tube that passes through the diaphragm, connecting the throat to the stomach. When acid from the stomach flows back up through the oesophagus, it burns the vocal folds and causes problems with swallowing, hoarseness and vocal disorders. People often attempt to lessen the pain caused by GERD by pushing their abdominals in and out as they breathe, not realising that this practice worsens the condition. Overusing abdominal muscles decreases length along the spine. This compression limits the complete excursion of the diaphragm. When students achieve coordinated breathing, they enjoy the benefits of what F. M. Alexander called the 'visceral massage'. The ongoing motion of breath creates a gentle massage for all the organs and intestines in the abdominal cavity. Efficient, complete digestion relies on integration of the muscles in the airway, gastrointestinal tract, abdomen, and respiratory system.

Despite the well-known dangers of smoking, we all work with students who smoke. These students are more prone to illness and vocal disorders. It is unsurprising that four actors who portrayed the 'Marlboro Cowboy' in cigarette ads died of COPD caused by smoking. Women who smoke are at even greater risk because oestrogen accelerates the absorption of nicotine. Former or current smokers can practise Art of Breathing to help release toxic air trapped in the lungs. Optimal breathing both discourages the habit and improves overall health.

Mood disorders – particularly anxiety and depression – are pervasive and the associated struggles can be debilitating. They also influence breathing patterns and how we use our bodies. Over-breathing and breathlessness are frequent complaints. In my practice, I observe how emotional inertia associated with depression leads to physical habits, like collapsing the chest, and impedes the adequate turnover of air. People with anxiety often breathe high in their chests and can experience sensations of suffocation. Exhalations that are sustained and effortless restore one's sense of confidence and fuel the length along the spine. Because breathing is moment-to-moment, each breath provides a new opportunity for change.

For the performing artist, it is particularly important to address any of these conditions. The demands on performers through rehearsal and production can often cause fear, which manifests in harmful breath-holding. There is nothing positive about habitual breath-holding. It is often an involuntary response to anxiety or stress. We often hold our breath when we concentrate or prepare to speak. We discussed ways we see performers 'get ready' to move and speak, and observed how breath holding interrupts the body's natural rhythmic patterns. This habit is detrimental to performers' endurance and well-being.

Although each of these conditions has different symptoms, I find they impact the respiratory system in similar ways. I identified certain procedures that can be helpful for all of the conditions mentioned above. For example, the whispered 'ah' is very effective in achieving an easy exhale, which bypasses the muscled 'gasp' and leads to a reflexive inhale. I guide students to maintain a balance of tension and relaxation through their vocal folds and facial muscles. The quality of their sound will reveal any excessive tension or pushing. The whispered 'ah' can be followed by a series of other active exhalations, all of which have a long, slow release. The diaphragm guides and modulates the air to slow the outflow. A hum or hiss, for example, will also help release air. Students can practise these procedures to ensure lengthening along the spine and awareness of the three-dimensional torso.

In the workshop we watched my rib animation film that illustrates the three-dimensionality of the torso as well as all the muscles, bones, and organs involved with respiration. In teaching the Art of Breathing, I believe it is crucial to remember that the movement of breath occurs throughout our entire torso. During the inhalation phase the diaphragm descends, expanding the ribs outward and upward, and gently increases volume in the abdomen. During the exhalation, the diaphragm rises high into the thoracic cavity as the ribs drape downward and inward. The abdominal organs respond to this motion and the entire circumference of the torso changes shape. I always stress that our ribs move in response to our breath; we do not need to move them consciously in order to breathe.

I led participants in a 'lie down'. We began in a semi-supine position on the floor, gently establishing connections throughout the body. To encourage the movement of the breath, I asked participants to notice their 'internal landscape', the ongoing motion of the diaphragm, the ways in which the abdominal cavity changes shape, and the increased mobility of their ribs. I guided them to release the jaw, tongue and neck to invite air to move in and out without unnecessary muscular effort. I suggested that people experiment and play with these procedures, not repeat them robotically. Since the respiratory system is predominantly involuntary, we work *indirectly* to redevelop and tone the diaphragm. These procedures aim to achieve conscious control. We explored a series of exhalations to become more aware of how the body and breath support movement and sound. Sound is essential for redevelopment. It provides resistance in the vocal folds, thereby requiring greater coordination among respiratory muscles. *Sound resounds* and leads to vibration throughout the body.

Next, I invited teachers to stand, so we could observe the use of ourselves on our feet and in monkey. We were able to observe the three-dimensionality of the torso and the way our voices resonate from within. Building on this observation, I led teachers through exercises to try on the different respiratory conditions we discussed on the workshop's first day. Replicating those conditions helps us better empathise with the student's experience. We experimented with different postures and breathing patterns, staying present and open. I taught participants to 'follow their breath to its natural conclusion', and never to use force to push the air out. With a partner, we used 'listening hands' to invite the breath to the back, and observed how the torso changes shape. I asked teachers to avoid breathing mechanically and notice their individual breathing cycle. I conveyed the importance of Alexander's principle 'the use of the whole'. We do not think in parts, but rather explore the potential for harmony among all muscles of respiration.

In bringing my workshop to a close, I spoke about the connection between breath and well-being. Our heart lives next to our lungs; the nervous and respiratory systems are intimately connected. By bringing awareness to the internal support of the breath, we bring about positive changes for our physical and emotional health. Through the practice of *Art of Breathing*, we rediscover our unique breathing rhythms, replace harmful habits, and bring vitality to our daily lives.

> Jessica Wolf trained at the American Center for the Alexander Technique and has been teaching for more than thirty-five years. Throughout her career, she has explored and conducted research into respiratory function. In 1998 Jessica established the Alexander Technique programme at Yale School of Drama, where she now holds the position of Assistant Professor. In 2002 she became the founder and director of the first post-graduate training programme for Alexander teachers in 'Jessica Wolf's Art of Breathing'. Other faculty appointments include the Aspen Music Festival, the Juilliard School, SUNY Purchase, Circle in the Square Theater School, Hunter College, Sarah Lawrence College, and the Verbier Music Festival. Jessica published *Jessica Wolf's Art of Breathing: Collected Articles* in 2013. She coaches many performing artists who appear on and off Broadway, as well as in film and television. Jessica travels extensively giving workshops to performers and health care providers.
>
> *jessicawolf170@gmail.com*
> *www.jessicawolfartofbreathing.com*

Notes from the Artist-in-Residence

Aisling Hedgecock

> The hands want to see, the eyes want to caress.
> *Goethe*

> My objective is to test to what extent my hands already feel what my eyes see.
> *Rodin*

> The loss of focus can liberate the eye from its patriarchal domination.
> *Juhani Pallasmaa* in *The Eyes of the Skin, Architecture and the Senses*

An artist's life is time and time again punctuated by the omnipresent word, exhibition. On arriving at the Congress in Limerick I realised my ears were ringing with this new word to my vocabulary: inhibition. A close antonym of exhibit, from the Latin *inhibire* 'to hold in, hold back, keep back', or perhaps the softer later definition to 'check, hinder, or restrain', as opposed to the public focus of the artistic career, to exhibere 'to hold out, display, present or deliver'. This linguistic paradox mirrored my feelings on how to bring visible the seemingly hidden subtleties of touch employed when observing the work.

Over the course of the week I attended workshops, continuous learning sessions, lectures and panel discussions, whenever possible armed with sketchbooks and materials. I drew from the exchange rooms and from the Swoosh Board in Trisha Hemmingway's workshop. I came with a fundamental curiosity about the relationship between the Alexander Technique and the visual arts, particularly drawing and sculpture. This is an area now more than ever rich in potential for interdisciplinary exchange. After spending a week immersed so fully, with a wealth of ideas and research, I left knowing the experience would inform a new direction in my work.

www.aislinghedgecock.com

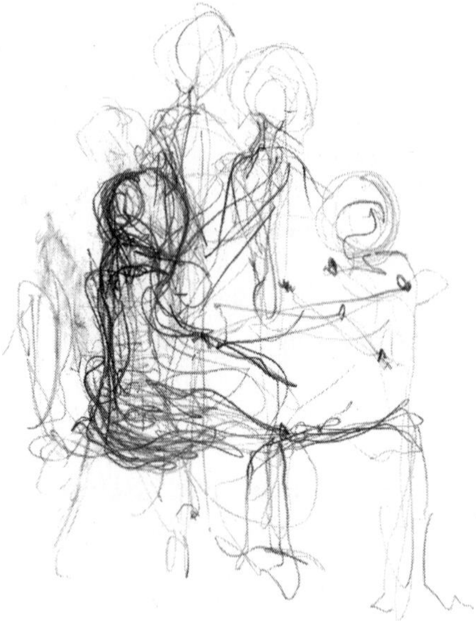

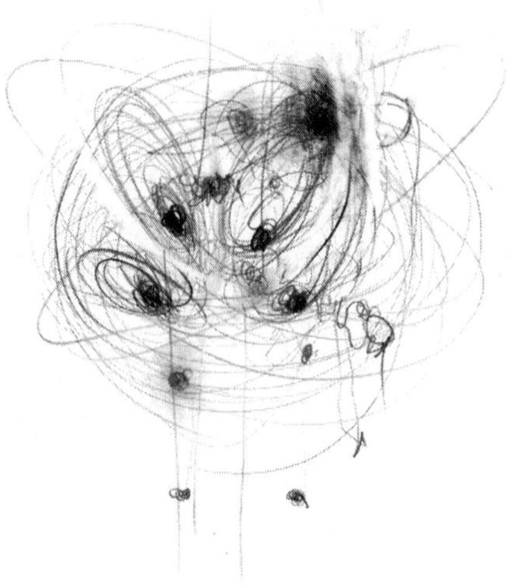

Aisling Hedgecock ~ Notes from the Artist-in-Residence

INDEX

Alphabetical Listing of Authors

Aoki, Paul Norikazu	177
Ballard, Kathleen	13, 300
Barber, Julie	230
Barker, Sarah	107
Battye, Anne	22
Bendix, Erik	116
Biggs, Korina	181, 300
Blanc, Pamela	26
Boggs, Carol	13
Bouchard, Ed	13
Breen, Katherine H.	242, 250
Brennan, Richard	29
Brucker, Jane	143
de Brunhoff, Agnès	156
Cassini, Corinne	150
Clappison, Jane	300
Dimon, Ted	34
Easten, Penelope	41
Fagg, Henry	47
Farkas, Alexander	121
Ferguson, Becca	268
Fitzgerald, Terry	13
Forsstrom, Brita	123
Freeman, Caitlin	275
Frost, Joan	185
Gaary, Diane	53
Gibbens, David	300
Glover, Lesley	300
Gross, Monika	60
Hadar-Borthwick, Mika	280
Hanefeld, Nicola	69
Hedgecock, Aisling	317
Johnson, Anne	73
Kingsley, Anthony	78
Lieb, Brooke	89

Alphabetical Listing of Authors

Machover, Ilana	283
Madden, Cathy	162
Magonet, Dorothea	129
Maxwell, Clare	188
Moore, David	13
O'Connor, Penny	136
Reese, Elizabeth	289
Rodiger, Ann	13
Ruben, Zadok	194
Simmons, Robin John	206
Süss, Martina	308
Thomas, Alun	169
Vasiliades, Tom	95
Walker, Lucia	209
Wasser, Jeremy	143
Weiser, Wolfgang	216
Weixler, Christine	308
West, Sharyn	98
Wolf, Jessica	313
Woodman, Julia	300
Woodward, John	220

Work Exchange
Photographs by Ralf Hiemisch